Financial Policies and the
World Capital Market

A Conference Report
National Bureau of
Economic Research

Financial Policies and the World Capital Market: The Problem of Latin American Countries

HG
185
.L3
F54
1983

Edited by Pedro Aspe Armella, Rudiger Dornbusch, and Maurice Obstfeld

The University of Chicago Press

Chicago and London

PEDRO ASPE ARMELLA is chairman of the Department of Economics at the Instituto Tecnológico Autónomo de México. RUDIGER DORNBUSCH is professor of economics at the Massachusetts Institute of Technology and is the author of *Open Economy Macroeconomics*. MAURICE OBSTFELD is associate professor of economics at Columbia University.

The University of Chicago Press, Chicago 60637
The University of Chicago Press, Ltd., London

Library of Congress Cataloging in Publication Data
Main entry under title:

Financial policies and the world capital market.

(A Conference report / National Bureau of Economic Research)
"Result of the National Bureau of Economic Research Conference on Financial Policies and the World Capital Market: The Problem of Latin American Countries, held in Mexico City, 26–27 March 1981"—Pref.
Includes bibliographies and indexes.
Contents: Stories of the 1930s for the 1980s / Carlos F. Díaz Alejandro — Optimal economic integration / Michael Mussa — Seigniorage and fixed exchange rates / Stanley Fischer — [etc.]
1. Finance—Latin America—Congresses. 2. Debts, External—Latin America—Congresses. 3. Capital market—Latin America—Congresses. 4. Foreign exchange problem—Latin America—Congresses. 5. Latin America—Foreign economic relations—Congresses. I. Aspe Armella, Pedro. II. Dornbusch, Rudiger. III. Obstfeld, Maurice. IV. National Bureau of Economic Research Conference on Financial Policies and the World Capital Market: The Problem of Latin American Countries (1981 : Mexico City, Mexico) V. National Bureau of Economic Research. VI. Series: Conference report (National Bureau of Economic Research)
HG185.L3F54   1983   332'.042'098   82-24820
ISBN 0-226-02996-4

Contents

Preface

The present volume is the result of the National Bureau of Economic Research Conference on Financial Policies and the World Capital Market: The Problem of Latin American Countries, held at the Instituto Tecnológico Autónomo de México in Mexico City, 26–27 March 1981.

Introduction

The story of interwar Latin American finance is one of high inflation, exchange rate crisis, and debt default. Today, once again, the Latin American financial scene attracts attention and demands analysis. The decade of the 1970s brought a huge increase in Latin American borrowing from the world capital market. Greater financial integration opened new opportunities—and created new risks—for both borrowers and lenders. Concurrently, the growing external linkages have imposed tighter constraints on domestic macroeconomic policies.

The essays brought together in this volume share a common objective: To bring a unifying methodological approach to the analysis of financial problems in developing, open economies. While the primary focus is on contemporary Latin America, the methods employed and the lessons learned are of wider applicability. The papers address the financial integration issue from three different perspectives. In some cases, a country study is the vehicle for an econometric investigation of a particular external linkage. In other cases, an individual country's experience suggests an economic model in which the stylized facts may be analyzed and developed. A third direction is unabashedly theoretical and formulates more general principles which are broadly applicable rather than country-specific.

Two examples will highlight the issues. In the late 1970s, Argentina embarked on a long-term program of financial stabilization. The key elements were a preannounced exchange rate path, complete freedom of capital movements, and a substantial reduction in trade barriers. Argentina's rush to financial integration produced severe real effects, most importantly a sharp and persistent overvaluation of the currency and extraordinarily high real interest rates reaching 100 percent and over. The cause of the high real interest rates, at least, is now clear, for a

1

number of large devaluations—deviations from the preannounced policy—have turned out to validate the expectations that market interest
rates reflect. In the area of external debt, Brazil is surely the biggest (if
not the leading) problem case. In June 1981 its external indebtedness to
banks stood at roughly $46 billion. External borrowing has been large, in
good measure financing current public and private consumption rather
than productive investment. But how should external borrowing be
analyzed in an economic framework? In particular, is Brazil's debt too
large? Is it worth making the extreme growth sacrifice Brazil has chosen
in the 1981 recession to improve the external balance?

These are only examples of the issues this book addresses. But they do
convey the importance of the issues and the need for a serious, coherent
investigation of the linkages between the world capital market and the
domestic policies of industrializing economies.

The volume opens with two general papers which provide a backdrop
for the study of Latin America's links to the world capital market. Carlos
Díaz Alejandro approaches the question from a historical perspective,
exploring the Latin American currency experience of the 1930s. What
lessons are to be learned from that period, when Latin America imported
the effects of the Great Depression and sought an internal and often
successful path to recovery? Díaz Alejandro concludes, "After the initial
external blows, the active countries steadily gained in both ability and will
to maintain growth regardless of foreign conditions." Study of the 1930s
is revealing, for it illustrates the costs of close integration when the world
economy malfunctions. A further lesson is that by getting out of step with
the world economy, countries may, at times, do better. Michael Mussa's
paper addresses the same set of issues from a purely theoretical standpoint. How much integration should a country seek? The answer, to a
first approximation, is as much as possible. As Mussa notes, however, the
answer is less simple when there is a trade-off between domestic objectives and first-best resource allocation. Here, the limited case for insulat-
ing home markets is investigated, albeit with little sympathy.

The papers by Stanley Fischer and by Guillermo Ortiz focus on three
closely related topics: The costs and consequences of different exchange
rate regimes, the choice of a monetary standard, and the viability of
country-specific money when the economy is open. Fischer makes a
theoretical case for exchange rate flexibility and a national money. When
public good provision is financed by distorting taxes on labor and commodities, the aggregate deadweight burden of taxation is higher than it
would be if a tax on money—the inflation tax—were employed as well. A
flexible rate regime is desirable, Fischer concludes, because it allows the
government to choose the optimal steady state level of seigniorage from
money creation. Ortiz offers a chronicle of Mexico's monetary experience from the standpoint of currency substitution. A central message of

his is that a close link exists between the public's willingness to use government-issued money and the public's beliefs concerning future government financial policies. Ortiz explores in detail the stability over time of the currency composition of Mexican money holdings, which consist of peso-denominated deposits and currency and U.S.-dollar-denominated deposits. He finds that the Mex-dollar component of domestic money holdings rises significantly when the public comes to anticipate a sharp currency devaluation after a period of exchange rate fixity.

The essays by Nissan Liviatan and by Michael Bruno analyze in a theoretical fashion the key relationships relevant to an economy that is subject to real and financial shocks. Liviatan studies these problems from the perspective of indexation arrangements. He asks: Does indexation make any difference to the operation of the economy? His conclusion is that private parties will choose optimal—less than complete—indexation arrangements that reflect their ability to diversify certain risks in labor and capital markets through portfolio selection. Importantly, the paper concludes that full indexation is in general *not* optimal. Bruno's paper deals with the following questions: What are the real and financial characteristics of a semi-industrialized country that are especially relevant to the international linkage? How do these characteristics interact with the exchange rate regime and with economic openness in affecting the impact of disturbances and the scope for macroeconomic management? This is a natural setting in which to explore not only the choice between accommodation or moderation of domestic and external shocks, but also the choice between exchange rate policies ranging from exchange control and dual rates to fully fixed or fully flexible rates. While theoretical in its approach, the paper is nonetheless highly relevant in its policy implications. Indeed, it is very much inspired by Israel's experience with these problems.

Two papers focus on Argentina and the extraordinary events that have unfolded in the past four years between stabilization and collapse. Guillermo Calvo concentrates on the problem of exchange rate overvaluation between 1976 and 1980. Through what channels—real and financial—is it possible to explain the large increase in the exchange-rate-adjusted level of prices in Argentina compared to the outside world? Was the phenomenon a reflection of slow domestic adjustment to inflation—a disequilibrium situation—or was it rather an equilibrium real appreciation? This is, of course, a very important question in the Argentine context. But it is important too in understanding the experience of Chile, which also has pursued a disinflation policy centered around a preannounced exchange rate path. The work of Domingo Cavallo and Humberto Petrei is concerned with the implication of extremely high *real* interest rates in Argentina. How have these high real interest rates on financial capital affected the profitability and ultimately the viability of private business? Remarkably high real rates have been a feature of stabilization programs in most Latin American countries, and one must ask how financial rates can move so far out of line with any reasonable expectation of the productivity of capital. One cause might be a sharply contractionary monetary policy. But another cause, perhaps more consistent with subsequent experience, is the expectation of a reversal of policies and a resumption of inflation.

Mexico is again the subject in the papers by José Lizondo and by Robert Cumby and Maurice Obstfeld. The approach is empirical and the question is the exact extent to which Mexican financial integration with the U.S. capital market provides scope for domestic credit policy. This is, of course, a question of central importance to policymakers, and these studies approach it through a careful analysis of data and institutions, coupled with econometric sophistication. Lizondo explores the large deviations from covered interest parity, finding that bank regulations and the taxation of capital gains due to exchange rate movement can account for most of the observed covered interest differentials. The Cumby-Obstfeld study uses an empirical structural model of Mexican financial markets to investigate the capital account offset to domestic credit policy under fixed exchange rates. The authors conclude that although the offset was substantial during the 1970s, the Banco de México did possess some short-run control over the money supply.

Olivier Blanchard takes up the subject of Brazil's external debt. To analyze solvency risk, Blanchard develops and simulates a formal growth model. Two main conclusions emerge: First, that there is no debt problem. Second, that current account adjustment, if it occurs at all, should come at the expense of consumption rather than at the expense of investment. The paper's approach may well be controversial, but it does provide a refreshing contrast to traditional country risk analysis.

The volume concludes with a panel discussion of capital markets under conditions of high and varying inflation. In informal statements, the panel brings up many of the issues that remain on the agenda for future research.

At first sight, this book suggests a diversity of topics and approaches, ranging from wage indexation to Mexican offset coefficients and from country studies to purely theoretical models. But that apparent diversity should not conceal a basic unity: All of these papers address issues of financial integration in the world capital market from a common and shared conceptual framework, and they are all concerned with live policy issues.

1   Stories of the 1930s for the 1980s

Carlos F. Díaz Alejandro

Once upon a time foreign money doctors roamed Latin America prescribing fixed exchange rates and passive gold exchange standard monetary rules. Bankers followed in their footsteps, from the halls of Montezuma to the shores of Daiquirí. To the delight of local dignitaries, the not-so-exigent financiers would yield convertible cash for IOUs. Such normalcy during the late 1920s appeared even more attractive than that immediately preceding the First World War. In some countries, such as Brazil, convertibility and fixed rates appeared to have been purchased at the price of sluggish growth; in other countries, such as Colombia, gold standard rules permitted significant inflation. Yet most observers emphasized the virtues of a monetary system which minimized possible shocks from irresponsible domestic politicians and maintained international creditworthiness. Concern also existed in the 1920s about the weakness in some markets for staple export products, often aggravated by rising protectionism at the Center, but both foreign loans and the optimism of the times made such concerns fleeting ones.

The Latin American balance of payments equilibrium of the late 1920s was rudely and repeatedly shocked from the outside, starting in 1929 and throughout the 1930s and 1940s. The occasional domestic earthquake, crop failure, or indigenous madman in authority paled into insignificance compared with the external shocks (in the case of the latter, it could often be argued that he was an endogenous product of the disturbed external circumstances and examples).

This paper will chronicle the major external shocks of the 1930s and some of the ways various Latin American economies coped with them. It will be seen that the performance of several economies was remarkably

Carlos F. Díaz Alejandro is a professor in the Department of Economics, Yale University.

good, under the circumstances. This will lead us to examine the mechanisms of adjustment at work during that decade, and the extent to which they were prodded along by autonomous policy. Exchange rate developments will be examined first. This will be followed by a look at monetary and fiscal policies, a section hobbled even more than the others by lack of data. During the 1930s most Latin American countries performed moratoria on their external public debts; discussion of the causes and consequences of that controversial and memorable step deserves a section of its own. Some reflections close the paper.

1.1   Shocks and Performance

In a world of fixed exchange rates, the slowdown in the Center economies already visible in 1929 was quickly translated into a decline of export values in the Periphery. The deepening slump plus additional protectionist measures at the Center, such as the U.S. Smoot-Hawley tariff of 1930, the British Abnormal Importations Act of 1931, the Ottawa Commonwealth preferences of 1932, and similar actions by the French, German, and Japanese empires, led to sharp declines in the Latin American terms of trade and a milder fall of their export quantum. The purchasing power of exports, which for countries such as Brazil and Cuba was already declining in the late 1920s, took a sharp dive between 1928–1929 and 1932–1933, as may be seen in table 1.1 for a sample of Latin American countries.[1] A vigorous recovery after 1932–1933 was interrupted by the 1937–1938 recession in the United States; for the decade as a whole, the purchasing power of exports showed declines between 25 and 40 percent. The early years of the Second World War had mixed effects on Latin American economies: loss of European markets and shipping shortages led to fresh export troubles in 1940 and 1941 in several countries.

While overall trends in the Center countries dominated the Latin American export picture, the export performance of individual countries was also marked by good or bad luck in the "commodity lottery" as well as by attempts at export promotion and diversification, even under the gloomy conditions of the 1930s. Examples of export gains after 1933, with good fortune and policy efforts playing different roles, include the cases of Peruvian and Colombian gold, Mexican silver (on which more will be said later), Argentine corn and fruits, Brazilian cotton, and Venezuelan oil.

As already noted, during the 1920s Latin American balance of payments were bolstered by large capital inflows, with New York replacing

---

1. For a closer look at the evolution of terms of trade and export quantum see Díaz Alejandro 1980a, pp. 351–382. For Chile both the terms of trade and the export quantum collapsed, leading to the steepest decline in the purchasing power of exports registered in Latin America.

Table 1.1   Foreign Trade Indicators in Selected Latin
American Countries, 1928/29–1942/43
(Percentage Changes between Years Shown)

Years	Argentina	Brazil	Colombia	Cuba	Mexico
	A. Purchasing Power of Exports				
1928/29–1932/33	−41.2	−42.3	−36.0	−56.1	−61.9
1932/33–1936/37	63.4	33.3	24.0	61.8	77.5
1936/37–1938/39	−28.2	−9.2	−5.0	−8.4	−9.9
1938/39–1942/43	−10.7	3.7	−9.7	40.6	−6.2
1928/29–1938/39	−31.5	−30.1	−24.7	−34.9	−39.0
	B. Import Quantum				
1928/29–1932/33	−50.0	−56.2	−59.6	−68.0	−55.4
1932/33–1936/37	45.1	63.3	93.0	94.6	82.2
1936/37–1938/39	−1.4	−2.0	10.9	−2.0	−11.0
1938/39–1942/43	−57.5	−28.1	−53.3	17.3	8.2
1928/29–1938/39	−28.4	−29.9	−13.5	−39.0	−27.7

Sources and method: Basic data, except for Cuba, obtained from CEPAL 1976. Percentage
changes were computed between two-year averages. Cuban data obtained by dividing
indices of the value of exports and imports by the United States wholesale price index.
Dirección General de Estadística 1959, pp. 24–25.

London as the source of long-term portfolio funds. Direct foreign investment was also significant and began to go into manufacturing activities.
Well before Latin American countries showed signs of skipping sched-
uled servicing of the external debt, gross capital inflows fell sharply. After
1930 little fresh capital came in. With the dollar price level falling unexpectedly by around one-quarter between 1928–1929 and 1932–1933, debt
servicing rose dramatically in real terms, compressing the capacity to
import beyond what is suggested in table 1.1A. As may be seen in table
1.1B, the import quantum fell even more than the purchasing power of
exports between 1928–1929 and 1932–1933, except in Mexico. By 1934
all countries except Argentina, Haiti, and the Dominican Republic had
suspended normal servicing of the external national debt. From then to
the end of the decade, import volumes as a rule recovered faster than the
purchasing power of exports.

The early years of the Second World War provided a different kind of
shock to most Latin American economies: even when the foreign exchange was available, imports could not be obtained, either because of
strict rationing by the Allied powers or due to shipping shortages. The
more distant a country from the Allied powers, geographically and
politically, the more intense and longer lived was this supply shock; for
Argentina it could be said to have lasted well into the late 1940s, while it
was much milder and briefer for Mexico, with its overland links to the

United States, and for Cuba after the Axis submarines had been driven from her coasts.

The emergence of a protectionist and nationalistic Center, prone to deflation and war, was the greatest shock to Latin American economies during the 1930s. It is true that as early as 1934 Cordell Hull, U.S. secretary of state, started a policy of reducing U.S. tariffs, but such policy made slow progress and had to whittle down a tariff wall raised not only by the Smoot-Hawley Act but also by the deflation-induced increase in the incidence of specific duties (Haberler 1976, pp. 33–34). Other major industrialized countries retreated further into protectionism, bringing their colonies ever more closely under their commercial and financial "economic communities," with negative trade-diverting consequences for sovereign Latin American countries. The memory of this betrayal of Hume, Smith, and Ricardo would linger longer in the Periphery than in the Center.

The open Latin American economies of the late 1920s were quite vulnerable to this sequence of outside shocks, especially in the early 1930s. Yet bits and pieces of evidence indicate that at least some of those economies managed to weather the storm better than the United States and Canada. Table 1.2 presents available national accounts data for the four largest republics. Compared to the United States, aggregate output during 1929–1939 experienced less violent fluctuations and expanded faster in the four Latin American countries. One should note, however, that measurements of gross domestic product, shown in table 1.2, do not take into account losses of real income arising from deteriorating terms of trade. Taking these losses into account reduces Brazilian aggregate growth during 1929–1939, for example, from 4.3 percent per annum to 3.2 percent, according to the source listed in table 1.2. For Argentina, it may be estimated that a similar correction would reduce annual growth from 1.6 percent to 1.2 percent per annum. On the other hand, estimates for gross *national* product (not available) would show faster growth rates,

Table 1.2   **Aggregate Real Output in Selected Countries, 1929–1943 (Percentage Changes between Years Shown)**

Years	Argentina	Brazil	Colombia	Mexico	U.S.
1929–33	−9.7	7.6	9.9	−10.3	−28.9
1933–37	23.2	31.7	16.4	28.0	47.0
1937–39	4.9	7.1	13.0	7.2	1.7
1939–43	8.4	9.7	4.5	25.3	53.3
1929–39	16.7	51.7	44.6	23.0	6.3

Sources and method: Data for Argentina, Colombia, and Mexico were obtained from CEPAL 1978. Brazil data were obtained from Haddad 1978, table 1. All of these data refer to gross domestic product at constant prices. U.S. data were obtained from U.S. Bureau of the Census 1960, p. 139. These data refer to gross national product at constant prices.

as factor payments abroad fell sharply during the 1930s, as will be seen later.

Table 1.2 also shows an interesting contrast between U.S. and Latin American aggregate performance during the early war years. Supply shocks and fuller use of capacity around 1939 kept Argentine, Brazilian, and Colombian expansion during 1939–1943 at annual rates below those registered during 1937–1939.

It could be argued that the aggregate performance shown in table 1.2 is far from impressive, and that the favorable contrast with the United States is mostly explained by the larger weight of price- and income-inelastic rural output in Latin American aggregate production. In fact, the most impressive evidence of favorable Latin American performance during the 1930s will not be found in aggregate data. The 1930s were a decade of major structural changes: some sectors boomed while others collapsed. The major leading sector was industrial output, as may be seen in table 1.3. Here we do find a remarkable contrast between, say, Brazilian and Colombian industrial growth and that of the United States; Brazilian industrial expansion during the 1930s was also faster than that experienced by the same country during the 1920s.

So far the term Latin America has been used loosely. Table 1.3 shows one Latin American country whose performance was weaker and more erratic than that of the United States. The Cuban case suggests that a typology may be desirable; for reasons that will become clearer later on, one may differentiate between the larger or active Latin American republics and the smaller or passive ones. While data for the latter type are especially scarce, the conjecture is that the small or passive republics,

Table 1.3   **Real Industrial Production, 1929–1943**
(Percentage Changes between Years Shown)

Country	1929–33	1933–37	1937–39	1939–43	1929–39
Argentina	−6.5	31.5	10.0	18.0	35.2
Brazil	6.9	53.7	13.4	19.1	86.2
Colombia	24.7	49.2	24.7	16.1	132.1
Cuba	−50.0[a]	90.2	−8.8	4.7	−13.2[a]
Mexico	−7.9	46.8	12.7	45.9	52.3
Uruguay	na[b]	na	na	na	58.3[a]
U.S.	−36.9	66.7	−5.0	133.3	−1.7

Sources and method: As in table 2, except for Cuba and Uruguay. Except for Cuba, Latin American data refer to value added by the manufacturing sector, measured at constant prices. U.S. data refer to the Federal Reserve Board index of manufactures, given in U.S. Bureau of the Census 1960, p. 409. Cuban data obtained from Perez Lopez 1977, p. 53. Uruguayan data obtained from Millot, Silva, and Silva 1972, p. 251.

[a]Percentage change relative to 1930.

[b]na = data not available.

mainly those in the Caribbean and some in Central America, were dragged down by the U.S. performance as surely as the states of Mississippi and Arkansas. Size is not the only characteristic differentiating the two types of countries, as Cuba in the late 1920s had a domestic market not very different from that of Uruguay or Chile, two countries whose performance was similar to those of larger countries. Note that "small" and "large" in this typology do not necessarily refer to the capacity of different countries to influence their external terms of trade.

The early war years cooled the industrial boom in Argentina, Brazil, and Colombia; not surprisingly, Mexico shows a performance during 1939–1943 in between those of the other large Latin American countries and that of the United States.

The structural changes noted above for the economy as a whole can also be found within the industrial sector. Even as some manufacturing activities closely dependent on pre-1929 export-oriented prosperity were shrinking or stagnating (examples include meat packing, flour milling, and sugar refining), other activities, sometimes a handful, made dramatic output advances during the 1930s. Textiles, cement, petroleum refining, tires, pharmaceuticals, toiletries, and food processing for the home market are examples of booming sectors. For several countries textiles appear as quantitatively the most important leading sector, often providing more than 20 percent of the net expansion of manufacturing value added and growing at annual rates above 10 percent. The rural sector also witnessed a gain in the production of "importables" relative to "exportables."

Output growth in the booming industrial sectors far outstripped the expansion of total domestic absorption of those manufactured goods, which followed more closely the somewhat sluggish growth of aggregate output. Export expansion explains little of this gap: it was import contraction, in both absolute terms and relative to domestic absorption, which completes the picture. Import substitution, defined in its purely accounting sense as a decline in the ratio of imports to domestic absorption, became the engine of growth of the 1930s, and not just in manufacturing; several rural activities experienced trends similar to those described above for textiles, cement, and pharmaceuticals. Such import replacement, often squeezing productive capacity already installed during the 1920s, helped both to cope with balance of payments difficulties and to maintain levels of employment; for countries such as Argentina and Brazil there is evidence that the industrialization drive seems to have been quite labor absorbing, with output elasticities of employment around one.

The cement industry provides a concrete example of some aspects of the import substitution process sketched above. Table 1.4 compares three-year consumption averages in the late 1920s and 1930s and the

Table 1.4   **Cement: Consumption and Output**

Country	Apparent Cement Consumption 1936–37–38 (1927–28–29 = 100)	Domestic Output as Percentage of Apparent Consumption	
		1927–28–29	1936–37–38
Argentina	150	35	94
Bolivia	128	28	69
Brazil	112	14	89
Chile	115	44	99
Colombia	126	6	72
Mexico	152	87	97
Ecuador	140	15	57
Paraguay	145	0	0
Peru	127	46	66
Uruguay	76	79	92
Venezuela	116	14	28
Central American republics (six)	113	12	12
Cuba	37	90	93
Haiti	50	0	0
Dominican Republic	79	0	0
Canada	49	102	100
United States	64	100	100

Sources and method: Basic data in physical magnitudes obtained from European Cement Association 1967, pp. 27–43. Apparent consumption refers to cement production plus imports less exports.

share in that absorption produced domestically. Mexico and the South American republics, with a few exceptions, show both some increase in total consumption and an impressive jump in the share of home production. Public works programs in Argentina and Mexico led to especially vigorous expansion in consumption, while the leap in the coefficient of domestic supplies is most notable for Brazil and Colombia. The Caribbean islands, in contrast, present a picture as melancholy as that for Canada and the United States. The Central American republics show no gain in import substitution, but a surprisingly good performance in total consumption.

1.2   Exchange Rate Policies

All Latin American countries which experienced vigorous industrial expansion during the 1930s had, by 1932 at the latest, abandoned convertibility and other gold standard rules of the game. Exchange controls were adopted in many countries following the devaluation of the pound sterling in September 1931. Large or active countries by 1933 had exchange rates relative to the dollar significantly above the late 1920s parities, and the use of multiple exchange rates became widespread. These measures were adopted as gold and foreign exchange reserves dwindled or disappeared, and there was little enthusiasm in their enactment; the governments viewed them as regrettable emergency operations, and there was much improvisation and confusion in their management. Yet the governments had the good sense to reject advice, such as that proffered by Sir Otto Niemeyer to the Brazilian government in July 1931 to adopt deflationary measures to return to convertibility at fixed parities (de Paivă Abreu 1974, p. 15).

Small or passive countries, such as Haiti, Dominican Republic, Panama, and Cuba maintained their peg to the U.S. dollar throughout the 1930s. The last two countries did not even have a central bank or a corresponding central monetary authority (such as those of Brazil or pre-1935 Argentina). Exchange control measures in these small countries were timid or nonexistent.

Regardless of the exchange rate policy followed, a country subjected to an exogenous and permanent worsening of its international terms of trade should witness over the long run a decline in the price of its nontraded goods and services relative to the domestic price of importable goods, encouraging a movement of resources toward the import-competing sector, additional to that generated by the decline in exportable prices. A permanent decline in net long-term capital inflows would also induce a decline in the prices of nontraded goods relative to all traded goods. Under a gold exchange standard with fixed rates and with collapsing international prices for both imports and exports, nontraded goods prices and domestic liquidity had a long way to fall. It is the working hypothesis of this section that countries willing and able to devalue their exchange rate moved toward the new constellation of domestic relative prices more speedily than those with fixed rates, thus limiting both price and monetary deflation, and containing their negative impact on real output.

Table 1.5 shows nominal exchange rates with respect to the dollar in the four largest Latin American countries. Starting in 1933 these data refer to average rates relevant for imports. These is some erratic behavior during 1932–1934 in Argentina and Brazil, countries caught in tricky triangular relationships with the United States and the United Kingdom, involving in different mixes unbalanced commercial and financial flows. But the depreciating trend is clear. Like exchange controls, the depreciations were accepted by the authorities with some reluctance, and, even after abandonment of convertibility, attempts were made to limit their extent. Exchange rates applicable to traditional export earnings and the purchase of foreign exchange for debt service depreciated by less than those shown in table 1.5. Indeed, one immediate motivation for adopting exchange controls and multiple rates was to guarantee the treasuries'

Table 1.5   Nominal Average Import Exchange Rates, 1925–1939
                (Units of Local Currency per One U.S. Dollar)

Year	Argentina (pesos)	Brazil (cruzeiros)	Colombia (pesos)	Mexico (pesos)
1925	2.49	8.17	1.02	2.03
1926	2.47	6.87	1.02	2.07
1927	2.36	8.35	1.02	2.12
1928	2.36	8.29	1.02	2.08
1929	2.39	8.48	1.03	2.15
1930	2.74	9.21	1.04	2.26
1931	3.46	14.3	1.04	2.65
1932	3.89	14.1	1.05	3.16
1933	3.23	12.7	1.25	3.50
1934	3.49	14.7	1.66	3.60
1935	3.53	17.4	1.78	3.60
1936	3.45	17.2	1.75	3.60
1937	3.25	16.0	1.77	3.60
1938	3.42	17.6	1.79	4.52
1939	3.87	19.2	1.75	5.19

Sources and method: Argentine data are given in detail in Díaz Alejandro 1980*b*, p. 21. Brazilian data obtained from Malan et al. 1977, p. 515. Colombian data obtained from Ocampo 1980, p. 213, and from sources cited there. Mexican data obtained from Nacional Financiera 1977, p. 216.

cheap access to the foreign exchange required to service the external public debts. Hard-pressed treasuries also welcomed the fresh revenues generated by the spread between high-selling and low-buying exchange rates.

Purchasing power parity should not be expected to hold in an economy subjected to real shocks. As may be seen in table 1.6, price levels in major Latin American countries generally fell by less and rose by more than United States prices during the 1930s. But the differences are small relative to the magnitudes of exchange rate depreciation, as may be seen directly in table 1.7. This table calculates indices of real import exchange rates, deflating the nominal rates of table 1.5 by the price levels given in table 1.6; comparisons are only made vis-à-vis the United States.

As the price level indices of table 1.6 have as broad a coverage of goods and services as possible, the real exchange rates of table 1.7 can be taken as rough proxies for the domestic price of importable goods relative to the nontraded goods price or, alternatively, as an index of profitability in import-substituting activities. Table 1.7 data are only proxies because they do not take into account increments in Latin American protection, due to either tariffs or quantitative restrictions, which occurred during the 1930s, while using the United States GNP deflator as an indicator of international prices for Latin American importable goods. While the

Table 1.6   **Price Level Indicators, 1925–1939 (1929 = 100)**

Year	Argentina	Brazil	Colombia	Mexico	U.S.
1925	104.1	116.1	91.7	92.8	101.0
1926	101.0	95.1	103.7	93.5	101.0
1927	100.0	93.0	100.0	95.1	99.0
1928	99.1	103.7	111.2	97.0	100.0
1929	100.0	100.0	100.0	100.0	100.0
1930	101.0	87.6	79.2	105.7	96.0
1931	87.0	78.1	64.0	89.7	85.0
1932	78.0	79.3	53.6	79.1	77.0
1933	88.0	77.7	55.2	81.0	75.0
1934	78.0	82.6	76.8	80.2	80.0
1935	82.7	86.5	80.0	88.2	79.0
1936	89.7	87.9	84.8	98.5	82.0
1937	92.1	96.3	86.4	119.4	83.0
1938	91.5	99.3	97.3	124.0	83.0
1939	92.9	101.3	101.6	127.0	82.0

Sources and method: Argentine data as in table 5; they refer to the cost of living index in the federal capital. Brazilian data refer to an implicit GDP deflator, given in Haddad 1978, p. 166. Colombian data refer to a combination of wholesale food price indices (pre-1937) and a cost of living index (beginning in 1937), obtained as in table 5. Mexican data refer to an implicit GDP deflator, given in Solis 1970, pp. 104–105. U.S. data refer to the implicit GNP deflator, given in U.S. Bureau of the Census 1960, p. 139.

Table 1.7   **Indices of Real Import Exchange Rates, 1925–1939 (1929 = 100)**

Year	Argentina	Brazil	Colombia	Mexico
1925	101.1	83.7	109.0	102.7
1926	103.3	86.0	96.4	104.0
1927	97.7	104.9	98.0	102.6
1928	99.6	94.3	89.0	99.7
1929	100.0	100.0	100.0	100.0
1930	108.9	118.9	122.4	95.5
1931	141.4	183.5	134.1	116.9
1932	160.7	161.5	146.4	143.1
1933	115.2	144.6	164.9	150.7
1934	149.7	167.8	167.9	166.9
1935	140.7	187.4	170.6	150.0
1936	132.0	189.2	164.3	139.4
1937	122.9	162.7	165.1	116.3
1938	129.9	173.5	148.3	140.7
1939	142.9	183.3	137.1	155.8

Sources and method: Calculated from data in tables 5 and 6, as explained in the text.

Table 1.8   **Wholesale Price Indices Relative to
Cost of Living Indices (1929 = 100)**

Year	Argentina	Chile	U.S.
1930	94	88	93
1931	106	81	86
1932	120	115	86
1933	107	139	92
1934	131	138	101
1935	121	135	105
1936	113	137	105
1937	126	146	108
1938	119	133	100
1939	120	128	100

Sources and method: Argentine and Chilean data obtained from League of Nations 1945, pp. 193, 197. U.S. data as in table 6.

neglect of protection underestimates the increase in the relative price of importables, the second consideration probably contributes toward over-estimation.

An additional bit of insight may be obtained comparing wholesale price indices with those for the cost of living. Only two Latin American countries have reliable series for the 1930s; those are presented in table 1.8 and contrasted with United States data. Wholesale prices cover both importables and exportables; it is thus remarkable that for both Argentina and Chile wholesale prices since 1929 fell less and rose more than the cost of living index, a trend in marked contrast with that for the United States. Data on money wages are very scarce for the period under consideration; if one assumes wages followed the cost of living, the evidence presented in table 1.8 is compatible with the hypothesis of rising profitability in the production of tradable goods, mainly in the import-competing sector.[2]

It has already been observed that, contrary to what would happen in many Latin American countries after the Second World War, during the 1930s both exchange rates and protectionist measures moved in the same direction in active countries, i.e., real depreciations, tariff increases, and import and exchange quantitative restrictions were thrown into the balance of payments battle, particularly in compressing imports. A full discussion of commercial policies, including the complexities of bilateral clearing arrangements imposed on the region by British and German policies, is outside the scope of this paper. But in light of postwar policies and controversies, it is worth noting that in the important case of Argen-

2. A look at disaggregated cost of living indices can also be revealing. In Uruguay, for example, the clothing price index rose relative to that for foodstuffs.

tina, the real average export rate was not allowed to appreciate, in spite of the gloomy outlook for exports (see Díaz Alejandro 1980b, pp. 2–3 for documentation, including real rates with respect to both the U.S. dollar and sterling). Traditional exports facing market restrictions abroad were of course handled to avoid further price declines, but nontraditional exports were given favorable treatment, earning the more depreciated rates which had to be paid by importers lacking licenses. A major architect of these policies was Raul Prebisch.[3] Modest export diversification occurred in Argentina and in some other countries.

1.3   Monetary and Fiscal Policies

The rise of importable goods prices relative both to exportable and nontraded goods prices, resulting from the exogenous deterioration in the external terms of trade as well as from exchange rate and protectionist measures, encouraged investment in import substitution. But aggregate demand was subjected to powerful deflationary forces which could have overwhelmed those incentives. The decline in export values signaling the crisis was accompanied by immediate balance of payments deficits which drained reserves and money supplies, according to gold standard rules. The export fall had important multiplier effects. This section will examine how those deflationary pressures on aggregate demand were contained in active countries and eventually reversed. In countries without well-developed financial markets it is difficult to isolate purely fiscal policies from monetary policies. During the 1930s only Argentina had financial markets of some sophistication, so this section will discuss aggregate macroeconomic policies without establishing very fine distinctions between monetary and fiscal ones.

Table 1.9 presents data on money supplies. With the exception of Cuba, Latin American countries show briefer or shallower post-1929 declines in money supplies than the United States. By 1932 Brazilian money supply exceeded that of 1929; the corresponding Colombian date is 1933. The end of convertibility in Argentina, Brazil, Colombia, and Uruguay was helpful in stemming the loss of liquidity, while in Cuba the inability to break out of (then) orthodox monetary rules led to a monetary deflation even greater than that of the United States.

Maintenance of liquidity was not simply a matter of ending convertibility. On the one hand, even after the abandonment of the gold standard, some countries such as Argentina shipped gold abroad to service the external debt and sold foreign exchange to stem currency depreciation.

3. See the fascinating lectures given by Raúl Prebisch in Mexico during 1944, available in Banco Central de la República Argentina 1972, especially pp. 290–291. The link between exchange rate policies and industrial expansion is explicitly made in these lectures; see p. 295.

Table 1.9   Nominal Money Supplies (End of 1929 = 100)

End of Year	Argentina	Brazil	Colombia	Cuba	Uruguay	U.S.
1928	101.3	100.9	136.6	107.5	90.5	101.5
1929	100.0	100.0	100.0	100.0	100.0	100.0
1930	100.1	95.5	79.3	74.5	103.2	96.0
1931	89.3	99.5	70.2	61.5	100.9	81.4
1932	88.5	107.2	84.2	51.0	101.0	74.2
1933	87.3	103.0	104.5	49.9	103.7	67.2
1934	87.9	119.2	124.4	46.8	105.6	76.4
1935	87.6	130.7	127.5	49.5	112.2	87.9
1936	96.2	143.6	153.4	56.3	131.8	98.1
1937	102.2	150.3	158.2	66.4	146.6	95.9
1938	100.2	186.4	175.1	64.4	150.5	101.5
1939	103.3	195.2	180.8	68.0	154.5	111.7
1940	105.4	209.5	195.6	75.6	163.0	125.7
1941	122.1	271.1	217.4	89.1	175.6	139.7

Sources and method: Argentine data refer to an aggregate slightly higher than M_2, obtained from Comité Nacional de Geografía, 1941, 1943. This series follows closely the M_2 of Diz 1970, p. 146, for the period of overlap. Brazilian data refer to the M_2 series of Neuhaus, 1975, pp. 158–159. Colombian data refer to the M_1 series presented in Banco de la República 1971, pp. 104–105. Cuban data refer to the M_1 series presented in Wallich, 1950, pp. 38, 76, 152. Uruguayan data refer to the M_2 series presented in Banco Central del Uruguay, n.d. United States data refer to the M_2 series presented in Friedman and Schwartz 1963, table A-1, pp. 712–716.

On the other hand, as early as 1931 South American monetary authorities began to adopt measures which Professor E. W. Kemmerer and Sir Otto Niemeyer would have found unsound. Thus, the Argentine Caja de Conversión, whose old and only duty was to exchange gold for domestic currency and vice versa, began in 1931 to issue domestic currency in exchange for private commercial paper. By 1932 the old Caja even issued domestic currency against treasury paper (Banco Central de la República Argentina 1972, pp. 262–263). The Colombian Central Bank began in 1931 for the first time to engage in direct operations with the public, discounting notes endorsed by two first-class corporations and lending on the security of warehouse receipts. Government bonds were purchased in large quantities by the Colombian Central Bank since 1932. As noted by Robert Triffin, with the introduction of exchange control in 1931 in Colombia, international reserves ceased to govern monetary issue, which from then on was predominantly influenced by internal considerations of economic policy or budgetary expediency (Triffin 1944*a*, pp. 23–25). Very much the same could be said for all active Latin American countries.

The then heterodox South American monetary policies, which started around 1932, were in some ways a "relapse" into past inflationary propensities, a past which was meant to be exorcised by the adoption of gold standard rules. Thus, the Argentine Caja relied on nearly forgotten laws to rediscount private commercial paper; indeed, memories of wild inflation under inconvertible paper during the late nineteenth century, memories still fresh during 1929–1931, hampered and slowed down the adoption of more self-assured and expansionist monetary policies. It should also be borne in mind that as late as the early months of 1931 there were optimistic reports of an upturn in the major economies (Banco Central de la República Argentina 1972, p. 280).

In contrast with the United States, there are no reports of widespread bank failures in South American countries during the early 1930s. Also in contrast with the United States, monetary aggregates fail to reveal a flight into currency and away from bank deposits; if anything, during the early stages of the depression the opposite appears to have occurred, as may be seen in table 1.10. In active Latin American countries monetary authorities simply did not let many banks fail, casting fears of moral hazard to the wind. While moratoria on domestic bank debts were decreed in many countries (much earlier than in the United States), thereby freezing the banks' assets, commercial banks were supported in a number of ad hoc ways, not all of them conducive to maintaining actual liquidity. Thus, in Brazil, as early as October 1930, withdrawals of bank deposits were restricted by decree (Neuhaus 1975, p. 104). Rediscounting of private commercial banks' loans was also vigorously carried out by central banks and institutions such as the Banco do Brasil and the Banco de la Nación Argentina. These and other publicly owned banks held a substantial share of demand deposits in South America. Unorthodoxy was sometimes cloaked by gestures to the old financial orthodoxy; Argentina claimed to have used "profits" from increases in the peso price of gold to create an institution which supported the commercial banks (Banco Central de la República Argentina 1972, p. 264).

A fairly detailed look at the budget of the Argentine central government should cast some light on major trends in expenditures and taxes, and on the possibilities for aggregate demand management during the 1930s. The first column in table 1.11 shows total expenditures at current prices, which reached a low point in 1932 and expanded thereafter until 1939. Comparing nominal expenditures with the Buenos Aires cost of living index shown in table 1.6, it may be seen that 1929 real expenditures were surpassed even during the provisional regime of General Uriburu (September 1930–February 1932), who had pledged an elimination of the excesses of the populist government of President Yrigoyen. After touching a post-1929 bottom in 1933, real expenditures expanded significantly during the second half of the 1930s. A major road-building pro-

Table 1.10   **Currency Held by the Public as Percentage of Money Supply**

End of Year	Argentina	Brazil	Colombia	Chile	Cuba	Uruguay	U.S.
1928	18.1	30.5	63.8	na	43.5	30.9	8.2
1929	18.1	28.0	66.4	na	44.9	29.8	8.3
1930	17.1	26.9	64.6	na	39.7	26.1	8.6
1931	17.3	26.8	65.4	19.2	44.7	27.1	12.3
1932	16.4	27.2	58.0	21.8	37.7	23.3	14.2
1933	16.7	28.7	59.6	18.4	47.8	26.0	15.7
1934	18.2	26.4	58.4	18.1	45.9	28.2	13.0
1935	19.6	28.8	59.6	19.4	44.0	28.8	12.1
1936	19.9	30.2	60.6	19.6	41.2	33.2	12.2
1937	25.5	30.6	57.9	20.6	43.4	30.9	12.6
1938	20.6	25.3	57.2	21.8	42.8	30.9	12.0
1939	20.5	26.1	56.2	23.8	45.9	29.6	12.1
1940	21.5	25.8	50.3	24.6	49.2	31.6	12.6
1941	21.2	25.9	54.0	26.1	50.5	29.8	14.9

Sources and method: Sources as in table 9. Chilean money supply data refer to M_2, as given in Deaver, 1970, pp. 60–63. Comparable data before 1931 are not available.

Table 1.11   Indicators of Size and Structure of Argentine Central Government Budget

Year	Total Expenditures at Current Prices (1929 = 100)	Ratio of Total Expenditures to Merchandise Exports	Percentages of Total Expenditures				
			Tax Revenues	Changes in Floating Debt	Public Works	Debt Service	Military
1928	93.0	0.38	80.4	na	15.0	na	21.2
1929	100.0	0.46	75.7	20.7	19.0	na	19.1
1930	110.5	0.78	60.8	32.4	17.3	18.3	18.6
1931	91.9	0.62	75.5	17.7	8.6	22.4	21.0
1932	86.0	0.66	87.4	−39.1	5.4	29.2	20.0
1933	89.1	0.79	91.2	−13.7	9.4	28.3	19.7
1934	94.5	0.65	96.2	−1.7	14.1	23.4	20.6
1935	99.3	0.63	99.7	−77.6	16.0	20.5	21.6
1936	106.4	0.64	93.2	−3.2	17.5	19.3	23.8
1937	123.6	0.53	90.4	7.8	19.3	16.0	25.8
1938	129.4	0.91	86.4	19.8	20.2	14.7	na
1939	147.8	0.93	80.4	−1.9	15.8	15.3	na
1940	133.7	0.92	93.2	21.9	15.8	18.5	na

Sources and method: Budget data obtained from Comité Nacional de Geografía 1941, pp. 402–405; and Comité Nacional de Geografía 1943, pp. 206–210. Merchandise exports at current pesos obtained from Díaz Alejandro 1970, p. 479. Military expenditures obtained from Potash 1969, pp. 34, 99; they include pensions and some public works, which are (probably) included also in the "Public Works" column. Tax revenues are broadly defined to include various fees and charges.

gram was undertaken by the government of General Justo (1932–1938), himself a civil engineer, which added 30,000 kilometers of all-weather and improved roads by 1938 to a system that had only 2,100 kilometers of such roads in 1932 (Potash 1969, p. 85). The late 1930s also witnessed an expansion of military expenditures.

The second column of table 1.11 compares two major injections into the Argentine income stream: government expenditures and exports. The latter gained relatively to the former so that by the late 1930s they were almost of the same magnitude.

Tax revenues lagged behind expenditures during President Yrigoyen's administration; in 1930 nominal tax revenues, heavily dependent on import duties, fell in absolute amounts, as may be seen in table 1.12. Large deficits were registered in 1930 and 1931, which could be regarded as being induced by the decline in foreign trade rather than as autonomous acts of policy. Both the Uriburu and the Justo administrations (and the brilliant technocrats in charge of their economic policies) took a dim view of government deficits and made repeated pledges to correct the situation. As in other Latin American countries fiscal heterodoxy was discredited in Argentina by lax budgets during the late 1920s. Both the Uriburu and the Justo administrations attempted to reduce expenditures and to increase taxes during the early 1930s; an income tax was introduced in 1932 and tariff rates were increased earlier.

During the early 1930s, budget deficits were primarily financed by increases in the "floating debt," i.e., delays in payments to suppliers and civil servants or payments in public debt instruments of low liquidity. Such financing methods, of course, contributed to giving government deficits a bad name and raised doubts about their net expansionary effects, as they came close to forced loans. Only in the late 1930s was an active market developed for public debt instruments. It may be seen in table 1.11 that starting in 1932 the "floating debt" was reduced, but it is unclear to what extent it was settled in cash or in long-term public securities. Money supply data shown in table 1.9 suggests that the latter was the predominant form of settlement.

Another consideration reducing the countercyclical potency of fiscal policy during the early 1930s is the increased share in the budget of debt service payments, mainly made to foreigners. As may be seen in table 1.11, payments on the public debt reached 29 percent of expenditures in 1932; this may be contrasted with the meager 5 percent devoted to public works. The import content of the budget probably peaked at the worst possible moment.[4] Other Latin American countries were to find the

---

4. Within the military budget, outlays for imported equipment seem to have been reduced while those for salaries and pensions were increased (Potash 1969, pp. 74–75). But the quantitative impact of such a shift appears small relative to debt service data.

Table 1.12   Argentine Central Government Tax Revenues

| Year | Total Tax Revenues at Current Prices (1929 = 100) | Percentages of Total Tax Revenues | | |
		Customs and Harbor Duties	Exchange Differential Profits	Income Taxes
1928	98.8	54.6	0	0
1929	100.0	54.9	0	0
1930	88.7	52.1	0	0
1931	91.7	46.1	0	0
1932	99.3	38.7	0	7.2
1933	107.4	38.2	0.1	8.1
1934	120.3	33.1	12.6	7.4
1935	130.9	33.1	12.1	7.9
1936	131.2	31.9	9.0	7.3
1937	147.6	36.8	5.8	9.0
1938	147.7	34.1	6.5	9.8
1939	157.1	27.3	9.6	9.5
1940	164.5	22.0	16.2	10.2

Sources and method: As in table 11.

budgetary weight of debt service an additional inducement to suspend normal payments.

In short, there is no evidence that during the early 1930s the Argentine government sought to increase the full employment budget deficit as a means to compensate for the fall in aggregate demand. On the contrary, there is evidence that attempts were made to shift the tax schedule upward and to lower government expenditures. It may be said, however, that even during the early 1930s the efforts to reduce the deficit induced by the decline in foreign trade and aggregate demand were tempered by either certain common sense or by the sheer inability to cut expenditures and raise taxes fast enough. The relative size of public expenditures in the income stream thus grew by default in the early 1930s, helping to sustain economic activity. Since 1933 public expenditures expanded in a deliberate way. Such an expansion had at least a balanced-budget-multiplier effect on the rest of the economy. In addition, since 1935 the new central bank facilitated the creation of a market for the domestic public debt, allowing some modest deficit financing. Finally, the structure of expenditures during the late 1930s favored domestic expansion, in spite of some increase in the import content of military expenditures (Potash 1969, p. 99).

Fiscal trends in other active Latin American countries may be briefly contrasted with those for Argentina, using scanty or impressionistic evidence. Calamities, civil disturbances, or border wars in the early 1930s led to increased public expenditures in several countries, apparently financed directly by monetary expansion. Examples include political turmoil in Chile during late 1931 and 1932 (when that country had a short-lived socialist government); the war between Peru and Colombia over Leticia in 1932; the second Chaco War between Bolivia and Paraguay, also in 1932; the São Paulo rebellion of 1932 and a severe drought in northeastern Brazil.

Brazil provides an interesting and documented example of a compensatory increase in government expenditures in the early 1930s, besides those resulting from the northeastern drought and the São Paulo rebellion. Since 1906 Brazil had attempted to sustain coffee prices both abroad and at home via buffer stocks. As coffee prices fell in the early 1930s, the government purchased large quantities of that product. A good share of those purchases were financed either by foreign loans or by new taxes, but about 35 percent appear to have been financed essentially by money creation (Silber 1977, p. 192). The new taxes levied on exports, or the relative exchange rate appreciation generated by foreign loans, could be said to have improved Brazilian terms of trade, relative to the relevant counterfactual situation (Fishlow 1972; Cardoso 1979). Argentina also started regulating the production and export of major traditional exports during the 1930s, but without the massive fiscal impact of the Brazilian coffee purchases. The exchange differential profits shown in table 1.12, however, were the Argentine counterpart to the Brazilian export taxes, both attempting to raise revenues as well as to protect the terms of trade.

Brazil, like Argentina, clearly expanded public expenditures during the late 1930s and probably reduced the import content of those expenditures even more than Argentina, as it suspended normal debt servicing in September 1931. In 1937 Brazil announced the suspension of *all* debt servicing, and none occurred during 1938 and 1939 (de Paiva Abreu 1978, pp. 109, 119). Both Argentina and Brazil in the 1930s instituted an important diversification of public revenues with a remarkable expansion in noncustoms taxes, which by 1932 (Argentina) and 1933 (Brazil) had exceeded the levels reached in 1929, at current prices. A similar trend toward tax diversification has been reported for Colombia and Mexico (Wallich 1944a, pp. 122–123).

Whatever the hesitations and improvisations of the early 1930s, by the second half of the decade the active Latin American countries had developed a respectable array of both monetary and fiscal tools, as well as the will to use them to avoid deflation. Thus, the 1937–1938 recession in the United States was felt in the foreign trade statistics much more than in those for industrial output. South American countries damaged by the loss of European markets and shipping shortages in 1940 mobilized to adopt emergency stabilization measures, such as the Plan Pinedo in

Argentina (Díaz Alejandro 1970, p. 105). Soon thereafter, however, fiscal and monetary tools had to go into reverse gear to offset inflationary pressures arising from expanding foreign exchange reserves and supply shortages. That transition was not managed smoothly, perhaps with the exception of pre-1944 Argentina,[5] but that is another story.

The impotency of passive countries may be illustrated by the contrasting experiences of Cuba and Mexico in their tinkering with silver for monetary and fiscal purposes during the early 1930s. Both countries hit upon the expedient of issuing silver coins, which both added to liquidity and yielded seigniorage "profits" to the treasury, justifying expenditures. In Cuba modest issues were made during 1932–1933, and in 1934 a revolutionary government appeared to herald a bold new monetary system independent of the dollar by planning new issues and by making silver pesos full legal tender for the discharge of old as well as new obligations contracted in dollars or in old Cuban gold pesos. Shortly thereafter a mild form of exchange control was decreed. Foreign banks apparently threatened to export all dollars from Cuba; capital flight followed. The government caved in, lifting rather than expanding controls. Only the legal tender status of silver for all contracts in such currency remained of the 1934 reform. Even a central bank was not established until 1948 (Wallich 1944b, pp. 351–352).

Mexico, after some deflationary measures in 1930 and 1931, adopted a series of expansionary monetary and fiscal steps early in 1932, relying mainly on issues of silver pesos.[6] Central bank control over commercial banks was extended and strengthened. Foreign banks threatened to leave Mexico, and as the Mexican authorities held firm, most of them actually did. Mexican-owned commercial banks took their place. These and other policies, framed under the remarkable leadership of Alberto J. Pani, contributed to the vigorous recovery of the Mexican economy. Mexican reliance on a silver standard did not generate unmanageable problems when the United States raised silver prices; Mexico simply prohibited the export of silver money in April 1935 and ordered all coins to be exchanged for paper currency. A year and a half later, after the world price of silver had fallen, silver coinage was restored (Friedman and Schwartz 1963, p. 491). As a major producer and exporter of silver, Mexico of

---

5. In an article published in 1944, Robert Triffin asserted: "In the short period since 1935 the Central Bank of Argentina has developed into an outstanding institution among central banks not only in Latin America but in older countries as well. Credit for this achievement is due largely to the brilliant leadership of Raoul [sic] Prebisch, general manager of the bank during most of this period, and to an extremely able staff of executives and research workers" (Triffin 1944b, pp. 100–101).

6. For Mexico, I shamelessly follow the unpublished works of two young Mexican scholars, who happen to be graduate students at Yale: Enrique Cárdenas and Jaime Zabludowsky. My summary of their research does not do full justice to their papers. I am grateful for their permission to use their work.

course benefited from higher international silver prices, which accelerated her recovery. The Mexican case was in this respect different from the disastrous Chinese experience (Friedman and Schwartz 1963, pp. 699–700; contrast with the slip in Haberler 1976, p. 10).

1.4   The Service of Foreign Capital

Before the First World War, portfolio and direct investments, mainly from Europe, flowed into Latin America. Those from the United States were then relatively small and concentrated in the Caribbean, Central America, and Mexico. During the 1920s, U.S. investments soared throughout the region, while European investments stagnated or declined. The expansion of public borrowing in the New York bond market was particularly noteworthy.

Table 1.13 presents estimates of the stock of British and U.S. investments of all kinds in Latin America toward the end of the 1920s. In per capita terms they remained below corresponding figures for Canada, but impressive levels were registered in Argentina, Chile, Uruguay, Costa Rica, Mexico, and especially Cuba. Both in Canada and Latin America the two major foreign investors had accumulated a stock of claims around four times the value of annual merchandise exports. Assuming a 5 percent rate of return, profits and interests of foreign capital must have accounted for about 20 percent of annual export earnings.

Relations with foreign investors had remained prickly throughout the nineteenth and early twentieth centuries. Defaults had occurred on bonds issued in London, and numerous frictions were generated by direct investments. The Royal Navy was no stranger to South American waters, once even attempting a naval blockade of Bolivia, and the U.S. Marines were an important presence in the Caribbean and in Central America. During the 1920s, however, the investment climate appeared reasonably good, with the exception of Mexico. The continuous tensions between Mexico and the United States over oil and other U.S. investments led a perceptive observer to worry about "the conflict between the vested rights of Americans in the natural resources of the Caribbean countries and the rising nationalism of their peoples" (Lippmann 1927, p. 353).[7]

These long-term considerations were overwhelmed after 1929 by short-term budgetary and balance of payments difficulties in servicing foreign

---

7. While adopting a paternalistic tone, highly offensive today ("One persistent motive in these uprisings is the desire to assert the national independence and the dignity of an inferior race".), Lippmann concluded with words which could be read with profit more than half a century later in the United States State Department: "And nothing would be so certain to arouse still further this illwill as the realization in Latin America that the United States had adopted a policy, conceived in the spirit of Metternich, which would attempt to guarantee vested rights against social progress as the Latin peoples conceive it" (Lippmann 1927, pp. 357, 363).

Table 1.13   Ratio of Stock of all British plus U.S. Investments to Annual
               Merchandise Exports and Population, circa Late 1920s

Country	Stock of Investments to Exports	Investments per Capita (current U.S. dollars)
Argentina	2.8	$258
Bolivia	3.3	56
Brazil	4.4	47
Chile	3.9	195
Colombia	2.4	41
Ecuador	3.7	24
Paraguay	2.4	34
Peru	2.7	53
Uruguay	2.9	164
Venezuela	3.3	82
Costa Rica	3.5	134
Guatemala	2.8	39
Honduras	2.2	52
Nicaragua	3.1	43
Salvador	1.8	15
Panama	11.2	88
Cuba	5.5	494
Haiti	2.0	12
Mexico	8.8	172
Dominican Republic	0.8	24
Total: Latin America	4.0	$107
Canada (all foreign investments)	4.7	$635

Sources and method: For Latin American countries basic data come from Winkler [1928]
1971, pp. 276, 278, 283. Export data refer to 1927, while those for investments are said to be
for 1929 (forecasts?). Canadian data obtained from Urquhart and Buckley 1965, pp. 14,
169, 173. Canadian data refer to 1926 and cover direct and portfolio investments from all
sources.

capital. The unexpected fall in dollar prices sharply increased the real
cost of external obligations denominated in nominal terms. Protection
and depression abroad cut into exchange earnings, actual and potential.
While much of the external debt of those days was long-term, it still called
for some amortizations. The drying up of foreign capital markets after
1930 made rollover operations for both long- and short-term debt very
difficult. The collapse of import duty revenues cut a traditional budgetary
source for payments on the external debt.

Table 1.14 shows estimates of the ratio of long-term external public
debt to annual exports, both in current dollars. A steep increase occurred
between 1929 and 1935 because of the fall in exports. More complete data
are available for Argentina and Brazil; these are presented in table 1.15,
which also gives Canadian data. By 1931 all net profits and interests on
foreign capital amounted to 47 percent of exports in Canada, 41 percent in

Table 1.14   **Latin America: Ratio of Stock of Long-Term External Public Debt to Yearly Merchandise Exports, F.O.B.**

Year	Ratio	Year	Ratio
1929	1.49	1972–73	1.14
1935	2.25	1974–76	1.06
1945	0.77	1977–78	1.48

Sources and method: Data for 1929 through 1945 obtained from CEPAL 1964, pp. 24, 27. Data since 1972 obtained from Inter-American Development Bank 1980, pp. 431, 443. The coverage of Latin America differs between these two sources; such a difference, however, is unlikely to modify the broad trend shown above.

Brazil, and 27 percent in Argentina. All public debt services (including amortizations) reached 38 percent of exports in Brazil and over 15 percent in Argentina. It was seen in table 1.11 that debt service reached 22 percent of Argentine government expenditures in 1931. Chile in 1932 faced interest and amortization charges, including those on short-term maturities, far exceeding export earnings (Wallich 1943, p. 321).

Starting late in 1931, exchange control authorities delayed issuing permits to foreign companies for remitting profits abroad. Such profits had also been reduced by the crisis. More drastically, and also starting in 1931, most Latin American countries suspended normal payments on their external debts and asked foreign creditors for conversations aimed at rescheduling and restructuring those debts. Those negotiations were to stretch well into the 1940s, and in some cases into the 1950s. Different countries carried out the conversations with various degrees of enthusiasm; Cuba, for example, while servicing her debt irregularly during the 1930s, maintained better relations with her creditors than Brazil, whose dealings with creditors during the late 1930s, especially with the British, were acrimonious.

Rescheduling and liquidations of European-held debt plus the recovery of international trade had lowered sharply the debt/export ratio by 1945, as may be seen in table 1.14, a trend which probably continued until the early 1960s. Even in Argentina and Canada, which maintained normal debt service during the 1930s, profits and interests relative to export tended to decline in the late 1930s and early 1940s, as may be seen in table 1.15. For Latin America as a whole, interests plus profits as a percentage of all export earnings were down to 7 percent in the early 1950s; only during the 1970s were these indicators to reach again the levels of the late 1920s (Bacha and Díaz Alejandro 1981, table 7).

The contrast between Argentine and Brazilian policies toward debt service in the 1930s reveals the nature of international economic relations during those years. (The punctual debt servicing by the Dominican Republic and Haiti presents no mystery: the U.S. Marines stationed in those countries at the time provide a plausible explanatory variable.) In

Table 1.15   Argentine and Brazilian Financial Remittances
                  as Percentages of Merchandise Exports, F.O.B.

| | All Public Debt Services[a] | | All Net Profit and Interest Remittances[b] | | |
Year	Argentina	Brazil	Argentina	Brazil	Canada
1914	12.5	18.2[c]	29.3	na	44.5
1921–25	6.3	11.9	16.6	na	20.3
1926–28	5.6	14.9	18.1	na	17.1
1929	6.2	18.2	19.8	na	22.2
1930	11.2	30.0	28.6	38.7	32.8
1931	13.8	37.9	27.2	40.5	46.9
1932	14.5	21.3	29.4	25.4	53.5
1933	15.6	17.0	31.6	13.1	42.5
1934	13.1	12.2	24.6	15.7	32.6
1935	11.2	14.0	22.8	25.1	28.1
1936	9.9	12.2	21.3	23.9	24.7
1937	6.5	12.1	16.0	23.5	21.7
1938	8.3	...	23.4	...	28.6
1939	9.0	...	23.8	3.8	27.5
1940–43	8.7	4.3	21.3	10.4	11.9
1973	20.5	15.3	14.3	18.3	9.0
1974–76	23.0	18.7	13.3	22.9	7.8
1977–79	24.1	33.0	11.6	33.2	10.4

Sources and method: Pre-1944 Argentine data obtained from CEPAL 1956, table 18, p. 293. Pre-1944 Brazilian data obtained from de Paiva Abreu 1980, tables 1 and 2. Data since 1973 for both countries obtained from World Bank 1980, vol. 2; International Monetary Fund 1980a, 1980b. Pre-1944 Canadian data obtained from Urquhart and Buckley 1965, pp. 159–160. Data since 1973 obtained as above.
[a]Include both interest and amortization. To obtain Brazilian data before 1944 it was assumed that amortization amounted to 40 percent of all public debt services.
[b]Include both private and public net profit and interest remittances.
[c]Refers to 1911–1915.

merchandise accounts, Brazil traditionally had an export surplus with the United States and an import surplus with the United Kingdom. Argentina had an export surplus with the United Kingdom, and an import surplus with the United States. Both the Argentine and Brazilian debts had become diversified during the 1920s, but more than half were still held by British interests.

Argentina had an export surplus with a country organizing commonwealth preferences and threatening to impose bilateral exchange clearings, and where the financial interests of the city still exerted great political influence. Australia, Canada, and New Zealand appeared eager to replace Argentina in British markets. British pressures culminated in the Roca-Runciman treaty of 1933, whose features were not unlike those of 1930s economic treaties between Germany and eastern European countries. The bitterness felt both in Argentina and in the United States toward this treaty is aptly summarized in a long rhetorical question of Virgil Salera: "But could not more far-sighted [Argentine] leadership have avoided the granting of thoroughgoing preferences of the sort that were actually conceded under the terms of the Roca pact, concessions which, besides encouraging international ill-will in the case of those countries discriminated against, reduced Argentina to something close to an economic vassal of a power that had never preached nor practiced *universal* narrow bilateralism as a new and more satisfactory type of international economic policy?" (Salera 1941, p. 89). Under these circumstances, tampering with the normal servicing of the Argentine debt would have involved not only a bruising commercial clash with the United Kingdom, but also probably a major restructuring of the Argentine domestic political scene, at the expense of groups linked with Anglo-Argentine trade.

Brazil had an export surplus with a country committed to multilateral trade plus convertibility, and where the New Deal viewed financial interests with some suspicion. United States exporters to Brazil know that an additional dollar spent in Rio for debt servicing, mainly to British interests, would mean one less dollar for Brazilian imports from the United States (Brazil had run out of reserves as early as 1930). The British could do little when faced by erratic Brazilian debt service. Furthermore, during the second half of the 1930s there was a preoccupation in Washington with German influence in Brazil, leading to even more tolerant views of Brazilian debt service irregularities (de Paiva Abreu 1978). Similar geopolitical considerations may also explain the relatively mild response of the Roosevelt administration to the Mexican oil nationalizations of 1938.

International capital markets never quite recovered from the 1930s defaults. Such an experience, particularly that involving nonindustrial countries, is still used to buttress arguments favoring the organization of sanctions against possible defaults by less developed countries during the 1980s (Eaton and Gersovitz 1980, pp. 7–9, 53). Without heavy penalties on defaults, it is argued, international capital markets will mobilize too few funds, as bankers ration credit to offset the adverse selection imperfection. As there are no more recent examples of widespread defaults than those of the 1930s, it is important to inquire whether the defaults resulted mainly from virtual impossibility to pay and from unexpected changes in international rules, or whether debtor countries coolly broke their contracts because they calculated that they could get away with it because of the lack of sanctions.

Writing in *The American Economic Review* for 1943, Henry C. Wallich argued that, at least for Latin American dollar bonds, the causes of default were well-known and deserved little elaboration: "If the depression of the 1930's had been mild, and if the steady expansion of world trade and capital exports had continued thereafter, defaults probably would have been infrequent and could have been settled without much difficulty. . . . Without . . . attempting to deny that insufficient care was exercised, and that Latin American countries were encouraged to borrow excessively one may question whether these factors were decisive" (Wallich 1943, p. 321).

Other commentators of the 1930s and 1940s emphasized that imperfections in the 1920s capital markets did not derive solely from the inability of honest and competent bankers and underwriters to tell which borrowers really planned to service their debts, independently of their financial positions. Many underwriters were accused not only of negligence in seeking information about borrowers and their projects, but also of deliberately misleading the proverbial widows and orphans (Winkler 1932; Cumberland 1932). Much New Deal legislation sought to check dishonesty in financial intermediation.

The crisis of the 1930s went beyond macroeconomic collapse and the protectionist upsurge. The industrialized countries themselves led in the undermining of belief in the sanctity of contracts; examples include the British default on the war debt, Germany's failure to make payments on the greater part of her international obligations, and the derogation of the gold clause in the United States (Wallich 1943, p. 322). During the 1940s the United Kingdom froze growing sterling balances of many developing countries, balances whose real value was sharply eroded by inflation, and actually contemplated complete repudiation. A substantial body of British economic opinion even today regrets that repudiation was not adopted (Bolton 1972).

By the late 1930s the ability to service their debts had improved in many Latin American countries, and indeed some servicing did occur throughout the 1930s. There were gains to be made avoiding repudiation, even in the absence of Eaton-Gersovitz sanctions. Some countries purchased their own partially or wholly unserviced bonds, which were selling at a discount in foreign markets. This was regarded by some as perfidious: you default, ruin the prices of your bonds, and then quietly buy them back. As late as 1943, Henry Wallich argued that such repurchases were not only defensible but, under the circumstances, constituted the best method of dealing with the defaulted bonds "not merely from the viewpoint of the debtor but to some extent even from that of the bondholder" (Wallich 1943, p. 332).

The repurchase, Wallich argued, avoided a rigid settlement at a time when the international economic outlook was very uncertain. Repurchases had a technical advantage which today seems archaic: they could be carried out by central banks, whose exchange reserves were rising in the early 1940s, while normal servicing was the responsibility of treasuries, whose revenue situation had been hurt by the fall in imports and the corresponding decline in duties. Wallich noted that by the late 1930s and early 1940s the defaulted Latin American bonds had become unsuitable for the portfolios of their original holders, so it could be assumed that a large part was held by speculators. This consideration, plus the macroeconomic advantages derived by the United States from capital exports during the 1920s, plus the irregularities found on both sides in many loan transactions, made the ethics of resuming debt service highly problematical. The early use of Keynesian analysis led Wallich to write, somewhat tongue-in-cheek: " 'Tis better to have lent and lost than never to have lent at all" (Wallich 1943, p. 328). He recommended a generous policy toward the debtors, without a hint of new codes for sanctioning defaults. Indeed, he suggested that the service of loans which the EXIMBANK began to extend to Latin American countries in 1940 should be made contingent on the exports of each country.

Regardless of the ethics and legalities of defaults, the economics of the 1930s induce tolerance. What Gottfried Haberler has written justifying the suspension of German reparations applies a fortiori to Latin American defaults: ". . . when productive resources were allowed to go to waste in idleness and countries everywhere were restricting imports to protect jobs, it made no economic sense whatsoever to insist on the transfer of real resources as reparations" (Haberler 1976, p. 28). Reparations, like debt service, were fundamentally victims of the Great Depression: ". . . there can be hardly a doubt that the transfer of the reparations as fixed by the Young plan would have been possible—in the absence, to repeat, of a serious depression and depression-induced protectionism" (Haberler 1976, p. 31).

1.5 Concluding Reflections

For most Latin American countries, the 1930s and early 1940s were "the worst of times and the best of times." After the initial external blows, the active countries steadily gained in both ability and will to maintain growth regardless of foreign conditions. The public sector undertook new development tasks, while the national private sector seems to have experienced an upsurge. Countries learned to rely on domestic finance for capital formation and to do without many imports. Import substitution extended to economic policy: gone were Kemmerer, Niemeyer, and Fisher,[8] their places partly taken by Prebisch and Pani,

---

8. Kemmerer's prestige in the United States and in Latin America seems to have peaked in the late 1920s. For a summary of his views see his presidential address to the American Economic Association (Kemmerer 1927). Irving Fisher advised the Calles government in Mexico during the early 1930s, but the nature of his advice is unknown (Suarez 1977, pp. 51–52).

and partly by new "imports" such as Triffin and Wallich. Domestic economic policy witnessed a most creative period, encouraged by the new foreign advisors. Thus Triffin defended Latin American exchange controls (Triffin 1944b, pp. 112–113) and advised Paraguay to peg to a basket of currencies (Triffin 1944c, pp. 6–7). Latin American experiences sparked further insights in the late 1940s: Polak outlined the "absorption approach" in a paper written in connection with Mexico's 1948 devaluation (Polak 1948). Polak has also noted, in private conversation, that the early development of the monetary approach to the balance of payments was heavily influenced by Rodrigo Gómez and his staff at the Central Bank of Mexico.

Policies which made sense during 1929–1945 turned out not to be so desirable after the Second World War. Some countries adapted to the more prosperous and peaceful international economic conditions fairly quickly, while others remained obsessed by export pessimism and fears of unemployment and of a new world war. Thus, while Mexico sought new sources of foreign exchange and achieved price stability by the 1950s, Argentina and Brazil remained tangled in extreme protectionism and inflation. To what extent the Argentine and Brazilian policy errors of the 1950s were inevitable consequences of the 1930s is highly questionable and beyond the scope of this paper.

To conclude, two lessons of the 1930s seem particularly relevant for the 1980s. In a world of erratic changes in terms of trade, unpredictable protectionism, and high capital mobility, commitment to fixed exchange rates, unlimited convertibility, and gold-standard-type monetary rules seems rash and risky. The second lesson applies to creditor countries. If by their actions they seriously disturb the normal expectations existing at the time loans were made, they may destroy the reverse transfer mechanism. Such a lesson would apply either to old or new capital exporters, and unusual actions would include protectionism, the tolerance of prolonged depression, or extravagant increases in oil prices or interest rates.

References

Bacha, Edmar L., and Carlos F. Díaz Alejandro. 1981. Financial markets: A view from the semi-periphery. Yale Economic Growth Center Discussion Paper no. 367. Paper presented at the CIEPLAN seminar on External Financial Relations and Their Impact on the Latin American Economies, March 1981.

Banco Central de la República Argentina. 1972. La creación del banco central y la experiencia monetaria Argentina entre los años 1935–1943. 2 vols. Buenos Aires.

Banco Central del Uruguay. n.d. *Series estadísticas monetarias y bancarias*. Montevideo.

Banco de la República. 1971. *Informe anual del gerente a la junta directiva, 1970–1971*. Bogota.

Bolton, Sir George. 1972. Where critics are as wrong as Keynes was. *The Banker* 122:1385–1388.

Cardoso, Eliana A. 1979. Inflation, growth and the real exchange rate: Essays on economic history in Brazil. Ph.D. diss., Massachusetts Institute of Technology.

CEPAL. 1956. Document E/CN.12/429/Add.4. Santiago de Chile.

———. 1964. *El financiamento externo de America Latina*. New York: United Nations.

———. 1976. *America Latina: Relación de precios del intercambio*. Santiago de Chile: United Nations.

———. 1978. *Series históricas del crecimiento de America Latina*. Santiago de Chile: United Nations.

Comité Nacional de Geografía. 1941. *Anuario geográfico Argentino*. Buenos Aires.

———. 1943. *Anuario geográfico Argentino, Suplemento 1942*. Buenos Aires.

Cumberland, W. W. 1932. Investments and national policy of the United States in Latin America. *American Economic Review* 22:152–173.

Deaver, John V. 1970. The Chilean inflation and the demand for money. In *Varieties of monetary experience*, edited by D. Meiselman. Chicago: University of Chicago Press.

de Paiva Abreu, Marcelo. 1974. A Missão Niemeyer. *Revista de Administracão de Empresas* 14:7–28.

———. 1978. Brazilian public foreign debt policy, 1931–1943. *Brazilian Economic Studies* 4:105–141.

———. 1980. O Brasil e a economia mundial, 1929–1949. Rio de Janeiro. Mimeo.

Díaz Alejandro, Carlos F. 1970. *Essays on the economic history of the Argentine Republic*. New Haven: Yale University Press.

———. 1980*a*. A America Latina em depressao, 1929–1939. *Pesquisa e Planejamento Economico* 10:351–382.

———. 1980*b*. Exchange rates and terms of trade in the Argentine Republic, 1913–1976. Yale Economic Growth Center Discussion Paper no. 341.

Dirección General de Estadística. Ministerio de Hacienda. 1959. *Resumenes estadísticos seleccionados*. Havana.

Diz, Adolfo Cesar. 1970. Money and prices in Argentina, 1935–1962. In *Varieties of monetary experience*, edited by D. Meiselman. Chicago: University of Chicago Press.

Eaton, Jonathan, and Mark Gersovitz. 1980. Poor country borrowing in private financial markets and the repudiation issue. Princeton Research Program in Development Studies Discussion Paper 94.

European Cement Association. 1967. *The world cement market in figures.* Paris.

Finch, David. 1951–1952. Investment service of underdeveloped countries. *International Monetary Fund Staff Papers* 2:60–86.

Fishlow, Albert. 1972. Origins and consequences of import substitution in Brazil. In *International economics and development,* edited by Luis de Marco. New York: Academic Press.

Friedman, Milton, and Anna J. Schwartz. 1963. *A monetary history of the United States, 1867–1960.* Princeton: Princeton University Press.

Haberler, Gottfried. 1976. *The world economy, money, and the Great Depression, 1919–1939.* Washington, D.C.: American Enterprise Institute for Public Policy Research.

Haddad, Claudio L. S. 1978. *Crescimento do producto real no Brasil, 1900–1947.* Rio de Janeiro: Editora da Fundacão Getulio Vargas.

Inter-American Development Bank. 1980. *Economic and social progress in Latin America: 1979 report.* Washington, D.C.

International Monetary Fund. 1980a. *Balance of payments yearbook.* Washington, D.C.

———. 1980b. *International financial statistics.* Washington, D.C.

Kemmerer, E. W. 1927. Economic advisory work for governments. *American Economic Review* 17:1–13.

League of Nations. 1945. *Statistical yearbook of the League of Nations, 1942–1944.* Geneva.

Lippmann, Walter. 1927. Vested rights and nationalism in Latin America. *Foreign Affairs* 5:353–364.

Malan, Pedro S., Regis Bonelli, Marcelo de Paiva Abreu, and Jose E. de C. Pereira. 1977. *Politica economica externa e industrializacao no Brasil (1939–1952).* Rio de Janeiro: IPEA/INPES.

Millot, Julio, Carlos Silva, and Lindor Silva. 1972. *El desarrollo industrial del Uruguay.* Montevideo: Universidad de la República.

Nacional Financiera. 1977. *Statistics on the Mexican economy.* Mexico D.F.

Neuhaus, Paulo. 1975. *Historia monetaria do Brasil, 1900–1954.* Rio de Janeiro: IBMEC.

Ocampo, José Antonio. Comentarios. 1980. *Ensayos sobre historia económica Colombiana.* Bogota: FEDESARROLLO.

Perez Lopez, Jorge F. 1977. An index of Cuban industrial output, 1930–1958. In *Quantitative Latin American studies: Methods and findings,* edited by J. W. Wilkie and K. Ruddle. Los Angeles: UCLA Latin American Center Publications.

Polak, J. J. 1948. Depreciation to meet a situation of overinvestment. International Monetary Fund Document RD-707. Washington, D.C.

————. 1953. *An international economic system.* Chicago: University of Chicago Press.

Potash, Robert A. 1969. *The army and politics in Argentina, 1928–1945.* Stanford: Stanford University Press.

Salera, Virgil. 1941. *Exchange control and the Argentine market.* New York: Columbia University Press.

Silber, Simão. 1977. Analise da política económica e do comportamento da economía Brasileira durante o periodo 1929–1939. In *Formacão economica do Brasil: A experiencia da industrializacão,* edited by F. R. Versiani and J. R. M. de Barros. São Paulo: Saraiva S.A.

Solis, Leopoldo. 1970. *La realidad económica Mexicana: Retrovisión y perspectivas.* Mexico D.F.: Siglo Veintiuno Editores.

Suárez, Eduardo. 1977. *Comentarios y recuerdos (1926–1946).* Mexico D.F.: Editorial Porrua, S.A.

Triffin, Robert. 1944*a. Money and banking in Colombia.* Washington, D.C.: Board of Governors of the Federal Reserve System.

————. 1944*b.* Central banking and monetary management in Latin America. In *Economic problems of Latin America,* edited by Seymour E. Harris. New York: McGraw-Hill.

————. 1944*c.* New monetary and banking measures in Paraguay. *Federal Reserve Bulletin* (January):1–11.

————. 1945. Monetary developments in Latin America. *Federal Reserve Bulletin* (June):1–14.

Urquhart, M. C., and K. A. H. Buckley, eds. 1965. *Historical statistics of Canada.* Cambridge: Cambridge University Press.

U.S. Bureau of the Census. 1960. *Historical statistics of the United States.* Washington, D.C.: Government Printing Office.

Wallich, Henry C. 1943. The future of Latin American dollar bonds. *American Economic Review* 33:321–335.

————. 1944*a.* Fiscal policy and the budget. In *Economic problems of Latin America,* edited by Seymour E. Harris. New York: McGraw-Hill.

————. 1944*b.* Cuba: Sugar and currency. In *Economic problems of Latin America,* edited by Seymour E. Harris. New York: McGraw-Hill.

————. 1950. *Monetary problems of an export economy: The Cuban experience, 1914–1947.* Cambridge: Harvard University Press.

Winkler, Max. 1932. Investments and national policy of the United States in Latin America. *American Economic Review* 22:144–152.

————. 1971. *Investments of United States capital in Latin America.* Port Washington, New York: Kennikat Press.

World Bank. 1980. *World debt tables.* Washington, D.C.

Comment   Miguel Mancera

The title of the document presented by Díaz Alejandro, "Stories of the 1930s for the 1980s," is in itself very appealing. Economic policies for the future are always based to a large extent on the experience of the past. In this sense, the review the author makes not only of the 1930s, but of the end of the 1920s and the beginning of the 1940s—along with occasional observations of other periods—proves most useful. The review of these conjunctures has the additional interest of referring to a time not experienced by the majority of today's population, including those who are now economists. However, it was a time which should be better known since the then prevailing circumstances spurred a significant advance in the science of economics and also, as Díaz Alejandro points out, a profound change in the economies of some Latin American countries.

As the author recalls, two major blows were received from abroad by the Latin American economies during the 1930s. On the one hand, there was the decline in demand for their exports due to both recession and protectionist policies at the center, and on the other, there was the great increase in the burden of servicing the foreign debt, due as much to the rise in the real rate of interest in certain years, as to the fact that it was virtually impossible to negotiate new loans with which to make the usual rollover.

One of the most interesting results derived from the drop in Latin American exports was that the countries which the author calls "active" abandoned the system of fixed exchange rates.

It is likely that the system of fixed exchange rates ceased to be the rule in the 1930s not so much because many were convinced of the comparative advantages of a more flexible system, but because it was practically unfeasible to maintain the previous parities with respect to gold. Some monetary authorities probably hoped to attain a new stability in exchange rates, if only at a different level than before and not necessarily in terms of gold, but in terms of a new standard that, in practice, became the U.S. dollar.

Whatever the reasons or aspirations were when the currencies of active countries declined in value, something very important was expediently achieved to bring about a profound structural change in the economies of these countries. In so doing, the crisis, as Díaz Alejandro says, was absorbed with less negative impacts on both employment and growth.

What was actually achieved with the Latin American devaluations of the 1930s—that, most likely, remains in the subconscious of many but is rarely admitted because it is unpleasant to confess—was the reduction in real wages. This reduction, accomplished with such expediency through

Miguel Mancera is subdirector general of the Banco de México, S.A.

exchange measures, would have been much slower, if at all possible, maintaining a fixed exchange rate and trying to lower nominal wages.

Obviously, the reduction in real wages made import-substituting industries and those with a nontraditional export potential more profitable. The hypothesis could then be established that, by means of devaluation, the crisis implied less penalties for the populations of active countries, since the negative impact of the reduction in wages on the working population was probably less than that which would have been caused by the resulting contraction in employment had the exchange rate been maintained. Furthermore, from the viewpoint of social fairness, perhaps a certain reduction in the income of many is better than maintaining the income level of some while causing the unemployment of others.

In discussing the exchange measures taken in the 1930s by active countries, a distinction should be made between the effects of outright devaluation and of establishing exchange controls, with or without devaluation. The virtues of devaluation in the 1930s have already been discussed.

Exchange controls are sometimes established to avoid capital flight. Naturally, for such controls to be effective, the monetary authority must succeed in making residents surrender all foreign exchange they receive for whatever reason. This assumes the existence of an extensive and costly administrative apparatus not only in the central bank, but also in commercial banks and in customs. Such an apparatus requires numerous and highly qualified personnel. They should be uncorruptible and always up-to-date on the prices of a wide variety of goods that are imported and exported. They must be familiar with the mechanisms for transferring funds and with the usual payment terms in foreign trade operations, as well as with the nature and conditions of international financial transactions.

What the exchange controls established in Latin America during the 1930s were able to achieve to avoid capital flight, no one can know for certain. It is reasonable to assume, however, that, given the great difficulty and the length of time necessary to set up an effective exchange control, enormous capital outflows did occur despite existing controls, mostly during the initial years (the controls themselves could have been an additional reason for the outflows). It may not be absurd to think, even though no one can prove or disprove it, that more capital flight has taken place over the years under exchange controls than under free convertibility.

Exchange controls can be established not only with the aim of controlling capital movements, but as an instrument for rationing the foreign exchange needed for current transactions—an alternative to devaluation, especially when there is not enough political courage to undertake it. If established under these conditions, the exchange rate will remain overvalued and it will be harder to bring about the desirable structural changes in the economy. In addition, since the price of foreign currency is not in equilibrium, monetary authorities must resolve the tremendous problem of suitably distributing the insufficient foreign exchange they have at their disposal. Monetary authorities become exposed to the risk of making serious errors in judgment when deciding how to distribute the foreign currency at hand, while many officers and employees of banking institutions and of customs become vulnerable to corruption.

In time, exchange controls—originally established to avoid capital flight or devaluation—may also be used to wield influence on the structure of international transactions through multiple exchange rates. In this respect, however, it is doubtful that exchange controls accomplish anything that could not be achieved with free convertibility, properly combined with import and export duties.

Much has been written about exchange controls, and this paper cannot discuss the subject in depth. But these brief remarks are needed, since the author seems inclined to suggest exchange controls in lieu of a system of flexible exchange rates and free convertibility.

One more word about the then heterodox devaluations of the 1930s. Besides being responsible for a profound and desirable structural change in the economies of the active countries, the devaluations served as an antirecessionary element. By partially or totally offsetting the decline in domestic prices brought about by the drop in exports, devaluations caused real interest rates not to rise as much as they would have in certain years had such policies not been implemented.

The monetary and fiscal management of the 1930s is the object of a stimulating analysis on the part of Díaz Alejandro. The author points to the successes of the compensatory measures of active countries. One of the reasons for the success of these measures was that they were applied without excess, at least in the beginning. The annual increases in public spending and the money supply were within a range that today would correspond to rather conservative programs in most of Latin America.

It was not until the last years of the 1930s and the early 1940s when macroeconomic policies moved from compensatory to expansionary. The new theories of Keynes began to permeate Latin America and were cited as an endorsement for incurring fiscal deficits of a magnitude that would hardly have been approved by such an intelligent economist.

In connection with the Latin American foreign debt in the 1930s, it is possible to say—as does the author—that the problem stemmed much more from the external situation than from domestic difficulties. The rise in the real burden of servicing the debt was doubtless a serious matter. But perhaps even a greater one was the collapse of international financial markets. In this respect, it should be remembered that highly indebted countries resemble banks, in the sense that they can only pay important percentages of their international obligations on time if those that they settle can be replaced by others. If the possibility of rollover is closed to them, so is the possibility to pay on time. This should be kept in mind by those who take out credit, but even more so by those who offer it. Lenders actually have a two-fold responsibility: to maintain the possibility of rollover and, at the same time, not to induce prospective debtors— as lenders paradoxically often do—to take more credit than can realistically be paid or replaced at maturity.

In his final reflections, Díaz Alejandro states, with good reason, that the policies that made sense in the 1930s were no longer desirable after World War II.

One might ask whether the lessons of the 1930s are appropriate for the 1980s. The answer surely is in the affirmative, but only in the general context that all experiences leave usable lessons for the future. The 1980s, however, find countries within Latin America in a wide variety of circumstances.

Some Latin American countries, especially the non-oil-producing ones, have received blows from abroad that are somehow equivalent to those of the 1930s; the difference being that, generally, the new problems are due much more to the rise in the price of oil imports than to the decline in the value of exports.

Needless to say, for those Latin American countries that are oil producers, the present situation differs tremendously from that of a half century ago.

But, apart from the peculiarities of each country, the general economic framework of the 1980s is radically different from the 1930s. This is true inside as well as outside Latin America. Take, for example, the case of international credit. Financial markets, especially the Euromarket, are extremely active and liquid nowadays. The majority of Latin American countries have been able to increase the amount of their foreign debt or, at least, to maintain it. It would be hard to find cases of countries that have to make net payments on foreign credit.

Besides, interest on foreign debt, taken in real terms, has tended to be low during the last years and, at times, has turned out negative. Only during short periods, like some recent ones, has it been necessary to pay high real interest rates.

The relative ease with which many Latin American countries have been able to increase their foreign debt during the last ten of fifteen years has determined that, contrary to the 1930s, international financial transactions, taken by themselves, now constitute a very important inflationary element.

There are also sharp differences with regard to the openness of the economy. Beginning in the 1930s, an increasingly protectionist trend has been observed in many Latin American countries, although there have been signs of change in recent years. But in spite of these signs, the levels of protection prevailing in many countries would have been inconceivable a half century ago. This excessive protection has curbed the development of existing or potential export industries whose inputs of domestic origin are frequently very costly according to international standards. In this context, there seems to be a case for applying policies inverse to those of the 1930s, namely, less and not more protection.

How does the fiscal and monetary picture of the 1980s compare to the 1930s? A half century ago it made sense to battle recessionary forces of external origin with policies of a Keynesian cut. Today, the situation is entirely different in most countries. There is demand-pulled inflation stemming from substantial fiscal deficits financed with net credit from the central bank and with resources from abroad.

In some cases, such deficits began precisely at the wrong time, during years in which international markets were booming and the demand for exports was enormous. It is hard to explain how this could happen. But, whatever the reason was, the outcome has been unfortunate. Inflation, which at the start was only demand-pulled, built itself into the economy and became cost-pushed as well—an element that did not exist in the 1930s and which makes the return to stability much more difficult.

One clear example of the building of inflation into the economy is the indexation of wages in a good number of countries. This, of course, renders some instruments of economic policy—like devaluation—ineffective or less effective, whereas in the 1930s they were a good expedient to achieve needed adjustments.

The author concludes his paper with two sets of morals:

Addressing creditor countries, he states, "If by their actions they seriously disturb the normal expectations existing at the time loans were made, they may destroy the reverse transfer mechanism." Among the possible actions of this nature, he cites protectionism, tolerance of prolonged depression, and extravagant increases in interest rates or oil prices. Surely, the majority of economists would agree with the author in this respect.

The moral addressed to Latin American countries is rather unexpected: "Commitment to fixed exchange rates, unlimited convertibility, and gold-standard-type monetary rules seems rash and risky." Since most of present Latin America hardly needs further persuasion to act against such rules, the moral is surprising indeed.

Perhaps the moral that would serve the region best might be one underlying the need to avoid the use of prescriptions which are, precisely, at the opposite extreme from the painful and irrational rules of the gold standard.

2   Optimal Economic Integration

Michael Mussa

Economic activities in different areas of the world are linked through commodity trade, factor movements, flows of financial claims, and transfers of knowledge and technology. Economic integration of the world economy is not complete because there are both natural and artificial barriers that inhibit full integration. The natural barriers include the real costs of moving goods and factors from one place to another, the differences in language and culture that diminish the benefits and increase the costs of labor migration, the real costs of securing information and conducting transactions in financial claims issued in different areas of the world, and the differences in education and training that interfere with the transfer of knowledge and technology. The artificial barriers to full economic integration include all of the distortions and inefficiencies created by the failure of market mechanisms and by government policies that interfere with commodity trade, factor movements, flows of financial claims, or transfers of knowledge and technology.

The question of optimal economic integration is the question of how economic policies should be structured to achieve the degree of integration of economic activities in different regions that maximizes some sensible measure of social welfare. One possible answer is that economic policies should be structured so that they do not themselves create artificial barriers to integration and so that they countervail the artificial barriers that would otherwise result from defects in the operation of market mechanisms. No formal proof can be given that this policy prescription will always lead to an improvement in potential economic

Michael Mussa is a professor at the Graduate School of Business at the University of Chicago and a research associate of the National Bureau of Economic Research.

welfare in the sense of Samuelson (1950), but analyses of specific issues relating to economic integration (such as the analysis of the global benefits of a general policy of free trade) indicate that this prescription provides the only possible general answer to the broad question of optimal economic integration. Nevertheless, in this paper it will be argued that the general policy prescription to avoid creating artificial barriers to economic integration and to countervail other artificial barriers is not a realistic and appropriate guide for the structuring of policies that affect economic integration. Moreover, it will be argued that there is *no* general prescription for policies that will serve the broad objective of optimal economic integration. The most that economic analysis can provide is an evaluation of the policies that will serve reasonably well-defined and specific objectives with respect to economic integration, given the limitations within which these policies must operate.

The central thesis of this paper is developed by discussing the four major impediments to *any* general prescription of policies to achieve optimal economic integration and then suggesting some principles that are relevant in applying economic analysis to more limited questions of economic integration. The first impediment to a general theory of optimal economic integration, which is considered in section 2.1, is the problem of defining a welfare criterion to use when evaluating policies that affect economic integration. This problem is more severe than the usual difficulties associated with interpersonal utility comparisons. Decisions about policies that affect economic integration are usually taken by government authorities who both assign special weight to the economic welfare of their own citizens (or to particular groups of citizens) and sometimes pursue policies that are not clearly motivated by any reasonable concept of economic welfare. The second impediment (section 2.2) is that government authorities are subject to a wide variety of constraints on the policies that they can adopt and on the effectiveness with which these policies can be pursued. The extent and diversity of these constraints render the search for a general theory of optimal economic integration virtually hopeless. The third impediment to any such theory (section 2.3) arises from the fundamental principle of second-best welfare analysis. Specifically, in economies with a multiplicity of distortions, the optimal economic policy with respect to any particular distortion (such as an artificial barrier) depends, in general, on all of the other distortions of the economic system. The fourth impediment (section 2.4) is that policies that affect different dimensions of economic integration (commodity trade, factor movements, flows of financial claims, and transfers of technology) cannot, in general, be evaluated separately. This is true because the extent of economic integration is one dimension usually affects the desirable extent of such integration in other dimensions.

2.1 Problems with Specifying an Appropriate Welfare Criterion

In analyzing issues of optimal economic policy, a welfare criterion is needed on which to base measurements of the relative desirability of the outcomes of different policies. The standard welfare criterion that is employed in economic analysis is the criterion of potential welfare improvement; that is, a policy is said to be welfare improving if the adoption of the policy allows some individuals economic gain without causing other individuals economic loss. Frequently, to insure that no individual suffers economic loss, it would be necessary for compensation to be paid by those who gain from a particular policy to those who lose from the policy. However, such compensation need not be paid for a policy to be judged "welfare improving," if it can reasonably be argued that the government authority is capable of evaluating the welfares of different individuals and determining and effectuating the appropriate amount of compensation.

Unfortunately, this general criterion of potential welfare improvement cannot realistically be applied in analyzing many important issues relating to economic integration. One important problem relates to the scope of the welfare criterion: Whose welfare is counted in deciding on a desirable policy? This problem is well illustrated by the standard analysis of the optimum tariff. A country that is large enough to influence the price that it pays for its imports can improve the welfare of its residents by exploiting its monopoly power in trade through the imposition of an import tariff. If the scope of the welfare criterion is limited to the residents of that country, then the imposition of a tariff is welfare improving. However, a tariff is not welfare improving from the perspective of the world as a whole, since the benefits to the residents of the tariff-imposing country are smaller than the losses to the rest of the world. Nevertheless, a government that is exclusively concerned with the economic welfare of domestic residents would find it attractive to restrict trade through the imposition of an optimum tariff.

Another problem related to the scope of the welfare criterion is the absence of any assured means of paying compensation across international boundaries. If a tariff-imposing country were always required to pay appropriate compensation to other countries injured by its actions, then the argument for the optimum tariff would disappear. However, there is no mechanism to insure that such compensation would be paid, and it is probably appropriate to assume that most governments place greater emphasis on improving the economic welfare of their own residents than on improving that of the residents of other countries.

An interesting example of the problems arising from the lack of an adequate and assured means of compensation arises in connection with the migration of skilled labor—the "brain drain" problem (see the papers in Adams 1968). A policy of limiting migration of skilled workers is likely to be supported by skilled workers already resident in high-income countries because they would sustain an uncompensated loss from immigration of additional skilled workers. Similarly, unskilled workers in low-income countries may favor restrictions on migration of skilled workers because they too would suffer an uncompensated loss. The skilled workers who would like to migrate from a low-income country to a high-income country would undoubtedly enjoy benefits from migration, but their welfare may have low weight in the welfare index of policymakers in both countries.

From a cosmopolitan viewpoint, of course, it is attractive to argue that the scope of the appropriate welfare criterion used in analyzing issues of economic integration should be very broad—indeed, that it should encompass the economic welfare of the residents of all countries, and that it should envision appropriate compensatory payments both within and across national boundaries. However, decisions about policies that affect economic integration are usually made by sovereign governments that assign the greatest weight to improving the economic welfare of domestic residents and that generally deny responsibility for making compensatory payments to residents of other countries who may be harmed by their policies. Policies that either promote or restrict economic integration (such as tariffs or limitations on labor migration) frequently have different effects on the economic welfare of the residents of different countries. Together, these facts imply that even if attention is restricted to the economic effects of policies that affect economic integration, it is frequently difficult to make any prescription for optimal policy because what is optimal from the perspective of one country is not optimal from the perspective of another.

The analysis of optimal policies with respect to economic integration is further confounded by divergences between the usual conception of economic welfare and the broader conception of national welfare that appears to motivate the actions of many national governments. Portfirio Díaz, the long-time president of Mexico, once summarized the problems of his country as follows: "Poor Mexico, so far from God, so near to the United States." Eighty years later, similar sentiments are reflected in the policies of the Mexican government that are directed to maintaining a degree of economic independence from the United States, regardless of what may be the (narrowly defined) economic benefits of closer interdependence. Policies of the Canadian government which seek to promote greater domestic ownership of companies engaged in exploration and development of Canadian energy resources reflect a similar desire for economic independence.

Trading relations among countries are frequently influenced by political considerations that are not easily represented in any measure of economic welfare. The nature and extent of trading relations among the Eastern bloc countries are clearly related to their political relationship. The changing attitude of the United States toward trade with the People's Republic of China is also clearly related to political developments and broader strategic objectives. The development of the European Economic Community is, at least in part, an expression of the desire for greater political unity among its member countries.

Policies affecting labor migration are another area in which noneconomic concerns weigh heavily. Some of these concerns were expressed with unusual forthrightness by a senior Australian politician who proclaimed that his policy was, "Two wongs don't make a white." Some native Malay politicians have expressed opposition, perhaps in somewhat more refined terms, to further growth of the Chinese minority in Malaysia through immigration of former Chinese residents of Vietnam. In the United States, domestic political opposition has clearly been an important factor motivating recent attempts to limit immigration of refugees both from Southeast Asia and from the Caribbean. Nevertheless, the acceptable flow of refugees and other immigrants into the United States (which has a long tradition of a relatively liberal immigration policy) has been considerably greater than the flow into Japan (which has an even longer tradition of opposition to immigration).

Since policies concerning foreign investment, international trade, and labor migration are strongly influenced by noneconomic objectives, an exclusively economic criterion of national welfare cannot provide a reliable guide for the policies that sovereign governments will want to pursue with respect to these key dimensions of economic integration. Differences in the noneconomic objectives of different societies and conflicts between these objectives mean that it is impossible to construct a general welfare criterion that will serve as the basis for a general prescription of policies to meet the objective of optimal economic integration.

2.2   Constraints on Government Policy

A second major obstacle to any general theory of optimal economic integration arises from the many constraints that are imposed on government policies and the lack of uniformity in those constraints. These constraints may be divided into three broad categories: First, political and legal constraints are placed on policies that directly affect commodity trade, factor movements, flows of financial claims, or transfers of knowledge and technology. Second, practical constraints on the effectiveness of these policies arise from the desire and capacity of private agents to avoid or evade government controls, regulations, or taxes. Third, constraints on policies that governments can pursue with respect to economic integration arise from policies that are adopted to serve other political and social objectives.

Political and legal constraints severely restrict the policies that can be employed to affect regional economic integration within a sovereign nation. The state of California, which is economically about the same size as Canada, does not have the same flexibility as Canada in adopting policies that affect its economic integration with the rest of the United States. The state of California cannot impose tariff barriers or import quotas to protect its domestic industries from competition with the rest of the United States. Nor can it restrict the free movement of labor and capital to and from the rest of the United States (except to a minor extent through licensing of professionals and zoning restrictions on the use of property). Nor can it decide, like Canada, to float the exchange rate between its money and the money of the rest of the United States.

Political and legal constraints also restrict the policies that sovereign nations can adopt with respect to economic integration with other nations. The threat of foreign retaliation and the legal and moral force of international agreements concerning commercial and financial policies limit the freedom of national governments to restrict commodity trade and, to a lesser extent, international capital flows. Members of the European Economic Community, and other regional economic organizations, accept limits on their freedom to restrict movements of goods and factors to and from other member countries. These limits cannot always or easily be articulated at the margin, at the convenience of a member government.

The practical constraints on the effectiveness of government policies that directly affect economic integration are well illustrated by the practices of smuggling and under-invoicing and over-invoicing import and export transactions as means of evading tariffs, export taxes, and other restrictions on commodity trade. The relevance of such evasive practices for the theory of international commercial policy has recently received considerable attention in academic literature (Bhagwati 1973). The practical importance of such evasive practices is indicated both by the incapacity (or unwillingness) of government authorities to suppress the narcotics trade and by the limited success of economic sanctions and embargoes.

Policies that attempt to limit international mobility of factors of production are also avoided and evaded on a wide scale. Controls on movements of financial capital can sometimes be enforced with some degree of effectiveness on large institutions, such as banks and corporations. They are notoriously difficult to enforce, however, on individual asset holders. Illegal migration vitiates policies that attempt to restrict the international mobility of labor. This is especially true for migration of labor from

Mexico to the United States, which could be halted only by draconian measures that would be unacceptable to both the United States and Mexico.

Black markets in foreign exchange are a mechanism through which private economic agents can partially circumvent government policies that interfere with economic integration by maintaining unrealistic official exchange rates between domestic money and foreign monies. The importance of such black markets is illustrated by the fact that in many countries when the difference between a black market exchange rate and an official exchange rate becomes large, a government is usually compelled to alter the official exchange rate to bring it into closer correspondence with the black market rate.

The Eurodollar market provides an outstanding example of the means that private agents can use to circumvent government restrictions on international financial flows. A major stimulus to the original development of this market came from the interest equalization tax which was imposed by the Kennedy administration in an attempt to discourage capital outflows from the United States. The desire of banks and their customers to avoid the tax on bank intermediation activities, which is implicit in reserve requirements on domestic bank deposits and in other forms of bank regulations, has provided continued stimulus for the growth of the Euromarket (see, e.g., Swoboda 1968).

Replacement of domestic money holdings with foreign money holdings is one means by which the residents of a country can avoid the inflationary tax on their cash balances that is induced by excessive domestic money creation. Currency replacement also allows domestic residents to escape from the disadvantages of an unstable domestic standard of value by using foreign money as the nominal unit of account for private agreements and transactions. Fear of large-scale currency replacement can become a significant constraint on the policies that a government adopts with respect to both exchange rates and the domestic money supply.

Government policies that are not specifically directed at commodity trade, factor movements, or monetary relations may nevertheless have important indirect effects on economic integration. In many cases policies that are not directed toward economic integration serve very important social and political objectives and are, for this reason, difficult to alter. These policies should be regarded as constraints on the overall flexibility of government policy in addressing issues related to economic integration.

For example, many countries have established policies of providing assistance to individuals and businesses in economic difficulty. This assistance takes several forms, including unemployment compensation, relocation assistance, special tax benefits, public purchases of products of distressed industries, outright subsidies, implicit subsidies through low interest rate loans, and public financing of enterprises taken over by government authorities. Whatever its form, such assistance almost inevitably distorts the incentives that individuals and businesses have to adjust to changing economic conditions, thereby affecting the social benefit or cost of policies that promote or inhibit economic integration.

In many countries, the conduct of macroeconomic policy is strongly influenced by objectives of domestic economic stabilization, particularly the maintenance of a high level of employment and an acceptable rate of inflation. When these objectives appear to conflict with policies that promote monetary integration, integration of financial markets, or integration through commodity trade and factor mobility, these policies are frequently sacrificed. The breakdown of the Bretton Woods system in 1971 occurred primarily because the United States wanted to pursue an expansionary monetary policy to fight a domestic recession (and to finance a war), and because other countries, especially West Germany, were unwilling to accept a domestic inflation rate that was consistent with the U.S. monetary expansion. The resort to highly protectionist policies by many countries during the 1930s was motivated largely by a desire to stimulate domestic employment and a belief that restrictions on imports would have an employment-stimulating effect. The decision by the Reagan administration to forego its general commitment to free trade and persuade the Japanese government to impose "voluntary" restraints on exports of automobiles to the United States is more recent evidence of the same important influence that domestic political and social concerns have on the conduct of policies that affect international economic integration.

The implication of all these constraints on the formulation and conduct of government policies that directly or indirectly affect economic integration is that issues of economic integration cannot generally be addressed by first-best policies that would remove or countervail all artificial barriers to complete economic integration. In some cases, these first-best policies may simply not be available to the relevant government authority. In other cases, the government authority may not be able to effectively implement the required policies. In still other cases, policies that governments pursue for reasons not directly related to economic integration may have side effects that significantly influence the consequences of policies affecting economic integration. Since these constraints on government policy are not the same for all governments, a general prescription of policies to achieve optimal economic integration is not possible.

2.3 Difficulties of Second-Best Welfare Analysis

A third fundamental difficulty which confronts any general theory of optimal economic integration arises from the basic principle of second-best welfare analysis. This principle states that in an economy where a multiplicity of distortions induce divergences between privately perceived values and costs and true social values and costs, policies that reduce the magnitude of any one distortion (or group of distortions) may not improve economic welfare because they may exacerbate the deleterious effects of other distortions. For this reason, the second-best policy for any particular issue of economic integration is generally not the same as the first-best policy that would be appropriate if there were no other distortions in the economic system and no constraints on the policies that a government could adopt and effectively implement. The second-best policy for a particular issue of economic integration cannot be prescribed in general terms because it depends on the other distortions that are present in the economic system and on the constraints that impinge on government policy.

The difficulties of analyzing issues of economic integration that are created by the application of second-best welfare analysis are well illustrated by analysis of the economic benefits and costs of customs unions—the issue for which second-best welfare analysis was originally developed (Viner 1950; Lipsey and Lancaster 1956). A customs union promotes economic integration through commodity trade for the countries that are members of the union by removing tariffs and other artificial impediments to trade within the union and by erecting a common external tariff for goods imported from outside the union. The formation of such a union is beneficial to its members to the extent that the elimination of tariff barriers between members of the union creates trade that would not otherwise have existed. The formation of such a union is harmful to its members to the extent that the elimination of tariff barriers within the union and the retention of a tariff on imports from outside the union diverts trade which would otherwise have occurred between members and nonmembers. The total effect of the customs union may be either to increase or decrease the economic welfare of the member countries, depending on whether the benefits of trade creation do or do not outweigh the losses from trade diversion. No general answer can be given to the question of whether this form of economic integration is beneficial to the countries that undertake it.

This analysis of the benefits and costs of customs unions extends to arrangements that would allow free mobility of factors of production within a group of countries or regions, but that restrict factor movements between this group and the rest of the world. For example, it is a common practice in most countries to permit free movement of capital and labor between regions within the country but to restrict movements of capital and especially labor to or from other countries. Another example is the adoption by the European Economic Community of a policy of free mobility of labor for citizens of the member countries of the community, combined with a continuation of restrictions on labor immigration from countries outside of the community. Such arrangements presumably generate economic benefits to the extent that they allow for movements of factors within the community that would not otherwise have occurred, but they also generate losses by displacing factor movements that would have occurred between members and nonmembers of the community.

Another application of second-best welfare analysis to an issue of factor mobility is to the "brain drain" problem (see the papers in Adams 1968). The United States and other advanced countries apply easier standards for immigration of highly skilled labor than for immigration of unskilled labor. In accord with the general principle of second-best welfare analysis, there should be a direct benefit from reducing barriers to migration of skilled workers, as reflected in a reduction in the wage differential for skilled workers between the advanced and the less advanced countries. But there should also be an indirect loss from reducing barriers to migration of skilled while retaining barriers to migration for unskilled labor, as reflected in an increase in the wage differential for unskilled workers between the advanced and less advanced economies.

With respect to issues of financial integration, one key application of second-best welfare analysis is to the question of optimum currency areas (Mundell 1961; McKinnon 1963). If all prices and wages were perfectly flexible and if factors of production were freely mobile among regions, then the optimum monetary system would be a unified currency used in all regions. In other words, the optimum currency area would be the whole world. This is the first-best policy that allows for maximum exploitation of the social benefits of money. However, when there are rigidities of prices and wage rates and barriers to free mobility of factors of production, economic disturbances may lead to excess supply and unemployment in some regions, together with excess demand and production bottlenecks in others. In this situation, optimum currency areas would be regions within which there is a high degree of mobility of factors of production and for which the composition of output is relatively homogeneous. Flexible exchange rates between the monies of these regions would allow the effects of economic disturbances to be partially absorbed by variations in the relative prices of their outputs, achieved by variations in nominal exchange rates. Thus, the argument for regional currency areas is a second-best argument—this arrangement balances the losses from impairing the functions of money with the benefits of reducing the costs associated with the distortions created by barriers to factor mobility and sticky prices and wages.

A similar kind of second-best reasoning is employed in recent theoretical analyses of the relative virtues of fixed and flexible exchange rates (Fischer 1973). In the models that are the bases of these analyses, it is usually the case that a fixed exchange rate regime allows the economic system to deal better with certain types of disturbances, particularly monetary ones, but that a flexible exchange rate regime allows the economic system to deal better with other types of disturbances, particularly real disturbances requiring adjustments in the relative prices of the outputs of different nations. The choice of a fixed or a flexible exchange rate regime, therefore, is not the choice of the first-best regime that is best in dealing with all types of disturbances; it is the choice of the second-best regime that is best on average for the type and magnitude of disturbances that impinge on the economic system.

Another application of second-best reasoning to an issue of financial integration is in the analysis of dual exchange rate systems. Under such a system, a country usually establishes a fixed exchange rate for current account transactions, but allows the exchange rate for capital account transactions to fluctuate in response to market pressures. The argument in favor of such an exchange rate system is not a first-best argument. Such a system creates distortions by introducing two prices for the same good (foreign exchange), it imposes significant monitoring and policing costs on the government and on private agents, and it creates a barrier to the international mobility of financial claims. The argument for a dual exchange rate is that the costs of these distortions are outweighed by the benefits of reducing excessive fluctuations of the exchange rate for current account transactions that would otherwise be induced by speculative capital movements.

The general principle that emerges from all of these examples of the application of second-best welfare analysis to issues of economic integration is that it is not possible to arrive at a general prescription of the best policies to pursue with respect to commodity trade, factor movements, and financial relations. For each of these dimensions of economic integration, the best policy (from an economic viewpoint) depends on a multiplicity of distortions that cause privately perceived costs and benefits to diverge from true social costs and benefits. The inconclusive results of analyses of the costs and benefits of customs unions, of the appropriate size of optimum currency areas, of the relative merits of fixed and flexible exchange rates, and of the advantages and disadvantages of dual exchange rate regimes illustrate the impossibility of arriving at any general prescription of policies to achieve optimal economic integration.

2.4   Interaction among Channels of Integration

The fourth major barrier to a general theory of optimal economic integration arises from the interdependence among alternative channels of integration. The degree of international mobility of factors of production influences the costs and benefits of international trade in commodities. Conversely, the extent of natural and artificial barriers to commodity trade affects the incentives for, and the consequences of, movements of factors of production. The extent of economic integration through commodity trade and factor mobility has important implications for the effects of alternative arrangements governing flows of financial claims and exchanges of national monies. Because of these interactions, questions of optimal policy with respect to different channels of economic integration cannot be treated separately. A general theory of optimal economic integration would have to be a theory that dealt with all forms of integration simultaneously.

The classic example of interaction among alternative channels of economic integration is provided by the Heckscher-Ohlin theorem: A country tends to export the commodities that use intensively the factors of production in which that country is abundant. In establishing this theorem, it is assumed that productive technologies are similar in different countries, but that factors of production are not mobile among countries. It follows that at given commodity prices, a country that is relatively heavily endowed with some factor of production, say land, will produce relatively large amounts of commodities that are intensive in the use of land, in comparison with the production of such land-intensive commodities in countries where land is not abundant. International trade in commodities allows the land-abundant country to export some of the land-intensive commodities that are efficiently produced in that country, in return for imports of commodities that intensively use factors that are abundant in other countries. Thus, the essential idea of the Heckscher-Ohlin theorem is that commodity trade will substitute for movements of factors of production when such movements are restricted by either natural or artificial barriers.

The converse of the Heckscher-Ohlin theorem is embodied in Mundell's (1957) theorem concerning the effects of a tariff in a world of physical capital mobility. Under the assumptions of the two-sector model developed by Stolper and Samuelson (1941) and by Lerner (1952), Mundell shows that when one factor of production, capital, is mobile between countries, even a small tariff on commodity trade will lead to the complete elimination of all trade. The essential idea that underlies Mundell's result is that factor mobility is a substitute (in his model, a perfect substitute) for commodity trade. Hence, when international economic integration through commodity trade is interfered with by the imposition of a tariff, resort is made to the alternative channel, international capital movements, as the mechanism for achieving economic integration.

The theory of effective protection (Corden 1966; Johnson 1969) reveals another aspect of the substitution between commodity trade and factor movements. This theory recognizes that a tariff imposed on an intermediate good implies negative protection for producers of final goods that employ this intermediate good as an input. For this reason, a barrier to factor mobility in the form of trade restrictions applied to intermediate goods is likely to stimulate increased trade in the final goods that embody these intermediate goods. Conversely, a barrier to trade in final goods creates an incentive for factor movements in the form of increased trade in intermediate goods.

Recent experience provides a number of illustrations of substitution between commodity trade and factor movements. Protection afforded by the United States to domestic textile and shoe manufacturers has been a stimulus to legal and illegal immigration of low-wage workers into the United States. The common external tariff erected by the European Economic Community and the removal of tariff barriers within the community have been stimuli to American firms to locate production facilities within the community or to acquire European firms that possess such facilities. The barriers to the importation of foreign steel into the United States have been one of the factors that have contributed to the lack of competitiveness of the U.S. auto industry and to increased auto imports. High tariffs on imports of automobiles imposed by many Latin American countries, on the other hand, have created an incentive for domestic assembly of automobiles using imported parts.

From these examples, it should not be concluded that commodity trade and factor mobility are only and always substitute channels of economic integration. If production processes are subject to increasing returns to scale, then both commodity trade and factor movements will generally be required to achieve an efficient pattern of production. If the scale of operations required to achieve reasonable efficiency in an industry is large, then a relatively small country that stimulates domestic development of this industry by severely restricting imports of the industry's product may acquire a very inefficient domestic industry. This apparently has been a problem with the import-substitution policies that have been adopted by a number of developing countries.

The correct conclusion to draw from the interactions between commodity trade and factor movements is that optimal economic policy for commodity trade cannot be analyzed separately from optimal economic policy for factor movements. The general principle of second-best welfare analysis (discussed in section 2.3) implies that when both commodity trade and factor mobility are subject to important distortions, a policy that generates benefits by reducing distortions to one channel of economic integration may create losses by exacerbating distortions in another channel of integration.

The interactions among channels of economic integration also involve interactions between arrangements governing transfers of financial claims (both monies and securities) and commodity trade and factor mobility. One aspect of these interactions is the linkage between movements of capital as a factor of production and transfers of securities representing claims to future income. At the aggregate level, if a country wishes to accumulate productive capital more rapidly than at the rate permitted by domestic saving, it must finance the excess of investment over saving in the world "capital market"; that is, in the world market for financial claims to future income streams. At the microeconomic level, mobility of specific types of productive capital may be linked to mobility of specific types of financial claims. In particular, when productive capital includes specialized knowledge or technology that is the property of a foreign firm, and when use of this knowledge or technology cannot be acquired through a license, then limitations on foreign ownership may represent a significant barrier to domestic production of commodities requiring the special knowledge or technology.

Interactions between transfers of financial claims and movements of goods and factors are especially important in influencing the international transmission of macroeconomic disturbances. When the monetary units of two countries are linked through a fixed exchange rate, the general levels of prices in these countries should move together over long periods of time, as required by purchasing power parity (allowing, of course, for differential price-level movements required to compensate for changes in relative prices). The speed with which price disturbances are transmitted from one country to another is likely to depend on the extent of trade and factor mobility. If a large fraction of the goods produced and consumed in the two countries are traded between them and if factors can move easily between them, then price disturbances should be transmitted quite rapidly, as they appear to be within countries. However, if trade and factor movements are impeded by extensive natural and artificial barriers, then transmission of price disturbances will probably occur more slowly, and more as a consequence of money supply adjustments necessitated by payments imbalances than as a consequence of direct transmission of price changes from one country to another. Moreover, this principle applies not only to disturbances affecting price levels (whether these disturbances be "monetary" or "real"), but also to disturbances affecting output and employment levels. In general, the more integrated two economies are through trade and factor movements, the easier and more rapid the transmission of macroeconomic disturbances should be between them. It follows that the more integrated two economies are through trade and factor movements, the less latitude national governments have in pursuing independent macroeconomic policies (see Frenkel and Mussa 1981 for further discussion).

International capital mobility, in the sense of free movement of non-monetary financial claims between countries, contributes another mechanism for the rapid transmission of macroeconomic disturbances (Mundell 1968; Frenkel and Rodriguez 1975). When exchange rates are fixed, easy mobility of financial claims implies that changes in official reserve holdings requiring adjustments in national money stocks will occur rapidly in response to desired portfolio shifts by private agents. This allows monetary disturbances that affect prices and output in one country to be rapidly transmitted into monetary disturbances that affect prices and output in other countries. Easy mobility of financial claims also allows for international transmission of "real" disturbances (disturbances affecting desired spending in different countries) when exchange rates are flexible. Specifically, when financial claims are traded among private agents, the incipient trade deficit generated by an increase in desired spending (relative to income) in one country can be financed by a private financial capital flow, thereby creating an increase in demand for goods in other countries. In the absence of private capital flows, there would be no way to finance the incipient trade imbalance, and exchange rate adjustments would forestall transmission of much of a domestic spending disturbance to other countries.

All of these examples illustrate interactions among alternative channels of economic integration that have potentially important implications for the conduct of government policies. It follows from these examples that all of the problems of specifying an appropriate welfare criterion, of taking account of the constraints on government policy, and of conducting complicated and frequently inconclusive second-best welfare analyses apply not only to each of the channels of economic integration considered separately, but also to designing an optimal set of policies that affect all channels of economic integration simultaneously.

2.5 Conclusion

The preceding discussion has emphasized the impediments to a general theory of optimal economic integration that seeks to provide a prescription of the best policies to pursue with respect to commodity trade, factor movements, and transfers of financial claims. These barriers, however, do not preclude a great deal of useful economic analysis about the consequences of specific policies affecting economic integration undertaken by particular nations. In concluding this paper, a few relevant principles are suggested for considering specific issues of economic integration.

First, the performance of the world economy since the Second World War has demonstrated the substantial advantage accruing to all nations from an international economic order that permits a high degree of economic integration through commodity trade, movements of financial capital, and transfers of knowledge and technology. It is in the general interest of all nations to insure that the benefits derived from this liberal international economic order are not lost by a move backward into protectionism, rigid capital controls, and other policies of economic disintegration. This does not imply that complete free trade and removal of all barriers to movements of financial capital and physical factors of production lead to the optimal degree of economic integration for every nation. But it does imply a presumption against erecting artificial barriers to economic integration in the absence of convincing arguments in favor of such barriers. Moreover, since the imposition of such barriers by one nation may weaken general political support for a liberal international economic order, in that nation and in other nations, there is additional reason to be cautious when moving in the direction of greater barriers to international economic integration.

Second, since decisions about policies affecting international economic integration are usually made by sovereign governments primarily concerned with their national welfare, attention must be focused on policies that will improve the national welfare of the countries that adopt them. The effects of such policies on the welfare of particular groups within a country will, of course, frequently be an important concern. However, mechanisms exist within a nation for weighing the interests of different groups and reconciling conflicts between them. At the international level such mechanisms are poorly developed. For this reason, it is not relevant to consider policies that would "benefit the world as a whole," in accord with some global welfare criterion, unless it can be shown that these policies are likely to benefit the individual nations that are asked to adopt them.

Third, while the analysis of policies affecting international economic integration must take into account the noneconomic concerns relevant to the broad conception of national welfare, this does not warrant suspension of the analysis of the economic consequences of such policies. As Harry Johnson (1960) indicates in his analysis of the "scientific tariff," it is always appropriate to consider the economic cost of pursuing a noneconomic objective, and to select the policy that achieves the objective at the least possible cost. Moreover, in assessing policies justified by noneconomic arguments, it is useful to recall the old adage that "patriotism is the last refuge of a scoundrel."

Fourth, constraints on the policies that governments can adopt and implement, and distortions which government policies cannot countervail, imply that the appropriate policies with respect to many isues of economic integration will necessarily be second-best policies that take account of these constraints and distortions. The necessity of pursuing second-best policies, however, does not provide a blanket justification for erecting or expanding artificial barriers to economic integration. For example, under certain circumstances, the standard infant industry argument is a valid second-best argument for granting tariff protection to a domestic industry. The required circumstances are that there be increasing returns to scale in the domestic industry, that the benefits of these increasing returns not be fully appropriable by private investors, that the first-best policy of a production subsidy not be available, and that the domestic industry be able to achieve competitiveness (without protection) within a reasonable time span. The infant industry argument is not a general warrant for granting protection to all import-competing industries at very high rates and for prolonged periods.

Moreover, in applying second-best arguments to justify policies that interfere with economic integration, careful account must be taken of the distortions that such policies are likely to introduce into the economic system, as well as the distortions that they are likely to correct. For example, granting tariff protection to a final goods producer on the basis of an infant industry argument may lead to increased imports of inputs used in producing these final goods. Increased imports of such inputs may lead domestic producers of these inputs to demand protection. Granting such protection, however, is likely to work to the disadvantage of the domestic final goods producer who will, in turn, demand greater protection for his output. Of course, substantial (and temporary) protection of both the final and intermediate goods industries may be justified if the infant industry argument (or some other second-best argument for protection) validly applies to both industries. But, the extent of protection should not exceed the amount that can initially be justified. The extent of protection should not be leveraged upward, with each tariff increase for one class of producers providing the automatic justification for the next tariff increase for some other class of producers.

Finally, in analyzing policies affecting economic integration, account must sometimes be taken of important interactions among alternative channels of integration. Imposing or removing restrictions on trade in intermediate products will frequently have important consequences for final goods producers. Similarly, imposing or removing restrictions on commidity trade may sometimes have important effects on factor movements, and conversely. When these ancillary consequences of policies directed at one channel of economic integration on other channels of economic integration are important, then obviously they must be taken into account in policy formulation. However, the general principle that in economics everything depends on everything else should not be allowed to paralyze analysis of what should be presumed to be the primary effects of a particular policy. If a policy cannot be justified on the basis of careful analysis of its likely effects in its principal domain of operation, it is unreasonable to adopt it on the basis of its unspecified and unanalyzed secondary benefits.

References

Adams, Walter. 1968. *The brain drain*. New York: Macmillan.

Bhagwati, Jagdish N. 1973. *Illegal transactions in international trade: Theory and measurement*. Amsterdam: North-Holland.

Corden, Max. 1966. The structure of a tariff system and effective protective rates. *Journal of Political Economy* 74 (June):221–237.

Fischer, Stanley. 1977. Stability and exchange rate systems in a monetarist model of the balance of payments. In *The political economy of monetary reform*, edited by Robert Z. Aliber. London: Macmillan.

Frenkel, Jacob A., and Michael L. Mussa. 1981. Monetary and fiscal policies in an open economy. *American Economic Review* 71 (May):253–258.

Frenkel, Jacob A., and Carlos A. Rodriguez. 1975. Portfolio equilibrium and the balance of payments: A monetary approach. *American Economic Review* 65 (September):674–688.

Johnson, Harry G. 1960. The cost of protection and the scientific tariff. *Journal of Political Economy* 67 (August):327–345.

———. 1969. The theory of effective protection and preferences. *Economica* 36, no. 142 (May):119–238.

Lerner, Abba P. 1952. Factor prices and international trade. *Economica* 19 (February):1–15.

Lipsey, Richard G., and Kelvin Lancaster. 1956. The general theory of the second best. *Review of Economic Studies* 24, no. 3:11–32.

McKinnon, Ronald I. 1963. Optimum currency areas. *American Economic Review* 53 (September):717–725.

Mundell, Robert A. 1957. International trade and factor mobility. *American Economic Review* 47 (June):321–335 1961. A theory of optimum currency areas. *American Economic Review* 51 (September):657–664.

———. 1968. *International economics*. New York: Macmillan.

Samuelson, Paul A. 1950. Evaluation of real national income. *Oxford Economic Papers* 2 (January):1–29.

Stolper, Wolfgang, and Paul A. Samuelson. 1941. Protection and real wages. *Review of Economic Studies* 9, no. 1:58–73.

Swoboda, Alexander K. 1968. The eurodollar market: An interpretation. *Princeton Essays in International Finance*, no. 64 (February). International Finance Section, Princeton University.

Viner, Jacob. 1950. *The customs union issue*. New York: Carnegie Endowment for International Peace.

3 Seigniorage and Fixed Exchange Rates: An Optimal Inflation Tax Analysis

Stanley Fischer

In choosing fixed over flexible exchange rates, a country gives up the right to determine its own rate of inflation and thus the amount of revenue collected by the inflation tax. This constraint imposes an excess burden that should be included in the cost-benefit analysis of the choice of exchange rate regime. If the country goes further by giving up its seigniorage and using a foreign money in place of the domestic money, it loses more tax revenue and has to adjust government spending and other taxes accordingly. The choice of exchange rate regime is thus related to questions discussed in optimal inflation tax analysis.

This paper presents an analysis of the optimal inflation tax in section 3.1.[1] The consequences of a constraint on the rate of money creation are studied in section 3.2, while section 3.3 analyzes the effects of the loss of revenue from the inflation tax. Section 3.4 presents an interpretation of the preceding analysis as applied to alternative exchange rate regimes. The interest in the paper derives from the explicit calculation of optimal inflation taxes for a specific utility function and production function, embodied in an intertemporal framework, as well as from the application to exchange rate regimes.

3.1 The Optimal Inflation Tax

The representative infinitely lived family in the economy is growing at rate n and derives utility from private consumption, from the services

Stanley Fischer is a professor in the Department of Economics at the Massachusetts Institute of Technology; a research associate of the National Bureau of Economic Research; and at the time of presentation of this paper was a visiting scholar at the Hoover Institution.

The author is indebted to Jeffrey Miron for research assistance. Research support was provided by the National Science Foundation.

1. Phelps (1973) is the original reference in this tradition. See also Aghevli (1977), Drazen (1979), and Brock and Turnovsky (1980) for further developments.

provided by holding real balances,[2,3] from leisure, as well as from consumption of a public good. There are no nondistorting taxes, and the government finances its expenditures through the issue of money and taxes on labor income. It is convenient to assume there is no capital.

The utility function of the representative household is

(1) $$V = \int_0^\infty U(c, m, x, g) \, e^{-\delta s} \, ds,$$

where c is per capita consumption, m is per capita real balances, $x = \bar{\ell} - \ell$ is leisure (ℓ is labor supply), and g is government spending; $\delta > 0$ is the discount rate or rate of time preference.

The household budget constraint is

(2) $$c + \dot{m} + (\pi + n) \, m = w(1 - t) \, \ell,$$

where π is the rate of inflation, n the growth rate of family population, w is the wage rate, and t the tax rate on labor income. It is assumed throughout that w is constant.[4]

The household maximizes (1) subject to the budget constraint (2), taking g, government spending, as given. The government budget constraint is

(3) $$g = tw\ell + (\dot{M}/PN) = tw\ell + \dot{m} + (\pi + n) \, m,$$

where $\dot{M}/PN$ is the flow of real resources, per capita, the government obtains by printing money. (N is population.)

The analysis proceeds in stages. First, the household optimization problem, taking π and t as given, is solved. I then note that there is no inherent dynamics in this model, since there is no capital accumulation, and that for a given rate of nominal money growth, θ, the rational expectations solution for the price level will have the economy jump initially to its steady state, in which $\dot{m} = 0$ and $\pi = \theta - n$. The remainder of the analysis is therefore conducted under the assumption that the economy is in steady state.

2. Fischer (1974) discusses the issue of money in the production (and utility) function, which is emphasized by Thomas Sargent in his comments on this paper and the paper by Guillermo Ortiz appearing later in this volume. The essential point is that of revealed preference: putting money in the utility (or production) function is *equivalent* to postulating a demand function for money. Deeper analyses of the demand for money require a more detailed specification of the transactions environment. It is well known that the choice of a medium of exchange in any model of transactions is extremely delicate in that there is no good reason for one asset rather than another to serve as medium of exchange. The Kareken-Wallace (1981) indeterminacy of exchange rates in a multicountry world represents the same logical difficulty as that of accounting for the use of noninterest-bearing currency in a single country where there are alternative assets. This problem was stressed by Keynes (1936) and Samuelson (1947) as the essential difficulty of monetary theory. In the light of these difficulties at the theoretical level, it is remarkable that there is so little difficulty in getting private economic agents to use the domestic currency: it takes extraordinary rates of inflation before there is flight from a given national currency. The theoretical challenge is to explain this phenomenon.

3. For use of a similar framework in a multiasset context, see Fischer (1972).

4. If capital were included in the model, w would become variable.

At the second stage, a Cobb-Douglas utility function is used to study the optimal tax problem. For any given level of g, there is an optimal combination of taxes to finance the spending. The optimal tax combination and its variation as g changes are examined. Finally, I ask what the optimal level of g is, under the assumption that the government maximizes (1), subject to the private sector behavioral functions and its budget constraint (3).

The first order conditions for maximization of (1) subject to (2) are

$$(4) \qquad\qquad 0 = U_c - \lambda,$$

$$(5) \qquad\qquad 0 = U_x - \lambda w(1 - t),$$

$$(6) \qquad\qquad \dot{\lambda} = (\pi + n + \delta)\lambda - U_m,$$

where λ is the multiplier associated with the budget constraint (2) and, from (4), is also the marginal utility of consumption.[5]

Now, consideration of equilibrium paths in which π, the rate of inflation in (6), is equated to the rate of inflation implied by solution of the full system (4)–(6) for given constant θ will show that the only path that converges to a steady state is one that goes immediately to that steady state.[6] Thus we can set $\dot{\lambda} = 0$ and work henceforth with the steady state system, (4), (5), and

$$(6') \qquad\qquad 0 = U_m - \lambda (\pi + n + \delta).$$

The general optimal tax analysis approach could now be applied, but I prefer to use a specific, Cobb-Douglas, example to illustrate the relevant considerations.[7] Assume

$$(7) \qquad U(c, m, x, g) = c^\alpha m^\beta x^\gamma g^\epsilon, \quad \text{with} \quad \begin{array}{l} \alpha, \beta, \gamma, \epsilon > 0, \\ \text{and } \alpha + \beta + \gamma + \epsilon < 1. \end{array}$$

Then, using equations (4)–(6') and the budget constraint (2):

$$(8) \qquad c = \frac{\alpha w(1 - t)\bar{\ell}}{\alpha + (\beta\theta/\theta + \delta) + \gamma}, \qquad \frac{\partial c}{\partial t} < 0, \frac{\partial c}{\partial \theta} < 0,$$

$$(9) \qquad m = \frac{\beta w(1 - t)\bar{\ell}}{(\alpha + \beta + \gamma)\theta + \delta(\alpha + \gamma)}, \qquad \frac{\partial m}{\partial t} < 0, \frac{\partial m}{\partial \theta} < 0,$$

$$(10) \qquad \ell = \bar{\ell}\left[1 - \frac{\gamma}{\alpha + (\beta\theta/\theta + \delta) + \gamma}\right], \qquad \frac{\partial \ell}{\partial t} = 0, \frac{\partial \ell}{\partial \theta} > 0.$$

The properties of the functions (8)–(10) are unsurprising, except for the absence of a wage or labor tax effect on labor supply. This last result is

---

5. For a similar optimization problem, see Fischer (1979).

6. See Fischer (1979) for the type of argument needed.

7. The Cobb-Douglas form does not permit the level of government spending to affect the rates of substitution between other pairs of variables. Thus a utility function like (7) cannot, for instance, reflect the notion that government and private consumption are close substitutes.

a consequence of the canceling of income and substitution effects and ensures, in this model, that total taxes from labor rise as the income tax rate increases.

Note from (9) that for an interior maximum with $m > 0$, it is required that

$$(11) \qquad \theta > -\frac{\delta(\alpha + \gamma)}{\alpha + \beta + \gamma},$$

which also implies that $\theta + \delta > 0$.

The government budget constraint (3) implies that for any tax rates, t and θ,

$$(12) \qquad g = w\bar{\ell}\left[\frac{\alpha t(\theta + \delta) + \theta\beta}{(\alpha + \beta + \gamma)\theta + \delta(\alpha + \gamma)}\right],$$

where I have substituted from (9) and (10) into (3). It is convenient to define

$$(13) \qquad \mu \equiv \frac{g}{w\bar{\ell}},$$

which is a measure of the share of government spending in potential (full-time work) output.

Different combinations of θ and t can be used to finance any feasible level of government spending. Locus BB in figure 3.1 shows those combinations in (t, θ) space for a given value of μ. The locus does not necessarily cross the t and θ axes, since there is a maximum μ that can be financed through exclusive use of either the income tax or seigniorage. In particular, if there is no use of seigniorage ($\theta = 0$), then it is required that

$$t = \frac{\alpha + \gamma}{\alpha}\mu.$$

When $t = 1$, the government is using the income tax to appropriate all income, and government spending is given by:[8]

$$(14) \qquad \mu_1 = \frac{\alpha}{\alpha + \gamma}.$$

In the case of nonuse of the income tax, maximum g is achieved as θ goes to infinity, and

$$(15) \qquad \mu_2 = \frac{\beta}{\alpha + \beta + \gamma}.$$

Since β is likely to be small relative to α and γ, the maximum steady state

8. I am grateful to Olivier Blanchard for correcting an error at this point in a previous draft.

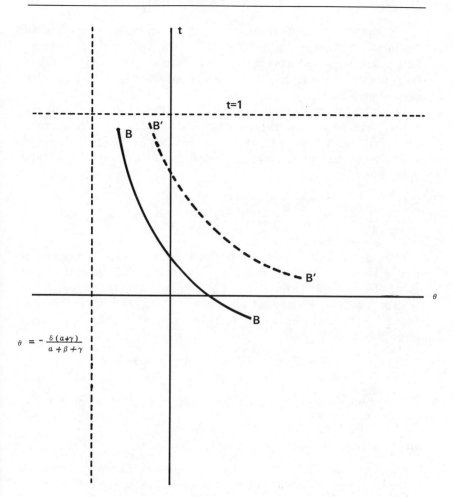

$$\theta = -\frac{\delta(a+\gamma)}{a+\beta+\gamma}$$

Fig. 3.1   Alternative tax combinations to finance a given level of government spending.

$(g/w\overline{\ell})$ that can be financed by seigniorage alone is also likely to be small. Use of the inflation tax does increase the level of output through its effect on labor supply; thus when the inflation tax alone is used to finance government spending, the level of output is higher than when the income tax is used to finance the same level of government spending.

The maximum attainable level of government spending when both taxes are used, μ_3, is obtained by setting $t = 1$ and letting θ go to infinity in (12):

(16) $\mu_3 = \dfrac{\alpha + \beta}{\alpha + \beta + \gamma}.$

Whether the *BB* locus crosses the t and θ axes as shown in figure 3.1 depends on the value of μ. For the *BB* locus in figure 3.1, μ is less than both μ_1 and μ_2. As μ increases, the locus shifts up to the right. The $B'B'$ locus applies for a level of government spending larger than μ_2 but smaller than μ_1 and μ_3.

The *BB* locus shows combinations of t and θ that *can* be used to finance a given level of government spending. But of course only one of these combinations will be the optimal tax combination for given μ. Given t, θ, and g, the consumer demand and supply functions (8)–(10) imply the flow of utility

(17)
$$U^* = \xi[(\alpha + \beta + \gamma)\theta + \delta(\alpha + \gamma)]^{-(\alpha+\beta+\gamma)}$$
$$\times (\theta + \delta)^{\alpha+\gamma}(1 - t)^{\alpha+\beta}g^\epsilon,$$

where ξ is a constant of no significance.

The marginal disutilities of the two tax rates, and hence the slope of an indifference curve in (θ, t) space, are obtained from (17), treating g as given. Then, equating the slope of an indifference curve to that of the budget constraint *BB* and solving, pairs of θ and t that are optimal for each level of government spending are obtained. This *optimal tax locus* is given by:

(18)
$$\alpha t[(\alpha + \beta + \gamma)\theta + \delta(\alpha + 2\gamma)] - \alpha\theta(\alpha + \beta + \gamma)$$
$$= \delta[\alpha(\alpha + \gamma) - \beta\gamma].$$

The optimal tax locus, *TT*, is shown in figure 3.2. Its slope is

(19)
$$\frac{dt}{d\theta} = \frac{(1 - t)(\alpha + \beta + \gamma)}{\theta(\alpha + \beta + \gamma) + \delta(\alpha + 2\gamma)},$$

which is positive. Thus both the seigniorage and the labor income tax increase as government spending rises. Corresponding to each point on *TT* is a level of government spending. Whether the *TT* locus crosses the $\theta = 0$ axis at $t > 0$, as shown, depends on the sign of $\alpha(\alpha + \gamma) - \beta\gamma$, the right-hand side of (18). Since β is related to the share of spending on real balance rentals, it is likely to be small; thus the case shown in figure 3.2 is more likely.

The optimum government policy is found by choosing the best point on figure 3.2. This is done by maximizing (17) with respect to θ and t after substituting for g from the government budget constraint (12): the resultant expression for the optimal rate of seigniorage is

(20) $$\theta^2(\alpha + \beta)(\alpha + \beta + \gamma) + \theta\delta[(\alpha + \beta)(\alpha + \gamma) + \alpha(\alpha + \beta + \gamma) - \gamma\epsilon]$$
$$+ \delta^2[\alpha(\alpha + \gamma) - \gamma(\beta + \epsilon)] = 0.$$

Three comments about (20) are in order. First, assuming that the coefficient of θ in the equation is positive, there will be no positive root of (20) unless

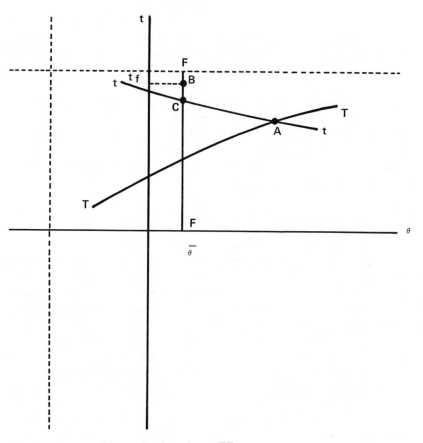

Fig. 3.2   The optimal tax locus *TT*.

$$\alpha(\alpha + \gamma) < \gamma(\beta + \epsilon).$$

This condition requires government spending optimally to take a relatively large share of output. For values of the parameters that generate approximately the observed ratios of consumption to income, consumption to real balances, labor to leisure, and government spending to consumption in the U.S. economy, the condition is not satisfied. Thus the current analysis does not give support to the notion that optimal rates of seigniorage can be high. In part, no doubt, this is a result of the functional form being used.[9] It may also reflect the absence of a banking system in this model.[10]

9. For instance, the likelihood of positive use of seigniorage at the optimum would be increased if real balances entered the utility function in Stone-Geary form as $(m - \bar{m})$. See Diamond and Mirrlees (1971) for an example, In the present paper use of the Stone-Geary form turns (20) into a quartic equation and thus is not appealing. Barro (1971) argues that optimal rates of inflation are low.

10. In unpublished work, Guillermo Calvo and Jacob Frenkel have shown that the

Second, nowhere has the analysis had occasion to enter the variables θ and π separately. Thus in this example the optimal use of seigniorage is independent of the rate of population growth.[11] The optimal steady state rate of inflation therefore falls one for one as the population growth rate rises.

Third, the optimal rate of seigniorage use, θ, is directly proportional to δ, the rate of time preference. If optimal θ is positive, it increases proportionately with δ, which may be thought of in this context as the interest rate. If optimal θ is negative, then higher δ would mean a lower optimal rate of inflation, which is consistent with the optimal quantity of money argument.

3.2   Constrained Optimal Taxation

The optimal position for this economy is a point like A in figure 3.2. In this section I consider the effects of constraining the rate of money growth, θ, to a level $\bar{\theta}$. Such a constraint would apply, for example, if the exchange rate were kept fixed. In terms of figure 3.2, the government is constrained to the locus FF. Two questions about the rate of income tax to be used are considered.

First, we could ask what rate t_f would be necessary to maintain any specified level of government spending, for instance, the optimal level associated with point A. That is a purely technical question to be answered using the budget constraint (12). The implied point B is shown illustratively, in figure 3.2.

The second question is: What, given the constraint $\bar{\theta}$, is the optimal level of government spending? The answer is found by maximizing (17) with respect to t, after substituting in for g from the government budget equation (12) and treating θ as a constant. The resultant locus, giving optimal t (by implication from (12), also g) as a function of $\bar{\theta}$, is

$$(21) \qquad t = \frac{\epsilon}{\alpha + \beta + \epsilon} - \frac{\bar{\theta}\beta(\alpha + \beta)}{\alpha(\alpha + \beta + \epsilon)(\bar{\theta} + \delta)}.$$

This *optimal income tax locus*, tt, in figure 3.2 is negatively sloped and lies above TT to the left of the optimal point A. When some seigniorage is taken away from the government, it optimally reduces government spending and increases its use of the labor income tax. Given the constraint on θ in figure 3.2, the optimal point is C.

Figure 3.3 shows the utility implications of giving up control over θ. The curve describes the level of utility traced out along tt. Point C shows

---

introduction of a banking system with fractional reserves in an optimal inflation tax analysis increases the optimal inflation rate.

11. Cf. Friedman (1971).

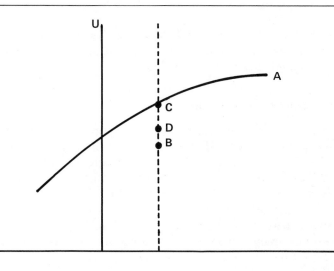

Fig. 3.3   Utility implications of alternative monetary and exchange arrangements.

the utility level corresponding to optimal policy when θ is fixed at $\bar{\theta}$. The utility level corresponding to B, where government spending is held to the level that obtains at A, lies below C. The utility loss from A to C can be compensated for by some amount of resources, which is not in general equal to the amount of seigniorage lost in moving from A to C. In the context of discussion of fixed exchange rates, that amount of compensation is the excess burden of accepting fixed exchange rates.

3.3 Losing the Inflation Revenue

Finally, suppose that the revenue generated by seigniorage is no longer available to the government. This would occur if, for instance, a country used a foreign money. The maximal attainable level of utility is certainly less than that shown by C in figure 3.3. The government loses a source of revenue and will again optimally reduce government spending below its level at C and increase the income tax rate above its level at C. The optimal tax rate is now

$$(22) \qquad t = \frac{\epsilon}{\alpha + \beta + \epsilon},$$

which is independent of $\bar{\theta}$; however, government spending optimally increases with $\bar{\theta}$. This occurs because an increase in $\bar{\theta}$, which may be thought of as an increase in the rate of inflation, increases labor supply and thus income tax revenue.

Corresponding to the higher rate of income tax when the government loses seigniorage, optimal holdings of real balances will be lower than the level corresponding to point C in figure 3.3, even though the inflation rate is the same. Point D in figure 3.3 represents the maximum utility attainable when the government loses its seigniorage.

3.4 Exchange Rate Regimes

The above analysis is relevant to one aspect of the differences among exchange rate regimes. The full optimal tax analysis presented in section 3.1 describes the options available when the exchange rate is flexible. The excess burden imposed by the constraint on θ in section 3.2 describes one of the costs of adopting a fixed rate regime which, however, uses domestic money. The rate of money creation $\bar{\theta}$ in section 3.2 is that rate required to maintain fixity of the exchange rate. Section 3.3 calculates the further cost of giving up domestic money, using instead a foreign money. The rate of inflation in this case will also be consistent with the rate of money growth $\bar{\theta}$.

The ranking of utilities of these sets of arrangements is unambiguous. Free choice of the rate of money growth is preferred to the situation where the rate of money growth is fixed at θ, with use of domestic money. Utility at point A in figure 3.3 is undoubtedly above (or no lower than) that at C. Use of a foreign money imposes a further cost, implying that point D is below C in figure 3.3.

It is entirely reasonable to ask whether the seigniorage considerations emphasized in this paper are of any empirical significance. The possibly surprising answer is yes. For the industrial countries over the period of 1960–1978, seigniorage provided 5.7 percent of government revenue, representing 1 percent of GNP on average. In some other countries, such as Greece and Spain, seigniorage revenue exceeded 10 percent of government revenue.[12] Such high rates of seigniorage are perhaps nonoptimal in the light of the preceding analysis, but they certainly indicate that seigniorage is a factor to be taken into account in the choice of an exchange rate regime. But of course it is not the only consideration determining the desirability of alternative exchange arrangements.

References

Aghevli, Bijan B. 1977. Inflationary finance and growth. *Journal of Political Economy* 85, no. 6:1295–1308.

Barro, Robert J. 1972. Inflationary finance and the welfare cost of inflation. *Journal of Political Economy* 80, no. 5:978–1001.

12. More detailed estimates of the amount of revenue collected from seigniorage are presented in Fischer (1982), along with a less formal discussion of the analysis presented in this paper.

Brock, William A., and Stephen J. Turnovsky. 1981. The analysis of macroeconomic policies in perfect foresight equilibrium. *International Economic Review* 22, no. 1:179–209.

Diamond, Peter, and James A. Mirrless. 1971. Optimal taxation and public production: II. *American Economic Review* 61, no. 3:261–278.

Drazen, Allan. 1979. The optimal rate of inflation revisited. *Journal of Economic Theory* 5, no. 2:231–248.

Fischer, Stanley. 1972. Money, income, wealth, and welfare. *Journal of Economic Theory* 4, no. 2:289–311.

———. 1974. Money and the production function. *Economic Inquiry* 12, no. 4:517–533.

———. 1979. Capital accumulation on the transition path in a monetary optimizing model. *Econometrica* 47, no. 6:1433–1440.

———. 1982. Seigniorage and the case for a national money. *Journal of Political Economy* 90, no. 2:295–313.

Friedman, Milton. 1971. Government revenue from inflation. *Journal of Political Economy* 79, no. 4:846–856.

Kareken, John H., and Neil Wallace. 1981. On the indeterminacy of equilibrium exchange rates. *Quarterly Journal of Economics* 96, no. 2:207–222.

Keynes, John Maynard. 1936. *The general theory of employment, interest, and money*. New York: Harcourt Brace.

Phelps, Edmund S. Inflation in the theory of public finance. *Swedish Journal of Economics* 75, no. 1:67–82.

Samuelson, Paul A. 1947. *Foundations of economic analysis*. Cambridge, Mass.: Harvard University Press.

4 Dollarization in Mexico: Causes and Consequences

Guillermo Ortiz

4.1 Introduction

The term "dollarization" will be interpreted in this paper as the degree to which real and financial transactions are actually performed in dollars relative to those performed in domestic currency. Since this is an unobservable variable, an obvious choice for measuring the extent of dollarization in the economy is the proportion of dollars to domestic currency circulating at any time.

This concept of dollarization is closely related to the literature on "currency substitution." This literature explains the conditions under which diversified portfolios of domestic and foreign money balances will be held and adapted in response to expected changes in relative risks and returns among the various currencies. The general idea of several recent papers (Miles 1978; Brillenbourg and Schadler 1980; Girton and Roper 1981) is that monetary policy will be ineffective in a country where foreign currencies are regarded as good substitutes for domestic currency. An important implication of this hypothesis is that the elasticity of substitution between domestic and foreign currency is likely to increase in periods when the exchange rate is floating and, consequently, the perceived risks of changes in the value of domestic currency are greater. This implies, of course, that the ability of the monetary authorities to pursue independent monetary policies is severely restricted—even in a world of floating rates. Hence, if the issue of currency substitution turns out to be

Guillermo Ortiz is manager, Research Department, Banco de México.

The author is grateful to Víctor Guerrero for statistical advice and help, and to Patricia Abreu for competent research assistance. Maurice Obstfeld made extensive and useful comments on an earlier draft. The responsibility for all remaining errors as well as for the ideas contained in this paper is the author's. This paper does not reflect the official views of the Banco de México.

empirically relevant, one of the stronger arguments for floating rates—greater national monetary independence—is seriously weakened.

The relevance of the dollarization problem for Mexico and other Latin American countries is not so much related to fixed versus floating exchange rates—since most countries in the area are not feasible floaters anyway—but to the potential problems of short-run monetary instability that currency substitution can create. If the demand for domestic currency is strongly influenced by "foreign" variables, a substantial degree of instability may be imported from abroad (from volatile interest rates, for example) even if the monetary authorities follow consistent monetary and exchange rate policies.

A fluctuating foreign-domestic composition of bank deposits is likely to be reflected on the asset side of the portfolios of financial institutions and, consequently, on the availability of the credit in domestic currency extended to firms and individuals. Also, in the absence of adequate protection mechanisms, firms may be reluctant to accept foreign currency denominated loans (or may engage in speculative inventory activities if highly leveraged in foreign currency). These effects may be more important if dollarization extends to time and savings deposits, especially in countries, such as Mexico, where the banking system provides most of the external financing to firms.

This paper focuses mainly on the dollarization of demand deposits, since most of the discussion on the effects of currency substitution has been concerned with narrow definitions of money. Section 4.2 contains a historical account of the dollarization process from 1933 to date. In section 4.3 an attempt is made to explain and quantify the main forces determining the behavior of the dollar/peso deposit ratio. Section 4.4 deals with the problem of monetary instability caused by currency substitution, and section 4.5 is a brief summary of the results and conclusions.

4.2 Dollarization: A Historical Perspective

The earliest regulations on exchange rate policy and monetary control in Mexico were implemented during the long (and politically stable) administration of General Porfirio Díaz. The Comisión de Cambios y Moneda (Council on Money and Exchange Rate) was created in 1905 with the intention of administering a fund of "monetary regulation" that would control the flows of gold, foreign exchange, and trade credit resulting from international transactions. The circulation of foreign currency in Mexico was explicitly prohibited by the Comisión; this constitutes one of the first—and last—attempts at establishing any form of exchange controls in Mexico.

The incipient financial system of General Díaz was completely dismantled by the Mexican Revolution of 1910–1917. The breakdown of the system began around 1913 and was reflected in a rapid depreciation of paper money, extreme inflation and falsification of bank notes, defaults in payments by the government and other debtors, and a general dislocation of economic activity.

In 1916, monetary circulation consisted of gold and silver coins and twenty-one types of paper money issued by different institutions and revolutionary factions; these notes were mostly inconvertible into metallic coins and were heavily discounted with respect to gold and silver. In an effort to unify fiduciary circulation, the Carranza government authorized the issue of 500 million pesos of "unforgeable" bank notes with a 20 percent gold guarantee in April 1916. However, these notes were not well received by the public, and by November they had depreciated to less than 1 percent of their face value in terms of gold. The following year, the "unforgeable" was finally demonetized and became "inconvertible;" as a result of this experience and other previous unsuccessful efforts, from 1917 to 1932 the Mexican monetary system consisted almost exclusively of gold and siver coins. Evidence also exists that during that period a substantial amount of foreign currency (mostly U.S. gold and silver coins) circulated alongside Mexican currency.[1]

The most important step toward the reorganization of the financial system after the Revolution, was the creation of Banco de México in 1925. Although the official charter granted the bank monopoly over the issuance of paper money, it was not until the early thirties that the *billetes* of Banco de México began to circulate effectively. The original idea was to establish a central bank in the British tradition; however, Banco de México began operating as an ordinary commercial bank, lending and receiving deposits directly from the public.

Although a gold standard was formally adopted with the creation of Banco de México, the importance of the country as a silver producer determined the existence of a de facto bimetallic standard.[2] The newly created central bank attempted to stabilize the price of silver with respect to gold to avoid excessive fluctuations of the real money stock. The price of this metal remained stable during 1925 and 1926, but dipped about 10 percent in 1927 in response to the slowdown of the economic activity in the United States. Banco de México stopped minting silver coins during that year, and the price of silver made some gains in 1928. However, the crash of 1929 and the Great Depression that followed had a very strong impact on the price of the metal; from 1929 to 1932 the price of silver declined by more than 50 percent (see table 4.1).

1. Martínez-Ostos (1946) and Cavazos (1976) provide an interesting discussion of monetary events of the epoch.
2. Martínez-Ostos (1946). Although only gold coins had legal tender, both gold and silver coins circulated widely. Fluctuations in the price of silver with respect to gold were reflected in the discount of silver pesos with respect to gold pesos.

Table 4.1   **Economic and Financial Indicators, 1925–1932**

Average (year)	GDP	GDP Deflator	Money Supply	Intl. Reserves Banco de México (million dollars)	Price of Silver (dollars per troy ounce)	Exchange Rate (peso/dollar)
	(nominal growth rates)					
1926–1928	−1.3	−2.0	10.8	17.9	.59	2.09
1929	−3.1	0.8	4.5	25.0	.52	2.15
1930	−4.0	2.4	4.3	13.6	.38	2.26
1931	−9.6	−12.5	−60.2	9.7	.27	2.65
1932	−24.0	−10.7	31.1	31.2	.34	3.16

Source: Medio Siglo de Estadísticas Económicas Seleccionadas. Subdirección de Investigación Económica y Financiera, Banco de México, S.A., in Fernández-Hurtado (1976).

The decline in the price of silver had a clear contractionary effect on the money supply (measured in terms of gold) since an important proportion of the money stock consisted of silver coins. In 1929 this decline was compensated with an increase of Banco de México's international reserves; however, in 1930 and 1931 the trade surplus was more than offset with a capital (gold) outflow, and the central bank's reserves actually declined. The combination of these price and reserve movements, compounded with the decision of the monetary authorities to stop minting silver coins to avoid a further erosion of the price of silver (derived from the Ley Calles of 1931), resulted in a drastic reduction of the money stock in 1931.[3]

The contraction of the money stock in 1931 apparently had a severe deflationary effect on economic activity. Prices fell by more than 10 percent per year in 1931 and 1932, while real output dropped nearly 15 percent in 1932, the greatest decline registered in Mexican economic history in a single year.

While it remains true that the deflationary spirit of the 1931 legislation was responsible at least for part of the decline of the money stock, it is not clear that effective countercyclical measures could have been taken by Banco de México even if the government had deliberately embarked on an expansionary monetary policy. Given the public's reluctance to accept bank notes as part of their money holdings, the only means available to the monetary authorities for expanding the quantity of money in circulation was the minting of silver coins. However, an increase in the supply of silver relative to gold would have put additional downward pressure on the gold price of the newly minted coints, frustrating, at least partially, the efforts to increase the (gold) money supply.

The deflationary policy was abandoned in 1932 when a new legislation changing the statutory provisions governing the activities of Banco de México was enacted. The new law strengthened Banco de México's control over the issuance of bank notes, limited the amount of transactions that the bank could undertake with the public and subjected monetary reserves to direct control by the central bank. Also, the law required all commercial banks to associate with Banco de México, purchasing stock and maintaining reserve deposits there. The minting of silver coins was then resumed, the exchange rate was allowed to float, and the first successful issues of bank notes were made. The scarcity of means of payment was so acute in that year that a national campaign promoting the

---

3. In view of the substantial loss of metallic reserves and foreign currency that occurred in the late 1920s, the Ley Calles of 1931 suspended convertibility of silver coins and retired gold out of circulation; gold was to be used exclusively for international transactions. The minting of silver coins was also stopped in an effort to prevent a decline of the silver peso exchange rate.

Table 4.2   Composition of the (Narrowly Defined) Money Supply
                   (in percentages)

Average (years)	Coins	Bank Notes	Checking Deposits
1925–1931	73.99	0.3	25.73
1932–1940	34.41	29.02	36.58
1941–1950	9.69	43.82	46.51
1951–1960	4.16	45.34	50.48
1961–1970	3.05	39.65	57.29
1971–1975	3.26	39.44	57.30

Source: Banco de México, S.A.

acceptance of the central bank's notes was endorsed by trade unions, chambers of commerce, and various local associations.[4]

As a result of the new silver mintings and note issues, and the favorable impact on the trade balance of the peso's downward float, the money supply increased 31 percent in 1932 and 15.4 percent in 1933. Also the proportion of bank notes to the money supply increased from 0.4 percent in 1931 to 10.5 percent in 1932 and 16.5 percent in 1933. (The structure of the domestic money supply has evolved, as shown in table 4.2.) In November 1933, Banco de México fixed the exchange rate for the first time at 3.60 pesos per dollar, this rate would prevail until 1938.

Figure 4.1 shows the ratios of foreign to domestic currency demand deposits and total deposits held by households and firms in Mexican private financial institutions from 1933 to 1979.[5]

During the first fixed exchange rate period (from November 1933 until March 1938) the demand deposits ratio fell consistently; by the end of 1937 less than 6 percent of checking deposits were denominated in foreign currency. The years 1933–1936 were relatively stable and prosperous. GDP grew at an average real rate of 8.3 percent, prices increased by less than 5 percent on the average, and a continued trade surplus—sustained by a hefty increase in the price of silver from 1933 to 1935—resulted in a net increase of Banco de México's international reserves of nearly 60 million dollars.

The ambitious social and economic development program launched by President Cárdenas in the mid-1930s required greater financial flexibility

4. See Cavazos (1976) and Carrillo-Flores (1976).
5. Consistent figures on total dollar deposits were obtained only after 1938. The institutional distinction between private and official banking institutions in Mexico is important for the purposes of this paper. Official banking institutions (such as Nacional Financiera) have traditionally handled external foreign currency denominated borrowing by Mexican public sector agencies, and their holdings of foreign currency liabilities reflect this borrowing pattern. It is therefore more convenient to consider exclusively the liabilities of private financial institutions (which held an average of 88 percent of total liabilities to the public from 1960 to 1980).

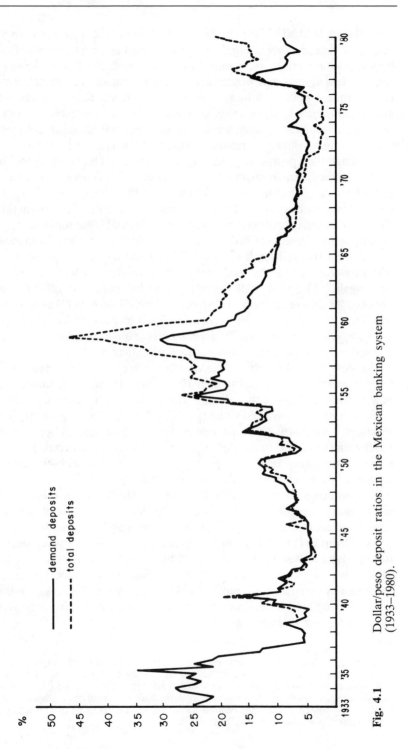

Fig. 4.1   Dollar/peso deposit ratios in the Mexican banking system (1933–1980).

from Banco de México. In 1936, the statutory law of the bank was revised one more time, further strengthening its position as a central bank. Two important innovations were introduced then: first, the flexible reserve requirement system that would serve as the instrument for the selective credit control policies followed later; and, second, the authorization granted to Banco de México to issue fixed-yield securities on behalf of the federal government. Taking advantage of expanded financial facilities, the government deficit increased substantially in 1936 and 1937.

Although the upsurge in government expenditures had only a moderate impact on the trade surplus, the U.S. recession and the capital outflow caused by the populist policies followed by the Mexican government resulted in a strong decline of international reserves in 1937. It was in this climate of international recession and domestic troubles in the balance of payments that President Cárdenas signed the decree of nationalization of the oil industry on March 18, 1938. That same day Banco de México withdrew from the foreign exchange market and the peso was allowed to float again.[6] The year 1938 turned out to be extremely difficult for Mexico; foreign retaliation in response to the oil takeover was felt immediately (for example, oil exports declined 60 percent from 1937 to 1938), aggravating the already depressed economic situation. GDP increased only 1.6 percent in real terms during that year.

The peso floated for thirty-one months. After two failed attempts at fixing the exchange rate, in October 1940 Banco de México announced a new parity: 4.85 pesos to a dollar. The depreciation of the peso with respect to its previous fixed value (in 1938) amounted to 34 percent. It is apparent from figure 4.1 that a new process of dollarization began with the floating of the peso; the dollar/peso deposit ratio reached its highest point in September 1940 and declined substantially following the establishment of a fixed, peso-dollar exchange rate.

The outbreak of World War II provided Mexico some relief from international pressures. Foreign demand for Mexican goods and services stimulated economic activity (GDP increased at an average rate of 6.07 percent from 1941 to 1945), and a consistent trade surplus was registered throughout the war years, reinforced by important inflows of capital seeking refuge from war-ravaged Europe; Banco de México's reserves increased by more than 250 million dollars from 1941 to 1945. Again, the dollarization coefficients showed an initial decline, stabilizing around a value of 5 percent in 1944 and 1945.

6. The possibility of implementing exchange controls at the time of the expropriation was apparently given serious consideration. However, President Cárdenas himself, in his 1938 State of the Union address, declared that "exchange controls can only function in highly disciplined countries where customs regulations are well organized and borders can be effectively patrolled; exchange controls (in Mexico) would surely be overridden by a black market" (Cavazos 1976, p. 83).

The fast pace of economic activity sustained during the war years was also accompanied by a relatively high rate of inflation. The wholesale price index increased 60.4 percent more in Mexico than in the United States from 1941 to 1945; by the end of the war the peso was probably overvalued. The following years, in 1946 and 1947, the largest historical trade balance deficits were recorded, probably as a result of deferred consumption during the war, and Banco de México lost practically all the reserves accumulated during the war years. In view of the continued loss of reserves, the monetary authorities decided to float the peso in July 1948. This new experiment with a floating exchange rate lasted only eleven months; in June 1949, the exchange rate was fixed at 8.65 pesos per dollar (a devaluation of 76 percent). The dollarization coefficient increased from 7.5 percent to 11.5 percent during the float, and there is also evidence that substantial capital outflows occurred during these months.

The 8.65 parity lasted from 1949 to 1954. Once more, the Korean War stimulated export growth in 1950 and 1951; the favorable trade balance of 1950 was reinforced with new capital inflows (mostly returning capital now that the float was over), and international reserves more than doubled. In contrast, the economic activity was negatively affected in 1952 and 1953 by the new U.S. recession, causing a rapid deterioration of the trade balance. In April 1954 the peso was devalued approximately 45 percent. This time the monetary authorities did not experiment with a floating period, and the new parity was announced outright to the surprise of many. This devaluation had a very strong psychological impact on the public. In only two months following the announcement, capital outflows reduced the central bank's reserves to one-half of their April level, and the dollarization ratios jumped dramatically.[7]

The exchange rate was maintained at 12.5 pesos to a dollar from April 1954 until September 1976. This period, the longest recorded with a fixed exchange rate, includes two distinct subperiods. The first, known in the literature as "stabilizing development" began after the adjustments to the 1954 devaluation had been completed and lasted until the early 1970s. A rapid rate of economic growth and low rates of inflation (averaging 6.5 and 2.95 percent from 1956 to 1971) were sustained through the combination of favorable international economic conditions and consistent domestic monetary and fiscal policies. Foreign borrowing was used to finance the persistent, but mostly moderate, trade deficits, preventing a direct impact from the short-run behavior of international reserves on the exchange rate as was experienced in the past.[8]

---

7. The dollar/peso demand deposit ratio increased from 11.5 to 25 percent from March to December; the total deposit ratio increased by a similar proportion. See figure 4.1.

8. This period of Mexican economic and financial development has been thoroughly surveyed in recent literature. See, for example, Nassef (1972) and Solís (1981).

The stable period ended with the upsurge of world inflation in 1973 and the government's decision to spare Mexico from the parallel effects of international recession by means of higher government expenditures. Although a liberal use of foreign credits was utilized for this purpose (the foreign long-term public debt jumped from 4 to 16 billion dollars from 1972 to 1976), the average growth rate of GDP in 1972–1976 (5.4 percent) was lower than in the stable period, while the inflation rate turned out to be significantly higher (14.76).[9]

The dollarization ratios, which increased substantially after the 1954 devaluation and then stabilized around a 20–25 percent level in 1955 and 1956, began to climb again in the second quarter of 1957 and reached an all time high at the end of 1958: the dollar/peso demand deposit ratio exceeded 30 percent, while the total deposit dollar/peso ratio went over 46 percent. Both ratios commenced a steady decline again in 1959 that continued through the 1960s and the first half of the 1970s; in the fourth quarter of 1975, the value of the checking deposits ratio was only 6.2 percent, and the total deposit ratio was even lower.

The 1957–1958 dollarization was motivated both for economic and political reasons. First, the downturn of economic activity in industrialized countries during those years put strong pressure on the balance of payments. The trade deficit almost trebled in 1957 (with respect to 1954) and continued at very high levels in 1958; in that year, the reserves of Banco de México declined almost 20 percent. Second, 1958 was the last year of President Ruiz-Cortinez's administration, and the private sector felt queasy about the seemingly leftist overtones of Mr. López-Mateos's rhetoric (the official presidential candidate). However, in 1959 the trade balance improved and the private sector was temporarily appeased, ending the speculative burst against the peso.

On August 31, 1976, the monetary authorities decided to float the peso once more and "let the market determine its equilibrium level" instead of devaluing outright as in 1954. The exchange rate rose quickly, reaching levels of around 20–21 pesos to a dollar; two weeks later a temporary rate was tried (19.5–19.7 pesos/dollar), but it had to be abandoned after five weeks because of strong speculative activity. Since then, the peso has been formally on a float, although the exchange rate has fluctuated within very narrow margins since the second quarter of 1977. The magnitude of the depreciation (about 45.50 percent in terms of dollars) was probably greater than what was generally anticipated and, not surprisingly, had a profound impact on economic activity.[10]

9. For a more detailed account of events that led to the 1976 devaluation, see Ortiz and Solís (1979).

10. For instance, the three-month forward rate for the Mexican peso quoted in the Chicago Mercantile Exchange Market in June 1976 was about 13 pesos, implying a premium of only 4 percent. For a discussion on the effects of the devaluation, see Córdoba and Ortiz (1979).

Table 4.3   **Dollarization Coefficients, 1976–1980**

Ratios	1976 (I–III)	1976 (IV)	1977	1978	1979	1980
Checking deposits (dollars/pesos)	6.6	12.5	13.3	8.7	8.7	11.2
Total deposits (dollars/pesos)	6.5	11.8	16.4	14.5	17.0	18.7

Source: Banco de México, S.A.

The behavior of the dollarization coefficients after the 1976 devaluation has been different from that observed in the previous periods with floating exchange rates. While the checking deposit peso/dollar ratio declined after the third quarter of 1977, the total deposit ratio has remained at substantially higher levels (see table 4.3). The explanation seems to be the liberalization of the Mex-dollar deposit rate in 1977.

Although private financial institutions were traditionally authorized to receive deposits denominated in foreign currencies from the public, the interest rate payable in these types of deposits was regulated by Banco de México and moved at infrequent intervals. In the more volatile world of the 1970s, the authorities attempted to keep the Mex-dollar deposit rate more in line with those prevailing abroad for similar types of deposits; however, large and persistent differentials between Mex-dollar and international rates often developed. Finally, in view of the large capital outflows that occurred after the peso was allowed to float, the monetary authorities decided to peg the Mex-dollar deposit rates for different maturities to the corresponding Eurodollar rates (March 1977). This measure had the effect of slowing considerably the outflow of capital since Mex-dollar deposits became perfect substitutes, except for political risk factors, for dollar deposits held abroad.[11]

4.3   Fixed versus Flexible Exchange Rates and Devaluation Expectations: Effects on the Dollarization of Demand Deposits

The literature on currency substitution outlined in section 4.2 has pointed out that, in the context of the existing international environment, domestic residents have strong incentives to diversify the composition of their currency holdings.[12] The same motives that exist for holding domestic money apply to the demand for foreign currency. Individuals and firms engaged in international exchange have similar transaction and portfolio incentives for holding foreign currencies as they do for maintaining

11. The implication of this measure for domestic monetary policy has been explored recently by Ortiz and Solís (1982).
12. Miles (1978) and Alexander (1980).

domestic money balances. It is clear, for example, that people who travel abroad for business or pleasure, residents of border areas, and importers or exporters have incentives to hold foreign currency balances. Also, large firms with liabilities denominated in foreign currencies will probably want to diversify their financial portfolios, particularly their holdings of liquid assets.

The case of border transactions is particularly important in the Mexican case. Given the length of the Mexican-U.S. border and its economic importance, it can almost be considered a different currency area from the rest of the country. Prices are usually quoted in dollars and payments are mostly made in dollars; pesos, although accepted as a means of payment on both sides of the border, are in less demand. The structure of financial intermediation clearly reflects this pattern of transactions. The average checking deposit dollar/peso ratio in the six more important border cities from 1977 to 1980 was 51 percent, compared with a national average of 12 percent.

Among the diverse reasons for holding foreign currency balances, the currency substitution hypothesis emphasizes the importance of foreign exchange risk effects. According to this hypothesis, the perceived risk of holding exclusively domestic currency increases when the exchange rate is floating. Consequently, there is a greater incentive to diversify the portfolio of liquid money assets under floating rates than when the exchange rate is fixed, and one would expect the dollarization of demand and time deposits to behave accordingly.[13] Table 4.4 summarizes the behavior of the demand deposit ratio during periods of fixed and floating exchange rates.

The figures presented in table 4.4 seem to indicate precisely the opposite behavior of the dollarization coefficient: the dollar/peso demand deposit ratio has been lower and more stable, on the average, during the periods when the exchange rate has been floating. This is true even if the first fixed exchange rate period (highly dollarized and unstable, 1933–

---

13. It is not obvious why greater variability of the exchange rate should increase the degree of risk of domestic currency holdings, since it could just as easily be interpreted as increasing the risk of holding foreign currency. However, a number of arguments have been advanced in favor of interpreting the variability of exchange rates as an incentive to diversify currency holdings. Akhtar and Putnam (1980) argue that domestic currency provides less information concerning international transactions when the exchange rate is floating and may not serve as an optimal store of value for a given level of transactions, creating incentives for diversification. Also, if fluctuations of the exchange rate between third currencies are uncorrelated with movements of the domestic/foreign currency exchange rate, some portfolio holders will find incentives to diversify, reducing the share of domestic currency in their portfolios. Miles and Stewart (1980) also investigate the effects of exchange rate risk (measured again by the variability of the exchange rate) using a "production function of money services." Both papers find a statistically significant negative effect of movements in the deutsche mark/dollar exchange rate, both in the demand for dollars and in the demand for marks.

Table 4.4   **Demand Deposit Dollar/Peso Ratio (percentages)**

Period	Exchange Rate Regime	Mean		Standard Deviation	
1933(I)–1937(IV)	fixed	20.6		8.4	
1938(I)–1940(IV)	floating	9.1		4.2	
1941(I)–1948(I)	fixed	6.4		1.9	
1948(II)–1949(II)	floating	10.5		1.8	
1949(III)–1954(I)	fixed	11.4		2.9	
1954(II)–1976(II)	fixed	12.9		6.8	
1976(III)–1980(IV)	floating	10.7		2.4	
Average	fixed[a]	12.5	11.3[b]	5.63	5.22[b]
Average	floating[a]	10.0		3.1	

Source: Banco de México, S.A.
[a]Weighted by relative length of the period.
[b]Excluding the 1933(I)–1937(IV) period.

1937) is not taken into account. It should be kept in mind, however, that the floating exchange rate periods have been relatively short (about thirty quarters from 1933 to 1980), and also that Banco de México has intervened constantly in the foreign exchange market when the peso has been "floating." Hence, the fixed/floating exchange rate distinction does not seem to shed much light on the dollarization process.

Going back to figure 4.1, it can be observed that the largest jumps of the dollarization ratio (after 1937) occurred in 1940, 1952, 1954, 1957–1958, and 1976; of these dates, 1940, 1952, 1958, and 1976 correspond to the last year of the incumbent administrations, while a devaluation also occurred in 1954 and in 1976. It seems, then, that both political variables and devaluation expectations must play a crucial role in explaining the historical record of Mexican dollarization; this proposition deserves a closer examination.

Consider the following simple money demand formulations:

(1)
$$\frac{M^d}{P} = L^d(\pi^d, \pi^f, r, \theta, \xi, w),$$

(2)
$$\frac{M^f}{P} = L^f(\pi^d, \pi^f, r, \theta, \xi, w),$$

where M^d/P and M^f/P are real domestic and foreign desired money balances; π^d, π^f, and r are the real returns on domestic currency, foreign currency, and an alternative asset; θ is a measure of foreign exchange risk; ξ is a proxy for political risk factors, and w is real wealth. Assuming that (1) and (2) can be expressed as exponential functions, and writing the relative returns in differential form, the money demand functions can be written:

(3) $\quad \dfrac{M^d}{P} = \alpha_0(w) \exp\left[\alpha_1(\pi^d - \pi^f) + \alpha_2(\pi^d - r) + \alpha_3\theta + \alpha_4\xi\right],$

$\qquad\qquad\qquad +\qquad\qquad +\qquad\qquad\quad +\qquad\;\; -\qquad -$

(4) $\quad \dfrac{M^f}{P} = \beta_0(w) \exp\left[\beta_1(\pi^f - \pi^d) + \beta_2(\pi^f - r) + \beta_3\theta + \beta_4\xi\right],$

$\qquad\qquad\qquad +\qquad\qquad +\qquad\qquad\quad +\qquad\;\; +\qquad +$

where the signs under the coefficients indicate partial derivatives. Subtracting (3) from (4), taking logarithms and rearranging terms, the following equation is obtained:

(5) $\qquad \ln\left(\dfrac{M^f}{M^d}\right) = \ln\left(\dfrac{\alpha_0(w)}{\beta_0(w)}\right) + \alpha_1(\pi^d - \pi^f) - \beta_1(\pi^f - \pi^d)$

$$- \beta_2(\pi^f - r) + (\alpha_3 - \beta_3)\theta + (\alpha_4 - \beta_4)\xi.$$

Imposing the following symmetry condition to equation (5): $\alpha_i = \beta_i$ for $i = 0, 1, \ldots 4$, and adding a random term u_t, the following expression is obtained:

(6) $\qquad\qquad \ln\left(\dfrac{M^f}{M^d}\right) = a_1(\pi^f - \pi^d) + a_2\theta + a_3\xi + u_t,$

where $a_1 = (2\alpha_1 + \alpha_2)$, $a_2 = 2\alpha_1$, and $a_3 = 2\alpha_4$.[14] Equation (6) was incorporated in a partial adjustment model to obtain a final estimating equation,

(7) $\qquad\qquad \ln\left(\dfrac{M^f}{M^d}\right) = b_1(\pi^f - \pi^d) + b_2\theta$

$$+ b_3\xi + b_4 \ln\left(\dfrac{M^f}{M^d}\right)_{t-1} + \epsilon_t,$$

where $b_1 = \lambda a_1$, $b_2 = \lambda a_2$, $b_3 = \lambda a_3$, $b_4 = (1 - \lambda)$, and $\epsilon_t = \lambda u_t$.

M^d and M^f are peso and dollar demand deposits held by the public in Mexican private financial institutions.[15] For a Mexican resident, the real return of the holdings of domestic currency, π^d, can be approximated by the rate of inflation. The real return on foreign money is simply $\pi^f = \pi^d$ plus the expected percentage rise in the peso price of dollars. Hence, the differential $(\pi^f - \pi^d)$ is just the expected depreciation of the exchange rate. Since a futures market for Mexican pesos did not exist during most of the period under consideration, an obvious proxy for the expected rate

14. The restrictions imposed on equation (5) prevent the identification of the substitution coefficients α_1 and α_2 in equation (6). However, this is not important for the purpose of this exercise. Note also that β_3, $\beta_4 < 0$.

15. Since no data on dollar currency circulation in Mexico are available, only demand deposits were included in the definition of M^d.

of devaluation of the exchange rate is the difference between the official and the real exchange rate.

As mentioned above, previous studies have used some measure of variability of the exchange rate as a proxy for foreign exchange risk. However, given the length of the period in which the exchange rate was fixed, the deviations of the real exchange rate from the trend rate were used here as a measure of foreign exchange risk. Finally, a dummy variable was included in the years when administration changes occurred to take into account the "political risk" factor mentioned earlier. Equation (7) was estimated using quarterly data from 1933(I) to 1980(IV), and the results are shown in equation (8). ED stands for the expected devaluation proxy, ER for the foreign exchange risk measure, and PRD for the political risk dummy.[16] After some experimentation, a simple two-period lag structure for the independent variables was found to perform adequately.

$$
(8) \qquad \left(\frac{M^f}{M^d}\right) = \underset{(1.70)}{0.059\,\mathrm{ED}_{t-1}} + \underset{(1.83)}{0.053\,\mathrm{ED}_{t-2}} + \underset{(2.23)}{0.066\,\mathrm{ER}_{t-1}}
$$

$$
+ \underset{(1.32)}{0.045\,\mathrm{ER}_{t-2}} + \underset{(2.75)}{0.079\,\mathrm{PRD}} + \underset{(17.3)}{0.932}\left(\frac{M^f}{M^d}\right)_{t-1} ;
$$

$$
R^2 = 0.907, \ \mathrm{DW} = 2.20, \ \mathrm{SE} = 0.157.
$$

Figures in parenthesis correspond to t-statistics.

The regression results are satisfactory in spite of the somewhat crude measures of differential returns and of the risk of exchange rate variations. All the coefficients estimated have the correct sign and are significantly different from zero at the 5 percent level of confidence, except for the second lagged term of the risk variable which is insignificant. It should also be kept in mind that only part of the monetary aggregates (namely demand deposits) were included in M^f and M^d, and consequently, the variations of the currency/deposit ratio that affect the dollarization coefficient were not taken into account.

The difficulties of obtaining good measures of devaluation expectations for such a long period of time in the absence of a forward market are quite obvious. However, the effects of the devaluations of 1954 and 1976, as well as the impact of the devaluation expectations prevailing in 1976, on the dollarization of demand deposits can also be studied using intervention analysis directly from the time series.

Intervention analysis is a statistical method developed by Box and Tiao (1975) for the purpose of detecting and quantifying the effect of an

---

16. ER was generated from the residuals of a regression between the real exchange rate and a trend variable.

exogenous event on the behavior of time series.[17] However, this procedure requires the series to be stationary (that is, to have constant mean and variance), so the original dollar/peso demand deposit ratio could not be studied directly. The analysis was performed on the growth rate of the original series, and the results show that the growth rate of the dollarization ratio increased 45.6 percent in the second quarter of 1954, returning immediately (the following quarter) to its original level. The 1976 devaluation's effect on the growth of the dollarization coefficient was also concentrated in one quarter: the fourth of 1976, when the ratio jumped 63 percent.

4.4 Effects of Dollarization

The monetary and real effects of dollarization on economic activity will obviously depend on the degree to which domestic currency is being displaced by dollars. If the substitution process goes to the extreme of eliminating or substantially reducing the circulation of domestic coins and currency, the monetary habitat of the country will be changed. This implies, of course, handing to the United States (or the country issuing the substitute currency) the seigniorage of money creation and seriously eroding the base of the inflation tax.[18] Even in less drastic situations, it has been pointed out in the currency substitution literature that substantial monetary instability might arise as a result of diversified currency holdings by domestic residents. The relevance of this substitution problem for monetary policy can only be evaluated empirically, and the evidence to date is scarce.[19]

One method of estimating the potential monetary instability problems of currency substitution is to simply examine the properties of alternative definitions of monetary aggregates. If dollar deposits are effectively regarded by the public as money, they should be included as part of the money stock for policy making purposes. Alternatively, if the currency substitution problem is important, domestic money demand estimations that fail to account for the foreign currency component should be unstable. To explore the relevance of this question for the case of Mexico, a

17. See Appendix A for details.
18. See the chapter by Stanley Fischer in this volume (chapter 3).
19. Miles (1978) used Canadian data to estimate a "production function of monetary services" obtaining direct measures of elasticities of substitution between U.S. and Canadian dollars. He finds that both currencies are close portfolios substitutes, especially during period of floating rates. Also utilizing Canadian data, Alexander (1980) included several "foreign influence" variables on the demand for money (such as expected returns on foreign currency holdings and exchange rate risk), obtaining low elasticities of substitution. In contrast to Miles, this author concludes that the currency substitution phenomenon has not posed important problems for the achievement of monetary policy objectives in Canada.

conventional money demand equation based on a partial adjustment model was estimated using quarterly data from 1960 to 1979, using two definitions of the monetary aggregate: M^j = currency (pesos) + peso demand deposits, and M^k = currency (pesos) + peso demand deposits + dollar demand deposits. The estimated equation was:

$$(9) \qquad \ln\left(\frac{M^{j,k}}{P}\right) = \alpha_0 + \alpha_1 \ln Y_t^c + \alpha_2 RL_t + \alpha_3 FR_t + \alpha_4 IR$$

$$+ \alpha_5 \ln\left(\frac{M^{j,k}}{P}\right)_{t-1} + d_1 + d_2 + d_3 + \epsilon_t.$$

where $(M^{j,k}/P)$ is the real monetary aggregate; Y_t^c is current real income; RL_t is the interest rate payable on short-term Mexican peso deposits; FR_t is the three-month Eurodollar deposit rate; IR is the expected rate of inflation; d_1, d_2, and d_3 are dummies included to correct for seasonal variations, and ϵ_t is a random error term.[20] Since the monetary authorities in Mexico fix the normal deposit rate, this variable does not always capture expected inflation. This is why both variables are included in equation (9).

Estimates of equation (9) from 1960 to 1979 are reported in table 4.5. The regression results for both definitions of money are very similar; perhaps the most striking difference is the income elasticity term which turns out to be not significantly different from zero for the M^k aggregate. Note also that the foreign interest rate coefficient is not significantly different from zero for either equation. Static and dynamic simulations were performed to examine the question of stability. Equation (9) was estimated from 1960 to 1972, and simulated from 1973 to 1979; a summary of the simulation results is included in table 4.6.

The simulation results are very similar for both aggregates and only slightly better for M^k. The truly remarkable outcome of the simulations is the smallness of the errors both in the static and in the dynamic exercises. The largest dynamic errors obtained correspond to the last observations of 1979 and represent less than 2 percent of the dependent variable. The magnitude of average errors for the postdevaluation period, 1976(IV)–1977(IV), is less than 0.5 percent for both equations. On the basis of this performance, the demand for domestic currency appears to be highly stable, and either definition M^j or M^k seems appropriate for purposes of policy making.

---

20. The estimation of equation (9) was taken from Ortiz (1982). The expected rate of inflation was calculated simply as a weighted average of current and lagged values. Several measures of expected inflation (including instrumental variables and a Box-Jenkins generated series consistent with the rational expectations approach) were tried in Ortiz (1982), but the results did not differ substantially from those reported here. See Appendix B for data sources.

Table 4.5   Regression Results of Equation (9), 1960–1979

Dependent Variables	$\ln Y_t^c$	RL_t	IR	FR_t	$\ln(M^{j,k}/P)_{t-1}$	R^2	Durbin-h	ρ	SE
M^j	.100	−.122	−.034	.010	.937	.9952	1.59	−.50	.0262
	(1.69)	(−3.34)	(−5.65)	(.94)	(15.69)				
M^k	.045	−.118	−.051	.004	.968	.9952	1.53	−.59	.0253
	(.81)	(−3.60)	(−5.84)	(.46)	(16.80)				

Note: Figures in parentheses correspond to t-statistics. The Cochrane-Orcutt procedure is used to correct for first order serial correlation. The estimated coefficients of constants and dummies are not reported for convenience.

Table 4.6   Simulation Results (1973[I]–1979[IV])

Simulations	Root-Mean-Square Percent Error	Mean Percent Error	Theil's Inequality Coefficient
Static:			
M^j	.4508	.2263	.00227
M^k	.4210	.2030	.00230
Dynamic:			
M^j	.5201	.4017	.00261
M^k	.5144	.4072	.00259

4.5 Concluding Remarks

The discussion of the previous sections suggests that the difficulties associated with the presence of currency substitution have not been empirically significant for Mexico. The dollarization of demand deposits has not been more pronounced during periods of floating exchange rates and, apparently, no instability has been introduced in the demand for domestic currency by the fact that both pesos and dollars are held by the public in the form of monetary assets. This conclusion is reinforced by the good performance of the money demand simulations in the difficult months following the 1976 devaluation.

The behavior of the dollar/peso demand deposit ratio has been influenced by economic as well as political considerations; among the former, devaluation expectations seem to be the most important factor. An interesting observation is that the last two devaluations seem to have fostered exchange rate risk expectations, at least temporarily, instead of appeasing them.

Although the empirical analysis was restricted to the behavior of demand deposits, the dollarization of time deposits has followed closely the movements of the dollar/peso demand deposit ratio until recent times. It was mentioned that the liberalization of Mex-dollar deposit rates had the effect of making Mex-dollar deposits near perfect substitutes for dollar deposits held abroad, and this explains the relative increase of the dollarization of time deposits. However, this need not concern the monetary authorities. Now that the Mexican banking system offers a competitive menu of foreign currency denominated financial assets, domestic investors will find little incentive to maintain deposits abroad, and consequently, short-run speculative capital flows should be reduced.[21] To the extent that the dollarization consists of locally produced

21. A recent theoretical paper by Alain Ize (1981) lends support to this view. Ize also concludes that the existence of Mex-dollar deposits has resulted in a more efficient allocation of financial resources.

dollars, the negative effects on economic activity can probably be minimized with appropriate exchange rate insurance mechanisms on the credit side.

4.6   An Addendum

On 18 August 1982 (almost a year and a half after the first draft of this paper was completed), the monetary authorities decreed that mexdollar deposits could no longer be transferred out of the country. Henceforth, mexdollar deposits would be paid in domestic currency at the rate of 70 pesos to a dollar. A few days later, on 1 September, a system of full exchange controls was imposed in Mexico for the first time in several decades. These decisions marked the end of the mexdollar market.

It is clear that the effectiveness of the mexdollar market to absorb short-term capital flows depended on the public's perception of close substitution between mexdollars and dollars held abroad. Hence, the commitment of the monetary authorities to maintain full convertibility of the peso and unrestricted capital flows was a key element of the public's trust of the system. As the Mexican economy's financial troubles deepened during the first months of 1982 and the public's confidence that the authorities would undertake the necessary macroeconomic adjustments faltered, the mexdollar market ceased functioning as a shock absorber. Large capital outflows occurred, and the authorities decided to cancel the potential threat of a run on mexdollars that could not possibly have been met with the available foreign exchange reserves.

Appendix A: Intervention Analysis

This procedure involves the following steps: First, the series to be analyzed is represented as a stochastic model of the Box-Jenkins (1976) type, such as an ARIMA model. Second, a dynamic intervention function, constructed a priori to represent the type of exogenous event under consideration, is constructed. Third, the iterative Box-Jenkins technique is used again to represent the complete model, including the intervention function. The effect of the exogenous event can then be quantified by the magnitude of the intervention function coefficients.[22]

The exogenous events (or interventions) considered here are: (a) the 1954 devaluation that occurred during the second quarter of 1954; and (b) the devaluation expectations of 1976 and the devaluation itself that occurred in September of that year. The objective, then, is to explore the effects of these events on the demand deposit dollar/peso ratio DDR_t

22. See Box and Tiao (1975).

(taken quarterly from 1939[I] to 1980[IV]). As a first step, the transformation $(1 - B) \ln (\text{DDR}_t)$, where B is a lag operator, such that $BZ = Z_{t-1}$ for any variable Z, was applied to DDR_t to obtain a stationary series with constant mean and variance. Note that the transformed series

$$(1 - B) \ln (\text{DDR}_t) = \ln \left(\frac{\text{DDR}_t}{\text{DDR}_{t-1}} \right) \approx \gamma_t,$$

where γ_t is the growth rate of the dollarization coefficient. A Box-Jenkins type model was estimated for each of the following periods: 1939(I)–1954(I), 1939(I)–1976(I), and 1939(I)–1980(IV); the results are shown in table 4.7.

The θ coefficients in the above models represent moving average parameters and the sequence $\{a_t\}$ is a white noise Gaussian process with mean zero and constant variance σ_a^2. The ω's are parameters of the intevention functions.

$$P_t^i = \begin{cases} 1 \text{ for } t = i \\ 0 \text{ otherwise} \end{cases}, i = \text{I, II},$$

where P^i is a pulse indicator designed to detect an instantaneous jump of the series at the time when the "interventions" seem to have occurred, namely, I = 1954(II) and II = 1976(II). This particular form of intervention function $\epsilon_I = \omega_0 P_t^{II}$ (chosen after testing other functional forms) seems appropriate to model the effects of the first depreciation because of the surprising character of the 1954 devaluation. In contrast, devaluation

Table 4.7   **Box-Jenkins Models Estimated for the Period 1939(I)–1980(IV)**

Period	Model	Estimated Parameters and Standard Deviations	$\hat{\sigma}_a$	Q Statistic[a] (h) Degree of Freedom
1939(I)–1954(I)	$(1 - B) \ln (\text{DDR}_t) = (1 - \theta B^6)a_t$	$\hat{\theta} = 0.246$ (± 0.126)	0.1933	10.70, (23)
1939(I)–1976(I)	$(1 - B) \ln (\text{DDR}_t) = \omega_0 P_t^I + (1 - \theta B^6)$	$\hat{\omega}_0 = 0.456$ (± 0.139) $\hat{\theta} = 0.201$ (± 0.082)	0.1419	13.17, (22)
1939(I)–1980(IV)	$(1 - B) \ln (\text{DDR}_t) = \omega_0 P_t^I + \omega_1 P_t^{II} B^2 + (1 - \theta B^6)$	$\hat{\omega}_0 = 0.456$ (± 0.137) $\hat{\omega}_1 = 0.630$ (± 0.139) $\theta = 0.207$ (± 0.081)	0.1403	14.23, (21)

[a]The Q statistic should be compared with the value of X^2 with (k) degrees of freedom (see Box and Jenkins 1976).

expectations seem to have been widespread in the months prior to the devaluation of 1976; substantial capital outflows were registered in the first half of the year, particularly during the second quarter. A dynamic intervention function designed to pick up the effects of devaluation expectations of 1976(II) was constructed and incorporated into the model; however, preliminary estimation failed to show any significant effects during the second and third quarters.[23] Finally, the model for the whole period was estimated incorporating a simple intervention function $\epsilon_{II}(t) = \omega_1 B^2 P_t^{II}$ to capture the effects of the 1976 devaluation. Figure 4.2 depicts graphically the effects of the estimations presented in table 4.7.

As mentioned in the text, the growth rate of the dollarization ratio increased 45.6 percent in the second quarter of 1954, then returned to its original level. The 1976 devaluation's effect on the series was concentrated in the fourth quarter of that year (increasing 63 percent). Also, the devaluation expectations of the preceding months did not significantly affect the dollarization ratio.

Appendix B: Data Sources

Demand deposits in pesos and dollars are regularly published in the *Informes Anuales* and *Indicadores Económicos* of Banco de México. Data on earlier years (since 1925) will soon be published by the *Oficina de Cuentas Financieras*, Subdirección de Investigación Económica, Banco de México, S.A.

Interest rates on Mexican time deposits have been published regularly only since 1972. However, a statistical appendix in Ortiz (1982) provides a previously unpublished series, weighted by the relative participation of the different financial instruments.

The Mexican consumer price index was utilized to deflate income and monetary variables. Quarterly data on prices before 1968 were constructed by applying seasonal variations observed in the consumer price index to the GDP deflator. Quarterly income data were also obtained by applying seasonal movements of the Mexican index of industrial production to real GDP. These series are also available in the statistical appendix of Ortiz (1982).

---

23. The intervention function postulated for the 1976 devaluation was of the form:

$$\epsilon_{II}(t) = \left\{ \frac{\omega_1 - \omega_2 B - \omega_3 B^2}{1 - \delta B} \right\} P_t^{II},$$

but only $\hat{\omega}_3$ turned out to be significantly different from zero.

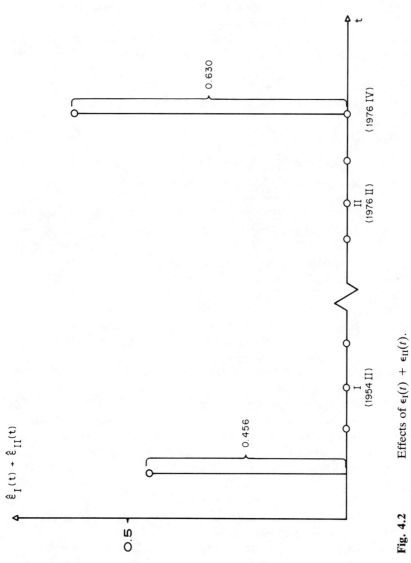

Fig. 4.2   Effects of $\epsilon_{I}(t) + \epsilon_{II}(t)$.

References

Akhtar, M. A., and Bluford H. Putnam. 1980. Money demand and foreign exchange risk: The German case, 1972–1976. *Journal of Finance* 35:787–798.

Alexander, William. 1980. Foreign influences on the demand for money in an open economy: The Canadian case. Bank of Canada, XVII Reunión de Técnicos de Bancos Centrales del Continente Americano. Bogotá, Colombia, 24–29 November.

Box, George E., and Gwilym M. Jenkins. 1976. *Time series analysis forecasting*, 2d ed. San Francisco: Holden-Day.

Box, George E., and George C. Tiao. 1975. Intervention analysis with applications to economic and environment problems. *Journal of the American Statistical Association* 70:70–79.

Brillenbourg, Arturo, and Susan Schadler. 1980. A model of currency substitution in exchange rate determination, 1973–1978. *IMF Staff Papers* 3:513–542.

Carrillo-Flores, Antonio. 1976. Acontecimientos sobresalientes en la gestación y evolución del Banco de México. *Cincuenta Años de Banca Central*, pp. 27–54. Fondo de Cultura Económica.

Cavazos, Manuel. 1976. Cincuenta años de política monetaria. *Cincuenta Años de Banca Central*, pp. 55–123. Fondo de Cultura Económica.

Córdoba, José, and Guillermo Ortiz. 1980. Aspectos deflacionarios de la devaluación del peso mexicano de 1976. *Demografiá y Economicá* 14:291–324.

Fernández-Hurtado, Ernesto. 1976. Reflexiones sobre aspectos fundamentales de la Banca Central en México. *Cincuenta Años de Banca Central*, pp. 15–26. Fondo de Cultura Económica.

Girton, Lance, and Don Roper. 1981. Theory and implications of currency substitution. *Journal of Money, Credit and Banking* 13:12–30.

Ize, Alain. 1981. A portfolio model of financial equilibrium with devaluation expectations. El Colegio de México. Mimeographed.

Martínez-Ostos, Raúl. 1946. El Banco de México. In M. H. de Koch, *La Banca Central*. Fondo de Cultura Económica.

Miles, Marc. 1978. Currency substitution, flexible exchange rates, and monetary independence. *American Economic Review* 3:428–436.

Miles, Marc, and Marion B. Stewart. 1980. The effects of risk and return on the currency composition of money demand. *Weltwirstschaftlickes Archiv* 116, no. 4:613–626.

Nassef, Sayed. 1972. *Monetary policy in developing countries: The Mexican case*. University of Rotterdam Press.

Ortiz, Guillermo. 1982. La demanda de dinero en México: Primeras estimaciones. *Monetaria* 5:37–82.

Ortiz, Guillermo, and Leopoldo Solís. 1979. Financial structure and exchange rate experience: Mexico 1954–1977. *Journal of Development Economics* 6:515–548.

————. 1982. Currency substitution and monetary independence: the case of Mexico. In P. Keven, J. V. Ypersele, and J. Braga de Macedo (eds.), *The international monetary system*. New York: Ballinger.

Solis, Leopoldo. 1981. *Economic policy reform in Mexico: A case study for developing countries*. New York: Pergamon Press.

Comment   Thomas J. Sargent

The subjects of "dollarization" and seigniorage involve fundamental and still controversial aspects of monetary economics. Views on these subjects stem directly from judgments about the theoretical models appropriate to explain why inconvertible (or "fiat") currencies command value. Currently, a variety of theories about the "demand for money" have adherents. These theories differ in terms of the economic forces that they adduce to assign a currency value, the relevance that they attach to distinctions between "inside" and "outside" money, and whether they give rise to well-defined and stable demand functions for national monies in a world of flexible exchange rates.

Theories of money begin from the observation that there is no role for unbacked fiat currency in the standard general equilibrium model of Arrow and Debreu, with its complete array of frictionless, state contingent futures markets. To provide room for an inconvertible currency, it is necessary to deviate from the Arrow-Debreu assumptions and to posit some source of friction that inhibits at least some of the trades envisaged by Arrow and Debreu. Theories of money differ in the ways that they introduce these frictions and the explicitness with which the theorizing is done.

One popular way of motivating a demand for money in a general equilibrium model is to resort to Sidrauski's (1967) device of adding real balances to the instantaneous utility function of a model that is otherwise isomorphic to a version of a Cass-Koopmans optimum growth model. The representative individuals in such a model are posited to maximize a criterion such as

$$(1) \qquad \sum_0^\infty u\left(c_t, \frac{m_t}{p_t}\right) e^{-\delta t},\ u_1 > 0,\ u_2 > 0,$$

where $\delta > 0$ is an instantaneous rate of time preference, c_t is per capita consumption of a single good, m_t is "nominal balances," and p_t is the nominal price level. Such a model is capable of generating a well-behaved, smooth demand function for the aggregate of assets included in

Thomas J. Sargent is a professor in the Department of Economics, University of Minnesota, and a Research Associate of the National Bureau of Economic Research. His comments are directed to both the paper by Stanley Fischer and the paper by Guillermo Ortiz.

nominal balances, m_t. This demand schedule permits the assets m_t to be dominated in rate of return by the alternative assets (corporate and government bonds, equities, or physical capital) that households have access to. Real balances are dominated in rate of return by those other assets to the extent that they provide utility directly, that is, to the extent that $u_2 > 0$. An important aspect of this theory is that very different principles are used to assign value to real balances, on the one hand, and to all other assets, on the other. All other assets are valued according to the utility value of the streams of consumption that they support in equilibrium. There is an asymmetry here, in that all assets except real balances are valued according to the principle of modern finance theory, which prices assets in such a way that no asset's return is dominated in equilibrium by the return on any other collection of assets.

In a theory of this kind, the analyst in effect decides a variety of important issues when he defines precisely what collection of assets enters the category of "real balances," or m_t/p_t. Is m_t/p_t high-powered money, as in the formal models of Sidrauski (1967), Brock (1974), and Fischer, thereby excluding inside money or that portion of demand deposits and time deposits that is not fully backed by high-powered money? The arguments that are used to justify including m_t/p_t in the utility function are widely interpreted as arguing for a broader aggregate including some components of inside debt, such as demand deposits, bank notes, and bills of exchange.[1] A closely related question is: For residents of a given country, are real balances denominated in foreign currencies included in m_t/p_t in (1)? It certainly seems plausible to posit, for example, that, for a two-country world, agents in country j maximize

$$(2) \qquad \sum_0^\infty u\left(c_{jt}, \frac{m_{1t}^j}{p_{1t}} + \frac{m_{2t}^j}{p_{2t}}\right)e^{-\delta t},$$

where c_{jt} is consumption in country j, m_{it}^j is nominal balances of country i held by residents of country j, and p_{it} is the price level in terms of country i currency. At this level of theorizing, positing (2) seems as plausible as positing that agents in country 1 maximize

$$(3) \qquad \sum_{t=0}^\infty u(c_{1t}, m_{1t}^1/p_{1t})e^{-\delta t},$$

while agents in country 2 maximize

$$(4) \qquad \sum_{t=0}^\infty u(c_{2t}, m_{2t}^2/p_{2t})e^{-\delta t}.$$

---

1. By introducing some heterogeneity of endowments and preferences across agents in a Sidrauski-like model, markets for consumption and production loans can be included, so that inside debt can be incorporated into the model. The properties of such a model would depend sensitively on what fraction of inside debt one included in the concept of real balances that enters the utility function.

Equations (3) and (4) assert that country 1 residents just happen to have "dollars" in their utility function and not "pounds," while country 2 residents just happen to have "pounds" and not "dollars." While these assumptions give rise to smooth and well-behaved demands for national currencies and a determinate theory of exchange rates, they are not useful for addressing the dollarization phenomenon described by Mr. Ortiz. However, the use of the criterion function (2) in a two-country Sidrauski model can readily be shown to imply a severe dollarization problem under a regime of flexible exchange rates and no capital controls. In particular, the resulting model has the properties that there are *not* smooth, well-defined demand schedules for particular national currencies, and that there is not even a unique equilibrium exchange rate. Thus, the predictions of the model depend very sensitively on the particular aggregate that the analyst chooses for "real balances." No first principles seem available to guide that choice for an analysis conducted at this level.

The same set of questions arises in models with "cash in advance" constraints, of the kind analyzed by Clower and by Lucas (1980). Here the idea is to have individuals maximize a Cass-Koopmans utility functional model involving only consumption

$$(5) \qquad \sum_{t=0}^{\infty} u(c_t)e^{-\delta t},$$

but to add the "cash in advance" constraint,

$$(6) \qquad p_t c_t \leq m_{t-1},$$

to the other intertemporal constraints of a version of a Cass-Koopmans model. A smooth, well-behaved demand schedule for real balances is obtained by forcing individuals to transact in the particular set of assets included in m_{t-1} in the Clower constraint (6). This constraint permits the assets included in m_{t-1} to be dominated in return by the other assets in the model. As in the Sidrauski model, the choice of assets to include in m_{t-1} sensitively conditions the conclusions of the analysis, especially from the point of view of the issues raised in the preceding papers by Fischer and Ortiz.

The same questions again arise if one attempts to use the reasoning underlying the Baumol (1952) and Tobin (1956) transactions costs models: to generate a demand for a particular class of assets called "money" that is dominated in terms of rate of return because business is less costly to transact with it. For example, it is hard to imagine a reasonable specification of a physical transaction cost technology that would naturally give rise to a situation in which, in equilibrium, each country turns out to have its own national money. Again, the Baumol-Tobin setup is silent on the question of the particular class of assets that is to be called money and with which business is less costly to transact.

The final brand of monetary theory that I will mention is based on the insight of Paul Samuelson (1958) that if sufficient "missing links" are introduced into a general equilibrium model, via spatial or temporal separation of agents, then a role for a properly managed inconvertible currency can emerge. Such models obtain a valued fiat currency by direct restrictions on the endowment patterns, locations in time and space, and technological possibilities for transforming goods over time and space. One popular example of this class of models is Samuelson's model of overlapping generations of two-period-lived agents, which has been used by Cass-Yaari (1966), Lucas (1972), Wallace (1980), and others to examine outstanding questions in macroeconomics. However, other models with agents who live more than two periods, such as those analyzed by Townsend (1980) and Tesfatsion (1980), embody the same general kind of missing-links friction that characterizes Samuelson's model. As in the previous kinds of models, issues of inside and outside money and of international currency substitution also arise in the context of these missing-links models. However, in these models the analysis is conducted at a more primitive level that naturally directs the analyst's attention toward the forces that make inside money displace (and devalue) outside money, and that make foreign currency compete with domestic currency.

Kareken and Wallace (1978, 1981) have used a version of Samuelson's model to analyze currency substitution, while Wallace (1980) and Sargent and Wallace (1981) have used such a model to analyze inside-outside money issues. To illustrate the issues raised by this brand of monetary theory for the subject of this paper, I shall briefly consider the following parametric, nonstochastic, two-country, pure exchange overlapping generations model.

At each date $t \geq 1$, there are born in country j N_j two-period-lived agents. Within each country, the agents are identically endowed both within and across time periods. There is a single, nonstorable consumption good. Let $w_s^j(t)$ be the endowment of t period goods of an agent in country j who is born at time s. Let $c_s^j(t)$ be the consumption of t period goods of an agent in country j who is born at time s. I assume the stationary endowment pattern

$$(7) \qquad \begin{aligned} w_t^1(t), w_t^1(t+1) &= (\beta_1, \beta_2), \\ w_t^2(t), w_t^2(t+1) &= (\alpha_1, \alpha_2). \end{aligned}$$

The young of each generation in each country are assumed to maximize the logarithmic utility function

$$(8) \qquad \ln c_t^h(t) + \ln c_t^h(t+1).$$

This utility function implies the saving function

(saving of an agent in country j who is young at t) $=$

(9)
$$w_t^j(t) - c_t^j(t) = \left[\frac{w_t^j(t)}{2} - \frac{w_t^j(t+1)}{2R(t)} \right],$$

where $R(t)$ is the real gross rate of return on saving between times t and $t+1$, denominated in time $(t+1)$ goods per unit of time t goods.

At time $t = 1$, there are N_j old people in country j. The old in country 1 are in the aggregate endowed with $H_1(0)$ units of government-supplied inconvertible paper currency, denominated in "dollars." The old in country 2 are in the aggregate endowed with $H_2(0)$ units of government-supplied inconvertible paper currency, denominated in "pesos." The government of country j has a *policy* of financing a real deficit of $G_t^j \geq 0$, $t = 1, 2, \ldots$ by creating additional fiat money. The government budget constraints are

(10)
$$G_t^j = \frac{H_j(t) - H_j(t-1)}{p_j(t)}, j = 1, 2,$$

where $p_j(t)$ is the price of time t goods, measured in units of j country currency per unit of time t goods. Below I shall characterize policy by $H_j(t)$ paths, and *not* G_t^j paths. The G_t^j path will be endogenous.

Consider a free-trade, flexible exchange rate regime in which agents in the two countries are permitted to borrow from and lend to each other freely and to hold each other's national currencies. Since there is no uncertainty, if the fiat currencies are to be valued (i.e., if $p_j(t) < \infty$), they must bear the same real rates of return with each other and with consumption loans (or "inside debt").[2] The real gross rate of return on currency j is $p_j(t)/p_j(t+1)$ at time t. Thus, we have the requirement that

$$\frac{p_1(t)}{p_1(t+1)} = \frac{p_2(t)}{p_2(t+1)}.$$

This implies

(11)
$$\frac{p_1(t)}{p_2(t)} = \frac{p_1(t+1)}{p_2(t+1)}.$$

The ratio $p_1(t)/p_2(t) = e(t)$ is the exchange rate, measured in dollars per peso. Equation (11) states that the exchange rate $e(t)$ must be constant over time if the currencies are to bear the same gross real rates of return. So we have $e(t) = e$ for all $t \geq 1$.

---

2. Tobin's (1958) theory of the demand for money also requires that the return on money not be dominated by the return on any possible portfolio of assets.

The sequence of equilibrium conditions for this two-country, world economy can be written, for $t \geq 1$, as

(net saving of young of country 1)
+ (net saving of young of country 2) =
(net dissaving of old of countries 1 and 2)
+ (net dissaving of government of country 1)
+ (net dissaving of government of country 2).

Net dissaving of the old at t is given by $H_1(t-1)/p_1(t) + H_2(t-1)/p_2(t)$, while net dissaving of government j is G_t^j. Substituting from (9) and (10), and using

$$p_1(t)/p_1(t+1) = p_2(t)/p_2(t+1) = R(t),$$

these equilibrium conditions can be written

$$N_1 \left[\frac{\beta_1}{2} - \frac{\beta_2}{2} \frac{p_1(t+1)}{p_1(t)} \right] + N_2 \left[\frac{\alpha_1}{2} - \frac{\alpha_2}{2} \frac{p_1(t+1)}{p_1(t)} \right]$$

$$= \left[\frac{H_1(t-1)}{p_1(t)} + \frac{H_2(t-1)}{p_2(t)} \right]$$

$$+ \frac{H_1(t) - H_1(t-1)}{p_1(t)} + \frac{H_2(t) - H_2(t-1)}{p_2(t)} .$$

This equation can be rewritten, using $p_2(t) = p_1(t)/e$, as

(12) $$\left(N_1 \frac{\beta_1}{2} + N_2 \frac{\alpha_1}{2} \right) - \left(N_1 \frac{\beta_2}{2} + N_2 \frac{\alpha_2}{2} \right) \frac{p_1(t+1)}{p_1(t)}$$

$$= \frac{H_1(t) + eH_2(t)}{p_1(t)} .$$

Multiplying by $p_1(t)$ and rearranging, we have the difference equation in $p_1(t)$

(13) $$p_1(t) = \lambda p_1(t+1) + \phi[H_1(t) + eH_2(t)], \quad t \geq 1,$$

where

$$\lambda = \left(\frac{\beta_2 N_1 + \alpha_2 N_2}{\beta_1 N_1 + \alpha_1 N_2} \right), \quad \phi = \frac{2}{N_1 \beta_1 + N_2 \alpha_1} .$$

If possible, the difference equation (13) is to be solved for a sequence of price levels $(p_1(t), t = 1, 2, \ldots)$ *and* an exchange rate $e \geq 0$. It happens, however, that the difference equation (13) cannot determine all of these endogenous variables. Kareken and Wallace (1981) describe this fact by stating that the equilibrium exchange rate is indeterminate or underdetermined. So long as all the price level $p_1(t)$ for *all* dates $t \geq 1$ is regarded as endogenous, Kareken and Wallace's characterization must be accepted.

We say that a *fiat money equilibrium* exists if the difference equation (13) has a solution with $p_1(t)\epsilon(0,\infty)$ for $t \geq 1$. The general solution of the difference equation (13) is

$$(14) \qquad p_1(t) = \phi \sum_{i=0}^{\infty} \lambda^i H_1(t+i) + e\phi \sum_{i=0}^{\infty} \lambda^i H_2(t+i)$$

$$+ c\left(\frac{1}{\lambda}\right)^t, t \geq 1,$$

where c is *any* arbitrary constant. So long as $G_t^j \geq 0$ and $t \geq 1$ in (10), a necessary condition for the difference equation (13) to have a solution with $\infty > p_1(t) > 0$ is $\lambda < 1$. The parameter $\lambda = (\beta_2 N_1 + \alpha_2 N_2)/(\beta_1 N_1 + \alpha_1 N_2)$ is the real gross rate on consumption loans in the pure consumption loans (or pure "inside debt") economy.[3] This is a version of Samuelson's result: For there to be a role for the "social contrivance" of inconvertible currency, an economy with inside debt alone must not provide a real gross rate of return in excess of the gross rate of growth of the economy.

If $\lambda < 1$, the existence of a fiat money equilibrium depends on the paths of $H_1(t)$ and $H_2(t)$ for $t \geq 1$. To take a concrete case, suppose that

$$H_1(t) = z_1 H_1(t-1), t \geq 1,$$
$$H_2(t) = z_2 H_2(t-1), t \geq 1.$$

We assume that $1 < z_1 < z_2$. Then we have the following situation: If $\lambda z_1 < 1$ and $\lambda z_2 < 1$, a continuum of fiat money equilibrium solutions of (13) is given by

$$(15) \qquad p_1(t) = \frac{\phi}{1 - \lambda z_1} H_1(t) + e \frac{\phi}{1 - \lambda z_2} H_2(t) + c\left(\frac{1}{\lambda}\right)^t$$

for *any* $\infty \geq e \geq 0$, and *any* $c \geq 0$. If $\lambda z_1 < 1$ and $\lambda z_2 > 1$, then a continuum of fiat money equilibrium solutions of (13) is given by

$$(16) \qquad p_1(t) = \frac{\phi}{1 - \lambda z_1} H_1(t) + c\left(\frac{1}{\lambda}\right)^t,$$

3. Notice that where there is no fiat currency, the equilibrium condition for the world economy is

(net saving of young of country 1)
+ (net saving of young of country 2) = 0,

or

$$N_1\left[\frac{\beta_1}{2} - \frac{\beta_2}{2}\frac{1}{R(t)}\right] + N_2\left[\frac{\alpha_1}{2} - \frac{\alpha_2}{2}\frac{1}{R(t)}\right] = 0.$$

The solution for the gross real rate of return of consumption loans is

$$R(t) = (\beta_2 N_1 + \alpha_2 N_2)/(\beta_1 N_1 + \alpha_1 N_2).$$

with $e \equiv 0$, and any $c \geq 0$. If $\lambda z_1 > 1$, the solution of (13) is $p_1(t) = +\infty$, so that neither fiat currency is valued.

The nature of these solutions reveals that the valuation of national currencies is *tenuous* for several reasons.[4] First, when $\lambda z_2 < 1$, so that solution (14) is pertinent, then the equilibrium exchange rate is underdetermined, with *any* constant e in the closed interval $[0, \infty]$ being an equilibrium exchange rate. This is Kareken and Wallace's celebrated result about the indeterminacy of equilibrium exchange rates under laissez-faire. Second, so long as $\lambda < 1$ and $\lambda z_1 < 1$, a continuum of equilibria exists (indexed by the parameter $c \geq 0$). All of these equilibria, except the stationary equilibrium with $c = 0$, have $p_1(t)$ following an explosive, self-fulfilling speculative bubble in which the real value of currency asymptotically goes to zero. Third, confining oneself to the stationary ($c = 0$) equilibrium, the more inside debt there is, or equivalently, the more private borrowers there are relative to private lenders, the higher is the equilibrium price level. Thus, equation (12) can be rewritten

$$\left(N_1 \frac{\beta_1}{2} + N_2 \frac{\alpha_1}{2}\right)p_1(t) = \left[\left(N_1 \frac{\beta_2}{2} + N_2 \frac{\alpha_2}{2}\right)p_1(t+1)\right]$$
$$+ [H_1(t) + eH_2(t)],$$

where the left-hand side is total nominal debt, the first bracketed term on the right-hand side is "inside" nominal indebtedness, and the second bracketed term on the right-hand side is nominal value of world currency supply; nominal values are measured in dollars. Notice that in a fiat money equilibrium the ratio of inside nominal debt to the total nominal debt is given by[5]

$$\left(\frac{N_1\beta_2 + N_2\alpha_2}{N_1\beta_1 + N_2\alpha_1}\right) \frac{p_1(t+1)}{p_1(t)} = \lambda \frac{p_1(t+1)}{p_1(t)}.$$

The larger the value of λ, the smaller the base of the inflation tax and the smaller the maximal sustained amount of real revenue that can be raised jointly by the two governments. Further, if $\lambda > 1$, we have seen that no fiat money equilibrium exists. Thus, private indebtedness competes with public indebtedness and limits the ability of the government to collect revenues through an inflation tax. Fourth, the valuation of national currencies is tenuous because it depends on the government not running deficits that are too large far into the future, that is, it depends on the government's repeated fiscal *policies*, as is exhibited directly by (14) or by the restrictions on z_1 and z_2 in the special versions of solutions (15) and (16).[6]

4. Neil Wallace (1980) has emphasized this feature of inconvertible currencies.
5. Equations (14) and (15) imply that $p_1(t + 1)/p_1(t) > 1$.
6. It is interesting to pose the following "optimal stationary seigniorage" question for this model. Given the exchange rate e, the real rate at which both governments together

Although the equilibrium value of the exchange rate is indeterminate, its value is important to the two governments, since it helps to determine the real value of the inflation tax revenues collected by each government (see [10] and [14]).[7] The scope of trade in inside debt is also significant from the viewpoint of the real amount of inflation tax that each government can potentially collect.[8]

This model thus implies, under a regime of flexible exchange rates and no capital controls, that dollarization will be a very important problem. This is particularly true if the economy with the larger deficits follows so expansionary a fiscal policy (e.g., $\lambda z_2 > 1$) that its currency is predicted to be valueless. The model indicates that a government intent on extracting an inflation tax from its own residents, or intent on preventing other countries from imposing such a tax on its residents, has substantial incentives to deviate from a regime of flexible exchange rates and capital mobility. That is, it has an incentive to impose currency and capital controls. The model also implies that such a government has a strong incentive to restrict and to regulate the scope of both domestic and international financial intermediaries that issue currency-like (i.e., small-denomination, low-risk) assets that compete with domestic currency in the portfolios of private agents.[9]

There are a variety of possible forms that the exchange interventions and regulations of intermediaries can take that are sufficient to render the equilibrium exchange rate determinate and the demand for domestic high-powered money well defined. Kareken and Wallace (1981) and Nickelsburg (1980) have studied several such intervention schemes. Here it should simply be mentioned that various kinds of implicit and state contingent threats, which perhaps need actually never be executed, are sufficient to render the exchange rate determinate. In interpreting time series data, in principle, it may be difficult to determine whether a system is truly operating under a laissez-faire regime "now and forever," or

---

collect revenues through the inflation tax is $G = H(t) - H(t-1)/p_1(t)$, where $H(t) = H_1(t) + eH_2(t)$. Let the "world money supply" follow the law $H(t) = zH(t-1)$. Then what value of z maximizes the sustainable value of G in stationary equilibrium? If the real gross rate of return on consumption loans in the nonfiat money equilibrium λ is greater than unity, no real revenues can be raised through the inflation tax. If $\lambda < 1$, the revenue-maximizing value of z turns out to be $\sqrt{(1/\lambda)}$.

7. Notice that in this economy there are not well-defined demand functions for the individual countries' currency stocks or for inside debt. Because all of these assets are perfect substitutes in lenders' portfolios, only a demand function for the total indebtedness, which can be thought of as the "total world money supply," is well defined. The real demand for this aggregate is equal to $(N_1\beta_1 + N_2\alpha_1)/2$.

8. The model is silent on the question of what currency inside debts are denominated in terms of.

9. I have set up the model so that residents within each country are identically endowed and have identical preferences. This means that all "inside debt" occurs in the form of international private loans. From the point of view of the points made here, it would have made no substantial difference if I had introduced heterogeneity of agents' preferences and endowments within each country to open up the possibility of within-country inside debt.

whether demands for inconvertible currencies are being influenced by some such implicit threats.

As do the other models of money that we have discussed, the Kareken-Wallace model has serious deficiencies. To get at the issues at an explicit and deep level, while maintaining analytical tractability, the model over-simplifies by severely restricting the technology, the life cycle, and the temporal distribution of agents. In fact, the physical and economic setup is so restricted that no one would seriously entertain econometrically estimating the free parameters of such a model by the appropriate econometric techniques of the post-Lucas critique (1976) era.[10] In interpreting the time series data, Kareken and Wallace do not seem to intend that their model be taken literally. In this sense, the model of Kareken and Wallace cannot yet serve as an entirely rigorous guide in formulating time series econometric specifications. However, it is possible to imagine generalizations of Kareken and Wallace's model along the lines of Townsend's (1980). Such a model would retain the missing-links features and isolate forces such as exchange rate indeterminacy and the tenuous character of fiat money equilibria. At the same time, it could accommodate more realistic and econometrically plausible infinite-period utility functions for households, so that one could think more seriously about formally using the model to interpret time series data. The problem is that such models quickly become analytically difficult to handle. In contrast, the Baumol-Tobin model and the real balances in the utility function models have more readily suggested econometric specifications.

Despite its abstractness and its remoteness from econometric applicability, the Kareken-Wallace model has the virtue of pointing toward forces that have seemed to operate in international currency markets and that other models have to some extent ignored. The history of exchange controls in England since the Second World War, for example, can be understood, at least partly, as a response to the forces pinpointed by their model.[11] So can the concern that monetary authorities in the United States and Europe have exhibited about the implications of Eurocurrency markets for monetary management. There is also Mr. Ortiz's observation that it was only with considerable difficulty that the Mexican authorities were able to induce Mexican citizens to hold domestically issued currency.

References

Baumol, William J. 1952. The transactions demand for cash: An inventory theoretic approach. *Quarterly Journal of Economics* 66 (November):545–556.

Brock, William A. 1974. Money and growth: The case of long run perfect foresight. *International Economic Review* 15 (October):750–777.

10. These techniques are described in various papers in Lucas and Sargent (1981).
11. See Leland Yeager (1975, chap. 22) for a history of British exchange controls.

Cass, D. 1965. Optimum growth in an aggregative model of capital accumulation. *Review of Economic Studies* 32 (July):233–240.

Cass, David, and Menahem Yaari. 1966. A reexamination of the pure consumption loans model. *Journal of Political Economy* 74 (August):353–367.

Kareken, John H., and Neil Wallace. 1978. Samuelson's consumption-loan model with country-specific fiat monies. Federal Reserve Bank of Minneapolis. Manuscript.

———. 1981. On the indeterminacy of equilibrium exchange rates. *Quarterly Journal of Economics*, forthcoming.

Koopmans, T. C. 1965. On the concept of optimal economic growth. *The econometric approach to development planning*, 225–287. Amsterdam: North-Holland.

Lucas, Robert E., Jr. 1972. Expectations and the neutrality of money. *Journal of Economic Theory* 4(April):103–124.

———. 1976. Econometric policy evaluation: A critique. In *The Phillips curve and labor markets*, edited by K. Brunner and A. H. Meltzer. Carnegie-Rochester Conferences on Public Policy, vol. 1. Amsterdam: North-Holland.

———. 1980. Equilibrium in a pure currency economy. In *Models of monetary economies*, edited by J. H. Kareken and N. Wallace. Federal Reserve Bank of Minneapolis.

Lucas, Robert E., Jr., and Thomas J. Sargent. 1981. *Rational expectations and econometric practice*. Minneapolis: University of Minnesota Press.

Nickelsburg, Gerald. 1980. A theoretical and empirical analysis of flexible exchange rate regimes. Ph.D. diss., University of Minnesota.

Samuelson, Paul A. 1958. An exact consumption-loan model of interest with or without the social contrivance of money. *Journal of Political Economy* 66 (December):467–482.

Sargent, Thomas J., and Neil Wallace. 1981. The real bills doctrine vs. the quantity theory: A reconsideration. Federal Reserve Bank of Minneapolis, Staff Report 64.

Sidrauski, Miguel. 1967. Rational choice and patterns of growth in a monetary economy. *American Economic Review, Papers and Proceedings* 57 (May):534–544.

Tesfatsion, Leigh. 1980. Distribution and competitive equilibria in a heterogenous overlapping generations model. Manuscript.

Tobin, James. 1956. The interest elasticity of the transactions demand for cash. *Review of Economics and Statistics* 38 (August):241–247.

———. 1958. Liquidity preference as behavior towards risk. *Review of Economic Studies* 25 (February):65–86.

Townsend, Robert M. 1980. Models of money with spatially separated agents. In *Models of monetary economies*, edited by J. H. Kareken and N. Wallace. Federal Reserve Bank of Minneapolis.

Wallace, Neil. 1980. The overlapping generations model of fiat money. In *Models of monetary economies*, edited by J. H. Kareken and N. Wallace. Federal Reserve Bank of Minneapolis.

Yeager, Leland B. 1975. *International monetary relations: Theory, history, and policy*, 2d ed. New York: Harper and Row.

5 On Equilibrium Wage Indexation and Neutrality of Indexation Policy

Nissan Liviatan

Recent literature on wage indexation[1] stresses its important role in the area of macroeconomic stability as reflected in the variability of aggregate output and the general price level. These papers compare economic stability under alternative wage indexation regimes: nonindexed, fully indexed, and partially indexed (according to some optimal criterion imposed externally). The results of these comparisons, as presented in Fischer (1977a), are that indexation tends to increase stability of output when the shocks are monetary while the reverse holds when the shocks originate from the real sector.

The approach taken in this paper is an entirely different one. The existing wage indexation regime shall not be treated as something imposed on the economy from the outside, but rather as an *endogenous* phenomenon which is part of the inflationary instability itself. Our approach is that an *equilibrium* degree of wage indexation exists which is determined by market forces. Therefore the question "How does indexation affect economic stability?" is, according to our approach, entirely meaningless if it refers to equilibrium wage indexation.

The only framework where the foregoing question can have meaning is when there is some sort of outside (say government) intervention policy to change the existing indexation arrangements. For example, given a formal fractional wage indexation of 50 percent for price inflation, the government may try to increase it to 80 percent. We would then argue that there are strong tendencies to offset the proposed policy and to leave the economic system effectively at its initial equilibrium.

The equilibrium degree of indexation in our analysis is a rather different concept from that of Gray's (1976) "optimal degree of indexation,"

Nissan Liviatan is a professor in the Department of Economics, Hebrew University, Jerusalem.

1. See especially Gray (1976, 1978), Fischer (1977a), and Cukierman (1980).

which is derived by minimizing some macroeconomic loss function based on differences between actual and spot equilibrium output. In particular, our concept of equilibrium degree of indexation depends on risk aversion of firms and workers. If, for example, firms are risk neutral, then the equilibrium solution is full indexation.

The idea of treating wage indexation as an endogenous phenomenon has been expressed in a paper by Shavell (1976). In fact, we follow his general analytic approach in deriving the Pareto-optimal degree of indexation, which we treat as corresponding to a market equilibrium. However, his formulation is a microeconomic one which does not utilize the macroeconomic framework in determining the equilibrium degree of indexation. The importance of macroeconomics in explaining the degree of indexation can be seen from our conclusion that an economy subject to purely monetary shocks tends to adopt full wage indexation. Also, Shavell did not consider the relation of indexation to labor input and economic stability which is a basic issue in our analysis.

Another paper which treats wage indexation as endogenous is Blanchard (1979). However, his indexing is not determined within the framework of a wage contract between parties of opposing interests. Instead, his concept is closely related to Gray's optimal degree of indexation mentioned earlier.

The conceptual framework for treating wage indexation which is closest to ours is that of Azariadis (1978). The details of the models are very different, however, and it is hoped that the endogeneity aspect of wage indexation and the determination of the indexing parameter will be presented in a much clearer fashion in our model.

The foregoing papers which treat the indexing parameter as an endogeneous phenomenon do not consider the effect of a government policy of changing the parameter directly, that is, through intervention in labor market negotiations. However, government often is in a position to affect this parameter. We shall therefore consider the consequences of direct government intervention in setting the indexing parameter, given that the behavior of the labor market is to a large extent regulated by labor contracts.

The other basic issue which will be considered in this paper is the interaction between wage indexing and asset indexing. This interaction has been pointed out by several writers (e.g., Blinder [1977] and Liviatan and Levhari [1977]), though not in the context of economic stability. We try to bring out the major significance of this interaction by proving a Modigliani-Miller-type theorem which states that under a perfect bond market the degree of wage indexing is indeterminate. In particular, any arbitrary change in the indexing parameter will generate offsetting forces in the capital market which will neutralize its effect on the real economy.

The neutrality property is also shown to hold under less stringent conditions.

5.1   Wage and Asset Indexation with a Perfect Bond Market

Let us consider an economy where all firms produce a single output with a variable labor input. The amount of labor is determined at the beginning of the production period, before uncertainty is resolved, and cannot be changed during the period. This is a case of ex ante determination of labor input. Later we shall extent the model to allow ex post adjustments in labor input. It is assumed that the only marketable assets are indexed and nonindexed bonds. There is no market for shares. As in the case of production, we assume that consumption takes place at the end of the period.

Wages to be paid at the end of the period can be considered as a payment by the employers to redeem their "bonds" held by the workers. We shall assume that these "employers' bonds" are not marketable. In addition, it will be assumed that the wage payments are perfectly safe (no risk of default) so that wages are equivalent to the redemption value of a nonmarketable bond. Although employers' bonds are nonmarketable, they are equivalent to ordinary (marketable) bonds if a perfect market exists for the latter.

Suppose that the workers would like to sell some of the employers' bonds in their possession to purchase some assets or to increase their money balances. Since they cannot do this directly, they can achieve the same thing indirectly by selling other bonds in their portfolios; this includes borrowing. If the workers can use their expected wages as collateral for borrowing, then it follows immediately that their employers' bonds are marketable indirectly. In our model, however, this may not be necessary since borrowing at the beginning of the period can be used only to acquire some assets, as consumption takes place only at the end of the period. Therefore the acquired assets may provide the main guarantee against default.

The production function of firms i is given by

$$y_i(s) = \gamma_i(s)\phi_i(n_{i1}L_{i1}, \ldots, n_{ij}L_{ij}),$$

where n_i denotes the number of workers of type j employed by firms of type i, L denotes hours of work, ϕ_i is an ordinary production function, and $\gamma_i(s)$ is a random factor which varies across states of nature s.

Wages are paid at the end of the period. The wage rate consists of the nominal base wage V and the cost of living allowance $V\theta[P(1/p^0) - 1]$, where P is the actual price level at the end of the period, and θ $(0 \le \theta \le 1)$ is a wage-indexing parameter. In the standard forms of wage indexing,

$(1/p^0) = (1/P_{t-1})$, so that $P(1/p^0) - 1$ is the relative rate of price inflation. For analytic purposes it is sometimes more convenient to define $(1/p^0)$ as the expected value of the purchasing power of money so that $(1/p^0) = E\pi$, where $\pi = (1/p)$. Using the notation $\bar{\pi} = (1/p^0)$, we may express the real wage rate as

$$\tilde{v}(s) = V[\theta\bar{\pi} + (1 - \theta)\pi(s)] \equiv V\tilde{\pi}(s).$$

We shall allow both V and θ to vary across firms and workers so that θ_{ij} is the indexing parameter for worker type j in firm type i.

The firms' profits are given by

(1) $$R_i(s) = \gamma_i(s)\phi_i - \sum_j n_{ij}L_{ij}V_{ij}[\theta_{ij}\bar{\pi} + (1 - \theta_{ij})\pi(s)].$$

We have noted that the total wage bill can be considered as a payment to redeem employers' bonds (B^w) held by the workers.[2] These bonds can be broken up into indexed and nonindexed components. From the point of view of the firms, the payments implied by these components are equivalent to holding negative amounts of ordinary bonds, the market values of which are given by

(2) $$B_{Ii}^w = -\frac{1}{1+r}\sum_j n_{ij}L_{ij}V_{ij}\theta_{ij}\bar{\pi};$$

$$B_{Ni}^w = -\frac{1}{1+i}\sum_j n_{ij}L_{ij}V_{ij}(1 - \theta_{ij}),$$

where I and N stand for indexed and nonindexed, r is the real interest rate on indexed bonds, and i is the nominal rate on nonindexed bonds.

In addition to the implicit liabilities in (2), the firms may invest in ordinary indexed and nonindexed bonds, denoted B_{Ii}^o and B_{Ni}^o, so that the employers' income (or resources) in state s is given by

$$Y_i(s) = \gamma_i(s)\phi_i + Q_{Ii}(1 + r) + Q_{Ni}(1 + i)\pi(s),$$

where $Q_{Ii} = B_{Ii}^w + B_{Ii}^o$ and $Q_{Ni} = B_{Ni}^w + B_{Ni}^o$.

The firms have an initial endowment of bonds equal to b_i. Since we do not consider a market for the firms' shares, it will be convenient to assume that the uncertain value of the firms' output cannot be capitalized. This means that the firms' future output can be used only as collateral to borrow from workers (i.e., to pay wages at the end of the period) and cannot be exchanged for ordinary bonds. This is, of course, an arbitrary assumption, but the exclusion of a market for shares is not essential for our analysis.

Under the foregoing assumptions and using the definition $w_i \equiv B_{Ii}^w + B_{Ni}^w$, we may write

---

2. The affinity of wage indexation to indexed bonds has also been pointed out in Brenner (1977).

(3) $$Q_{Ni} = b_i + w_i - Q_{Ii}.$$

We may then rewrite $Y_i(s)$ as

(4) $$Y_i(s) = \gamma_i(s)\phi_i + Q_{Ii}(1 + r) + (b_i + w_i - Q_{Ii})(1 + i)\pi(s).$$

For the workers, the indexed and nonindexed components of the wage bill constitute receipts which are equivalent to those originating from holding ordinary bonds, the market values of which are

(5) $$B_{Iij}^w = (L_{ij}V_{ij}\theta_{ij}\bar{\pi})\,\frac{1}{1 + r}\,;\; B_{Nij}^w = L_{ij}V_{ij}(1 - \theta_{ij})\,\frac{1}{1 + i}\,.$$

Since the workers may also invest in ordinary (nonwage) bonds, we may express their income in state s as

(6) $$Y_{ij}(s) = Q_{Iij}(1 + r) + Q_{Nij}(1 + i)\pi(s),$$

where

$$Q_{Iij} = B_{Iij}^w + B_{Iij}^o;\qquad Q_{Nij} = B_{Nij}^w + B_{Nij}^o.$$

Define

(7) $$w_{ij} \equiv B_{Iij}^w + B_{Nij}^w = L_{ij}V_{ij}\left(\frac{\theta_{ij}\bar{\pi}}{1 + r} \quad + \quad \frac{1 - \theta_{ij}}{1 + i}\right) \equiv L_{ij}X_{ij}.$$

In addition, if bonds are the only asset, we have a budget constraint on ordinary bonds of the form

(8) $$b_{ij} = B_{Iij}^o + B_{Nij}^o,$$

where b_{ij} is an initial endowment. Adding w and b, we obtain

(9) $$Q_{Nij} = b_{ij} + w_{ij} - Q_{Iij}.$$

In these formulations we omit, for simplicity, other forms of wealth, such as real balances, held by economic agents. The workers' income can then be expressed as

(10) $$Y_{ij}(s) = Q_{Iij}(1 + r) + (b_{ij} + w_{ij} - Q_{Iij})(1 + i)\pi(s).$$

The expected utility of workers is given by

(11) $$\underset{s}{E}U_j[Y_{ij}(s), L_{ij}],$$

with partial derivatives $U_{j1} > 0$ and $U_{j2} < 0$. Similarly, the expected utility of firms is

(12) $$\underset{s}{E}U_i[Y_i(s)].$$

We may use these functions to formulate an efficient contract problem between workers and firms as follows:

(13)   maximize EU_i subject to $EU_j = U_j^0$ $(j = , \ldots, J)$.

Using (7) and the fact that

(14)
$$\sum_j n_{ij} w_{ij} = w_i,$$

we see that the maximization is carried out with respect to the variables n_{ij}, L_{ij}, Q_{Iij}, Q_{Ii}, and X_{ij}. (We shall denote the optimal values of these variables by asterisks.) The optimal values of Q_{Ni} and Q_{Nij} are derived from (3) and (9).

In a general equilibrium of the economy, we must have

(15)
$$\sum_i Q_{Ii}^* + \sum_{ij} Q_{Iij}^* = 0; \qquad \sum_i Q_{Ni}^* + \sum_{ij} Q_{Nij}^* = 0.$$

This is so since $B_{Ii}^w + \sum_j B_{Iij}^w n_{ij} = 0$ for every firm and

(16)
$$\sum_i B_{Ii}^o + \sum_{ij} n_{ij} B_{Iij}^o = 0$$

for the economy as a whole. Note that if the total number of workers type j in the economy is $\bar{n}_j$, then full employment requires.

(17)
$$\sum_i n_{ij} = \bar{n}_j \qquad (j = 1, \ldots, J).$$

These J conditions make it possible, in principle, to determine the values of U_j^o which are treated as given parameters on the level of individual agents, while (16) and the corresponding market clearing condition for B_N^o enable us to determine i and r.

It should be stressed that, given L_{ij} and X_{ij}, the workers determine their *overall* indexed position Q_{Iij} rather than the individual indexed components B_{Iij}^w and B_{Iij}^o, and the same is true for the firms. Note also that the contract determines X_{ij} (the present value of the real wage rate) rather than V_{ij} and θ_{ij} on which it is based.

Consider the following conditions resulting from efficient contracts:

(18)
$$Q_{Iij}^* = L_{ij}^* V_{ij} \theta_{ij} \bar{\pi} \left(\frac{1}{1+r} \right) + B_{Iij}^o;$$

$$Q_{Ii}^* = -\bar{\pi} \sum_j n_{ij}^* L_{ij}^* V_{ij} \theta_{ij} \left(\frac{1}{1+r} \right) + B_{Ii}^o.$$

(19)
$$Q_{Nij}^* = L_{ij}^* V_{ij} (1 - \theta_{ij}) \left(\frac{1}{1+i} \right) + B_{Nij}^o;$$

$$Q_{Ni}^* = \sum_j n_{ij}^* L_{ij}^* V_{ij} (1 - \theta_{ij}) \left(\frac{1}{1+i} \right) + B_{Ni}^o.$$

(20)
$$X_{ij}^* = V_{ij} \left(\frac{\theta_{ij} \bar{\pi}}{1+r} + \frac{1 - \theta_{ij}}{1+i} \right).$$

In addition, we have the market clearing conditions in the bond market

(21) $\sum_{ij} n_{ij} B^o_{Iij} + \sum_i B^o_{Ii} = 0$; $\sum_{ij} n_{ij} B^o_{Nij} + \sum_i B^o_{Ni} = 0$.

These conditions are not sufficient to determine V_{ij} and θ_{ij} individually. However, given θ_{ij}, we see from (20) that V_{ij} is determined uniquely. The nondeterminacy of θ_{ij} can be seen as follows: Suppose we start with equilibrium values θ^*_{ij} and V^*_{ij}. Now, let all the θ^*_{ij} increase to θ'_{ij}. If we hold the left-hand side of (20) fixed, then $\Delta\theta_{ij} = \theta'_{ij} - \theta^*_{ij}$ implies a change in V_i, say $\Delta V_j = V'_{ij} - V^*_{ij}$. Specifically, we have

(22) $$\Delta V_{ij} = -\frac{[\bar{\pi}(1 + i) - (1 + r)]}{\pi(1 + i)\theta_{ij} + (1 - \theta_{ij})(1 + r)} \Delta\theta_{ij}.$$

It is evident that, in general, $\Delta\theta_{ij}$ will cause a change in $V^*_{ij}\theta^*_{ij}$ so that to maintain (18) B^o_{Iij} will have to change by, say, ΔB^o_{Iij}. Similarly, B^o_{Ii} will have to change by ΔB^o_{Ii} to maintain (18). It is clear, however, that for each firm $\sum_j n_{ij} \Delta B^o_{Iij} + \Delta B^o_{Ii} = 0$, so that the market for indexed bonds remains in equilibrium. A similar argument shows that the market for nonindexed bonds remains in equilibrium as required by (21). It follows that the economy as a whole is invariant to an arbitrary change in the θ_{ij}'s.

The sign $\Delta V_{ij}/\Delta\theta_{ij}$ in (22) depends on the sign of $[(1 + i)\bar{\pi} - (1 + r)]$. This latter expression will be positive when nonindexed bonds carry a premium over indexed bonds as a result of the inflationary risk. It has been shown in a paper by Landskroner and Liviatan (1981) that this risk premium tends to be positive when real factors contribute significantly to the variability of π. If the risk premium of nonindexed bonds is positive, then $\Delta V_{ij}/\Delta\theta_{ij} < 0$, which is in line with intuition.

Moreover, if $\Delta V_{ij}/\Delta\theta_{ij} < 0$, then the elasticity of V_{ij} with respect to θ_{ij} is less than unitary (in absolute value), provided $0 < \theta_{ij} < 1$.[3] This implies by (18) that an increase in θ_{ij} will increase the demand for indexed bonds by employers and increase supply of indexed bonds by workers (by an equal amount). By the same argument, an opposite development will take place in the market for nonindexed bonds. Thus, the bond market enables employers to hedge fully against changes in the degree of wage indexing.

It may be pointed out that the existence of perfect bond markets is not essential for neutrality of wage indexing. It is sufficient to assume that workers can make transactions in bonds only with their own employers. Let A_{Iij} and A_{Nij} denote the net redemption value of ordinary indexed and nonindexed bonds of employer i held by worker j. The incomes of workers and employers can then be expressed as

3. This elasticity is given by

$$-\frac{\theta_{ij}}{V_{ij}}\frac{\Delta V_{ij}}{\Delta\theta_{ij}} = \frac{(1 + i)\bar{\pi} - (1 + r)}{(1 + i)\bar{\pi} + (1 + r)[(1 - \theta_{ij})/\theta_{ij}]}.$$

(23)
$$Y_{ij}(s) = Z_{Iij} + Z_{Nij}\pi(s),$$
$$Y_i(s) = \gamma_i(s)\phi_i - \sum_j n_{ij} Z_{Iij} - \sum_j n_{ij} Z_{Nij}\pi(s),$$

where
$$Z_{Iij} = L_{ij} V_{ij} \theta_{ij} \bar{\pi} + A_{Iij},$$
$$Z_{Nij} = L_{ij} V_{ij}(1 - \theta_{ij}) + A_{Nij}.$$

An optimal contract will determine equilibrium values Z_{Iij} and Z_{Nij}. It then follows that an arbitrary change in θ_{ij} can be offset by an appropriate change in A_{Iij} and A_{Nij} even when V_{ij} is held constant. In this case there is no meaning to a trade-off between θ_{ij} and V_{ij}. If, however, we impose a constraint on capital transactions between workers and their employers, then a trade-off between θ and V may emerge.

For example, if we require that

(24)
$$A_{Iij} + \delta_{ij}\bar{\pi} A_{Nij} = 0,$$

then a change in θ_{ij} will require a specific change in V_{ij}. A simple calculation shows that in this case

(25)
$$\frac{dV_{ij}}{d\theta_{ij}} = -\frac{V_{ij}\left[\left(\dfrac{1}{\delta_{ij}}\right) - 1\right]}{\dfrac{1}{\delta_{ij}}\theta_{ij} + (1 - \theta_{ij})},$$

where the optimal values of Z, L, and n are held constant. It follows that we obtain a trade-off (negative sign for [25]) if $0 < \delta_{ij} < 1$. The latter condition means that nonindexed bonds carry a positive risk premium over indexed ones. In this respect the result is similar to that obtained earlier.

The analysis in this section is based on the existence of some form of indexed bonds. In practice a market for indexed bonds rarely exists. An exception is the Israeli economy where a highly developed market for the government's indexed bonds has been operating for a long time. It should be noted, however, that close substitutes for indexed bonds have been developed recently in the form of "variable interest loans." In these loans the linkage is to the short-term interest rate rather than to the price level, but when the interest is computed over short intervals (as in fact it is) the two types of bonds become quite similar in nature. Our indexed bonds are, of course, also a proxy for many other assets (shares, commodities, etc.) which contain a high degree of insurance against inflationary risk.

5.2   The Case Where Wage Indexing Matters, and the Determination of a Fractional θ

In the foregoing analysis we have seen how wage indexing is completely offset by transactions in bonds. The case where an arbitrary change in the wage-indexing parameter will affect the real system is where capital transactions are sufficiently imperfect. To clarify this case let us take the extreme example where transactions in bonds, or other assets, are completely ruled out.

In this case we may set i, r, and all terms involving B^o equal to zero in (18)–(20). We may then see that V_{ij} and θ_{ij} are determined uniquely by (18) and (19) or by (18) and (20). Alternatively, the optimization leading to an efficient contract may be carried out directly with respect to θ_{ij} and V_{ij}, leading to unique optimal values of these variables. In this case it is clear that if the government enforces an arbitrary value of θ, say θ^g, then the general equilibrium solution will change.

In the present case, where no offsetting by capital transactions is possible, θ becomes a significant variable in wage negotiations. We shall now argue that, in general, one should expect to find a fractional θ rather than the extreme case of full wage indexation or no indexation at all.

Two arguments can be produced to rationalize a fractional θ in equilibrium. The first argument is concerned with holdings of nominal money balances by firms and workers. In the case of workers, this will only strengthen their desire to increase θ as a hedge against inflationary risks. In the case of firms, however, a nominal obligation to pay wages acts as a hedge against inflationary risk with respect to real balances. This argument is discussed in detail in Liviatan and Levhari (1977). This may lead to a fractional θ in equilibrium.

A second argument concerns the sources of inflationary uncertainty. Assume for simplicity that all workers are identical and all firms are identical. The profit function is then given by

$$(26) \qquad R(s) = \gamma(s)\phi(nL) - nLV[\theta\bar{\pi} + (1 - \theta)\pi(s)$$
$$\equiv \gamma(s)\phi(nL) - nL\tilde{v}(s).$$

If the random shocks in the system originate only in the monetary side, so that $\gamma \equiv 0$, then $\text{var}(R) = (nL)^2 \text{var}(\tilde{v})$, which is also the expression for the variance of the workers' income. Suppose that the wage is fixed in nominal terms and is given by V^0. If $E(1/P)$ remains constant, then both parties can adopt full indexation to eliminate the variance of their incomes while maintaining the same expected value of incomes by setting $v = V^0 E(1/P)$. The assumption that $E(1/P)$ remains constant can be justified by using a money market equilibrium equation of the form $M = PYk$, where Y is aggregate output and k is the "Cambridge k." Since Y is held constant, this yields $E(1/P) = YkE(1/M)$, which is independent of θ. The model of exclusively monetary shocks therefore tends to support the case for full indexation. In this respect it is similar to the behavior of Gray's optimal degree of wage indexation.

Consider now the other extreme case, where M is constant and where the entire variance of prices stems from the *real* disturbance, γ. Recall that the real wage is given by

(27) $$v = V[\theta\bar{\pi} + (1 - \theta)\pi] \equiv V^0\widetilde{\pi},$$

so that the real wage bill can be expressed as

$$w = vLn = nLV^0\widetilde{\pi},$$

Then

(28) $$\text{var}(R) = \phi^2\,\text{var}(\gamma) + \text{var}(w) - 2\,\text{cov}(\gamma, w)\phi.$$

Using (27), we obtain

(29) $$\text{cov}(\gamma, w) = V^0nL(1 - \theta)\,\text{cov}(\gamma, \pi),$$

and

(30) $$\text{var}(w) = [(1 - \theta)nLV^0]^2\,\text{var}(\pi),$$

so that

(31) $$\text{var}(R) = \phi^2\,\text{var}(\gamma) + \left\{[(1 - \theta)nLV^0]^2 - 2\phi nLV^0(1 - \theta)\frac{\text{cov}(\gamma, \pi)}{\text{var}(\pi)}\right\}\text{var}(\pi).$$

While var (R) can be regarded as relating to an individual firm, we may compute cov (γ, π)/var (π) on a macroeconomic basis using the assumption that γ is identical for all firms. Expressing our variables on a *per firm* basis, we may use the money market equilibrium to write

(32) $$\gamma = \pi(M/\bar{y}k),$$

where $\bar{y} = \phi$. Then we have (assuming $E\gamma = 1$)

(33) $$\frac{\text{cov}(\gamma, \pi)}{\text{var}(\pi)} = \frac{M}{\bar{y}k} = \frac{1}{\bar{\pi}}.$$

Using this result we may express (28) as

(34) $$\text{var}(R) = \phi^2\,\text{var}(\gamma) + \left\{[(1 - \theta)nLV^0]^2 - 2\phi\frac{nLV^0(1 - \theta)}{\bar{\pi}}\right\}\text{var}(\pi).$$

Differentiating (34) with respect to θ, we obtain

(35) $$\frac{\partial\,\text{var}(R)}{\partial\theta} = 2(nLV^0)^2\,\text{var}(\pi)[1/S_L - (1 - \theta)],$$

where $S_L = \bar{\pi}V^0nL/\phi$ is a concept of expected labor share which must be less than unity. It follows (assuming $\theta \leq 1$) that the effect of indexation on the variance of R is negative. The reason for the difference compared with the monetary shocks assumption is that now we have a positive covariance between w and γ which tends to reduce the variance of $R = \gamma\phi - w$. In view of (35), a risk-averse firm will prefer less wage indexation.

The efficient wage contract is determined by

$$\max EF(R) \text{ subject to } EU(w, L) = U^0,$$

where F and U are the utility functions of the firm and workers, respectively. The maximization is carried out with respect to n, L, V, and θ. Let us concentrate on the partial indifference curves in the (V, θ) plane.

What can be said about the slopes of these curves? We can calculate[4]

$$(36) \qquad \partial EU/\partial V^0 = LEU_1'\,\tilde{\pi} > 0,$$

$$(37) \qquad \partial EU/\partial \theta = -V^0 LEU'(\pi - \bar{\pi}) = -V^0 L \operatorname{cov}(U_1', \pi) > 0,$$

where the last inequality follows from $\operatorname{cov}(U_1', \pi) < 0$ as a result of $U'' < 0$. Thus both V^0 and θ have a positive effect on EU.

Turning to the firm, we find

$$(38) \qquad \partial EF/\partial V^0 = -nLEF'\,\tilde{\pi} < 0,$$

$$(39) \qquad \partial EF/\partial \theta = V^0 nL \operatorname{cov}(F', \pi).$$

Since F' is a function of $w = \gamma\phi - V^0 L[\theta\bar{\pi} + (1 - \theta)\pi]$, we have an ambiguous sign for $\operatorname{cov}(F', \pi)$. This is so since γ is positively correlated with π by macroeconomic considerations, while $-V^0 Ln(1 - \theta)\pi$ is negatively correlated with π if $1 - \theta > 0$. To have a fractional θ in equilibrium, we must assume $\partial EF/\partial \theta < 0$, which can be justified by assigning sufficient importance to real shocks in the economy (as explained earlier).

If firms are risk neutral, as is assumed in various studies of implicit contracts, then $\partial F/\partial \theta = 0$ and the equilibrium solution will be $\theta = 1$. This can be seen by noting that we can regard the equilibrium solution alternatively as being derived from the maximization of EU subject to a given EF. When both firms and workers are risk averse and $\partial EF/\partial \theta < 0$, the solution will tend to be one of partial indexation, $0 < \theta < 1$.

Since both V^0 and θ are desirable items for workers, it follows that they will be willing to trade, at an appropriate exchange rate, a higher θ for lower V^0. In equilibrium exactly the same trade-off will apply to firms where both V^0 and θ are undesirable items.

The foregoing analysis is illustrated in figure 5.1 which is based on a given level of L. When firms are risk averse and real disturbances are important, then the firms' indifference curves will look like FF, with EF increasing as we move toward the origin. For a given level of the workers' $EU = U^0$, equilibrium is determined at E. If the firms are risk neutral,

---

4. U_R' denotes the partial derivative of U with respect to the Rth argument.

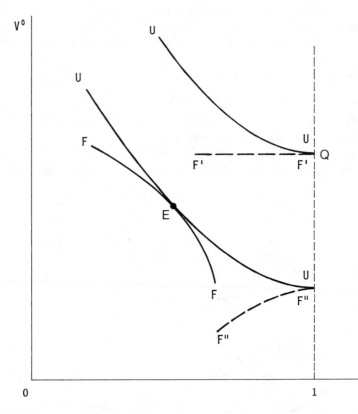

Fig. 5.1   It is assumed that all indifference curves have a zero slope at $\Theta = 1$. This is always true for the workers. For firm owners this is true under purely monetary shocks.

then their indifference curves will be horizontal, like $F'F'$, so that the solution will be at a point like Q with full indexation $\theta = 1$. Similarly, if firms are risk averse but real disturbances are insignificant, then θ is desirable for the firms so that their indifference curves will be upward sloping like $F''F''$. Clearly in this case the solution is again one of full indexation. (We assume that a solution with $\theta > 1$ is ruled out.)

Suppose that a fractional θ has been established in equilibrium, say θ^*, and let the government try to impose a higher θ, say θ^g. First, assume that the government passes a law which states that workers are entitled to require θ^g, and if they do so the firms must comply with their demand. If, however, we take into account that θ^* is the equilibrium rate, then the workers will ordinarily not be interested in using the option offered to them by the government.

The reason for this is that the option $\theta = \theta^g$ existed potentially when the negotiations leading to equilibrium took place. The reason that the workers did not insist on this option is because the firms would agree to it only if V^0 were reduced by an amount which exceeds the workers' subjective trade-off. There is therefore no reason to assume that the workers will opt to ask for θ^g after the law has been passed.

If the law takes a compulsory form, that is, firms are actually required to index wages by θ^g, then in general the equilibrium in terms of the real variables will be affected. This is a consequence of the restriction that no capital transactions are allowed. The implications of the nonneutrality of government wage indexation policy on economic stability will be discussed later.

5.3 Ex Post Adjustment of Labor Input and the Dual Labor Market

The foregoing analysis was concerned with the determination of equilibrium θ but had practically nothing to do with the problem of stability as analyzed in the recent Fischer-Gray models and related work. As we noted earlier, the foregoing works are concerned with the relation of indexation to the variability of output and prices during the period of production after the contract has been signed. Thus the conventional analysis of stability is concerned with ex post variability of output which has been ruled out in our earlier analysis.

The foregoing analysis allows, of course, ex post variability of prices. However, it is unlikely that the variability of the general price level will be significantly affected by indexation if labor input is determined on an ex ante basis. For if the money market equilibrium is $M\pi = \gamma \bar{y} k$, then the logarithmic variances satisfy var$(\log \pi)$ = var(γ/M) which is independent of $\bar{y}$.

In order to deal with the problem of stability let us turn to a model which permits ex post adjustments of labor input. In the Gray type of models the contract takes the form of setting V to conform with the "no-risk" competitive equilibrium. In addition, some value of θ is given externally. Then the workers are assumed to agree to supply, under the conditions of the contract, any quantity of services at the fixed terms when uncertainty is resolved.

This model of contracting is deficient in various respects. It is quite clear that we do not ordinarily observe this kind of contract in practice. Indeed, it seems to be an unreasonable arrangement from the point of view of the workers. The recent literature on implicit contracts stresses the risk aversion of workers, and it is clear that, quite apart from the question of indexation, the Gray contract will subject the workers' income to considerable variability resulting from the shifts of the firms' demand curves for labor. In a typical labor contract the workers will aim at stabilizing the amount of their employment at the cost of reducing their real wage (in fact, some implicit contract models lead to the result that employment will be fully stabilized).[5]

Another criticism concerning this type of model was raised by Barro (1977), who points out that the rigidity of the contract forces the parties to deviate considerably (ex post) from their best mutual interests as represented by the spot (or unconstrained) equilibrium. This implies that after the uncertainty is resolved both parties can benefit by moving toward the spot equilibrium.

The reply of Fischer (1979b) to this sort of criticism is that it is difficult to formulate a contract which will specify a formal procedure by which the ex post adjustment in employment à la Barro should be carried out, because there are obvious problems of moral hazard involved.

A sensible solution to these opposing views is to consider a dual system where part of the labor input is determined by ex ante contracts while another part is determined through a spot market. This is clearly the setup observed in many labor markets. There are always the long-term, wage-employment contracts which relate to the regular personnel, and there is the variable part which consists of temporary and part-time workers, ordinarily identified with special demographic groups. To the variable part we may often add overtime and special (unforeseen) assignments carried out by the regular personnel.

The employment conditions of the regular personnel which are determined in advance by a contract usually refer to a fixed amount of work determined by normal working hours. On the other hand, the conditions relating to wages and employment of the variable component are determined by something which resembles a spot market. If we consider the family as the basic decision-making unit with respect to labor supply, then we should consider the part-time work of one family member and the fixed labor input of another family member as originating from the same unit. We may therefore generally consider the ex ante determined labor input (by means of labor contracts) and the variable labor input as relating to the same optimization problem on the part of the workers. This is in fact the procedure which we shall adopt, although it is by no means essential for our conclusions.

We assume that the contractual part of the labor input is determined ex ante and fixed during the production period. This part will be denoted by L^0. In addition, the contract specifies the ex ante nominal wage, V^0, associated with L^0, and the degree of indexation, θ. The ex post amount of variable labor input supplied through the spot market will be denoted L_1^s and the corresponding real wage by v_1.

The workers' incentive to enter the contract is to reduce the risk of income fluctuations as a result of the variability of the real wage in the

---

5. See Sargent (1979, chap. 8).

spot market, which is in turn due to the variability of firms' demand for labor. This consideration holds quite independently of the problem of indexation. We shall begin the analysis of this model by ruling out the possibility of capital transactions and then consider the relaxation of this assumption.

When we deal with ex ante and ex post adjustment, both firms and workers face a two-stage optimization problem. The first-stage problem, which refers to the situation before uncertainty is resolved, must determine the contractual values of V^0, θ, n^0, and L^0 which are independent of the state of nature. In the second stage, uncertainty is resolved so that π and v_1 are known. At this stage, n_1 and L_1 (the number of workers and hours worked) are determined by firms and workers through an optimization process based on current market values of π and v_1. The second (ex post) stage of optimization depends, of course, on the predetermined values of the first-stage problem, but it is also clear that the first-stage optimization must take into account the distribution of π and v_1.

The firms' ex post profits are given by

(40) $$R = \gamma\phi(n^0L^0 + n_1L_1) - n^0L^0V^0\widetilde{\pi} - n_1L_1v_1.$$

Given the first-stage variables (n^0, L^0, V^0, and θ), the firms determine their spot market demand for labor by maximizing R with respect to the product n_1L_1. Since $n^0L^0V_0\widetilde{\pi}$ can be considered (ex post) as a fixed-cost element, it will not affect the optimal solution as long as it can be covered by the firms' revenue. Hence the optimal n_1L_1 can be considered as a function of v_1, n_0L_0, and γ, say

(41) $$n_1L_1 = L_1^d(v_1, n^0L^0, \gamma).$$

The workers' second-stage utility function is given by

(42) $$U(V^0\widetilde{\pi}L^0 + v_1L_1, L^0 + L_1); U_1' > 0, U_2' < 0,$$

which is maximized with respect to L_1. The second-stage supply of hours worked in the economy may then be considered as a function of $V^0\widetilde{\pi}$, L_0, and v_1, say

(43) $$\overline{n}L_1 = L_1^s(v_1, L^0, V^0\widetilde{\pi}),$$

where $\overline{n}$ is the given number of workers in the population on a per firm basis. (This formulation assumes that all workers are employed in the spot market.) In equilibrium $n_1 \doteq \overline{n}$ and $L^d = L^s$, so that v_1 and L_1 are determined. Thus for every set of first-stage variables a distribution of v_1 is determined.

Note also that through L_1 and L^0 the distribution of output and hence also that of prices is determined through the money market equation. In a full rational expectation equilibrium it is required that the distribution of π, determined in the foregoing manner, should be consistent with the a priori distribution of π on which the optimization problem is based.

In the first-stage problem the expected utility function of the firms is given by

$$(44) \qquad \underset{\gamma, \pi, v_1}{EF} \{\gamma\phi[L^0 n^0 + L_1^d(v_1, n^0 L^0, \gamma)] - V^0 \widetilde{\pi} L^0 n^0$$
$$- v_1 L_1^d(v_1, n^0 L^0, \gamma)\} \equiv F^*(v^0, \theta, L^0 n^0).$$

Similarly, the expected utility of workers is given by

$$(45) \qquad \underset{\pi, v_1}{EU} \left[V^0 \widetilde{\pi} L^0 + \frac{1}{n} L_1^s(v_1, L^0, V^0 \widetilde{\pi}) v_1, L^0 \right.$$

$$\left. + \frac{1}{n} L_1^s(v_1, L^0, v^0 \widetilde{\pi}) \right] \equiv U^*(V^0, \theta, L^0).$$

Note that n^0 does not appear in U^* since it relates to an individual worker.

Unlike the second-stage equilibrium which is determined in a spot market, the first-stage equilibrium is determined through contracts between workers and firms which are assumed to be efficient. Consequently the firms are assumed to maximize F^* subject to $U^* = $ constant, where the maximization is carried out with respect to n^0, L^0, V^0, and θ.

The maximization problem implies that, for internal solutions, V^0, θ, and L^0 should have opposite effects on F^* and U^*. The considerations leading to opposite effects of V^0 and θ were presented earlier (see [36]–[38]). As for L, it is assumed that the dominant factor is the workers' desire to ensure themselves against the real wage fluctuations in the spot market. In view of our earlier discussion in this section, we may assume that in equilibrium the effect of L^0 and U^* is positive while the effect on F^* is negative.

The structure of the first-stage problem has been reduced essentially to that of the model with ex ante determination of labor input which we have discussed in earlier sections. We may therefore apply some of the conclusions reached earlier. In particular, it is evident that when perfect bond markets exist, then θ will cease to be a relevant consideration for wage contracts. Consequently, an arbitrary imposition of θ^g will have no effect on L^0 nor on realized real wealth at the end of the period. As a result of this, the spot market supply and demand functions will be unaffected, and therefore the distribution of output will remain unchanged. Similarly, private loans between workers and firms, even when no general bond markets exist, will neutralize the effect of θ^g.

If follows from the foregoing remarks that external intervention in setting the degree of wage indexing can be effective only if the offsetting mechanism originating in the capital market is inoperative. A detailed analysis of the effect of a government's indexation policy under the latter conditions will not be undertaken in this paper.

As might be expected on the basis of earlier studies, the effect of indexation policy on economic stability is related to sources of random shocks to the economy. If, for example, the shocks are purely monetary, then, as we have seen, the equilibrium degree of indexing will be unitary. In this case, indexing will fully neutralize the effect of monetary shocks on the real system. If θ is reduced arbitrarily below unity, then part of the nominal shocks will be transferred to the real sectors. Thus reducing indexation is destabilizing. Alternatively, if the shocks originate entirely from the real sector, then an arbitrary increase in θ will tend to destabilize output. Thus, in the absence of capital transactions the results of our model tend to be in line with the Fischer-Gray analysis.

It should be stressed however that if an arbitrary change in θ^g increases stability of output (as is the case when θ is increased in a model where all shocks are "real"), it does not mean that this step is desirable. From the point of view of individual welfare, an arbitrary change in θ causes a deviation from the Pareto-optimal solution, which is undesirable. In particular, an increase in θ will ordinarily cause a reduction in the wage base V^0 (as we have seen when we dealt with perfect bond markets) to a greater extent than warranted by the workers' subjective trade-off between these variables.

References

Azariadis, C. 1978. Escalator clauses and the allocation of cyclical risks. *Journal of Economic Theory* 18:119–155.

Barro, R. J. 1976. Indexation in a rational expectations model. *Journal of Economic Theory* 13:229–244.

———. 1977. Long-term contracting, sticky prices and monetary policy. *Journal of Monetary Economics* 3:305–316.

Blanchard, O. J. 1979. Wage indexing rules and the behavior of the economy. *Journal of Political Economy* 87:798–815.

Blinder, A. S. 1977. Indexing the economy through financial intermediation. *Journal of Monetary Economics*, Supp. Series 5:69–105.

Brenner, R. 1977. Micro- and macroeconomic aspects of indexation. Ph.D. diss., Jerusalem.

Cukierman, A. 1980. The effect of wage indexation on macroeconomic fluctuations. *Journal of Monetary Economics* 6:147–170.

Fischer, S. 1977a. Wage indexation and macroeconomic stability. *Journal of Monetary Economics*, Supplement, pp. 107–148.

———. 1977b. Long-term contracting, sticky prices and monetary policy: A comment. *Journal of Monetary Economics* 3:317–323.

Gray, J. A. 1976. Wage indexation: A macroeconomic approach. *Journal of Monetary Economics* 2:221–235.

———. 1978. On indexation and contract length. *Journal of Political Economy* 86:1–18.

Landskroner, Y., and N. Liviatan. 1981. Risk premium and the sources of inflation. *Journal of Money, Credit and Banking* 13:205–214.

Liviatan, N., and D. Levhari. 1977. Risk and the theory of indexed bonds. *American Economic Review* 67 (June):366–375.

Liviatan, N., and D. Levhari. 1979. On the deflationary effect of government's indexed bonds. *Journal of Monetary Economics* 5:535–550.

Sargent, T. J. 1979. *Macroeconomic theory*. New York: Academic Press.

Shavell, S. 1976. Sharing risks of deferred payment. *Journal of Political Economy* 84:161–168.

Comment   Mario Henrique Simonsen

Wage indexation can be understood as a form of risk sharing between workers and firms. It only covers one single type of risk, the one corresponding to unanticipated changes in the general price level and, as such, it is a highly incomplete insurance scheme. Yet it is simple enough to be enforceable without problems of moral hazard and without the costs of describing and checking all the possible states of nature, as in the Arrow-Debreu (1971) model of general equilibrium under uncertainty.

Different views have been expressed recently on the effects of wage indexation based on different asumptions about how labor contracts are written. Let me summarize a few of them.

Gray's model (1976) accepts the degree of wage indexation as exogenously given. The wage basis is specified in the labor contract, being determined by a Walrasian auctioneer who clears the ex ante labor market under rational expectations. The level of employment is determined by the ex post labor demand curve after uncertainties have been realized. With such assumptions, one easily concludes that indexation protects output against demand shocks and monetary noises but overexposes it to supply shocks. In any case, the higher the degree of wage indexation, the higher the price instability is in face of either type of shock. Gray defines the optimal degree of indexation as the one which minimizes the variance of the difference between the actual and spot equilibrium output measured by their logs. A central planner aiming to stabilize employment would have strong reasons to choose such an indexation parameter. Yet there seems to be no reason why decentralized market forces would lead to such a result. According to Gray's analysis, the optimal degree of indexation is positive but less or equal to one. Full wage indexation is optimal in the above sense if and only if shocks are purely nominal.

Mario Henrique Simonsen is a professor at Fundacao Getulio Vargas, Rio de Janeiro.

Similar results obtained by Stanley Fischer (1977) were challenged by Barro (1977) who questioned why contracting parties should conform to Pareto-inefficient arrangements instead of moving to the welfare superior, spot market equilibrium. Barro's questions are of this type: "Why does the real world not behave like the Arrow-Debreu model with uncertainty?" or "Why does Coase's theorem not hold in so many cases?" But they stress an important point: the lack of consensus among economists about how labor contracts are actually written. Fischer's reply emphasizes that enforceable labor contracts cannot follow the Arrow-Debreu model of contingent claims because of moral hazard problems and because of the costs of specifying all the possible states of nature, and that labor contracts should conform to the simpler standards of efficiency described by Azariadis and Bailey. This is a sensible answer except that the Gray-Fischer indexation model assumes a Keynesian labor contract which is not efficient by the Azariadis (1976) standards. Problems of moral hazard and heterogeneous expectations can also oppose the enforcement of the Azariadis based contracts, and this is the only reason why wages and employment might behave according to the Gray-Fischer model.

Liviatan's paper takes a different look at the problem, treating wage indexation as an endogenous phenomenon. If a perfect capital market exists, with indexed and nominal bonds, the degree of wage indexation is irrelevant since any economic agent can choose his own indexation degree just as in the Modigliani-Miller theorem. If wages are not indexed and if a worker prefers to have them fully indexed, he just has to sell a nominal bond corresponding to his future pay and buy an indexed one, and so on. The case where the wage indexation degree does matter is the one where transactions with bonds are ruled out. In this case one should expect the degree of indexation to be determined by efficient labor contracting in the Azariadis sense. Workers are always assumed to be risk averse, and in two important cases efficient contracting will lead to full wage indexation: (a) when the firm is risk neutral; (b) when the firm is risk averse, but shocks are purely nominal. If both contracting parties are risk averse and if real shocks are brought onto the scene, the outcome may be fractional indexing.

According to Liviatan's analysis, a law which imposes a certain degree of wage indexation will be inoperative, provided firms can exchange indexed bonds for nominal bonds and vice versa with their own workers. (This is a much weaker assumption than the one of the existence of a perfect capital market.) Only if this escape valve is prevented from working will mandatory indexation produce meaningful economic results, the first of which would be to move the system to a Pareto-inferior equilibrium. Even in this case, the degree of wage indexation will not affect price and output stability if the labor input of each firm is determined before uncertainties are realized, as assumed by Liviatan in section 5.2 of his paper. To escape this neutrality theorem one must accept the possibility of ex post adjustment of the labor input. Liviatan's section 5.3 discusses this possibility through a dual labor market model, in which regular workers provide the ex ante labor input and where the variable labor force is supplied by temporary or part-time workers or by overtime assignments carried out by the regular personnel. Although the model fails to explain why regular workers may be laid off during recessions, its conclusions are in line with those of the Gray-Fischer analysis.

In the following comments I shall argue that the cases discussed by Liviatan which lead to full wage indexation exhibit strong efficiency properties which are absent in those corresponding to fractional indexation, which appears to be a poor hedge against supply shocks. This might help to explain why fractional indexation is not a popular clause in labor contracts which, at least implicitly, can adopt more efficient arrangements.

Throughout this discussion I will assume that labor contracts conform to the following hypotheses of Azariadis:

(a) An enforceable labor contract extends for N periods. In each period m different states of nature may occur, with probabilities g_1, $g_2, \ldots, g_m$. (The g_s are positive, and $g_1 + \ldots + g_m = 1$.) The possible states of nature and their probabilities are the same for the different periods covered by the contract.

(b) Expectations are homogeneous in the sense that the firm and its workers share the same description of the various states of nature and the same knowledge about their probabilities.

(c) The firm recruits N workers when the contract is signed and makes the commitment to employ N_s randomly chosen among then $(N_s \leq N)$ at the real wage W_s in every period in which the state of nature s occurs; $(s = 1, \ldots, m)$.

(d) No worker can contract his services with more than one firm, and firms are not allowed to employ individuals who were not assigned to them in the labor contract; any possibility of default is ruled out.

(e) There are only full-time jobs.

Let us indicate by $m_s f(N_s)$ the net real revenue of the firm, and hence by $R_s = m_s f(N_s) - W_s N_s$ its real profit in the state of nature s; $f(N_s)$ is assumed to be concave and nondecreasing in N_s; m_s represents the supply shock which may result from a proportional displacement of the production function or from a change in relative prices.

The firm will be assumed to be either risk averse or risk neutral with an utility function $F(R)$, where R indicates its real profit. Its expected utility will be given by:

(1) $$EF = \sum_{s=1}^{m} g_s F(R_s) = \sum_{s=1}^{m} g_s F[m_s f(N_s) - W_s N_s].$$

Let us assume that all workers are risk averse with the same utility function $V(Y, L)$, where Y indicates the individual real income, and L the leisure time per period. Since only full-time jobs are offered by the firm, there are only two possible values for L: L_0 for the unemployed individual and L_1 for the employed one ($L_1 < L_0$). Every worker is assumed to receive a capital income Y_0 and an unemployment compensation W_0 is paid by the government. (Of course, the possibilities $Y_0 = 0$ and $W_0 = 0$ are not ruled out.) This is to say that the utility of the unemployed individual in any state of nature is given by $V(Y_0 + W_0, L_0)$, moving to $V(Y_0 + W_s, L_1)$ when he is employed in the state of nature s.

Since the origin of a von Neumann-Morgenstern utility scale can be arbitrarily chosen, we shall take the utility of the unemployed individual $V(Y_0 + W_0, L_0) = 0$ and define $U(W_s) = V(Y_0 + W_s, L_1)$. $U(W_s)$ is the utility of the employed worker in state of nature s. Since the probability of being hired by the firm in that state is equal to N_s/N and since the utility of the unemployed is equal to zero, the expected utility of the individual in state of nature s is given by $(N_s/N) U(W_s)$, and his expected utility when the labor contract is signed is indicated by:

$$(2) \qquad EU = \sum_{s=1}^{m} g_s \frac{N_s}{N} U(W_s).$$

We shall assume $U(W)$ to be twice differentiable, with $U'(W) > 0$ (because of nonsatiation) and $U''(W) < 0$ (because of risk aversion). A similar assumption will be made for the firm's utility function, except that now $F''(R) \leq 0$, since the firm may be either risk averse or risk neutral.

Let us indicate by U_0 the expected utility offered to the individuals by a competitive labor market. The problem of the firm is to choose the wage-employment plan $(W_1, W_2, \ldots, W_m)$, $(N, N_1, N_2, \ldots, N_m)$ which maximizes EF subject to $EU \geq U_0$. For any given employment program $(N, N_1, \ldots, N_m)$, the Kuhn and Tucker theorem yields:

$$(3) \qquad \frac{F'(R_1)}{U'(W_1)} = \frac{F'(R_2)}{U'(W_2)} = \ldots = \frac{F'(R_m)}{U'(W_m)} = \lambda.$$

This is the well-known Arrow-Borch condition, according to which the ratio of the marginal utilities of the contracting parties should be independent of the state of nature in an efficient risk-sharing scheme.

Let us now analyze the two cases where full indexation is the outcome of efficient wage contracting: (a) when the firm is risk neutral; (b) when the firm is risk averse but shocks are purely nominal.

If the firm is risk neutral, the marginal utility of its income is a constant. Hence, by the Arrow-Borch condition, $U'(W_s)$ should be invariant to the state of nature. Since, because of risk aversion, $U'(W)$ is a decreasing function of W, the above result implies full wage indexation, that is, W_s should be independent of the state of nature. The theorem can be proved without differentiable hypotheses on the utility functions. It is enough to remember that when the firm is risk neutral, EF can be identified with the firm's expected profit. A wage-employment program $(W_1, \ldots, W_m)$, $(N, N_1, \ldots, N_m)$ with different real wages across the states of nature would be dominated by one which would make wages uniform at the unique real level W such that:

$$W \sum_{s=1}^{m} g_s N_s = \sum_{s=1}^{m} g_s W_s N_s.$$

In fact, making wages uniform by the above formula would not change the firm's expected profit and, because of strict concavity, would increase workers' utility.

If the firm is risk averse but shocks are purely nominal, then $m_s = 1$ for every state of nature. Let us assume that $(W_1, \ldots, W_m)$, $(N, N_1, \ldots, N_m)$ is a wage-employment program where real wages and employment are not invariant to the state of nature. We shall prove that this program is dominated by one with invariant wages $\bar{W}$ and employment $\bar{N}$ where:

$$\bar{N} = \sum_{s=1}^{m} g_s N_s,$$

$$\bar{N}\bar{W} = \sum_{s=1}^{m} g_s W_s N_s.$$

In fact, since both the firm's utility function and its production function are concave and nondecreasing,

$$EF = \sum_{s=1}^{m} g_s F[f(N_s) - W_s N_s] \leq F[f(\bar{N}) - \bar{W}\bar{N}].$$

Let us now observe that

$$\bar{N} \leq N,$$

and that because of strict concavity in the workers' utility function,

$$\sum_{s=1}^{m} g_s N_s U(W_s) \leq \bar{N} \, U(\bar{W}).$$

Since wages and employment are not uniform in the initial program, at least one of the above inequalities must hold with strict sign. Hence,

$$EU = \sum_{s=1}^{m} \frac{N_s}{N} U(W_s) < U(\bar{W}).$$

Summing up, if shocks are purely nominal, the firm's expected utility will not decrease and the workers' utility will increase if wages and employment are made invariant to the state of nature at $\bar{W}$ and $\bar{N}$. This, once again, implies full wage indexation.

The latter result is by no means surprising. In this very special case, full indexation of all contracts solves the Arrow-Debreu model with uncertainty.

What about fractional indexation? The problem is that now W_s cannot be freely determined for each state of nature but must be expressed as a function of two single independent variables, the wage basis V_0 and the indexation degree θ. Using Liviatan's symbols, if $\bar{\pi}$ is the inverse of the general price level when the labor contract is signed, and π_s the corresponding value to state of nature s, then

$$W_s = V_0[\theta\bar{\pi} + (1 - \theta)\pi_s].$$

This is to say, if there exist $m > 2$ possible states of nature, that $m - 2$ degrees of freedom will be lost by fractional indexation arrangements, and that these arrangements should not be expected to fulfill the Arrow-Borch condition. Of course, if fractional indexation is considered the only possible device to make real wages contingent on the state of nature, an optimal indexation degree will always be found, although not necessarily in the $(0, 1)$ interval. Yet the strong efficiency properties of full indexation when the firm is risk neutral or when shocks are purely nominal will not hold in the fractional indexation schemes. This is why, I think, economic agents will always find some strong incentive to move to more efficient forms of wage contracting.

One possible scheme is full wage indexation combined with a profit-sharing plan. When both parties are risk averse, the Arrow-Borch condition implies that real wages should be an increasing function of the firm's real profits. A plausible additional assumption is that the firm is relatively less risk averse than its workers, in the Arrow-Pratt sense, that is,

$$A_F = -\frac{RF''(R)}{F'(R)} < \frac{WU''(W)}{U'(W)} = A_W.$$

Differentiation of the Arrow-Borch condition yields

$$A_F \frac{dR}{R} = A_W \frac{dW}{W},$$

which means that real wages should change in the same direction, although proportionally less than real profits. A fixed real wage plus a fixed share in profits, $W_s = W + aR_s$, might be an acceptable first order approximation to the efficient wage plan.

Moral hazard problems or inadequacy of first order approximations might make the idea of linking wages to profits undesirable. In this event all one can get from the Arrow-Borch equation is that wages should be fully indexed but adjusted for supply shocks. Of course, the measurement of supply shocks, especially at the microeconomic level which encompasses the firm's relative price position, would be too much of a nightmare to be included as an explicit clause of any feasible labor contract.

Yet, as an implicit clause it might work. Wages are settled in nominal terms but periodically revised. In an inflationary environment, the increase in the consumer price index appears to be the main determinant of nominal wage adjustments. Still, enough flexibility is kept so as to adapt real wages to supply shocks.

The present world is crowded with both real and nominal shocks. According to Liviatan's model, fractional indexation should be the rule, full indexing or no indexing at all being the exceptions. Empirical evidence suggests the opposite, namely, that fractional indexation is the exception. It is not even a necessary intermediate step between nominal wage contracting and full indexation when inflation rates escalate, as shown by the experience of so many countries. This can be explained by the assumption that economic agents will instinctively move to some approximate solution of the Arrow-Borch equation.

References

Arrow, K. J., and F. H. Hahn. 1971. *General competitive analysis*. Edited by Oliver and Boyd-Edimbursh, eds. San Francisco: Holden-Day.

Azariadis, C. 1976. On the incidence of unemployment. *Review of Economic Studies* 43, no. 133:115–126.

Barro, R. J. 1977. Long-term contracting, sticky prices, and monetary policy. *Journal of Monetary Economics* 3:305–316.

Fischer, S. 1977. Wage indexation and macroeconomic stability. *Journal of Monetary Economics*, supplement, 107–148.

Gray, J. A. 1976. Wage indexation—a macroeconomic approach. *Journal of Monetary Economics* 2:221–235.

6 Real versus Financial Openness under Alternative Exchange Rate Regimes

Michael Bruno

6.1 Introduction

The semi-industrialized economy to be discussed here mainly imports raw materials and capital goods and is past the stage of using quantitative restrictions for import substitution of consumer goods. Traditionally it depended mainly on primary exports and is now rapidly moving into industrial exports. While it may still have a multiple protective tariff system and thus be more "closed" in the real sense than some optimum degree of free trade might dictate, it will rely quite heavily on the use of the formal exchange rate system to handle current account problems.

The typical problem for such an economy, unless it happens to be an oil exporter, is how to manage its exchange rate and internal macropolicies over time in face of a large structural deficit, as part of its long-run trade and development strategy.

Under reasonable assumptions it will be an optimal strategy for this economy to borrow abroad to finance a large deficit in the early stages of industrialization and to use these funds to develop its exports, providing the internal rate of return lies above the marginal social cost of foreign borrowing. Subsequently it will pay back these loans as the economy approaches independence. In the course of the growth process the real effective exchange rate will usually be required to grow over time, and it should do so at a rate that equals the difference between the internal and external real rate of return to capital (see Bruno 1976). This statement must be modified in the case where relative technical progress in export—

Michael Bruno is a professor in the Department of Economics, Hebrew University, Jerusalem, and a research associate of the National Bureau of Economic Research.

Helpful comments by Rudiger Dornbusch and other participants at the conference are gratefully acknowledged.

as compared to home—industries (or when the country's relative export price in world markets) is sufficiently high to make actual growth in the real exchange rate unnecessary. Even then it is usually the case that a real exchange rate level has to be maintained over time.

Governments, of course, seldom know how to solve optimality problems, nor do they know the path of long-run foreign credit availabilities with any certainty. More often than not, they have to live from hand to mouth. Yet the logic of theoretical constructs may still be followed in at least some respects. The marginal cost of foreign loans must not exceed the internal profitability of the resulting investment, and the tariff (or subsidy) inclusive real exchange rate must be related to the size of the allowable structural deficit. The main point is that there should be a clear long-run relationship between the ratio of present and future real exchange rates and between the internal and external real rates of interest. These simultaneously affect long-run borrowing, domestic savings and investment policies, as well as the real exchange rate as an allocative device.

Problems occur when short-term market prices do not give the "correct" long-run allocation signals for producers or consumers. Two major sources for such discrepancies may arise in the present context, both working in the same direction. The world financial market may temporarily register very low (or even negative) real rates of interest for short- and medium-run loans,[1] as it has done for some time in the 1970s and until very recently. The other, often more important, problem is that domestic stabilization policy, with its associated restrictive monetary policy, may cause the real marginal cost of domestic credit to rise considerably above the desired long-run rate. Either one of these or a combined opening up of the gap between the two interest rate signals will, in the absence of other intervention, cause substantial short-run capital inflows and a real appreciation of the exchange rate, depressing manufacturing exports and profits, an experience recently shared by a number of countries in Latin America[2] and elsewhere.

Prolonged periods of real exchange appreciation accompanying short-run capital inflow, when the long-run horizon dictates the converse, may not be harmful from the point of view of financial portfolio allocations. These are easily reversed at the cost of a phone call. They may, however, be costly in terms of irreversible production and investment decisions, which by nature have long gestation periods. This argument, of course,

---

1. The typical loan in the new post-1973 private capital market, even if taken for a long-run investment purpose, is basically short-run in nature, insofar as the interest rate has to be renegotiated at short-run intervals.

2. As noted in Díaz Alejandro's chapter in this volume (chapter 1), this problem was also relevant in the 1930s.

depends on some myopia in the expectation formation process of investors. Given the market imperfections in a typical semi-industrialized country, this is a reasonable assumption to make.

This type of conflict between short-term and long-term asset pricing also raises the question of financial openness, as distinct from real openness of a country. Real openness relates to the degree of substitutability of goods across borders and the efficiency advantages to be reaped from reducing intervention in the free flow of real trade. Financial openness has to do with the substitutability of foreign and domestic financial assets and the extent of interference with free capital mobility. Since the exchange rate enters the pricing of both tradable assets and tradable goods, conflicts of price signaling may occur when financial openness is pursued along with real openness.

We shall assume here that the problem of relating long-term borrowing (and investment) to the development strategy has somehow been taken care of, and we may, for our purposes, consider the long-run capital imports as largely determined outside the present framework. This leaves the question of openness toward the world financial market for short-run capital movements. Also, how does financial, as distinct from real, openness relate to the operation of the economy under alternative exchange rate regimes?

After laying out a simple analytical framework (section 6.2), we shall consider the main alternative exchange rate regimes and their bearing on macroeconomic management in the light of the extent of real and financial openness of the country. The regimes to be considered are a fixed peg, with or without a "crawling" commercial policy; the crawling peg; and the managed float (sections 6.3–6.5). This being a conference on the capital market, we shall emphasize the implications of different degrees of capital mobility under these regimes.

There is a separate question of how the extent of real and financial openness restricts or enhances domestic stabilization policy. Thus for brief transition periods it may pay to use the exchange rate as a price-stabilizing device, even at the cost of "wrong" long-term signaling. The last section (6.6) considers the two-way relationship of exchange rate adjustment and the inflationary process. Should the exchange rate always accommodate to the inflation rate (or overtake it), or can it sometimes be used in the opposite direction to moderate an excessive rate of inflation?

While this and other problems seem to be a hot subject of debate in the Latin American scene, I do not pretend to know enough about the empirical background of these countries to go into analysis of actual examples. This discussion has partly been inspired by the experiences of my own country (see also Bruno and Sussman 1979, 1980) which we hope may also be relevant to a wider set of countries.

6.2 Analytical Framework

We can represent the general equilibrium of the economy in a diagram in which the real exchange rate ($q = e/p$) and real money balances ($m = M/p$) appear on the two axes.[3] We shall consider the commodity market, asset supply and demand, and the balance of payments.

6.2.1 Commodities

Suppose the economy produces a composite good (Q), priced p, which is an imperfect substitute for a world export good priced abroad at $p^* = 1$. Exports will be a positive function of their relative prices, $q(1 + t_x)$, where $q(= p^*e/p)$ is the real exchange rate, and t_x is a possible export subsidy. Imports (N) in this economy are assumed to be an input into the productive system, together with labour (L), and capital (K), that is, we have $Q = Q(L, N, K)$. The short-run supply function is given by Q^s [$w, q(1 + t_n)p_n^*; K$], where w is the real wage ($= W/p$), t_n is a tariff rate, and p_n^* is the relative world price of the import. Domestic absorption depends on real income, the real money supply ($m = M/p$), expected inflation (π),[4] and a fiscal impact variable (g).

Under the usual assumptions, we can represent the excess demands for goods in the form:

$$(1) \qquad Q^d - Q^s = f_1(q, m; U_1),$$
$$+ \ \ + \ \ +$$

where U_1 stands for a vector of various exogenous shift factors (g, w, π, t_x, $t_n, -K$).[5]

The downward-sloped curve QQ in figure 6.1 gives the combinations of real exchange rate and real balances that keep the commodity market in equilibrium ($Q^d = Q^s$). It will shift inward with an increase in the government deficit (g), the real wage (w), expected inflation (π), or any of the other factors listed under U_1. Above the curve there is excess demand, and prices will tend to increase; below it there is excess supply, and prices may or may not decrease depending on price stickiness. Since the price level appears in the denominator of both variables on the axes, the movement of prices in this diagram will always take place along a 45° vector, toward the QQ curve.

---

3. At a later stage we shall put total real banking credit, instead of m, on the axis, see section 6.5.

4. The variables m and π enter firm asset market equilibrium (see below).

5. In this formulation we implicitly assume some real wage (w) rigidity, in which case the labor market need not clear. In a fully flexible wage case, one should include $-\bar{L}$ as the alternative parameter in U_1, assuming full employment. The basic form of equation (1) would remain the same. The negative sign placed on K makes the vector U_1 consist only of positive shift factors.

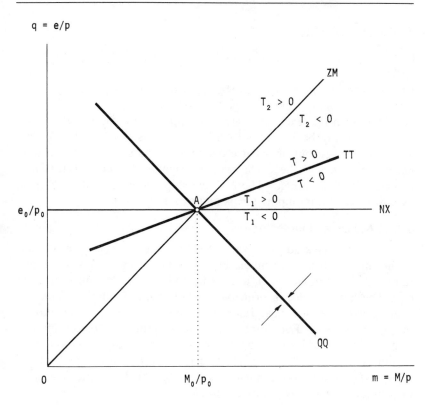

Fig. 6.1

6.2.2   The Basic Balance

The basic balance (T_1) will here be defined as the difference between exports and current import requirements plus exogenously given long-run capital flows (F).

The reason for distinguishing between current import requirements and what are normally registered as imports is to separate out the hoarding element in imports and add it to the capital account. Thus, import inventory movements will be a form of savings (in addition to being part of investment). The idea of separating out part of capital imports as receipts in the current account is meant to distinguish between long-run transfers and loans, which are usually handled and determined centrally by governments and will not affect private sector wealth directly, and short-term capital flows (and changes in exchange reserves), which are the only ones to be considered endogenous here. For simplicity, we assume F to include foreign investment and to be defined net of interest payments on the outstanding debt.

We can now write

$$(2) \qquad T_1 = T_1(q, U_2),$$
$$+ \ +$$

where U_2 is another vector of exogenous shift factors (F, t_x, t_n).[6]

Current account balance is represented by the horizontal line in figure 6.1, at a given real exchange rate $q_0 = e_0/p_0$. Below the line there is a deficit in the basic balance $(T_1 < 0)$, above it there is a surplus $(T_1 > 0)$. The adjustment when out of balance depends on the total balance of payments position and the exchange rate regime of which discussion is deferred for the moment. The NX line shifts up with a fall in F or an overall reduction in import tariffs and export subsidies.[7]

6.2.3   Money and Other Assets

There are three kinds of privately held assets in the system in addition to the capital stock: government bonds (B_g) carrying a nominal interest rate i, domestic money (M), and a foreign currency denominated asset (Z). The latter could, in principle, include paper money, an interest-bearing asset (net of debt and carrying an interest rate i^*), or inventories of imported goods. For simplicity, we shall ignore the foreign interest rate and only take into account the expected rate of devaluation (ϵ).

Money demand (M^d) is a negative function of the nominal rate of interest (i) and is proportional to gross output (Q). The money market is in equilibrium with given money supply (M).

$$(3) \qquad M^d/p = \lambda(i)Q = M/p.$$
$$-$$

For high rates of expected inflation, π may be substituted for i in (3). As is usually assumed, only domestic residents holds M, while both domestic and foreign residents may hold Z. The relative demand for the foreign asset (Z^d) is assumed to take the following simple form (see Miles 1978; Calvo and Rodriguez 1977):

$$(4) \qquad eZ^d/M^d = qZ^d/m^d = k(\epsilon),$$
$$+$$

where $q = e/p$ as before, and ϵ is the expected rate of depreciation.[8] The more elastic k, the closer substitutes are M and Z.

---

6. For simplicity we ignore the need to modify (2) when the commodity market is not balanced. Actually the NX line should have a kink at the point of intersection with QQ. When $Q^d < Q^s$, imports are a function of Q^d which in turn depends positively on m.

7. When we are in a multiple-tariff world, this need no longer be the case. Sometimes a tariff-cutting process may actually *improve* the current account. Even the case schematically given here, where there may be a common tariff on imports which is different from the export subsidy, could lead to this result.

8. The demand for government bonds (B_g) is not specified separately since it can be derived as a residual once total asset demand (supply) is given. If the latter is denoted by a, we get from (3) and (4) that the demand for real bonds (b^d) is: $b^d = a - \lambda(i) Q[1 + k(\epsilon)]$.

If total short-term foreign exchange assets held in the economy are B and central bank foreign exchange reserves are A, actual private assets (Z) will always equal the difference $Z = B - A$. B may change only as a result of an imbalance in the basic account as defined above, thus it will be assumed to be given at any moment of time. Foreign exchange reserves (A) may or may not be determined by the central bank, depending on the foreign exchange regime (see below).

If both the markets for M and Z are in balance, equation (4) can be turned into an asset market equilibrium relationship: $q = mk(\epsilon)/(B - A)$. This is represented by the line ZM in figure 6.1. To allow for different degrees of financial openness, we assume that the *actual* change in the privately held foreign exchange asset (ΔZ) is proportional to the *desired* change $Z^d - Z_0$ from any initial level, $Z_0 = B_0 - A_0$, while the money market (3) equilibrates. (This assumes that the bond market adjusts more slowly.)

$$(5) \qquad \Delta Z = \beta[k(\epsilon)m/q - (B_0 - A_0)],$$

where $\beta \geq 0$.

The relationship between asset formation and the balance of payments is taken up next.

6.2.4   The Balance of Payments

The balance of payments consists of the sum of the basic balance (T_1) and the short-run capital account (T_2), which in turn equals the net sale of private foreign exchange assets $(-\Delta Z)$. The overall balance of payments surplus $(T = T_1 + T_2)$ must equal the net accumulation of bank reserves (ΔA). We can thus write:

$$(6) \qquad T = T_1(q) + \beta[B_0 - A_0 - k(\epsilon)m/q] = T(q, m; U_3) = \Delta A,$$
$$\qquad\qquad\qquad\qquad\qquad\qquad\qquad\qquad\qquad + \;\; -$$

where U_3 includes all the shift variables appearing in U_2 as well as $(B_0 - A_0, -\epsilon)$.

The line ZM in figure 6.1 represents the short-run capital account balance $(T_2 = 0)$. Its slope is $k(\epsilon)/(B_0 - A_0)$. Above it $T_2 > 0$ and below it $T_2 < 0$. The curve TT which represents the overall balance $(T = 0)$ must lie between the lines NX and ZM. Below it $T < 0$ and above it $T > 0$.

This two-part graphical representation of the balance of payments, which was inspired by Frenkel and Rodriguez (1980), is also useful for considering different degrees of capital mobility.[9] A very low level of β (relatively flat TT curve) would correspond to the case of rather effective

---

9. We differ from their presentation in using the pair of real variables (q, m) on the axes rather than the nominal e and p and in having T_1 separate from the goods market. The capital flow term in their paper is written directly as a function of the interest differential $[i - (i^* + \epsilon)]$. There is some advantage in relating the capital flow to the underlying asset behavior.

exchange controls. In the extreme case ($\beta = 0$), only the current account matters. The other polar extreme ($\beta = \infty$) is the one in which only asset behavior ($T_2 = 0$) matters. There is instantaneous adjustment of Z to Z^d (as in Dornbusch 1976).

6.2.5   The Banking Balance Sheet

We end this preliminary description by stating the basic balance-sheet restriction of the banking system, within which monetary policy operates. Denoting central bank credit to the government by C_g, to the private sector by C_c, and private banking credit to the private sector by C_p we have:

$$(7) \qquad\qquad M = eA + C_g + C_c + C_p.$$

For subsequent reference we also note that by adding the net foreign exchange asset eZ to the left-hand side of (7) and remembering that $A + Z = B$, we get another constraint on the sum of the two assets:[10]

$$(8) \qquad\qquad M + eZ = eB + C,$$

where $C = C_g + C_c + C_p$ is total bank credit.

6.3   Operating a Fixed Peg under Limited Capital Mobility

We first consider the process of large-step adjustment of the exchange rate in response to shifts in the basic balance under a pegged exchange rate regime. An important issue in the present context is the limitation imposed by the role of expectations of exchange rate change and of short-run capital movements even when the economy is relatively (though not absolutely) closed to financial capital movements. These pose considerable short-term stabilization problems, especially for monetary policy. Let us discuss these problems and possible remedies.

Consider a fixed exchange rate economy with initial equilibrium at a nominal exchange rate e_0, quantity of money M_0, and price level p_0 (see fig. 6.2). Commodity market equilibrium is given by the curve QQ, the basic balance is given by NX. There is limited capital mobility (low β), so that the balance of payments equilibrium is given by the line TT whose slope is assumed to be between 0 and 1. Given are low expectations of exchange rate change ($\epsilon = \epsilon_0$, which may be zero). Suppose now that for some reason there is a shift in the basic balance (NX shifts up) which may be caused by a long-term fall in lending (F). A real devaluation from q_0 to q_1 is called for. For simplicity, assume that the change is confined to the

---

10. If B is added on the left-hand side, we get total financial assets ($M + eZ + B_g$) as financed from the three major sources: the basic balance (eB), the government deficit ($C_g + B_g$), and the banking system's finance to the private sector ($C_c + C_p$).

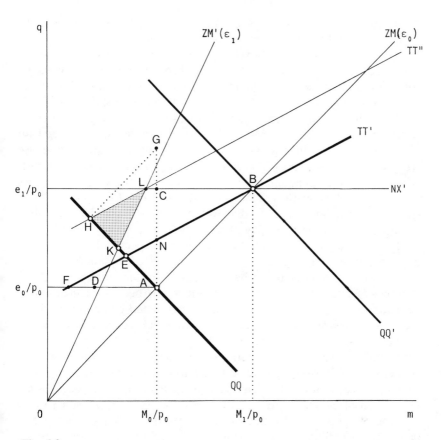

Fig. 6.2

current account and QQ is not immediately affected.[11] A possible new equilibrium for the economy would be at point B which is given at the intersection of NX' and the old ZM line, assuming that after the change its slope $k(\epsilon_0)/(B - A)$ and Z remain the same. A set of policies that might bring this about could be a combination of a nominal devaluation to e_1, fiscal and income restraint, a reduction in g or w (shifting QQ to QQ'), plus an increase in M to M_1 so that $M_1/M_0 = e_1/e_0$. Unless prices are downward rigid, the same real movement in M/p and e/p could also be achieved by a fall in p, keeping M constant ($= M_0$), coupled with a smaller nominal devaluation. We are less interested in the exact final

11. An exactly analogous situation would be created by an inflationary shift in the commodity market. Suppose we start at B on QQ' and NX' and for some reason (e.g., an increase in the budget deficit or in the real wage) QQ' shifts inward to QQ. Assuming the line AB to be on a 45° vector, inflation will move the economy back to equilibrium at A. From here on the analysis is the same.

outcome than in the dynamic sequence of events that may typically occur once the need for a step devaluation is signaled.

It is in the nature of a fixed exchange rate regime that a considerable lag exists between the first signal of a required change in e and the actual act of a devaluation, let alone the implementation of the internal demand restrictions that have to accompany it. The moment TT shifts toward TT' and foreign exchange reserves start falling ($\Delta A < 0$), two processes may be set in motion, one having to do with expectations, the other with fluctuations in the money base. As expectations of a devaluation rise ($\epsilon_1 > \epsilon_0$), there is import hoarding and delayed repatriation of export proceeds. The asset equilibrium curve rotates upward to ZM', say, with the balance of payments equilibrium line shifting to TT''. The result is a more intensive fall in reserves than would otherwise take place, signaling a larger devaluation than may objectively be required.

This can be illustrated as follows: given the expectation of a devaluation, a new temporary equilibrium could take place at point H. One way of exactly reaching H could be a nominal devaluation from A to G, keeping M constant, followed by a price increase (because of an inflationary gap in the goods market) which is represented by an inward move along a 45° vector from G to H. Whether the real exchange rate is above or below the level balancing the new basic account (NX') depends on the extent of the excessive, expectations-induced shift of TT'' which, in turn, depends on the asset-demand response to expectations change ($\partial k/\partial\epsilon$) and the effectiveness of foreign exchange control (β). Once a devaluation has taken place, expectations will stabilize again (at ϵ_0, or some lower number). Suppose ZM returns to its previous position and balance of payments equilibrium is represented by TT'. At point H, for example, there is now a surplus with renewed capital inflow (repatriation of export proceeds, dishoarding of import inventories, etc.) which more than compensates for the remaining basic deficit, and reserves will start rising again.

So far we have ignored changes in nominal money which can be assumed away only if there is central bank sterilization of the fluctuations in exchange reserves.[12] This brings us to the second dynamic process which may take place simultaneously with the one previously described. Let us go back to point A when foreign exchange reserves start falling. Unless sterilized, there will be a fall in M which in figure 6.2 would show as a horizontal leftward move from A toward D. Excess supply and unemployment develop unless prices (and wages) are downward flexible. Again, a possible move under price flexibility would be a fall in M by the amount DA and a reduction of prices along a 45° vector from D to E. If

---

12. Equilibrium at H or at E here implies a fall in real balances from M_0/p_0 to M_0/p_1 through a price rise.

expectations of a devaluation are kept at zero, the balance of payments would have reached temporary equilibrium at E without a devaluation but through a monetary squeeze and a forced deflation.

If prices are inflexible, the monetary contraction and the deepening slump could in principle continue until an unemployment equilibrium is reached at F.[13] It is the capital flows in response to the interest rate gap[14] that will finance the basic deficit. Obviously, this is neither a sustainable nor a socially desirable equilibrium. What usually happens is that the internal pressure on the monetary authorities makes for monetary expansion to counterbalance the loss of reserves.

The counterpart of this phenomenon, after an excessive devaluation, is the reverse upward pressure on the money supply coming from the renewed capital inflow and the rising reserves. Suppose we are temporarily at H when the balance of payments equilibrium is given by TT'. Lack of monetary restraint (and legitimate pressure on the part of sectors hurt by the real credit squeeze) will cause M to rise. In terms of figure 6.2, there will be a movement along a horizontal line from H toward TT'. At the same time inflationary pressure develops causing a rise in prices (move back toward QQ).

The large swings in short-run capital movements and in the money before and after large devaluations are hard to contain even under exchange controls and constitute one of their main drawbacks (see Bruno and Sussman 1979 for an account of the Israeli experience). The pressure to keep real money and credit high (e.g., for investment) may cause a continued inflationary process driving down the real exchange rate to a renewed balance of payments deficit, unless the devaluation is coupled with the appropriate measures that will shift QQ outward.[15]

If exchange controls are tight ($\beta = 0$) and the original level of real balances is desired, an equilibrium devaluation could be reached at C providing there is a sufficient accompanying budget cut to move the QQ line through that point. If controls are not tight and there are capital flows, temporary equilibrium could be reached at N, say, with a smaller budget cut and smaller real devaluation. This, however, can only be temporary since the current account deficit will gradually erode foreign exchange assets and require further cuts in the budget deficit, and an additional increase in e/p to make room for the expanded production of tradable goods, as TT' gradually shifts up. Only a larger budget cut to

13. Strictly speaking, equilibrium will probably take place at a point right of F (since now $Q = Q^d < Q^s$).

14. This may sometimes take the form of active government encouragement to firms to take foreign credit, which is expensive from a social point of view but is relatively cheap given the prevailing higher domestic interest rates.

15. The analysis was conducted with a given commodity market curve. When QQ shifts inward due to a rise in inflationary expectations or in real wages, these problems are clearly accentuated.

QQ' (and/or a larger drop in the real wage, coupled with a rise in m and q) can keep all markets in new, current-account equilibrium at point B.

The main problems that arise in the operation of a fixed peg which is adjusted in large jumps thus center around the sizable accompanying fluctuations in real reserves and in the money supply and the large one-time adjustments required in other expenditure items. The latter are unavoidable under any exchange rate regime, since a real resource transfer will always be required (unless there is a slack in the system which can be diverted to the tradable goods sector). On the other hand, the monetary upheavals and the real loss of reserves could in principle be delayed if the real exchange rate corrections are confined to the current account. Short of moving to a regime of small-step adjustment in the formal rate, one may operate the fixed formal peg on capital account transactions while correcting the real effective exchange rate in smaller steps through adjustments in commercial policy.

Consider the case in which we have a pure dual rate on the two accounts—a uniform tariff (t_n) on imports and a subsidy of the same rate $(t_x = t_n)$ on exports. When F falls, as in the above discussion, one could in principle increase t_n and t_x to keep the NX line in place, while manipulating the budget to compensate for the loss in revenue (when the balance is in deficit). In that case the economy may stay in equilibrium at A while at the same time reducing the basic deficit.

Countries hardly ever operate a uniform tariff rate on imports. However, a close substitute for the above idea is a flat export subsidy based on value added. Israel had operated such a system quite successfully through the 1960s and part of the 1970s. Large devaluations would take place only once every few years and in between the rate of export subsidy (and sometimes also the tariff rate on imports) would be adjusted upward gradually. The problem with such a system is usually two-fold. One problem is that it tends to get abused once the subsidy rate reaches high levels. There is considerable incentive to cheat in the calculation of value added which leads to trade distortions and the like. The other difficulty is that such measures usually meet with strong disapproval of the international agencies (e.g., GATT and IMF). It can be claimed that when used in small measure and with some prudence such a system may nonetheless have its merits. The alternatives, as we shall see, have their drawbacks too.

6.4   The Pros and Cons of a Crawling Peg

We now keep the assumption of a formal peg but assume that the adjustments are made in very small steps and at frequent intervals.[16]

---

16. In the Israeli case the crawling peg was operated for two years, between June 1975 and October 1977, and at first followed rather rigid rules but then became quite flexible in terms of size of change and allowed frequency of adjustment (see Bruno and Sussman 1980).

The advantage of a crawling peg over the previous regime lies in the two areas where the large-step adjustment regime is weakest. It usually avoids the political and social taboo attached to an act of currency depreciation and shifts the exchange rate adjustments from the front pages of the newspapers to back-page financial columns. The major exchange reserve crises and monetary upheavals may be avoided.

One by-product of the crawling peg is that no major political decisions or restrictive internal policies have to be taken at each step. This apparent advantage of minidevaluations sometimes may also be, paradoxically, a source of major weakness. In a government-deficit and inflation-prone economy the operation of the exchange rate is delegated to a ministerial or bank committee without the accompanying continuous urge for small-step fiscal and income policy discipline.[17] The fact that devaluations now take on a more continuous form make for built-in inflationary expectations ($i \simeq \pi = \epsilon = e/e$), thus exacerbating inflationary pressures.

Under a crawling peg, especially if it is predetermined, the capital account curve no longer fluctuates. Suppose expectations are fixed at ϵ_1 and the relevant asset demand curve is ZM' in figure 6.2, with equilibrium momentarily at K. Say a small-step adjustment to a new balance of payments curve TT'' is required. The small triangle marked by the points K, L, and H marks the policy trade-offs. If fiscal policy can be used along with a minidevaluation, we may move from K to L or at least refrain from getting a fall in real balances (i.e., maintain real credit levels). If fiscal or real wage restraint cannot take place, real money balances will have to fall as we move from K to H, by a cut in nominal money, by inflation, or by both. One of the problems of the crawling peg is the continuous built-in pressure for monetary restraint to keep domestic interest rates high relative to ($i^* + \epsilon$). To illustrate, at point K on ZM', m has to be lower than at N or at B.

6.5   High Capital Mobility and Flexible Rates

So far we have considered regimes in which the authorities directly peg the exchange rate, in which case the balance of payments need not be in momentary equilibrium and foreign exchange reserves are the short-run buffer. In section 6.1 we posed the problem of conflicting long-term and short-term price signaling. This may occur in a situation of relatively high capital mobility and exchange rate flexibility, to which we now turn. Consider the case in which the exchange rate automatically adjusts to equilibrate the exchange market. It helps to discuss first the case of a flexible rate under perfect asset mobility ($\beta = 0$) and no intervention ($\Delta A = 0$).

17. E.g., it may be easier to convince the trade unions of the need to forego one step in the indexation mechanism in a national crisis situation than to reduce indexation on a continuous basis.

In an inflationary situation and when the foreign asset is highly liquid [$k(\epsilon)$ is elastic], it may sometimes be advantageous to use total bank credit ($C = C_g + C_c + C_p$) rather than M as the financial instrument. The commodity market equilibrium curve QQ can be expressed in terms of $c = C/p$ (instead of m) and e/p, keeping all other properties as before (see fig. 6.3). The asset curve can be transformed by substituting from equation (8) into (4) and writing $Z^d = B - A$ to get:

$$(9) \qquad\qquad e/p = \frac{k(\epsilon)}{\beta - [1 + k(\epsilon)]A} \, C/p.$$

Equation (9) is represented by the curve ZC in figure 6.3 which has analogous properties to the curve ZM. It is a ray through the origin whose slope increases with ϵ and A and falls with B. Equilibrium takes place at the intersection of the asset market line (ZC) and the commodity market QQ (point A). In case of a disturbance, the exchange rate immediately adjusts to equilibrate the asset market first. Consider, as before, the case

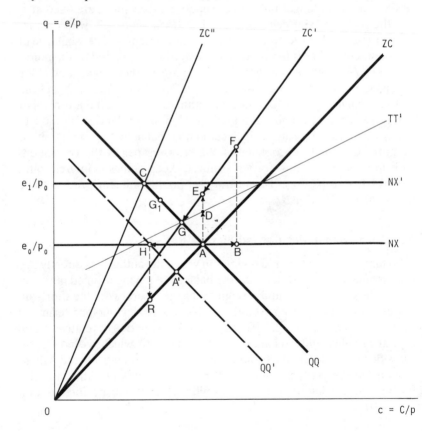

Fig. 6.3

in which there is an increase in the basic deficit (NX to NX') and, for simplicity, assume first that there is no change in the commodity market. The only channel by which this may have an effect on the economy is the asset market, through a possible impact effect on expectations (ϵ) and a long-run effect on the total supply of foreign exchange assets (B). Suppose there is a one-time effect on ϵ rotating ZC to ZC'. The nominal (and real) exchange rate will overshoot to point E and may quickly be eroded by inflation with real appreciation moving the economy from E to G along line ZC'. At point G the balance of payments is in short-run equilibrium, but there is a sustained basic deficit. This may disappear over time only gradually as B falls and the ZC curve continues to rotate upward. Final equilibrium will take place only when the asset equilibrium line and the commodity market line intersect at the new basic balance equilibrium (see point C). The story is only slightly modified if we consider that the disturbance that has shifted the basic balance (NX) also shifts the commodity market (e.g., shift of QQ to $Q'Q'$ as would happen in the case of an increase in import prices).

There are some clear drawbacks to this automatic adjustment process. One is that in the first stage there may be an excessive price increase with no real benefits to the current account. This is only one example of the "overshooting" tendency of an exchange regime in which the asset market takes a major role in the short-run determination of the exchange rate (cf. Dornbusch 1976, and the related literature). Similar effects characterize the case of unexpected domestic monetary changes. For example, a monetary expansion from A to B raises expectations of a depreciation, causes a jump of the exchange rate to point F on ZC', say, followed by inflation (more from F to G). The case of monetary contraction, from A to H, which may be needed to correct a commodity market imbalance (at QQ') leads to an appreciation (point R) coupled with excessive unemployment, unless prices are downward flexible.

The main drawback of asset market determination in the present context, quite apart from overshooting, is that the process of adjustment to a new long-run situation may be much too slow. The real exchange rate that is signaled by the asset market (at point G, say) does not reflect the true long-run rate from the point of view of real resource allocation. Given the gestation lags of exports and of investment in export industries and the imperfections in the expectation formation mechanism, this would seem to be the major cost of allowing short-run capital movements to determine the exchange rate.

One way of avoiding this signaling problem is to impose a direct tax on capital imports as was done in a recent Israeli episode (see Liviatan 1980; Bruno and Sussman 1980). In figure 6.3 this can be shown by noting that the imposition of a tax (τ) on capital imports is the same as raising the expected cost of foreign borrowing and thus causing the asset market curve to rotate in the required direction (say, from ZC' to ZC''). This may not overcome the overshooting problem but may, at least, avoid overvaluation of the currency.[18] A managed float, which takes the form of intervention in the foreign exchange market, in principle works in the same direction. Purchase of foreign exchange by the central bank raises foreign exchange reserves (A) and also rotates ZC counterclockwise.

What happens when capital mobility is not perfect and we do not have instantaneous arbitrage? Overshooting will clearly be mitigated. Consider again the case in which the current account flows also play a role in the market. Suppose that with the projected increase in the basic deficit balance of payments equilibrium is represented by the curve TT' (shifted from TT and assuming no immediate change in expectations). Under a float the exchange rate jumps to D and then adjusts along TT' to G. Note that there is less overshooting (and less inflation) in this case. If we now also assume a shift in expectations, the new equilibrium will be at a higher point, G_1, on QQ. Obviously, the flatter the TT line, the more important the basic balance is in the determination of market signals and the closer a float will bring us to the long-run signal.

Does this analysis imply that it is always advantageous to control capital movements, that is, limit financial openness for the sake of real openness? One should be careful not to jump to hasty conclusions. If it were possible to draw an absolute distinction between short-run and long-run capital movements in practice, then such a conclusion could perhaps be justified. However, we should bear in mind that the way we have distinguished between capital movements in terms of exogenously determined long-run funds (F) and endogenous short-term capital is somewhat artificial. Excessive foreign exchange controls could also drive away legitimate long-run capital, which may thus affect the options for the real economy (i.e., shift the NX curve). The costs and benefits must be weighed against each other. In any case, the argument for financial closeness may often be confined to particular short-term situations.

6.6 Exchange Rate Adjustment and Inflation: Accommodation versus Moderation

The last issue to be discussed briefly is the relationship between exchange rate change and inflation. This brings up the case in which short-run stabilization may take the lead over long-run objectives in exchange rate pricing. Specifically, should the rate of devaluation always be made to accommodate (or overtake) the inflation rate for the sake of

18. Note, however, that the imposition of a tax on capital imports has another negative by-product in the form of high domestic interest rates which may harm investment. The movement from A to C obviously involves a real credit squeeze which may be voluntary, through a fall in C, or involuntary, through inflation.

the long-run external balance? Or are there situations in which it pays to moderate exchange rate changes as a short-run stabilization device even at the cost of a real loss of reserves?

For simplicity, we shall conduct the discussion in terms of steady state rates of change, $\hat{p}$ and $\hat{e}$, and assume consistency of expectations, that is, $\pi = \hat{p}$ and $\epsilon = \hat{e}$.

One basic short-term relationship between the rates of inflation and depreciation in an open economy can be derived from the commodity and labor markets and represents the price-wage-price dynamic adjustment process. In reduced form this can be written as follows:

$$(10) \qquad\qquad \hat{p} = \pi_0 + \alpha\hat{e}.$$

The "path-through" coefficient α incorporates the role of the direct and indirect import coefficient as well as the implied wage-price linkages. The α is most likely to be less than one, providing we do not have 100 percent indexation. The intercept π_0 summarizes the role of excess demand factors in the commodity and labor markets as well as autonomous cost-push factors (world price of raw materials, indirect taxes on consumer goods, etc.).[19]

Equation (10) appears as the line PP in figure 6.4, with intercept π_0 on the π-axis and slope $\alpha < 1$. Given any rate of depreciation (ϵ), this curve gives the implied inflation rate that will be propagated by the real system given its underlying behavioral and institutional parameters. This inflation rate can in principle be lowered either by a reduction in the extent of linkage (α) or by fiscal and other stabilization measures, lowering π_0. In practice it is unlikely that the slope can be changed much (except momentarily under special circumstances), while the intercept of the PP line is more amenable to policy change.

Line XX in figure 6.4 represents the long-run depreciation that keeps the current account in balance. The intercept ϵ_0 (which may be zero or even negative) reflects the effect of the expected long-run reduction in capital flows net of autonomous time shifts in the basic balance (due to productivity growth, relative world price changes, etc.).[20]

A crawl that achieves steady state equilibrium under these assumptions is given at the rate ϵ_2, which is consistent with an inflation rate of π_2 (see point A in fig. 6.4). More restrictive internal policies (showing in a lower PP' curve) will allow a lower rate of depreciation, ϵ_1, with a correspondingly reduced inflation rate (cf. point C with A).

If there is a high degree of capital mobility in the system, the momen-

---

19. If we write $\hat{p} = \beta\hat{e} + (1 - \beta)\hat{W} + d$, $\hat{W} = \gamma\hat{p} + \ell$, we get $\hat{p} = \pi_0 + \alpha\hat{e}$, where $\alpha = \eta\beta$, $\pi_0 = \eta[d + (1 - \beta)\ell]$, and $\eta = [1 - (1 - \beta)\gamma]^{-1}$. $\alpha = 1$ if and only if $\gamma = 1$. This can also be expanded to incorporate real balance effects.

20. If we denote the autonomous time shift of T_1 by η_t and the elasticity of T_1 with respect to q by η_q, we can show that $\epsilon_0 = -(\hat{F} + \eta_t)/\eta_q$.

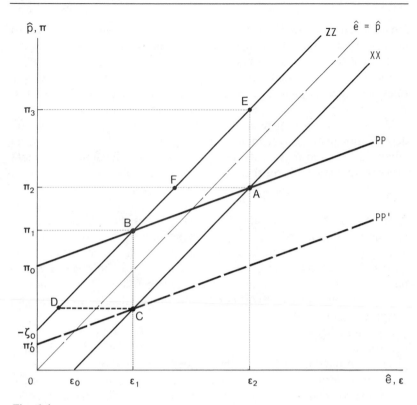

Fig. 6.4

tary equilibrium rate of inflation will not be given by the line XX, however, but rather by the combination of $\hat{e}$ and $\hat{p}$ that keep the asset market in balance over time (line ZZ in fig. 6.4).

This can be obtained by time differentiation of equation (9), leading to an asset equilibrium rate of real depreciation $\hat{e} - \hat{p} = \zeta_0$, where ζ_0 is a positive function of the rate of change of real credit ($\hat{c}$), central bank intervention in reserves (ΔA), and the rate of change of expectations ($\hat{\epsilon}$),[21] and depends negatively on the basic balance ($T_1 = \Delta B$).

In figure 6.4 the intercept of ZZ on the $\hat{p}$ axis measures $-\zeta_0$. If ZZ happens to coincide with line XX (ζ_0 is then positive), the system is in full steady state equilibrium at A. If ZZ lies to the left and above XX, however, there may be a difference between the rate of inflation that keeps the asset market in balance and that which is propagated by the real economy, at any given announced rate of depreciation (compare point E with A).[22] If left to itself, the fall in T_1 will gradually shift the ZZ curve

21. ΔA and $\hat{\epsilon}$ will be zero in equilibrium, but appear here since they can be used as policy instruments, along with $\hat{c}$.

22. One could argue that in this case the *expected* rate of inflation may be π_3 while the *actual* rate is π_2. If ϵ_2 is maintained and expectations play an important role, actual inflation may gradually rise above π_2 (Does this accord with developments during hyperinflation?).

down toward XX. Now suppose that the ZZ curve is deliberately shifted up to its position in figure 6.4 through a credit squeeze and by allowing reserves to fall ($-\Delta A > 0$). At the same time the authorities preannounce a lower rate of depreciation ($\epsilon_1 < \epsilon_2$). Equilibrium can now take place at a lower rate of inflation ($\pi_1 < \pi_2$ at point B), providing these steps are credible.[23] If the stabilization program also affects the real economy, π_0, is brought down to π_0' while the crawl and the expected inflation rate are further reduced (point D). At this stage the economy may be ready for renewed growth (raise $\hat{c}$, $\hat{\epsilon}$) and a shift to a new long-run rate of devaluation (ϵ_1) at C.

The sequence of steps $A-B-D-C$ may be a more feasible one to achieve than an attempt at a direct move from A to C. The main difference is that one uses the exchange rate much more drastically as a stabilizing device (at D, ϵ is almost zero), but one pays the cost in terms of short-term debt (or loss of reserves). This is an example in which short-term capital flows are deliberately used as a stabilizing device at the expense of long-term signaling. The main problem in practice is the speed at which these adjustments can be made to be credible and the size of the real social cost in terms of transitional production and employment slowdown.

References

Bruno, M. 1976. The two-sector open economy and the real exchange rate. *American Economic Review* 66 (September):566–577.

Bruno, M., and Z. Sussman. 1979. Exchange-rate flexibility, inflation and structural change: Israel under alternative regimes. *Journal of Development Economics* 6:483–514.

———. 1980. Floating versus crawling: Israel 1977–1979 by hindsight. Falk Institute Discussion Paper no. 803 (January).

Calvo, G. A., and C. A. Rodriguez. 1977. A model of exchange rate determination under currency substitution and rational expectations. *Journal of Political Economy* 85 (June):617–626.

Dornbusch, R. 1976. Expectations and exchange rate dynamics. *Journal of Political Economy* 84 (December):1161–1176.

Frenkel, J. A., and C. A. Rodriguez. 1980. Exchange rate dynamics and the overshooting hypothesis. NBER Working paper, August.

Liviatan, N. 1980. Anti-inflationary monetary policy and the capital import tax. Department of Economics, The Hebrew University of Jerusalem. Working paper.

Miles, N. 1978. Currency substitution, flexible exchange rates and monetary independence. *American Economic Review* 68 (June):428–436.

---

23. Also, in line with note 22, inflation may for a time rise above π_2 before it eventually comes down to π_1.

Comment   Peter M. Garber

In his paper, Michael Bruno constructs a framework for exploring the effects of various policy combinations on the dynamics of the real exchange rate, real interest rates, income, and elements of the balance of payments accounts. The focus of the study is to determine how such policy combinations may affect the reestablishment of an economy's long-term equilibrium after a disturbance in markets entering the current account balance. The discussion of policy choice is complicated because it considers a number of government objectives, many potential economic environments, and a large number of possible policy tools. Government objectives include a desire to maintain full employment, to allocate properly available capital among different investment projects, and to establish equilibrium in the balance of payments. The environment in which the economy operates may have either fixed or flexible prices and wages. Local capitalists may lack the ability or information to predict optimally the future course of the real interest rate dictated by the dynamics of the economy's path to a new equilibrium. More generally, expectations of other price changes may move sluggishly or they may display perfect foresight. Finally, the available policy tools are the use of commercial policy, the ability to impose exchange controls on short-term debt movements, control of domestic credit, fiscal policy, and the use of fixed versus flexible exchange rates.

Since many combinations of these objectives, policies, and environments are possible, the paper constructs an analytical framework of loci of equilibrium in the goods market, the current account, the short-term capital account, and the balance of payments. The framework is then used to gain a qualitative notion of the dynamics that may arise under alternative policies.

My comments are intended to suggest that these myriad scenarios can be unified by treating them as policies to be imposed by a government *conditional* on the behavior of some endogenous variables of interest to the government. Thus, the policies need not be treated as independent alternatives used to impose a single dynamic path on the economy. Rather, in line with the paper's emphasis on dynamics, they can be viewed as a sequence of policies which switch the economy's laws of motion from time to time as particular contingencies arise. That the government's policies may switch in the future will affect current prices and their dynamics if rational expectations or, as in this paper, perfect foresight is assumed. In this light, Bruno's paper can be interpreted as an exploration of the dynamics associated with a large number of "pure"

Peter M. Garber is a professor in the Department of Economics, University of Rochester, New York, and a research economist with the National Bureau of Economic Research.

policies; the next step is to weight these policies together to determine prices, using the probabilities that the contingencies on which they depend will materialize.

Of course, given the large number of possible policy combinations and contingency rules of thumb for their implementation, this is no easy task. The mere notion that there is one metapolicy which imposes policies according to given contingencies leads, as Sargent (1980) suggests, to the problem of the existence of free will. Aside from the philosophical problem, to study the system's dynamics, even with only a few markets and a few policy choices available, is a very large problem in differential or difference equations. Here I will simply point out a few examples of work that has been done to give a flavor of the potential of employing Bruno's results in this direction.

In the context of a fixed exchange rate model with a drain on a country's foreign reserve holdings, it is possible to foresee a run on a country's reserve which will either force a devaluation or a system of floating exchange rates. Bruno discusses this sort of situation in which the policy generating domestic credit may be incompatible with a viable fixed exchange rate system. Krugman (1979) and Flood and Garber (1981b) have shown how a foreseeable exchange market collapse will affect the dynamics of a country's exchange holdings. In these models the time of the end of a fixed exchange rate and a switch to a floating rate can be determined both by the agents in the economy and by the researcher.

Conversely, under certain contingencies a country may wish to switch from a floating exchange rate to a monetary policy which would fix the exchange rate, as in the British case in the 1920s. In Flood and Garber (1981a) the effects of such a regime switch on the current exchange rate and its dynamics are derived, together with a probability density function over the time of the switch.

Similarly, in the dual exchange rate system mentioned by Bruno in the context of using commercial policy, one can foresee situations in which the exchange rates will be unified. This affects the current values of the exchange rates in both the current and capital accounts, as demonstrated by Flood and Marion (1981).

The above papers deal with switches in the exchange rate regime. However, switches in other policies are possible. One of the major features of Bruno's paper is the explicit statement of short-term asset dynamics after exchange controls are imposed. Thus, we can envisage a foreseeable policy switch from a situation of perfect capital mobility $(\beta = \infty)$ to a situation of exchange controls $(\beta < \infty)$, with the switch imposing different laws of motion on the system. More concretely, suppose that the system is one of fixed exchange rates and that initially there are no controls. Also, the government has a rule which states that under some contingencies (e.g., too large a cumulative deficit in the balance of payments) a switch will be made to exchange controls. Finally, suppose that the process determining domestic credit is such that foreign reserve losses will eventually reach this limit. Then the knowledge that controls will be imposed will affect both the current deficit and the time that the limit is reached.

These examples all examine cases of a single policy switch. More complicated are cases in which various policies will be imposed in sequence. Alternatively, a given contingency may cause a random switch to a single policy from a set of possible alternatives. The tools used to study the above examples would be applicable to this more complex problem. While to my knowledge such multiple policy switches have not been extensively studied, the numerous scenarios studied by Bruno would fit naturally into such a framework.

References

Flood, R., and P. Garber. 1981a. A model of stochastic process switching. NBER Working Paper no. 626.

————. 1981b. Collapsing exchange-rate regimes and the indeterminacy problem. Working paper.

Flood, R., and N. Marion. 1981. The transmission of disturbances under alternative exchange-rate regimes with optimal indexing. *Quarterly Journal of Economics*.

Krugman, P. 1979. A model of balance-of-payments crises. *Journal of Money, Credit, and Banking* 11, no. 3:311–325.

Sargent, T. 1980. The ends of four big inflations. Working paper.

7 Financing Private Business in an Inflationary Context: The Experience of Argentina between 1967 and 1980

Domingo F. Cavallo and A. Humberto Petrei

This paper attempts to describe how inflation and different kinds of anti-inflationary policies affect the financial structure of private firms. The Argentine experience between 1967 and 1980 is examined, using information for the whole economy and a sample of individual firms. Section 7.1 relates main stabilization attempts, examines the characteristics of sources and costs of financing faced by private firms, and pays particular attention to conditions created by the last stabilization plan. Section 7.2, using information from a sample of individual firms for the 1976–1980 period, analyzes the changes in the structure of assets and liabilities and the composition of costs and profitability of firms brought about by changes in general financial and economic conditions.

7.1 Stabilization Policies and Their Impact on Private Sector Financing

Section 7.1.1 outlines major aspects of the inflationary process of the 1967–1980 period and describes key anti-inflationary measures pursued in each of the five subperiods identified for analytical purposes. Section 7.1.2 shows the development of different sources of finances for private business over the last fifteen years, relating them to changes in financing costs in various markets. Section 7.1.3 concentrates on the last stabilization plan, comparing it with the 1967–1969 program, with which it shares several features.

Domingo F. Cavallo and A. Humberto Petrei are respectively Director and Director of Research of the Instituto de Estudios Económicos Sobre la Realidad Argentina y Latinoamericana (IEERAL), Fundación Mediterranea, Cordoba, Argentina.

Table 7.1   Selected Indicators of Economic Policy and
Performance of the Argentine Economy, 1967–1980

Year	Rate of Growth: GDP[a]	Rate of Growth: Real Wages[a,b]	Government Deficit as Percentage of GDP[c]	Rate of Growth: Domestic Credit[d]	Rate of Growth: Money Supply[d]
1967	2.6	5.2	1.7	16	26
1968	4.3	0.4	0.9	30	30
1969	8.5	2.3	1.1	23	18
1970	5.4	4.1	1.0	20	22
1971	3.6	3.2	3.6	61	49
1972	1.6	−9.0	4.3	51	53
1973	3.4	12.3	6.4	82	92
1974	6.5	18.0	6.7	60	56
1975	−0.9	−4.3	14.4	148	125
1976	−0.2	−36.7	9.4	356	366
1977	6.0	6.2	3.1	195	227
1978	−3.9	1.4	3.6	184	183
1979	7.0	6.2	3.9	190	192
1980	0.0	—	4.0	129	73

[a]*Source:* Banco Central de la República Argentina. 1975. *Sistema de cuentas del producto e ingreso de la Argentina*, vol. 2, and quarterly updating reports.
[b]Instituto Nacional de Estadísticas y Censos. *Boletín Trimestral*, several issues.
[c]Secretaría de Hacienda. Unpublished manuscripts.

7.1.1   Inflation and Stabilization Attempts during 1967–1980

The 1967–1980 period was characterized by high and variable rates of inflation, ranging from 4 to 386 percent per year as measured by the wholesale price index. Five different subperiods may be identified by their various anti-inflationary policies. The main characteristics of the economic policies and the performance of the economy in these subperiods, using key economic indicators, are given in table 7.1. Cost of financing faced by private business is a central variable in the discussion that follows. Table 7.2 lists the various rates in each of the relevant markets.

1967–1969: The Krieger-Vasena Plan

While combating inflation was the central objective of the Krieger-Vasena plan, emphasis was also given to stimulating the growth of the economy. The plan consisted of an initial 40 percent devaluation of the peso (partially compensated by the introduction of taxes on traditional exports and a reduction of tariffs on imports), the adoption of a fixed

Rate of Inflation[b]		Rate of Devaluation[d]		Balance of Payments Current Account Deficit[d,e]	Accumulation of Foreign Reserves[d,e]	Excess Black Market Dollar Price over Official Price[f]
Wholesale	Cost of Living	Commercial	Financial			
21	27	40		13	35	—
4	10	0		−1	4	—
7	7	0		−13	−33	—
27	22	14		−8	10	—
48	39	37	106	−20	−20	13
76	64	57	19	−10	8	16
31	44	9	0	24	19	13
36	40	−2	0	3	−1	63
348	335	432	471	−34	−21	95
386	348	407	377	16	31	31
147	160	115		18	42	—
142	170	70		32	36	—
130	140	62		6	55	—
58	88	24		−35	−20	—

[d]Banco Central de la República Argentina. *Boletín Estadístico Mensual* and *Memorias Anual*, several issues.

[e]As percentage of exports, plus imports, divided by 2.

[f]Organización Techint. 1979. *Boletín Informativo*, no. 214.

exchange rate, the relaxation of constraints on trade and capital movements, and a system of voluntary price agreements and wage controls. In addition, steps were taken to make fiscal and monetary policies compatible with inflation targets. The government deficit was drastically reduced and kept around 1 percent of GDP, while the rate of growth of domestic credit roughly averaged the sum of the rate of growth of real income plus the planned rate of inflation. Inflation went down to 7 percent per year from 21 percent and 27 percent as measured by the wholesale and cost of living indices, respectively. The annual rate of growth of GDP went up from 2.6 to 8.5, and real wages increased by an average of 2.5 percent per year. The plan's major constraint was the balance of payments, where a crisis developed as a result of a reduction in beef production and exports caused by the relatively low beef prices of previous years.

The central bank directly controlled interest rates in domestic financial markets without, however, reaching negative rates in real terms (see table 7.2). Except for 1967, the devaluation year, the cost of credit was higher in the domestic market than in the foreign markets. The cost of foreign resources during 1968 and 1969 was higher if the borrower pur-

Table 7.2   Cost of Financing in Different Markets, Argentina 1967–1980 (Effective Interest Rates in Annual Percentages)

	Nominal Rates[a]				Real Rates[b]			
	Domestic		Foreign		Domestic		Foreign	
Year	Controlled Interest Rate	Free Interest Rate	Exchange Insurance	No Exchange Insurance	Controlled Interest Rate	Free Interest Rate	Exchange Insurance	No Exchange Insurance
1967	14.9	—	37.4	51.5	-3.8	—	15.1	26.9
1968	14.9	—	13.6	9.2	9.4	—	8.2	4.0
1969	15.0	—	15.1	12.8	7.4	—	7.4	5.3
1970	14.4	26.7	22.7	27.1	-9.7	0.0	-3.2	0.3
1971	14.0	28.1	20.3	129.7	-22.7	-13.1	-18.4	55.8
1972	15.6	34.5	29.8	28.8	-34.4	-23.7	-26.3	-26.9
1973	21.5	33.7	24.7	12.3	-7.3	2.0	-4.9	-14.3
1974	20.9	30.0	24.5	14.2	-11.2	-4.5	-8.5	-16.1
1975	21.0	49.2	124.0	791.6	-73.0	-66.7	-50.0	99.2
1976	48.0	124.6	117.7	262.8	-69.6	-53.8	-55.2	-25.4
1977	152.7	196.6	52.3	133.9	2.3	20.0	-38.4	-5.3
1978	—	195.4	—	89.9	—	21.4	—	-22.0
1979	—	144.8	—	86.8	—	6.9	—	-18.4
1980	—	104.9	—	42.8	—	29.9	—	-9.5

Sources: Banco Central de la República Argentina. *Boletín Estadístico Mensual*, several issues. Unpublished information from the databank. Fundación Mediterránea. *Novedades Económicas*, several issues.

[a]Nominal Rates.

[b]Obtained, $[(1 + i)/(1 + \pi)] - 1$, where i is the nominal rate and π is the rate of inflation during the year as measured by the Wholesale Price Index.

chased exchange insurance. The large difference between these two costs in 1968–69 reflects devaluation expectations, which in turn explain the reduction of foreign reserves by more than the current account deficit, even though without exchange insurance foreign financing was still cheaper than domestic borrowing.

1970–1972: Anti-inflationary Targets Abandoned

This period was dominated by the objective of solving the balance of payments problem. Anti-inflationary targets were abandoned as the government, involved in a political plan to transfer power to politicians, put emphasis on avoiding recession. The year 1970 was transitional. A 14 percent devaluation of the peso occurred but the fiscal and monetary discipline still existed that characterized the previous period. During 1971 and 1972 that discipline was relaxed; a dual exchange rate system was put into effect with a big initial devaluation of the peso for financial transactions while the exchange rate for real transactions was being devalued more gradually. The balance of payments problem was being solved gradually, helped by very favorable terms of trade existing at the end of the period. Real growth slowed down, though a deep recession was avoided and, on average, real wages remained unchanged over the period. Since nominal interest rates in the domestic markets were still controlled by the central bank, real rates became increasingly negative as inflation accelerated throughout the period. With the exception of the cost of credit from foreign markets in the big devaluation year (1971), real interest rates were negative in all the markets, including the incipient "bill bank acceptances" market with free interest rates.

1973–1974: The Gelbard Plan

The main objective of the Gelbard plan, under the Peronist government, was to increase real wages and achieve high levels of economic activity. Very strict price controls and the establishment of a fixed exchange rate were the main instruments used to fight inflation. The government deficit rose to almost 7 percent of GDP, and credit expanded at a rate of 82 in 1973 and 60 in 1974. The natural result of these policies was the development of increasingly important black markets for almost every good. At the beginning of the period, very favorable export prices helped to maintain the exchange rate as previously fixed, but soon strict exchange controls and import restrictions were necessary to keep it. In 1974 the price differential between the dollar in the black market and the official rate averaged 63 percent and was rising. Inflation was kept between 30 percent and 40 percent per year, according to the different indicators, but it was an evident situation of repressed inflation. Real wages increased over the period by 30 percent and real output by 10 percent. As in the previous period, interest rates, controlled by the government, were predominantly negative, and by the end of the period credit rationing became more and more important.

1975–1976: Inflationary Explosion

As a natural consequence of repressed inflationary conditions and a climate of political crisis caused by internal disputes in the Peronist party and by the intensification of terrorism, a dramatic increase in the rate of inflation took place in 1975. The rate of devaluation of the peso was around 450 percent, and still the price of the dollar in the black market almost doubled the official price. The government deficit more than doubled, and controls of credit expansion and money supply were lost. In 1975 the annual inflation rate rose to around 350 percent, and by the first quarter of 1976 it reached a figure of 900 percent. Real output declined for the first time since 1963, and real wages began to deteriorate.

In April 1976 a new military government put an emergency plan into operation which included a big devaluation, the imposition of nominal wage ceilings, the lifting of existing controls on commodity prices, and several measures to reduce the government deficit. The expansion of credit was still out of the central bank's control as the government faced huge losses because of the subsidized sales of dollars in the futures market that had been committed during the last part of the previous government period to induce an inflow of foreign capital necessary to cope with the balance of payments crisis. In 1976 the rate of inflation was similar to that of the previous year, real output declined again, and real wages were reduced by almost 37 percent. By the second part of 1976 the rate of inflation had been more than halved. The balance of payments crisis had been overcome by an increase in export earnings due to a strong supply response to the price incentives given to exporters by the devaluation of the peso and the elimination of export taxes. During this period, domestic borrowing and foreign borrowing with exchange insurance received subsidies at an annual rate of around 60 percent. However, the real cost of foreign credit without exchange insurance was almost 100 percent in 1975.

1977–1980: The Martínez de Hoz Plan

During this period fighting inflation again became an explicit aim of economic policy. Together with this objective, economic policy addressed the reestablishment of the conditions of a free market economy opened to the rest of the world. After a temporary period of price control on leading firms, anti-inflationary policy between mid-1977 and the end of 1978, was based on the control of money supply, and after 1978 was based on an announced declining rate of devaluation. Neither of these two different anti-inflationary strategies were clean examples of what is taught in conventional macroeconomic theory. On the one hand, the attempt to control money supply was not accompanied by a floating exchange rate. The government reacted to the inflow of foreign capital, resulting from the contraction of domestic credit, by imposing controls on international capital movements. During 1978 a zero interest rate deposit in domestic currency, equivalent to 20 percent of the amount of the loan, was imposed on borrowers in foreign markets. On the other hand, during 1979 and 1980 the announcement of a devaluation rate was made in such a way that did not create enough certainty in the market. The relatively short periods for which the announcements were valid and the announcements' lack of clarity, together with the reluctance of the minister to make firmer commitments to his program (as that would have meant the intervention of the central bank in the futures market for the exchange rate), caused a high degree of uncertainty regarding the exchange rate policy. This uncertainty was greater during 1980 as the deficit in the current account of the balance of payments widened. In addition to the imperfect design of these monetary policies, the government deficit, although significantly smaller than in previous years, still amounted to 3–4 percent of GDP. This made the attempts to control credit expansion very costly in terms of high real interest rates and the control of the nominal exchange rate very costly in terms of real exchange rate deterioration and accumulation of a current account deficit.

Between September 1977 and March 1978 the annual interest rate in real terms was around 100 percent as a consequence of the attempt to reduce, in the second half of 1977, the rate of growth of the money supply from 10 percent a month to 4 percent. The price of traded goods relative to nontraded goods declined by more than 30 percent during 1979 and 1980, as reflected by the difference between changes in wholesale and cost of living indices, which can be taken as proxies for traded good and nontraded good prices. Inflation remained almost constant for three years at 150 percent per year, a figure which was reached in the second part of 1976. It was only during the last quarter of 1979 that the inflation rate began to decline significantly.

Real output grew during the second part of 1976 and most of 1977, but declined sharply during 1978 as a result of a substantial increase in real interest rates that took place in the last quarter of 1977 and the first part of 1978. Real output recovered again during 1979 as real interest rates were declining, thanks to a relatively high level of confidence in the government and to a declining rate of devaluation that provided an inflow of foreign capital and kept down domestic interest rates. During 1980 real output was stagnant as real interest rates increased again because of increasing uncertainty regarding the exchange policy and because of the deterioration of the real exchange rate which affected incentives in the production of traded goods. During the whole period, real wages tended to recover from the deep fall of 1976, but they did not reach the pre-

Peronist levels. Since 1977 the cost of credit in real terms was very high in the domestic financial market while borrowing in foreign markets had negative costs, ranging from −22 percent to −5.3 percent per year.

7.1.2   Sources and Costs of Finance

Table 7.3 shows sources of investment funds for private firms in real terms for each of the policy periods described in section 7.1.1. Table 7.4 presents the same information as percent of gross investment.

Sources of finances are classified as external and internal to the firms. The external sources contain debt financing from different domestic stock markets and from direct foreign investment. The internal sources in turn are classified as net results from operating in each of the financial markets and as depreciation allowances and profits. The former was estimated from information on the real financial cost in each market as reported in table 7.2, and the latter was obtained as the difference between gross private investment and all the other sources of financing.

The first observation emerging from tables 7.3 and 7.4 is that significant amounts are listed under debt financing and internal sources of financing. Sources of external equity capital financing were generally unimportant, except for direct foreign investment during the Krieger-Vasena period. The stock market has been negligible as a source of finances, and it has remained so irrespective of different stabilization plans. Debt financing became important during the stabilization programs of Krieger-Vasena (1967–1969) and Martínez de Hoz (1977–1980). When anti-inflationary policies were abandoned or when repressed inflation exploded, as in the 1970–1972 and 1975–1976 periods, internal sources of finances became dominant.

Depreciation allowances and operating results are the most important and stable components of internal sources. A clear correlation exists between the proportion they represent and the rate of growth of real output. The proportion of finance gained from operating in financial markets varied substantially between the periods in a way which is negatively correlated with the share of debt financing.

Debt financing and net results from operating in financial markets are consolidated in tables 7.5 and 7.6. A relatively stable pattern prevails over the last fifteen years, indicating that the contribution of domestic and foreign financial markets to the financing of private business is independent of the composition of that contribution. When inflation is being fought, as in the Krieger-Vasena and Martínez de Hoz programs, firms rely strongly on additional debt. When inflation accelerates and real interest becomes negative, as in 1970–1972 and 1975–1976, firms collect important subsidies in financial markets which add up to profits.

With respect to the relative importance of different financial markets, tables 7.5 and 7.6 show clearly the declining role of the domestic market.

Table 7.3   **Sources of Finances for Private Business in Argentina, 1967–1980**
(Annual Averages in Millions of Pesos at Constant Prices of 1970)

External Sources

Period	Debt Financing (increments in debt at constant prices)					Equity Capital Financing		Total
	Debt with Domestic Market		Debt with Foreign Markets				Direct	
	Controlled Interest Rate	Free Interest Rate	Exchange Insurance	No Exchange Insurance	Total	Stock Market	Foreign Investment	
1967–1969	2,324.9	—	111.6	373.8	2,810.3	66.7	534.5	3,411.5
1970–1972	−1,270.9	619.4	446.7	986.8	782.0	106.0	395.1	1,283.1
1973–1974	2,667.9	519.8	−636.9	−691.5	1,859.3	53.3	116.8	2,029.4
1975–1976	−6,720.0	1,149.0	433.2	−4.6	−5,142.4	32.8	92.1	−5,017.5
1977–1980	−854.1	5,623.6	−334.7	751.5	5,186.3	75.9	268.5	5,530.7

Internal Sources

Period	Net Results from Operating in Financial Markets					Depreciation Allowances and Operating Results	Gross Private Investment
	Domestic Market		Foreign Markets				
	Controlled Interest Rate	Free Interest Rate	Exchange Insurance	No Exchange Insurance	Total		
1967–1969	−480.3	—	−11.3	−408.5	−900.1	7,639.1	10,150.5
1970–1972	3,138.6	108.0	231.6	−357.9	3,120.3	8,652.6	13,056.0
1973–1974	1,276.6	40.2	90.2	1,015.5	2,422.5	8,749.1	13,201.0
1975–1976	8,484.1	1,339.5	1,381.7	−1,341.9	9,863.4	6,040.4	10,886.3
1977–1980	−19.4	−1,626.0	128.4	1,037.5	−479.5	7,579.6	12,630.8

Sources: See Appendix A.

Table 7.4   Structure of the Sources of Finances for Private Business in Argentina, 1967–1980 (Percentages That Each Source Represents of Gross Private Investment)

External Sources

| | Debt Financing (increments in debt at constant prices) | | | | | Equity Capital Financing | | |
| | Debt with Domestic Market | | Debt with Foreign Markets | | | | | |
Period	Controlled Interest Rate	Free Interest Rate	Exchange Insurance	No Exchange Insurance	Total	Stock Market	Direct Foreign Investment	Total
1967–1969	22.9	—	1.1	3.7	27.7	0.7	5.3	33.7
1970–1972	-9.7	4.7	3.4	7.6	6.0	0.8	3.0	9.8
1973–1974	20.2	3.9	-4.8	-5.2	14.1	0.4	0.9	15.4
1975–1976	-61.8	10.6	4.0	0.0	-47.2	0.3	0.8	-46.1
1977–1980	-6.8	44.5	-2.6	6.0	41.1	0.6	2.1	43.8

Internal Sources

| | Net Results from Operating in Financial Markets | | | | | Depreciation Allowances and Operating Results | Gross Private Investment |
| | Domestic Market | | Foreign Markets | | | | |
Period	Controlled Interest Rate	Free Interest Rate	Exchange Insurance	No Exchange Insurance	Total		
1967–1969	-4.7	—	-0.1	-4.0	-8.8	75.1	100.0
1970–1972	24.0	0.8	1.8	-2.7	23.9	66.3	100.0
1973–1974	9.7	0.3	0.7	7.7	18.4	66.2	100.0
1975–1976	77.9	12.3	12.7	-12.3	90.6	55.5	100.0
1977–1980	-0.2	-12.8	1.0	8.2	-3.8	60.0	100.0

Sources: See Appendix A.

Table 7.5   **Net Amount of Financial Resources Obtained by Private Business via New Debt and Results from Operating in Financial Markets, Argentina, 1967–1980 (Yearly Averages in Millions of Pesos at Constant Prices of 1970)**

| Period | Domestic Market | | Foreign Markets | | |
	Controlled Interest Rate	Free Interest Rate	Exchange Insurance	No Exchange Insurance	Total
1967–1969	1,844.7	—	100.3	− 34.7	1,910.3
1970–1972	1,870.5	727.4	678.4	628.9	3,905.2
1973–1974	3,944.3	560.1	− 546.7	324.0	4,281.7
1975–1976	1,764.7	2,488.5	1,814.6	− 1,346.5	4,721.3
1977–1980	− 873.5	3,997.7	− 206.3	1,788.0	4,705.9

Sources: See Appendix A.

The higher the inflation rate, the less the controlled markets are chosen by investors, and the more difficult it is for the government to exercise effective controls. Because of this problem, the Martínez de Hoz anti-inflationary plan was aimed at freeing interest rates.

The role of foreign financial markets does not show a clear trend or a neat association with the degree of control exercized over inflation by government. While the role of foreign financing was almost negligible during the years of the Krieger-Vasena plan, it played an important role during the Martínez de Hoz years. Its role was also important during the 1970–1972 period of neglected anti-inflationary targets as a result of the restrictions imposed by the government on foreign-owned firms which wanted to get financing in the domestic market and as a result of the widespread use of exchange insurance to make foreign financing attractive to private firms. The net resources provided by foreign financial markets during the 1975–1976 inflationary explosion were very small and

Table 7.6   **Structure of Net Amount of Financial Resources Obtained by Private Business from Operating in Financial Markets, Argentina, 1967–1980 (Percentages That Each Source Represents of Gross Private Investment)**

| Period | Domestic Market | | Foreign Mrakets | | |
	Controlled Interest Rate	Free Interest Rate	Exchange Insurance	No Exchange Insurance	Total
1967–1969	18.2	—	1.0	− 0.3	18.9
1970–1972	14.3	5.6	5.2	4.8	29.9
1973–1974	29.9	4.2	− 4.1	2.5	32.5
1975–1976	16.2	22.9	16.7	− 12.4	43.4
1977–1980	− 6.9	31.7	− 1.6	14.2	37.4

Sources: See Appendix A.

would have been still smaller had the government not resorted to a subsidized exchange insurance and other strong incentives to keep firms borrowing from abroad. The different role that foreign financial markets played in the Krieger-Vasena plan compared with the Martínez de Hoz program is discussed in section 7.1.3.

The preceding discussion has concentrated on comparing the anti-inflationary policy years, on the one hand, and the uncontrolled inflation years, on the other, but specific comments have not been made on the Gelbard years (1973–1974). The Gelbard plan, although attempting to control inflation, included a set of internally inconsistent policies, such as strict price controls, a fixed exchange rate, large government deficits, and an expansionary monetary policy, which made a very poor anti-inflationary plan. Economic conditions in which different sources of finances played their roles during 1973 and 1974 were in part similar to the anti-inflationary policy years and in part to the periods of uncontrolled inflation.

7.1.3   A Closer Look at the Krieger-Vasena and Martínez de Hoz Periods

Let us now concentrate on the differences in the structure of the sources of finances between the Krieger-Vasena and the Martínez de Hoz plans.

Depreciation allowances and operating results played a more important role during the first period. They represented 75 percent of overall private investment as compared to 60 percent in the second period, suggesting that private business was more profitable during the Krieger-Vasena years. This is not surprising because the voluntary wage and price controls that were included in that plan aimed precisely at making the fight against inflation consistent with the expansion of economic activity. In the case of the Martínez de Hoz plan, more emphasis was placed on introducing structural changes, like the opening up of the economy; these turned out to be costly in terms of the level of economic activity in the short run, since recession has a negative effect on profitability.

While the bulk of foreign resources came as direct foreign investment during the Krieger-Vasena period, during the Martínez de Hoz period the most important part of foreign sources was debt financing. This difference is, in part, the result of the same policies that led to the different levels of profitability of private business between the two periods. The expanding economy of the Krieger-Vasena years offered better opportunities for profitable, direct foreign investment than the structurally changing economy of the Martínez de Hoz period. The significant role of foreign debt financing during the latter period was related to the magnitude of the interest rate differential between domestic and foreign markets that was created by attempts to control domestic credit expansion in an economy with a significant government deficit.

Private business had to pay a positive real cost for debt financing during both periods, but in the Krieger-Vasena case those real costs did not differ much whether domestic or foreign funds were used. That was not the case during the Martínez de Hoz period, because firms paid higher costs when borrowing in domestic markets and collected an important subsidy when borrowing in foreign markets. Part of this difference could have been eliminated if the uncertainties about the ability of the government to keep the devaluation within the announced schedules had been removed, but an important proportion of these differences is related to attempts to reduce domestic credit expansion when the government deficit was not reduced simultaneously.

7.2 Changes of Firms' Balance Sheets, 1976–1980

In order to analyze the behavior of different sources of finances as well as changes in the structure of assets, data were gathered for a sample of seventy-eight private corporations for the period 1976–1978. The data were gathered from firms whose shares are traded in the Buenos Aires Stock Exchange, using quarterly balance reports. The aggregation was made from balance sheets whose dates were close to mid-year. Results for the whole sample are analyzed first, then two divisions are made between small and large firms and between firms producing traded goods and nontraded goods.

7.2.1 Results for the Whole Sample

Table 7.7 reports in proportional terms the main results for the sample as a whole. In addition, several key balance sheet ratios, which are shown in table 7.8, were computed to illustrate the analysis.

The assets side of the balance sheet shows no major changes between the proportion of total assets held as physical or financial capital. A significant decline in the relative importance of inventories since 1977 is perceived, which is an expected result from policy changes regarding interest rates during the period.

The liabilities side shows important changes. There is an increase in long-term debt financing and a consequent decline in the proportion of net worth. This change is the consequence of the drastic reduction of profitability, as may be seen in the profit and loss statements.

The shortening of the terms of deposits and loans as a consequence of inflation and the variability of interest rates is a well-known phenomenon not only in Argentina. As a result of institutional arrangements, this shortening of terms was accentuated in the Argentine domestic market at the initial stage of the financial reform, that is, immediately after June 1977. The main factor working in that direction was a system of compensation for interest paid by banks on that part of time deposits that could not be lent due to the high proportion of reserve requirements

Table 7.7   Argentina 1976–1980. Balance Sheets, Profit and Loss Statements
                 for a Sample of Seventy-Eight Private Corporations

	1976	1977	1978	1979	1980
	Balance Sheets				
Assets	100.0	100.0	100.0	100.0	100.0
Cash	1.9	2.9	1.9	1.5	1.8
Short-term investments	2.5	2.6	1.8	2.4	3.3
Credit	14.2	17.8	16.5	15.3	14.5
Inventories	21.8	20.4	16.7	16.3	16.4
Long-term assets	59.6	56.4	63.1	64.5	64.0
Short-term debt	30.2	36.5	31.7	31.1	31.7
Commercial	14.1	12.0	9.6	8.8	8.4
Foreign	8.3	6.1	7.7	6.5	8.3
Banks	3.4	13.5	10.2	11.8	10.6
Others	6.0	4.9	4.2	4.0	4.4
Long-term debt	10.2	9.5	18.2	20.1	19.8
Foreign	6.7	5.6	8.3	9.0	8.8
Banks	0.0	0.0	6.4	7.7	7.8
Others	3.5	3.9	3.5	3.4	3.2
Net worth	59.6	54.0	50.1	48.8	48.5
	Profit and Loss Statements				
Sales	100.0	100.0	100.0	100.0	100.0
Cost of sales	68.6	72.9	71.4	73.8	78.8
Gross margin	31.4	27.1	28.6	26.2	21.2
Financial costs	9.3	10.4	13.0	9.8	8.5
Other costs (marketing, administrative, etc.)	18.0	15.1	18.6	17.3	18.0
Net profits	4.1	1.6	−3.0	−0.9	−5.3

Sources: See Appendix B.

imposed by the central bank. The required compensation changed every month and was known only for the current month. Therefore, banks, when lending long, not only faced the risk of changing interest rates but also the risk of changes in the proportion of nonlent time deposit costs that the central bank decided to compensate (see Arnaudo, Cavallo, and Dadone 1978). How did this increase in long-term liabilities of firms come about? Part of it came through foreign financial markets, that is, foreign financing was chosen by firms not only because it was cheaper but also because it provided terms appropriate to the role those resources were called to play: to substitute for the deterioration of the internal sources of financing. The other part of the increase in long-term financing came from the domestic financial system as special financing for long-term investment by the state-owned banks; some of this was the result of debt refinancing by firms that faced financial problems. As can be seen in table 7.7, this long-term debt shows up immediately after the period when

Table 7.8   Argentina 1976–1980. Balance Sheet Ratios for a Sample of Seventy-Eight Private Corporations

Ratios		1976	1977	1978	1979	1980
Immobilization (1):	$\dfrac{\text{long-term assets}}{\text{net worth}}$	99.3	103.1	125.1	130.1	129.3
Immobilization (2):	$\dfrac{\text{long-term assets}}{\text{net worth + long-term debt}}$	84.8	87.7	91.8	92.2	91.8
Liquidity:	$\dfrac{\text{cash + investments(s-t) + credits}}{\text{short-term debt}}$	61.8	64.5	63.7	61.7	61.8
Leverage (total):	$\dfrac{\text{total debt}}{\text{net worth}}$	67.9	85.2	99.6	104.9	106.2
Leverage (short-term):	$\dfrac{\text{short-term debt}}{\text{net worth}}$	53.4	67.6	63.3	63.7	65.4
Leverage (long-term):	$\dfrac{\text{long-term debt}}{\text{net worth}}$	17.1	17.6	36.3	41.2	40.8
Leverage (in foreign currencies):	$\dfrac{\text{debt in foreign currencies}}{\text{net worth}}$	25.2	21.7	31.9	31.8	35.3
Net financial position in domestic currency		−7.2	−9.0	−5.6	−5.5	−3.8
Net financial position in foreign currencies		−12.7	−9.8	−14.2	−15.4	−17.1

Sources: See Appendix B.

interest rates went up to almost 100 percent per year in real terms, provoking economic losses and financial crises in many firms. This re-financing was mainly undertaken by the state-owned banks. However, in early 1980 the central bank allowed the banks to use an index based on the deposit rate to facilitate the granting of long-term indexed loans, even though the banks were still receiving only short-term deposits (see Cavallo and Dadone 1979). This institutional arrangement, together with the new spurt of financial crises that showed up in 1980, accelerated the transformation of short-term liabilities into long-term ones.

The composition of short-term liabilities shows an important decline in commercial credit compensated by an increase in bank credit. This change is a natural outcome of the growth of financial intermediation brought about by the liberalization of interest rates.

The profit and loss statements reveal important facts that seem to be related to the changing nature of the stabilization plan within the Mar-tínez de Hoz period. The drastic decline of profitability experienced in 1978 was basically the result of a significant increase in financial costs, while a similar decline in profitability registered in 1980 is explained by a big reduction of gross margin. In other words, by the end of 1977 and the beginning of 1978, the stabilization plan, based on the control of the money supply, was pressing inflation down by an important increase in the real rate of interest. By the end of 1979 and the beginning of 1980, the inflation was being pressed down by foreign competition and the control of the exchange rate. By the middle of 1981, balance sheets will surely register a still more drastic decline in profitability which will be the effect of both the control of the nominal exchange rate and an important increase in real rates originating in the increasing uncertainty about the future exchange rate policy, unless the Martínez de Hoz stabilization plan collapses as current political events seem to suggest as this paper is being written (January 1981).

The ratios reported in table 7.8 summarize the main changes in the financial structure of firms during the period. The deterioration of net worth produced an increase in the first immobilization index from 100 to almost 130, but firms managed to keep more or less constant the relationship of long-term assets and net worth plus long-term liabilities, as it is registered by the second immobilization index. In spite of the deterioration of profitability and the associated difficulties, firms seem to have been cautious in keeping liquidity within the usual rates. Overall leverage increased dramatically from 67.9 to 106.2, with the bulk of the increase registered in long-term leverage. Firms tried, on average, to collect the subsidy associated with operations in the foreign financial markets and to avoid the high real rates of the domestic markets. That is registered by the leverage in foreign currencies index and by the opposite movement of the net financial position in both domestic and foreign currencies.

7.2.2   Differences between Small and Large Firms

Tables 7.9 and 7.10 report for small firms the same type of information given in tables 7.7 and 7.8, and tables 7.11 and 7.12 do the same for large firms.

The structure of large firms is almost identical to that of the aggregate of firms. Therefore, differences in behavior will be observed mainly in table 7.9. What emerges from it is the observation that smaller firms had a smaller increase in leverage and a reduced access to long-term credit and foreign financing. The smaller reliance on debt financing should have helped the firms get higher profits, but this effect was largely outweighed

Table 7.9   **Argentina 1976–1980. Balance Sheets, Profit and Loss Statements for a Sample of Small Private Corporations**

	1976	1977	1978	1979	1980
Balance Sheets					
Assets	100.0	100.0	100.0	100.0	100.0
Cash	2.7	2.5	2.9	2.6	3.0
Short-term investments	2.4	1.3	3.1	2.0	4.2
Credits	24.1	23.7	21.5	20.6	17.4
Inventories	15.5	17.9	17.6	18.1	18.7
Long-term assets	55.3	54.6	54.9	58.7	56.7
Short-term debt	34.0	35.9	38.8	42.8	39.6
Commercial	14.1	12.8	14.0	13.9	13.3
Foreign	2.1	1.9	2.1	2.1	4.5
Banks	5.5	13.3	13.7	15.1	10.8
Others	12.3	7.9	9.0	11.7	11.0
Long-term debt	4.6	7.2	8.6	5.3	6.4
Foreign	1.4	0.6	0.6	0.9	1.7
Banks	0.0	0.2	3.0	1.4	1.3
Others	3.2	6.4	5.0	3.0	3.4
Net worth	61.4	56.9	52.6	51.9	54.0
Profit and Loss Statements					
Sales	100.0	100.0	100.0	100.0	100.0
Cost of sales	63.0	59.7	56.3	60.7	62.5
Gross margin	37.0	40.3	43.7	39.3	37.5
Financial costs	6.0	17.6	27.8	29.7	17.2
Other costs (marketing, administrative, etc.)	19.7	22.0	24.3	25.5	28.1
Net profits	11.3	0.7	−8.4	−15.9	−7.8

Sources: See Appendix B.

Table 7.10   Argentina 1976–1980. Balance Sheet Ratios for a Sample of Small Private Corporations

Ratios		1976	1977	1978	1979	1980
Immobilization (1):	$\dfrac{\text{long-term assets}}{\text{net worth}}$	90.1	88.2	90.5	102.3	83.1
Immobilization (2):	$\dfrac{\text{long-term assets}}{\text{net worth + long-term debt}}$	83.8	78.3	77.9	92.8	74.3
Liquidity:	$\dfrac{\text{cash + investments(s-t) + credits}}{\text{short-term debt}}$	85.9	75.8	70.9	58.9	62.1
Leverage (total):	$\dfrac{\text{total debt}}{\text{net worth}}$	62.9	75.7	90.1	92.7	85.2
Leverage (short-term):	$\dfrac{\text{short-term debt}}{\text{net worth}}$	55.4	63.1	73.8	82.5	73.3
Leverage (long-term):	$\dfrac{\text{long-term debt}}{\text{net worth}}$	7.5	12.7	16.3	10.2	11.9
Leverage (in foreign currencies):	$\dfrac{\text{debt in foreign currencies}}{\text{net worth}}$	5.7	4.4	5.1	5.8	11.5
Net financial position in domestic currency		-4.9	-8.2	-10.9	-15.5	-10.5
Net financial position in foreign currencies		-1.3	-0.8	-1.0	-3.0	-6.2

Sources: See Appendix B.

Table 7.11   Argentina 1976–1980. Balance Sheets, Profit and Loss Statements
                    for a Sample of Large Private Corporations

	1976	1977	1978	1979	1980
	Balance Sheets				
Assets	100.0	100.0	100.0	100.0	100.0
Cash	1.8	3.0	1.8	1.5	1.5
Short-term investments	2.5	2.7	1.8	2.4	3.1
Credits	13.7	17.4	16.3	15.0	15.9
Inventories	22.2	20.5	16.6	16.2	17.0
Long-term assets	59.8	56.4	63.5	64.9	62.5
Short-term debt	29.7	36.6	31.4	30.7	31.8
Commercial	12.8	12.0	9.4	8.6	8.5
Foreign	8.3	6.2	8.1	6.7	7.5
Banks	3.0	13.7	10.0	11.6	11.6
Others	5.6	4.7	3.9	3.8	4.2
Long-term debt	10.6	9.4	18.5	20.5	19.9
Foreign	7.4	6.0	8.6	9.3	7.3
Banks	0.0	0.0	6.6	8.0	7.8
Others	3.2	3.4	3.3	3.2	4.8
Net worth	59.7	54.0	50.1	48.8	48.3
	Profit and Loss Statements				
Sales	100.0	100.0	100.0	100.0	100.0
Cost of sales	68.9	73.6	72.1	74.3	79.5
Gross margin	31.1	26.4	27.9	25.7	20.5
Financial costs	9.5	10.1	12.3	9.0	8.1
Other costs (marketing, administrative, etc.)	18.0	14.7	18.3	17.0	17.6
Net profits	3.6	1.6	−2.7	−0.3	−5.2

Sources: See Appendix B.

by the negative effect on profits caused by the inability of small firms to
collect the subsidy associated with foreign financing. This is clearly
reflected by the behavior of the net financial position on domestic and
foreign currencies, and it is the source of the huge losses shown in the
1978 and 1980 statements. Financial costs for small firms were almost
three times those of large firms.

7.2.3   Differences between Producers of Traded and Nontraded Goods

Tables 7.13 and 7.14 report balance sheet structures and ratios for
corporations producing nontraded goods, and tables 7.15 and 7.16 do the
same for corporations producing traded goods.

While profitability did not vary much through the period for the
producers of nontraded goods, it did vary greatly for the producers of
traded goods. This difference is related to the behavior of the real

Table 7.12   Argentina 1976–1980. Balance Sheet Ratios for a Sample of Large Private Corporations

Ratios		1976	1977	1978	1979	1980
Immobilization (1):	$\dfrac{\text{long-term assets}}{\text{net worth}}$	100.1	104.4	126.7	133.0	129.4
Immobilization (2):	$\dfrac{\text{long-term assets}}{\text{net worth} + \text{long-term debt}}$	71.1	88.9	92.6	93.6	91.6
Liquidity:	$\dfrac{\text{cash} + \text{investments(s-t)} + \text{credits}}{\text{short-term debt}}$	60.6	63.1	63.6	61.6	64.5
Leverage (total):	$\dfrac{\text{total debt}}{\text{net worth}}$	67.5	85.2	99.6	104.9	107.0
Leverage (short-term):	$\dfrac{\text{short-term debt}}{\text{net worth}}$	49.7	67.7	62.6	62.9	65.8
Leverage (long-term):	$\dfrac{\text{long-term debt}}{\text{net worth}}$	17.7	17.4	36.9	42.0	41.2
Leverage (in foreign currencies):	$\dfrac{\text{debt in foreign currencies}}{\text{net worth}}$	26.3	22.6	33.3	32.8	30.6
Net financial position in domestic currency		−3.4	−7.3	−3.4	−5.1	−3.8
Net financial position in foreign currencies		−13.4	−10.3	−14.9	−15.8	−14.8

Sources: See Appendix B.

Table 7.13   **Argentina 1976–1980. Balance Sheets, Profit and Loss Statements for a Sample of Private Corporations That Sell Nontraded Goods**

	1976	1977	1978	1979	1980
	Balance Sheets				
Assets	100.0	100.0	100.0	100.0	100.0
Cash	1.5	2.3	1.2	1.0	1.9
Short-term investments	2.9	3.1	1.6	3.3	5.5
Credits	15.6	21.6	18.3	16.1	15.6
Inventories	29.1	23.0	17.7	18.4	18.0
Long-term assets	50.9	50.0	61.2	61.2	59.0
Short-term debt	32.7	37.2	26.3	28.7	28.4
Commercial	14.2	14.9	9.8	10.4	10.2
Foreign	8.4	5.0	4.9	6.3	6.7
Banks	4.4	11.3	7.4	7.7	6.7
Others	5.7	6.0	4.2	4.3	4.8
Long-term debt	11.6	10.1	27.4	26.5	22.5
Foreign	10.3	6.2	16.6	11.8	10.6
Banks	0.0	1.4	8.6	10.8	9.4
Others	1.3	2.5	2.2	3.9	2.5
Net worth	55.7	52.7	46.3	44.8	49.1
	Profit and Loss Statements				
Sales	100.0	100.0	100.0	100.0	100.0
Cost of sales	72.8	72.7	70.4	75.1	80.0
Gross margin	27.2	27.3	29.6	24.9	20.0
Financial costs	9.9	9.9	10.7	7.6	5.6
Other costs (marketing, administrative, etc.)	16.3	14.2	20.0	15.8	15.6
Net profits	1.0	3.2	−1.1	1.5	−1.2

Sources: See Appendix B.

exchange rate during the period as a consequence of the balance of payments crisis at the beginning and the reliance on controlling the money supply and the nominal exchange rate in the following years. In addition, structural adjustments made as a result of the opening of the economy obviously affected the producers of traded goods more. Access to foreign credit, as to other long-term loans, seems to have been easier for producers of nontraded goods, although producers of traded goods should have demanded a higher proportion of credit in foreign currencies because of the link between their sale prices and the exchange rate. Difficulties created for the finances of private business by the stabilization policy were much more important for producers of traded goods than for producers of nontraded goods.

Foreign financing was channeled mainly into the domestic economy by the local branches of foreign banks. These banks applied evaluation rules that were more easily fulfilled by large firms and producers of nontraded

Table 7.14   **Argentina 1976–1980. Balance Sheet Ratios for a Sample of Private Corporations That Sell Nontraded Goods**

Ratios		1976	1977	1978	1979	1980
Immobilization (1):	long-term assets / net worth	91.4	94.9	132.2	136.6	120.2
Immobilization (2):	long-term assets / net worth + long-term debt	75.6	79.6	83.0	85.8	82.4
Liquidity:	cash + investments(s-t) + credits / short-term debt	61.2	72.6	80.2	71.1	81.0
Leverage (total):	total debt / net worth	79.5	89.8	116.0	123.2	103.7
Leverage (short-term):	short-term debt / net worth	58.7	70.6	56.8	64.1	57.8
Leverage (long-term):	long-term debt / net worth	20.8	19.2	59.2	59.2	45.8
Leverage (in foreign currencies):	debt in foreign currencies / net worth	33.6	21.3	46.4	40.4	35.2
Net financial position in domestic currency		−8.6	−5.2	−0.3	−2.0	1.3
Net financial position in foreign currencies		−14.4	−7.6	−19.7	−18.0	−7.2

Sources: See Appendix B.

Table 7.15   **Argentina 1976–1980. Balance Sheets, Profit and Loss Statements for a Sample of Private Firms That Sell Traded Goods**

	1976	1977	1978	1979	1980
	Balance Sheets				
Assets	100.0	100.0	100.0	100.0	100.0
Cash	2.1	3.3	2.2	1.8	1.7
Short-term investments	2.2	2.3	1.9	1.8	1.8
Credits	13.2	15.7	15.5	14.7	13.8
Inventories	17.1	18.9	16.1	15.0	15.2
Long-term assets	65.4	59.8	64.3	66.7	67.5
Short-term debt	27.8	36.1	34.9	32.6	34.0
Commercial	11.4	10.4	9.7	7.8	7.1
Foreign	7.9	8.1	6.5	6.7	9.5
Banks	2.2	13.4	14.6	14.4	13.4
Others	6.3	4.2	4.1	3.7	4.0
Long-term debt	9.8	8.8	12.5	15.6	17.5
Foreign	4.7	3.8	6.4	7.2	7.5
Banks	0.5	0.8	2.4	6.1	6.6
Others	4.6	4.2	3.7	2.3	3.4
Net worth	62.4	55.1	52.6	51.8	48.5
	Profit and Loss Statements				
Sales	100.0	100.0	100.0	100.0	100.0
Cost of sales	65.6	73.1	71.9	72.9	78.0
Gross margin	34.4	26.9	28.1	27.1	22.0
Financial costs	8.9	10.7	14.3	11.3	10.5
Other costs (marketing, administrative, etc.)	19.3	15.5	17.8	18.3	19.8
Net profits	6.2	0.7	−4.0	−2.5	−8.3

Sources: See Appendix B.

goods. Smaller firms and the producers of riskier, traded goods had to get their financing from institutions which operated almost exclusively with domestic funds.

7.3   Conclusions

The experience of Argentina between 1970 and 1976 shows that relaxation of anti-inflationary targets, uncontrolled inflation, and negative real interest rates provide an automatic solution to the financing of private business. The most important aspects of private business financing in such a context are to sort out the limitations imposed by the credit rationing criteria and to be able to collect the highest possible amount of subsidies in the financial markets. In this context, foreign financing is avoided unless it can be contracted with exchange insurance.

Table 7.16   Argentina 1976–1980. Balance Sheet Ratios for a Sample of Private Corporations That Sell Traded Goods

Ratios		1976	1977	1978	1979	1980
Immobilization (1):	$\dfrac{\text{long-term assets}}{\text{net worth}}$	104.8	108.5	122.2	128.8	139.2
Immobilization (2):	$\dfrac{\text{long-term assets}}{\text{net worth} + \text{long-term debt}}$	90.6	93.6	98.8	99.0	102.3
Liquidity:	$\dfrac{\text{cash} + \text{investments(s-t)} + \text{credits}}{\text{short-term debt}}$	62.9	59.0	56.2	56.1	50.9
Leverage (total):	$\dfrac{\text{total debt}}{\text{net worth}}$	60.3	81.5	90.1	93.1	106.2
Leverage (short-term):	$\dfrac{\text{short-term debt}}{\text{net worth}}$	44.6	65.5	66.3	62.9	70.1
Leverage (long-term):	$\dfrac{\text{long-term debt}}{\text{net worth}}$	15.7	16.0	23.8	30.1	36.1
Leverage (in foreign currencies):	$\dfrac{\text{debt in foreign currencies}}{\text{net worth}}$	20.2	21.6	24.5	26.8	35.1
Net financial position in domestic currency		-2.4	-6.7	-8.8	-7.6	-7.2
Net financial position in foreign currencies		-11.6	-11.0	-11.1	-13.7	-17.0

Sources: See Appendix B.

When stabilization plans are applied, financial management again becomes relevant for private business because internal sources of financing are insufficient, and the real cost of debt financing becomes positive and relevant in most of the financial markets. This is shown by the analysis of the Krieger-Vasena and Martínez de Hoz plans. The comparison of these two experiences shows that the financial problems of private business can significantly increase by special features of the stabilization plans, like large credit requirements by the public sector originating in big government deficits and the imposition on firms of costly structural adjustments caused by long-term policies (e.g., the opening of the economy). The simultaneity of these two sources of complications can be damaging to the success of the stabilization plan, because large government deficits are the source of large interest rate differentials between domestic and foreign markets and the overvaluation of the domestic currency when domestic credit creation is controlled. Under these conditions an uneven distribution of the stabilization burden is likely to result as small firms and producers of traded goods face difficulties in obtaining financing in foreign markets and are compelled to pay the high real costs of domestic credit. These differences are clearly shown by the balance sheet structures and ratios for a sample of corporations during the period 1976–1980.

Balance sheet figures show that after 1976 there was a significant reduction of inventories on the assets side, and on the liabilities side, short-term bank debt replaced, in part, short-term commercial debt. These are expected results of the higher real interest rates and the increase in short-term financial intermediation resulting from the liberalization of interest rates.

More surprising is the increase in leverage, especially in the form of long-term debt. Although domestic banking regulations did not favor the development of the long-term debt market, the increase in long-term debt relative to net worth took place mainly as a result of an increase in financing from abroad, special investment financing provided by state banks, and refinancing of debts for firms facing financial problems. Net worth was negatively affected by the drastic reduction of profitability that is observed especially in 1978 and 1980.

The central analytical question that emerges from the observation of the Argentine experience during the Martínez de Hoz period is: Why do firms rely more and more on debt financing even though it is very costly in real terms? When entrepreneurs are faced with this question, the usual answer is that losses have to be financed and debt financing is the only available alternative. But why not a more drastic reduction of fixed investments accompanying the observed reduction of inventories? There are several institutional reasons that can explain why there is no big reduction of fixed investments: the existence of long-term and relatively cheaper credit from the state-owned banks which is earmarked for new investments; the existence of fiscal incentives, like reduced tariffs on capital good imports and tax credits. The recent Argentine experience suggests that still another explanation of more general interest exists. Doubts about the soundness of the government's commitment to maintain its anti-inflationary strategy create uncertainties that keep alive the expectation that the high real cost of credit is a transitory phenomenon. Previous experience suggests that every anti-inflationary plan is followed by a period of accelerating inflation that reverses the sign of financial costs. Of course, there are instrumental aspects of anti-inflationary policies which can create unnecessary uncertainties, like the simultaneous announcement of contradictory targets and the reluctance of the government to adopt a firm commitment to its policies, the success of which depends crucially on people's confidence that those policies will be maintained for a long period of time.

Appendix A *Sources and Methodology for Table 7.3*

Debt financing was computed as the difference between the amount of debts at the end and the beginning of the periods, deflated by the Wholesale Price Index of December of the respective year. The sources and coverage of the different components are the following:

Debt with Domestic Markets. Banco Central de la República Argentina. *Boletín Estadístico Mensual*, several issues. These figures were obtained by subtracting from M_3 (financial assets held by the nonfinancial private sector) the debt of the public sector net of deposits with the financial system and net foreign assets of the financial system. The disaggregation between free and controlled interest rate markets was done by allocating to the free interest rate market the amount of the "bill bank acceptances" from 1970 to 1975, and the "bill bank acceptances" plus the amount of time deposits in 1976. From 1977 the whole debt is with the free interest rate market.

Debt with Foreign Markets. A. Arnaudo and R. Bartolomei. 1967–1971. *Mercado cambiario e inflación, Argentina*. México: CEMLA; and Banco Central de la República Argentina. *Memorias Anual*, several issues. The disaggregation into debt with and without exchange insurance was done by allocating to the first one the net sales of foreign exchange in the futures market by the central bank at the end of each year, as reported by the Banco Central de la República Argentina. *Boletín Estadístico Mensual*, several issues.

Equity capital financing was computed from annual flow figures, deflated by the annual average of the Wholesale Price Index. The sources of the two components were:

Stock Market. Banco Central de la República Argentina. *Memorias Anual*, several issues.

Direct Foreign Investment. Ministerio de Economía. 1967–1976. Unpublished manuscript; and Banco Central de la República Argentina. 1977–1980. *Memorias Anual*, several issues.

Net results from operating in financial markets were obtained using the information on debt financing and table 7.2 as follows: the profit (+) or loss (−) in each market is obtained for each year by multiplying the initial debt at constant price times the real interest rate.

Depreciation allowances and operating results were calculated as the difference between gross private investment and all other sources.

Gross private investment was calculated as the difference between overall gross investment and gross public investment. The former was taken from Banco Central de al República Argentina. 1975. *Sistema de cuentas del producto e ingreso de la República Argentina*, vol. 2, and quarterly updating reports; and Banco Central de la República Argentina. 1980. *Gerencia de investigación estadísticas Económicas*. Gross public investment was estimated from the information reported in Ministerio de Economía. 1980. *Evolución económica de la Argentina*.

Appendix B *Sampling Criteria*

A list of all corporations whose shares are traded in the Buenos Aires Stock Exchange was prepared, recording their names, main industrial groups, and amounts of sales from their last balance sheet reports. A sample comprised of approximately 25 percent of the firms was taken.

Corporations were classified by industrial group and by three size categories. Size was determined on the basis of sales. Limits for size stratification were determined in order to have an equal number of firms in each stratum. Therefore, a two-entry table (one by size and the other by industrial group) was constructed.

Firms were selected from the first-size stratum (big firms) and the third-size stratum (small firms) only. The criterion was to select a sample of 20 percent of all the firms from each cell (similar size and same industrial group) with a minimum of three. In the case of incomplete or missing information, firms were replaced by others within the same cell when possible.

The classification of firms in the traded goods and nontraded goods categories was made on the basis of a correlation between changes in wholesale prices of the group of products corresponding to the industrial groups used in the study and changes in the price of the dollar. Those groups that showed a simple correlation coefficient of greater than 60 were classified as traded good producers, and those with a lower correlation coefficient as nontrade good producers.

References

Arnaudo, Aldo A., Domingo F. Cavallo, and Aldo A. Dadone. 1978. Evaluación de la eficiencia del actual régimen financiero Argentino. *Estudios* 2:50–58.
Cavallo, Domingo F., and Aldo A. Dadone. 1979. Índice implícito en la tasa testigo. *Estudios* 12:169–176.

Comment   Charles E. McLure, Jr.

Inflation-induced shifts in financial policy, such as those described by Cavallo and Petrei, would be expected by most economists. But they often can be captured only through the most imaginative and sophisticated use of advanced econometric techniques. A country such as Argentina, in which large shifts have occurred in macroeconomic policy, the rate of inflation, and real interest rates, provides the economist with virtually a laboratory experiment in which responses to changes in economic incentives can be observed much more easily. Even so, I am rather amazed at the degree to which Cavallo and Petrei have been able to discern clear patterns of response to changes in financial incentives created by changes in inflation and anti-inflation policies. Most of these responses are quite in line with what one would expect. There are some apparent anomalies, but the authors are able to provide reasonably convincing explanations, even in those cases.

Unanticipated inflation reduces real interest rates. This may, of course, affect saving and the availability of foreign capital. More to the point, if inflationary expectations are not symmetric, so that business firms expect a higher level of inflation than do lenders, and therefore a lower real rate of interest, there should be a decisive shift toward the use of debt financing by business.

Much of what appears to have occurred in Argentina confirms economic intuition. When inflation produced low real interest rates, firms

Charles E. McLure, Jr., is a senior fellow at the Hoover Institution, Stanford University, and a research associate of the National Bureau of Economic Research. At the time these comments were prepared, he was vice-president of NBER. The views expressed here are his own and not those of either the Hoover Institution or NBER.

attempted to capitalize on the situation through debt financing. But when interest rates were controlled at nominal levels that produced negative real rates, domestic funds dried up. Firms also seem to have responded in the way expected when restricted credit creation produced differentials in domestic and foreign interest rates or when subsidized insurance against exchange rate risk reduced the cost of borrowing abroad.

The one really anomalous result is the apparent lengthening of debt that occurred when inflation accelerated. I would have welcomed more evidence for the proposition that this lengthening can be traced to financing of long-term investment by state-owned banks. This might have been provided by a more detailed classification of sources of finance, if such is available. It would probably be difficult to document the assertion that refinancing of debts by firms in financial trouble was a further contributor to the increase in long-term financing.

My next comments reflect my background as a tax economist. We all know that inflation and the various policies governments adopt to fight it should have important influences on the way private businesses choose to operate and finance themselves. In the United States we think especially of effects working through the taxation of business income. If tax depreciation is based on the historical cost of assets, there will be a tendency for costs of goods sold to be understated and for profits subject to tax to be overstated. Similar effects can occur with inventories. If firms use first-in, first-out (FIFO) methods for valuing inventories, whether because they are required to do so by fiscal authorities or because they simply prefer to do so, perhaps in order to show larger book profits, taxable income will tend to be greater than economic income. Both these effects will tend to discourage investment in physical assets, and patterns of finance may adjust. Offsetting these tendencies is the allowance of deductions to firms for nominal interest payments. In many instances this more than offsets the first two tendencies to overstate profits. The incentive for firms to employ debt financing resulting from the interaction of inflation and the deductibility of nominal interest costs is accentuated if businessmen expect greater inflation than is reflected in the cost of funds in financial markets.

Not until the very end of their paper do Cavallo and Petrei mention the fiscal system of Argentina. But one can hardly help wondering the extent to which fiscal influences, including those mentioned earlier, were active in Argentina during the period of variable inflation under examination. In particular, I am not sufficiently familiar with the Argentine tax system to know whether depreciation allowances are based on historical cost depreciation or if replacement cost depreciation or indexing is allowed. Similarly, is FIFO required, or is LIFO (last-in, first-out) an acceptable method of inventory evaluation? Finally, is there any indexing of the value of debt that would eliminate the advantage of debt financing in an inflationary period? Perhaps even more important, there is no indication of whether the tax system has been stable over the period covered by the paper. Without attempting a very long shopping list, I might note that one wonders whether the treatment of depreciation or inventories might have changed in any important way during the period, whether provisions relating to the taxation of the return to lenders might have been altered, and whether the deductibility of interest (and nondeductibility of dividends, for that matter) changed during the period. Beyond that, one needs to know whether there are explicit subsidies to credit of one kind or another that might have been changed during the period.

The division of internal sources of finance into "net results from operating in financial markets" and "depreciation allowances and operating results" is, I believe, quite useful. Particularly noteworthy is that when the first of these is added to external debt financing this combined source of investment funds is a relatively stable contributor to the total. Calculating "depreciation allowances and operating results" as a residual has the virtue that one need not worry that they are calculated directly from financial statements, without adequate allowance for the effects of inflation. The same cannot, of course, be said for the information contained in tables 7.7–7.16. One does not know the extent to which inventories and long-term assets have been revalued to reflect inflation. Nor can one determine this from the data in the paper, since only ratios are provided. Do the commonly accepted financial standards in Argentina allow (or require) the revaluation of assets? This question has its counterpart in the profit and loss statements. Do the depreciation allowances and deductions for inventories used in the figures for cost of sales reflect inflation? Are the relatively modest rates of profits real, or do they contain fictitious profits resulting from inflation? Without satisfactory answers to these questions, I am a bit uneasy about attributing changes in financial patterns to intertemporal differences in profitability of firms.

I believe that this study could be usefully extended in several directions. First, I would expect producers of traded goods to be relatively large, and small firms to be especially heavily involved with the production of nontraded goods. Given that patterns of effects of inflation on financial practices are quite different for small firms and producers of traded goods, on the one hand, and for large firms and producers of nontraded goods, on the other hand, it may be that results from either two-way classification (traded vs. nontraded; large vs. small) really understate significant differences that would be revealed from a four-way (two-by-two) classification. That is, one might expect large producers of nontraded goods to be affected quite differently from small producers of traded goods, with the remaining two categories falling somewhere in between. It would be useful to have such a cross-classification, if the data would allow it.

A further exercise that would be useful, if data are available, would be to attempt to gain information on Argentine subsidiaries of foreign firms similar to that used for firms traded on the Buenos Aires Stock Exchange. While it is important to know how firms with primarily domestic ownership respond to inflation and anti-inflationary policies, it would be equally interesting to know how foreign-owned firms have responded to the same economic stimuli.

Comment   Andrew Abel

Domingo Cavallo and Humberto Petrei address the issue of financing private business in Argentina in the presence of high and variable rates of inflation. Their paper is an interesting blend of three sections: a brief review of Argentine macroeconomic performance from 1967 to 1980; an analysis of the sources of finance for investment based on aggregate data over this entire fourteen-year period; and an analysis of a sample of individual firm balance sheets during the Martínez de Hoz period (1977–1980).

The review of the Argentine economy provides an excellent introduction to readers not completely familiar with the Argentine experience. Cavallo and Petrei divide the fourteen-year period into five subperiods according to the extent to which government policies were directed against inflation. Because the paper focuses on the financing of private business, the macroeconomic summary properly devotes much attention to the behavior of interest rates—both nominal and real. However, the real interest rates tabulated by Cavallo and Petrei are apparently *ex post pretax* real interest rates. The interest rate relevant for decision making by firms is the *ex ante after-tax* real interest rate. The difference between ex ante and ex post real interest rates is equal to the forecast error of the rate of inflation. Although it may be reasonable to suppose that the forecast error has a mean of zero so that the ex post real rate is an unbiased measure of the ex ante real rate, the variance of this forecast error was probably quite large in Argentina. Since the reported ex post real interest rate is the sum of the ex ante real interest rate and the forecast error of inflation, the variance of the reported ex post real interest rate may greatly exceed the variance of the relevant ex ante real interest rate.

The distinction between pretax and after-tax real interest rates depends on the tax treatment of interest payments. It is well known that if nominal interest payments are tax deductible, then the after-tax real

Andrew Abel is an assistant professor in the Department of Economics, Harvard University, and a faculty research fellow of the National Bureau of Economic Research.

interest rate can be negative even though the pretax real interest rate is positive. Furthermore, the observation that the pretax real interest rate was higher in 1967–1969 than in 1970–1972 does not imply that the after-tax real interest rate was higher in 1967–1969 than in 1970–1972, even if the tax rate was the same in both periods. Of course, these comments apply to a situation in which nominal interest payments are tax deductible. It would be useful if the authors could briefly describe the tax treatment of interest payments in Argentina.

Perhaps the most interesting result of the analysis of the aggregate sources of finance is the finding that firms use external debt financing when inflation is being successfully fought, but they use internal financing when inflation is not being fought successfully. The most volatile component of internal financing is net results from operating in financial markets. Cavallo and Petrei point out that the sum of external debt financing and internal financing is much more stable than either of the two separate components. To interpret this finding, we observe that

$$(1) \qquad\qquad b = \frac{vB}{P} \, ,$$

where b is the real value of bonds outstanding, B is the number of bonds outstanding, v is the nominal value of a bond, and P is the price level. Differentiating (1) with respect to time and then subtracting rb from both sides of the equation, we obtain

$$(2) \qquad\qquad \dot{b} + \left(\pi - r - \frac{\dot{v}}{v}\right)b = \left(\frac{v}{P}\right)\dot{B} - rb \, ,$$

where r is the nominal interest rate, and $\pi = \dot{P}/P$ is the rate of inflation.

The first term on the left-hand side of (2) is the change in the real value of outstanding bonds and corresponds to the Cavallo-Petrei measure of external debt financing.

The second term on the left-hand side of (2) represents net results from operating in financial markets and is equal to the decrease in the real value of existing bonds $[\pi - (\dot{v}/v)]b$ minus the real value of nominal interest payments rb. Observe that the real value of existing bonds decreases both because of general price inflation (π) and because of any decrease in v, perhaps as a result of an increase in interest rates. Cavallo and Petrei measure the net results from operating in financial markets as $(\pi - r)b$, thereby ignoring capital gains or losses arising from the changing nominal valuation of existing bonds resulting from changing interest rates or interest rate expectations. Recognizing that $r = \rho^e + \pi^e$ is an identity (ignoring any taxation of interest) in which ρ^e is the ex ante real rate of interest and π^e is the expected rate of inflation, the Cavallo-Petrei measure of net results from operating in financial markets is $[(\pi - \pi^e) - \rho^e]b$. One interpretation of their finding that net results from operating in financial markets is high when inflation is not fought successfully, and low when inflation is successfully combated, is that the ex ante real interest rate, ρ^e, is fairly stable over time and that variations in $[(\pi - \pi^e) - \rho^e]b$ are mostly the result of variations in forecast errors about inflation. When inflation is lower than expected, the net operating results in financial markets are low; when inflation is higher than expected, net operating results in financial markets are high.

The Cavallo-Petrei result that the sum of external debt financing and net operating results in financial markets is more stable than its two components is equivalent to noting that the right-hand side of (2) is more stable than each of the two terms on the left-hand side of (2). The right-hand side of (2) is the excess of the real value of newly issued debt over the real value of interest payments on existing debt. This remains fairly stable in the presence of large swings in unanticipated inflation which cause large but opposite swings in the two terms on the left-hand side of (2). The swings in observed external debt financing and in observed net operating results are not the outcome of explicit action on the part of firms. Rather, much of the variation in the observed measures of these two sources of financing is due to variations in unanticipated inflation.

From the analysis of the sample of individual firm balance sheets in the period 1976–1980, it was found that a major source of profitability differences between large firms and small firms and between producers of nontraded goods and producers of traded goods is access to foreign credit. The real cost of credit was substantially lower in foreign markets than in domestic markets. Small firms and producers of traded goods tended to use foreign credit less than large firms and producers of nontraded goods, and their profitability suffered. The observation that small firms were generally confined to the domestic credit market with a higher interest rate than in the foreign market leads to an anomaly in the data on inventories. Cavallo and Petrei point out in table 7.7 a decline in the relative importance of inventories since 1977 and link this to policy changes regarding interest rates. However, table 7.9 reveals that for small firms, which as a group faced higher interest rates than the aggregate, the share of inventories in total assets actually rose over the period 1976–1980.

Cavallo and Petrei have skillfully combined data from different sources to provide some insights into the financing of private business in the presence of inflation. As they point out in their conclusion, further research is required to understand the behavior of investment during the Argentine experience with inflation.

8 Debt and the Current Account Deficit in Brazil

Olivier Jean Blanchard

One of the premises underlying the debate about economic policy in Brazil is that the country is accumulating too much external debt. Therefore, most of the proposed policies attempt, through either depreciation or a reduction in economic activity, to reduce the current account deficit. The purpose of this short paper is to question the validity of that premise and thus the necessity of such painful remedies.

Brazil indeed has a level of debt which is both high by international standards and increasing fast. The ratio of external guaranteed debt to GDP is approximately 25 percent, slightly lower than the Latin American average. The ratio of total external debt to GDP is probably around 35 percent. The current account deficit has increased rapidly since 1973, reaching 5 percent of GDP. This increase was initially the result of a larger trade balance deficit, and more recently the result of the higher nominal interest payments on existing debt.

Does this represent too high a level of debt and too high a current account deficit? As the current account is the difference between income and spending, the question can be rephrased as follows: Given the current levels of debt and capital, is consumption or investment spending too high? The underlying rate of growth is still high and expected to remain high. This suggests the feasibility of maintaining high levels of consumption together with the ability to repay debt in the future. The

Olivier Jean Blanchard is an associate professor in the Department of Economics, Harvard University, and a faculty research fellow of the National Bureau of Economic Research.

This paper was written while the author was on leave at the Hoover Institution. Financial assistance from the Hoover Institution and from the John Stauffer Charitable Trust is gratefully acknowledged.

The author wishes to thank Andrew Abel, Eliana Cardoso, Rudiger Dornbusch, and especially Jeff Sachs for suggestions and discussions.

rate of return on investment still largely exceeds the world real interest rate charged for similar projects; this suggests the desirability of further investment.

In order to answer the question, I proceed in three steps. In section 8.1, I specify what is probably the simplest model needed to address the question and show the qualitative features of the answer. In section 8.2, I refine the model just enough so that it can be used for simulations and give quantitative answers which have a semblance of relevance for Brazil. The results suggest that a country like Brazil can safely run a current account deficit at its present level. In section 8.3, I extend the question slightly by considering the possibility that Brazil may want, nevertheless, to reduce its current account deficit. The problem then becomes the allocation of the reduction in spending between consumption and investment. This section suggests that most of the decrease in spending should come from consumption rather than from investment.

8.1

To ask whether the current account deficit is too high is to ask whether investment or consumption spending is too high. Investment spending may be too high, even if the rate of return on capital exceeds the borrowing rate, if it is proceeding too fast and too inefficiently, wasting too many resources in return for future output. Consumption spending may be too high if the implied accumulation of debt leads to drastic reductions in future consumption.

To answer these two questions, a model must have at least two components. It must have a description of technology such that high rates of investment are associated with waste or high installation costs. It must have an objective function which allows the ordering of different paths of consumption. The following model is probably the simplest one:[1]

$$\max_{\{C,I\}} \int_0^\infty e^{-\Theta t} U(C_t)\,dt, \text{ subject to}$$

$$\dot{B}_t = C_t + I_t[1 + \psi(I_t)] + \Theta B_t - F(K_t, \bar{L}),$$

$$\dot{K}_t = I_t,$$

$$K_0, B_0, \text{ given}; \ \psi' > 0, \ F_K > 0, \ F_{KK} < 0.$$

Spending is the sum of consumption, C_t, and investment spending. Investment spending itself is the sum of investment, I_t, and "installation

1. This model is implicit in much of the literature on debt and the current account. This includes in particular work by Bardhan and Bruno in the 1960s, and more recently by Helpman, Obstfeld, Razin, Sachs, and Svensson, among others. An exhaustive bibliography is given in Svensson (1983).

costs" $I_t\psi(I_t)$; $\psi(\cdot)$ is an increasing function of I_t, implying higher installation cost per unit of investment for higher levels of investment.

The country can borrow or lend at the world interest rate, Θ. The excess of spending plus interest on debt, ΘB_t, over output, $F(K_t, \bar{L})$, is equal to the current account deficit, itself equal to the change in debt, $\dot{B}$. There are, in this simple model, no population growth ($L = \bar{L}$), no productivity growth, and no depreciation of capital; furthermore, the subjective discount rate is equal to the world interest rate; all these assumptions will be relaxed later.

The solution to the above problem as stated is probably difficult to advocate. It is to go deeper and deeper in debt forever, issuing new debt to meet interest payments. To avoid such Ponzi games, an additional condition is needed. The following will do:

$$\lim_{t \to \infty} e^{-\Theta t} B_t = 0.$$

Solving the first order conditions and rearranging gives the following characterization of the solution:

(1) $$1 + \psi(\dot{K}_t) + \dot{K}_t \psi'(\dot{K}_t) = q_t,$$

(2) $$\dot{q}_t = \Theta q_t - F_K(K_t, \bar{L}); \ \lim_{t \to \infty} e^{-\Theta t} q_t = 0,$$

(2') $$q_t = \int_t^\infty e^{-\Theta(s-t)} F_K(K_s, \bar{L}) ds,$$

and

(3) $$C_t = \bar{C},$$

(4) $$\dot{B}_t = \Theta B_t + C_t + \dot{K}_t[1 + \psi(\dot{K}_t)] - F(K_t, \bar{L}).$$

Equations (1), (2), and (2') characterize investment spending. Equation (1) says that investment should take place until the marginal cost of investing equals q_t. Equation (2) implies (2'), which gives q_t as the present value of future marginal products. The important characteristic of the solution is that investment spending depends only on the technology and the world rate of interest and does not depend on the objective function or the initial level of debt.

Once the investment problem has been solved to give the path of investment and the capital stock, the consumption problem can be solved using (3), (4), and the transversality condition we have imposed on debt. If, as we have assumed, the subjective discount rate is equal to the world interest rate, the preferred path of consumption is constant. The problem is then to find the highest sustainable level of consumption. Solving (4), using the transversality condition, gives consumption as function of net wealth:

$$C_t = \Theta[\int_t^\infty e^{-\Theta(s-t)}\{F(K_s,\bar{L})$$
$$- \dot{K}_s[1 + \psi(\dot{K}_s)]\}\,ds - B_t].$$

Consumption depends positively on the sequence of net output, negatively on existing debt.

Returning to the current account, this model suggests an essential asymmetry between investment and consumption. Whatever the initial level of debt, investment should proceed if the current marginal product exceeds the interest rate. Whether consumption should be high or not and, thus, whether the current account should be balanced or not depends very much on the initial level of debt and cannot be determined a priori. To get some idea of what the answer might be for Brazil, this initial model needs to be refined a little.

8.2

The purpose of this section is to derive, under different assumptions about growth, feasible paths of consumption for a country like Brazil. To do this, I must allow for population growth, n, time varying Harrod neutral technological progress β_t, a positive rate of capital depreciation δ, and let the subjective rate of discount Θ_t possibly vary over time. The model thus becomes:

$$\max_{\{C,I\}} \int_0^\infty L_t U\left(\frac{C_t}{L_t}\right) e^{-\int_0^t \Theta_s ds}\,dt,$$

subject to:

$$\dot{B}_t = C_t + I_t\left[1 + \psi\left(\frac{I_t}{K_t}\right)\right] + rB_t$$

$$- F(K_t, L_t e^{\int_0^t \beta_s ds}),$$

$$\dot{K}_t = I_t - \delta K_t,$$

$$K_0, B_0, \text{ given}.$$

The world interest rate is still assumed constant and is now denoted by r. The only additional modification is in the functional form of the installation cost of investment. The installation cost is now assumed to be a function of the ratio of investment to capital rather than of the level of investment. This assumption is more appropriate in a growing economy.

As usual, it is convenient to work with all variables divided by labor in efficiency units. They will be denoted by lower case letters. Solving the first order conditions gives a characterization very similar to the previous one. Investment and capital accumulation are characterized by:

$$(5) \qquad \frac{i_t}{k_t} \psi'\left(\frac{i_t}{k_t}\right) + \psi\left(\frac{i_t}{k_t}\right) = q_t - 1 ;$$

$$\dot{k}_t = i_t - (\delta + \beta_t + n)k_t ,$$

$$(6) \qquad \dot{q}_t = (\delta + r)q_t - \left[\left(\frac{i_t}{k_t}\right)^2 \psi'\left(\frac{i_t}{k_t}\right) + f'(k_t)\right].$$

Again, the rate of investment takes place until the marginal cost of investing is equal to the present value of marginal products, q_t. The slightly different specification of installation costs is responsible for the difference between equations (5) and (6) and the previous equations (1) and (2). Again, investment does not depend on tastes or the level of debt.

Consumption is now characterized by:

$$(7) \qquad \epsilon\left(\frac{\dot{c}_t}{c_t} + \beta_t\right) = \Theta_t - r; \; \epsilon \equiv \frac{C_t e^{\int_0^t \beta_s ds} U'}{U''} ,$$

$$(8) \qquad \dot{b}_t = (r - \beta_t - n)b_t + i_t\left[1 + \psi\left(\frac{i_t}{k_t}\right)\right] - f(k_t).$$

Equation (7) characterizes the path of consumption. If $\Theta_t = \Theta = r$, consumption in efficiency units decreases at rate β so that consumption per capita is constant as in the first model. If $\Theta_t = r + \epsilon\beta_t$, consumption in efficiency units is constant so that, along the optimal path, consumption per capita grows at the rate of technological progress. Equation (8) together with a nonexplosion condition for debt determines the highest feasible path of consumption.

To get quantitative answers, functional forms, initial conditions and values of the parameters must now be specified. I shall concentrate on the effects of varying two parameters. The first one, related to technology, is the rate of growth of technological progress. The second, related to the objective function, is the discount rate; varying it will allow consideration of different feasible consumption paths, given the technology. The rest of the model is specified as follows:

On the technology side, $f(\cdot)$ is Cobb-Douglas, with a share of capital of 25 percent. Depreciation is equal to 10 percent, population growth 1 percent. $\psi(\cdot)$ is linear: $\psi(i/k) = 2(i/k)$. This implies that a ratio of gross investment to capital of 10 percent per year leads to an installation cost of 20 percent of investment. The world real interest rate is 5 percent. This implies from equations (5) and (6) a steady state gross marginal product of 19 percent. The initial condition for capital is chosen so that the initial marginal product is 25 percent.

The utility function is logarithmic, so that $\epsilon = -1$. The initial ratio of debt to GNP is chosen to be approximately 50 percent, higher than the current Brazilian ratio.

The first set of simulations, reported in table 8.1, gives the highest sustainable *constant level of per capita consumption*. Variable Θ_t is set equal to r in all three simulations which represent three different hypotheses about the rate of technological progress. In all three cases, it is assumed to have a 1980 value of 6 percent. In the first case, this rate is assumed to decline by 5 percent per year, in the second by 10 percent, and in the third by 20 percent.

In view of the constant consumption per capita (which corresponds in the table to a decreasing consumption per efficiency unit) in a growing economy, the dramatic results in table 8.1 are easily understood. Optimal investment is approximately equal to 22 percent of GNP and relatively insensitive to the anticipated rate of growth. Consumption is, however, very sensitive; even in the "pessimistic" case, consumption is initially larger than production, and debt increases to 3 times GNP. The required trade balance surplus in steady state represents 10 percent of GNP.

What these three simulations show is the high level of sustainable consumption in a rapidly growing economy and the associated large

Table 8.1   Constant Consumption per Capita

Year	β	$f(k)$	c	i	cad	tbd	b
			Optimistic				
1980	.060	.70	1.27	.16	.83	.81	.40
1981	.057	.71	1.19	.16	.77	.71	1.20
1985	.047	.73	.95	.15	.59	.42	3.45
1990	.037	.75	.76	.14	.45	.20	5.01
2000	.023	.76	.57	.13	.30	−.01	6.49
2020	.014	.76	.40	.11	.16	−.21	7.57
			Intermediate				
1980	.060	.70	.96	.15	.50	.48	.40
1981	.055	.71	.90	.15	.45	.40	.87
1985	.037	.73	.73	.14	.29	.19	2.09
1990	.023	.74	.62	.12	.18	.04	2.83
2000	.009	.76	.53	.11	.10	−.07	3.39
2020	.001	.77	.49	.11	.04	−.14	3.61
			Pessimistic				
1980	.060	.70	.80	.14	.33	.31	.40
1981	.050	.71	.75	.14	.28	.24	.70
1985	.024	.73	.63	.13	.14	.07	1.40
1990	.010	.75	.58	.12	.07	−.01	1.76
2000	.002	.76	.55	.11	.02	−.07	1.97
2020	.000	.77	.55	.11	.02	−.08	2.01

Note: All variables in efficiency units. cad = current account deficit. tbd = trade balance deficit.

initial trade balance deficits. Constant consumption per capita in a growing economy is, however, neither politically feasible nor desirable. A more relevant path of consumption may be a path where consumption per capita grows at the rate of technological progress, or where, equivalently, consumption per efficiency unit is constant. Returning to equation (7), we can find the best feasible paths satisfying this condition by putting $\Theta_t = r + \epsilon\beta_t$. As ϵ is negative, this implies a discount rate smaller than the world interest rate. This assumption is made in the three simulations reported in table 8.2. In all three cases, the 1980 value of β_t is 6 percent. In the first simulation, this rate declines by 5 percent per year, in the second by 10 percent, and in the third by 20 percent.

As the assumptions about technology are the same as before, investment and output are the same as in table 8.1. The level of consumption is different, however. Because of the assumption linking the discount rate to the rate of technological progress, the initial level of consumption is approximately insensitive to the rate of technological progress. What allows consumption to be relatively high initially compared to income is

Table 8.2   **Constant Consumption per Efficiency Unit**

Year	β	$f(k)$	c	i	cad	tbd	b
			Optimistic				
1980	.060	.70	.58	.16	.14	.12	.40
1981	.057	.71	.58	.16	.13	.10	.51
1985	.047	.73	.58	.15	.09	.05	.79
1990	.037	.75	.58	.14	.06	.02	.96
2000	.023	.76	.58	.13	.04	−.01	1.10
2020	.014	.76	.58	.11	.03	−.03	1.25
			Intermediate				
1980	.060	.70	.59	.15	.14	.12	.40
1981	.055	.71	.59	.15	.13	.10	.51
1985	.037	.73	.59	.14	.07	.04	.77
1990	.023	.74	.59	.12	.05	.01	.92
2000	.009	.76	.59	.11	.03	−.02	1.05
2020	.001	.77	.59	.11	.01	−.04	1.11
			Pessimistic				
1980	.060	.70	.59	.14	.13	.11	.40
1981	.050	.71	.59	.14	.11	.09	.49
1985	.024	.73	.59	.13	.07	.03	.75
1990	.010	.75	.59	.12	.05	−.00	.91
2000	.002	.76	.59	.11	.02	−.03	1.03
2020	.000	.77	.59	.11	.01	−.04	1.04

Note: All variables in efficiency units. cad = current account deficit. tbd = trade balance deficit.

the anticipated capital accumulation and capital deepening. The highest feasible path of consumption implies an initial trade balance deficit of 16 percent, and the trade balance remains in deficit for approximately ten years. In steady state, the country must run a trade balance surplus equal to 4 percent of GNP to meet interest payments on debt. All three simulations suggest that the present levels of trade balance and current account deficits in Brazil can be run quite safely.

The steady state level of debt, as opposed to the steady state capital stock, depends on both the initial conditions and the path of the economy. In all three simulations, the optimal path of consumption is associated with a high level of steady state debt, equal to approximately 1.5 times GNP. Such a level of debt may be considered unacceptable, not, as we have seen, because of issues of solvency, but for reasons of political risk. This may be particularly true if most of the capital inflow is in the form of direct investment. In section 8.3, I include this potential cost of high levels of debt and consider its implications.

8.3

The simplest way of taking account of the nonmonetary costs of foreign debt is to extend the objective function to include a "disutility of debt" function, so that the maximization problem now has as an objective function:

$$\max_{\{c, i\}} \int_0^\infty [U(c_t e^{\int_0^t \beta_s ds}) - G(b_t)] e^{nt - \int_0^t \Theta_s ds} dt.$$

The function is directly stated in terms of efficiency units. The "disutility of debt," $G(b_t)$, is a function of the level of debt per efficiency unit. Not much would be changed if it was made a function of debt per capita or of the ratio of debt to income. $G(\cdot)$ is such that $G' > 0$; $G'' \geq 0$.

The first order conditions are similar to the conditions of section 8.2, except for the equations characterizing the movement of q and c over time. Those are now:

(6') $$\dot{q}_t = (\delta + r + \lambda_t) q_t - \left[\left(\frac{i_t}{k_t} \right)^2 \psi' \left(\frac{i_t}{k_t} \right) + f'(k_t) \right],$$

(7') $$\epsilon \left(\frac{\dot{c}_t}{c_t} + \beta \right) = \Theta_t - r - \lambda_t,$$

where

$$\lambda_t \equiv G'(b_t) / e^{\int_0^t \beta_s ds} U'(c_t e^{\int_0^t \beta_s ds}).$$

The interpretation of these conditions is straightforward. The presence of a disutility of debt function implies that the relevant interest rate for both consumption and investment decisions is not r, but $r + \lambda_t$, where λ_t is simply equal to the ratio of the marginal disutility of debt to marginal utility of consumption. A high marginal disutility of debt implies a high shadow interest rate, a substitution of consumption in favor of consumption in the future and a decrease in investment.

I shall use as a benchmark the first simulation of table 8.2, so that I derive the highest feasible path of consumption under the assumptions that $\Theta_t = r + \epsilon\beta_t$ and that the rate of technological progress decreases by 5 percent per year. The assumption that $\Theta_t = r + \epsilon\beta_t$, together with the assumption that $U(\cdot)$ is logarithmic, implies that

$$\frac{\dot{c}_t}{c_t} = \lambda_t .$$

In steady state, if it is ever reached, λ_t must therefore be equal to zero. This in turn implies $G'(b) = 0$, so that this equation determines the steady state level of debt. In the light of this, I specify $G(b)$ to be:

$$G(b_t) = g(b_t - .4)^2, \ g \geq 0 .$$

This implies that the level of debt must return eventually to its initial value of .4. Different values of g will imply different paths of debt over time but leave the steady state level unchanged. Table 8.3 gives the results for three values of g: 0, .005, .075.

Table 8.3 indicates that, if a reduction in the growth of debt has to be achieved, it must be done by reducing consumption rather than investment. The investment path remains approximately unchanged as the marginal cost of debt is increased, as g increases from 0 to .075. A decrease in investment, although it decreases the current trade deficit, would lead to a decrease in potential output, either increasing future trade deficits given consumption or requiring a decrease in future consumption. The implication of this result is that even if the cost of debt is high ($g = .075$) so that debt never reaches more than 75 percent of GNP, it is better to run a trade balance deficit initially, when investment spending is high.

The main conclusion of this last set of simulations is that, if a reduction in the growth of debt must be achieved, investment spending and consumption spending should not be treated identically. Measures such as an exchange rate depreciation or a recession are likely to affect both investment and consumption, or even to alter investment more than consumption, and are therefore not attractive in this respect.

8.4 Conclusion

The above analysis suggests that from the point of view of solvency, Brazil's current account deficit is not a major problem. It also suggests

Table 8.3   Debt-Constrained Paths

Year	$f(k)$	c	i	cad	tbd	b
			$(g = 0)$			
1980	.70	.58	.16	.14	.12	.40
1981	.71	.58	.16	.13	.10	.51
1985	.73	.58	.15	.09	.05	.79
1990	.75	.58	.14	.06	.02	.96
2000	.76	.58	.13	.04	−.01	1.10
2020	.76	.58	.11	.03	−.03	1.25
			$(g = 0.005)$			
1980	.70	.56	.16	.11	.09	.40
1981	.71	.56	.15	.09	.07	.48
1985	.73	.56	.14	.06	.02	.66
1990	.74	.56	.13	.03	.00	.72
2000	.75	.57	.12	.02	−.01	.71
2020	.76	.59	.11	.01	−.02	.64
			$(g = 0.075)$			
1980	.70	.53	.15	.07	.05	.40
1981	.71	.53	.15	.05	.03	.44
1985	.73	.54	.14	.03	.00	.48
1990	.74	.56	.13	.02	−.00	.46
2000	.75	.57	.12	.00	−.01	.45
2020	.76	.60	.11	.00	−.01	.41

Note: cad = current account deficit; tbd = trade balance deficit.

that, if Brazil does not want to accumulate high levels of debt, the reduction in the deficit should come mostly from consumption rather than from investment.

The model used to reach these conclusions is quite simplistic, and it is useful to point to some of the ways in which these conclusions could potentially be overturned:

The implicit assumption of the model is the "one good" assumption, or equivalently, that the terms of trade are constant. If there is an anticipated adverse shift in the terms of trade, this would lead to lower levels of feasible consumption and trade balance deficit.

The explicit assumptions of the model about technology may be challenged. Government guarantees on private loans make these loans less risky than they truly are, and the difference between the rate of return and the true interest rate may be smaller than assumed above.

Finally, even the consumption sequences of tables 8.2 and 8.3 may be politically infeasible. Any trade balance deficit must be followed at some time by a trade balance surplus. If, for example, we required consumption to be growing at the same rate as income—rather than at the rate of technological progress, as in table 8.2—the initial level of consumption would be reduced and so would the trade deficit. This raises issues about the ability of fiscal policy to affect consumption and domestic savings, which have not been considered here.

Reference

Svensson, Lars E. O. 1983. Oil prices, welfare, and the trade balance. *Quarterly Journal of Economics*, forthcoming.

9   Trying to Stabilize:
         Some Theoretical Reflections
         Based on the Case
         of Argentina
         Guillermo A. Calvo

During the period of 1976–1980, the Argentine peso suffered a "real" appreciation against the U.S. dollar of about 100 percent (see table 9.1). This phenomenon is also noticeable if one takes into account the estimates of Rodriguez and Sjaastad (1979), which suggest that part, but not all, of the reason is that the "long-run" equilibrium real exchange rate also appreciated during the same period.

One possible reaction to these facts is to interpret the difference between the actual and long-run equilibrium exchange rate as an indication of short-run "disequilibrium," and then build up models to explain it. This was the course followed by Rodriguez (1979) and Dornbusch (1980). The former assumed adaptive (nonrational) expectations, while Dornbusch assumed that there is inertia in the actual rate of inflation or, more formally, that the rate of inflation is a "state" variable. In both models a reduction in the rate of devaluation (the policy explicitly undertaken since January 1979) appreciates the real exchange rate. This is so because the papers assume that the price of tradables is proportional to the nominal exchange rate; thus, in Dornbusch (1980) the implication is immediate because the growth rate of the price of tradables would be reduced, whereas the price growth rate of nontradables is, by assumption, given in the short run; in Rodriguez (1979), on the other hand, perfect capital mobility implies that a lower rate of devaluation results in a lower domestic nominal rate of interest. Since inflationary expectations

Guillermo A. Calvo is a professor in the Department of Economics, Columbia University.

The work on this paper was performed while the author held a fellowship from the John S. Guggenheim Foundation and was a Visiting Professor at Centro de Estudios Macroeconómicos de Argentina, Buenos Aires, and the University of Chicago. Special thanks are given to Leonardo Auernheimer, Juan Carlos De Pablo, Roque Fernandez, and Carlos Rodríguez for their advice, but not necessarily their consent.

199

Table 9.1   Real Exchange Rates

	(a)	(b)		(a)	(b)
1977	162.8	144.0	1979	92.0	92.9
1978	137.5	114.0	1980	74.0	82.4

Source: Same as table 9.2; (a) U.S. Wholesale Price Index times the peso/dollar exchange rate divided by CPI of Argentina; (b) same denominator as in (a), but numerator is 0.7 times Agriculture-Cattle Raising Price Index *plus* 0.3 times Import Price Index.

are given in the short run, we also have a fall in the real interest rate that, by stimulating aggregate demand, appreciates the real exchange rate.

Another way of reacting to these facts is to search for "general equilibrium" explanations where behavioral equations could, in principle, be derived from optimization processes and where individuals have rational expectations (in the sense used in the current macroeconomic work; see, e.g., Sargent and Wallace 1975).[1] This is the type of model that we will discuss in this paper.

To familiarize the reader with the Argentine economy from March 1976 (when the military coup took place), section 9.1 will be an outline of the main policies and the available empirical evidence for that period. This will also serve as background and motivation for the models of the next section.

Section 9.2 will start with a brief review of the important work of Rodriguez and Sjaastad (1979) on which, as noted before, rests the idea that the real value of the peso lies above its long-run level. Then we will present essentially three types of models. The first one studies the impact of a portfolio shift from dollars to domestic capital (land); the second model emphasizes the substitutability of domestic and foreign monetary assets. Finally, the third model examines the effects of the announced exchange rate policy's lack of credibility on the minds of the public.

The main message of this paper is that there are simple, realistic, general equilibrium models that have the potential to account for at least some of the divergence between the actual and the long-run equilibrium real exchange rates. How much these models can explain, however, is an open question that must await further study.

9.1   Some Stylized Facts

The explicit objectives of the military government were to substantially reduce the rate of inflation from world-record levels and to start a process of trade and banking liberalization. All of this was supposed to take place

1. Dornbusch (1980) would also belong to this class of models if one could find a rationale for his price-setting equation.

without causing a sizable increase in the rate of unemployment.[2] To carry out these almost-impossible sounding objectives, J. A. Martínez de Hoz was put at the helm of the Ministry of Economics; he, in turn, appointed Adolfo Diz as head of the central bank.[3]

Despite the stability of the economics team and a visible trend toward fulfilling the original objectives, economic policy was not always clearly understood by the public. Part of the reason for this "lack of clarity" was, of course, that at the beginning the new administration was engaged in both dismantling long-inherited price distortions and trying to substantially cut a large budget deficit (the fiscal deficit in 1975 was over 12 percent of GNP and revenue was less than 25 percent of expenditure), a program that was hard to carry out by means of across-the-board, clear-cut measures, especially given the above-mentioned unemployment constraints. But, in addition, there is some consensus among economic observers that an important source of private-sector confusion also had to do with the minister's admitted bias toward discretionary policy ("pragmatism" in the Argentine jargon).

The period from March 1976 to December 1978 was by far the most turbulent in terms of radical changes; the one that was most completely accomplished was the decontrol of the banking system. The latter developed from a system with very negative interest rates, where the central bank was the only "owner" of deposits (except for savings banks, "financieras," that were heavily controlled), to a situation where interest rates on time deposits were left to fluctuate in response to market forces, banks were free to choose their loan portfolios, and barriers on international capital mobility were substantially lifted.

The second important change during that period (1976–1978) was the (partial) elimination of wage, price, and trade controls. Price controls were practically removed in April 1976. Guidelines on minimum wages were kept, but by all accounts, the latter became nonbinding (i.e., the market equilibrium wage lay above the minimum). Subsidies on nontraditional exports were phased out as was also the case with taxes on traditional exports (meat, wheat, etc.). Import tariffs were substantially reduced with the exception of steel, which is considered to be a strategic sector. Apparently, however, by December 1978, tariff reductions did little more than just eliminate redundant protection.

Monetary policy was perhaps the least clear aspect of the economic program during this period. It started with an inexplicitly defined "crawl-

2. Apparently unemployment was seen as a potential breeding ground for the guerrilla groups that were still very active and powerful in 1976.

3. They, as most of the other officials appointed in 1976, kept their positions until the official end of their appointments (March 1981), a fact that, as noted by De Pablo (1980), makes this by far the longest-lived economics team in recent Argentine history. According to De Pablo, from 1945 to 1976 the average term of a minister of economics was 347 days, and only eleven out of thirty-two ministers lasted for more than a year.

ing peg" system and finally converged, in 1978, with an equally unclear "dirty float" regime. These points are worth keeping in mind, for while we observe a decline in the fiscal deficit and in the growth rate of the monetary base, these otherwise important components of a stabilization program are bound to lose their effectiveness, or to operate in perverse ways, if economic agents do not understand the (implicit) policy rules.[4]

The period from January 1979 to December 1980 was relatively calm in terms of fundamental structural changes. In addition, in contrast to the previous period (1976–1978), monetary policy became relatively transparent. Beginning in January 1979, the government announced the future exchange rate until October of that year (with a declining rate of devaluation) and *promised* to continue with that type of policy until March 1981 (when a new administration would take charge). Although in January 1979 a prefixed schedule for the dollar exchange rate was not set for after October, it was understood that from then on the rate of devaluation was going to steadily decline until it reached zero by March 1981. Restrictions on capital mobility were relaxed further, although an important imperfection was kept: except for some minimal amounts, foreign capital could not be repatriated until it had been in the country for a year. This is important because the administration never prefixed the exchange rate for more than six months. In July 1980, however, free capital mobility was allowed (practically). Until November 1980 the prefixed rate was fully honored. From December, there was a slight upward revision of the "rate" of devaluation relative to that announced in July 1980 (it went from 1 percent to about 2 percent a month).[5]

As seen in table 9.2, from 1977 to 1980 the annual (November-to-November) CPI inflation rate fell from 177 percent to 89 percent, the sharpest decrease being in 1980 (particularly in the last months). This contrasts with the rate of devaluation that went from 117 percent to 27 percent. As a result, all reasonable estimates of the "real" exchange rate show a marked decline over the entire period (see table 9.1). For future reference, the appreciation of the real rate started before January 1979.

4. Here we come across an example of the "pragmatism" that prevailed, especially during the 1976–1978 period.

5. A more precise chronology is as follows (I owe this to De Pablo): On December 20, 1978, the government announced the dollar exchange rate for the period from 1-1-79 to 8-31-79; on April 10, such schedule was extended up to the end of 1979. In October 1979, the rate was announced up to (virtually) March 1980, after which it was understood that the rate of devaluation of a given month was going to be the same of the previous one minus 0.2 percent. September 1980 marks what, with the benefit of hindsight, we might call "the beginning of the end," because contrary to what was declared in December 1978, the rate of devaluation for October and succeeding months was announced to be 1 percent per month; however, in December the "ask" rate was allowed to grow at 2 percent, while the "bid" rate was kept as 1 percent per month. Finally, toward the end of the Videla-Martínez de Hoz administration (2-2-81 to be exact), the peso was unexpectedly devalued by 10 percent and a rate of devaluation of 3 percent per month was announced for the "future" (see section 9.3).

Table 9.2

Year	CPI Rate of Inflation	U.S. Dollar Rate of Devaluation
1977	177.5	117.4
1978	165.5	73.9
1979	150.1	66.1
1980	88.9	26.8

Source: C.E.M.A., Seminario de discusión sobre economía Argentina; data compiled on the basis of information of the Central Bank of Argentina, Instituto Nacional de Estadísticas y Censos, International Finance Statistics, and other sources. These are percentage rates as of November of each year.

As measured by published GDP figures, the cost of the program in terms of lost output appears to be quite substantial. The annual growth rate during the 1974–1980 period dropped to 1.1 percent compared to a secular 4 percent (see table 9.3). However, these figures are not very reliable because the base is 1960—a fact that may have tended to underestimate changes in output associated with the above-mentioned structural changes—and because the rate of unemployment apparently fell from 4.8 percent in April 1976 to 2 percent in April 1980 (De Pablo 1980).[6]

A remarkable development over most of the period was the sizable increase of international reserves held by the central bank. As seen in table 9.4, reserves increased more than seven times from April 1976 to April 1978. The rate considerably diminished over the next two years but was still relatively large (over 12 percent per annum). However, from April to October 1980, a period that started with the collapse of three major private banks, reserves fell by about 12 percent; this declining tendency continued toward the end of the year.

Two forces seem to be operating here. During 1976–1977 there is likely to have been a portfolio shift from foreign to domestic assets, because the government made it very clear from the beginning that private property would be fully respected; later the interest rates were decontrolled, thus widening the set of attractive domestic assets. Prior to March 1976 the menu of assets held by the public consisted mainly of goods and foreign assets (for most people just dollars in safety boxes). With this in mind, it is not implausible that a large proportion of the less than 5 billion dollar increase of reserves from April 1976 to April 1978 just came from private portfolios of Argentines, since it only represents about 20 percent of

6. It should be noted, however, that even leaving capital accumulation effects aside, one could conceive of a situation where GDP stagnates while unemployment falls. This would be the case, for example, if wages became downward flexible (by the elimination of labor unions) and firms were price setters which preferred to underutilize capacity. See section 9.2.3 for further discussion.

Table 9.3

	GDP (millions of 1960 pesos)		
1970	15,284.5	1976	18,186.9
1971	16,182.37	1977	19,085.4
1972	16,798.29	1978	18,429.7
1973	17,589.4	1979	19,972.6
1974	18,664.9	1980	19,940.9
1975	18,502.9		

Source: Central Bank of Argentina.

Table 9.4

	(a) Reserves (million dollars)	(b) Claims on Government (billion pesos)	(c) Real High-Powered Money
1976	1,812	477	6,193
1977	4,039	1,089	8,370
1978	6,037	1,324	7,097
1979	10,480	1,352	5,757
1980	7,683	7,744(d)	6,547

Source: International Financial Statistics and Central Bank of Argentina; (a), (b), and (c) as of December of each year; (c) deflated by the Wholesale Price Index; (d) as of October.

GNP.[7] Another possible reason for the accumulation of reserves is that, especially after 1978, the rate of growth of the central bank's credit to the government (the main component of domestic credit) was held considerably below the rate of inflation and, more fundamentally, also below the prefixed rate of devaluation (see tables 9.2 and 9.4).[8]

After the banking reform (last quarter of 1977), interest rates skyrocketed; the real lending rate for December 1977 reached the record equivalent annual level of 194 percent (see table 9.5). The real rate was positive for 1978 and 1980 and near zero for 1979.

9.2   The Road to an Explanation

In view of the previous description, it is clear that the central question we ought to answer is: What are the main reasons for the slow convergence of the inflation rate to the prefixed inflation rate (plus the international inflation rate)? This question has already been partially answered in an important paper by Rodriguez and Sjaastad (1979). They start from the observation that the equilibrium real exchange rate is, inter alia, a

7. To get this estimate, we conservatively assumed that per capita income was $1,000 (U.S.).
8. The opposite happened in 1981, thus explaining the loss of reserves over that period.

Table 9.5   **Real Interest Rate**

Month	1977	1978	1979	1980	1981
January	—	3.18	−2.45	2.43	3.94
February	—	5.86	−0.90	1.85	2.84
March	—	0.23	−1.03	1.74	5.66
April	−1.25	−0.74	0.61	1.44	—
May	−1.82	−0.81	−1.87	0.03	—
June	0.79	3.51	−3.22	−0.94	—
July	1.47	3.11	0.08	4.17	—
August	−4.37	−0.85	−6.54	3.19	—
September	1.89	0.68	2.85	2.62	—
October	−1.30	−2.55	6.95	−0.11	—
November	5.76	−0.93	3.56	2.76	—
December	9.39	1.50	4.38	5.51	—

Source: Same as table 9.1, obtained by subtracting the monthly rate of growth of wholesale prices from the nominal interest rate of table 9.5.

function of the domestic terms of trade (i.e., international terms of trade adjusted by tariffs and subsidies), and thus, they run a regression of the latter against the former. An implication of their estimates is that, for instance, the removal of an export tax will tend to appreciate, while the reduction of a binding import tariff will tend to depreciate the equilibrium real exchange rate. As noted earlier, both experiments were tried. If, as argued above, tariffs were reduced to eliminate redundant protection, then their paper would imply that there was a downward shift in the real exchange rate. In a fixed exchange rate regime this would take the form of an increase in the inflation rate. As reported by the authors, and by extrapolations for 1980 made by C. A. Rodriguez, however, the price level appears to be even higher than warranted by their formulas. Estimates vary, but their analysis suggests that by the end of 1980 the price level was at least 15 percent above its long-run, equilibrium level.

Another, more fundamental, reason why the Rodriguez-Sjaastad analysis could not tell us the whole story is that their estimates are based on Cochrane-Orcutt techniques, suggesting that there exist some other, perhaps slow-moving, variables crucial to the process.

In what follows we will present several models that try to account for some of the "missing" variables in a general-equilibrium, rational-expectations context. It should be made clear from the outset that the models do not intend to capture all the aspects of the Argentine experience.

9.2.1   The Portfolio Shift Model

The first model tries to capture the impact effect of a portfolio shift, like the one mentioned in section 9.1. More specifically, here we will be concerned with shifts away from foreign and toward domestic physical assets.

Let us assume that there are three assets: land (inelastically supplied), domestic money, and foreign money (M and f, respectively). Thus, wealth in terms of foreign exchange, a, satisfies

$$(1) \qquad\qquad a = z + q,$$

where

$$(2) \qquad\qquad z \equiv \frac{M}{E} + f$$

is "financial" wealth, q is the price of land in terms of foreign exchange, and E is the exchange rate (i.e., price of foreign currency in terms of domestic money). We assume the existence of tradable and nontradable goods, no international inflation, and that the country is "small" in international markets; thus, the domestic price of tradables could be identified with E.

Given that we wish to emphasize the substitutability between land and foreign assets and that, as shown in table 9.4, the stock of real, high-powered money was relatively constant, we will assume that the demand for money is inelastic with respect to the interest rate(s). Assuming that the relevant price level is the price of nontradables,[9] P, we get

$$(3) \qquad\qquad \frac{M}{P} = \alpha, \text{ a constant}.$$

Furthermore, we assume that

$$(4) \qquad\qquad q/f = k.$$

This is simply a portfolio demand equation. To simplify the exposition, we will assume k to be exogenous. However, straightforward extensions will be briefly mentioned at the end.

We assume (see Calvo and Rodriguez 1977 for a similar procedure):[10]

$$C_H(p, a) = \text{demand for nontradable}$$
$$\quad - \quad + \qquad \text{(or "home") goods},$$
$$C_T(p, a) = \text{demand for tradable goods},$$
$$\quad + \quad +$$

$$y_H(p) = \text{supply of nontradables},$$
$$\quad +$$
$$y_T(p) = \text{supply of tradables}.$$
$$\quad -$$

9. Results are qualitatively the same as long as in the relevant "price level" P has a positive weight.

10. Signs underneath an argument indicate those of the corresponding partial derivatives.

In equilibrium,

(5) $$C_H(p, a) = y_H(p),$$

and thus, at equilibrium,

(6) $$p = v(a).$$
$$+$$

We will study the case where E is prefixed (although it may vary over time). Thus, assuming that foreigners do not demand domestic land,[11] it follows that financial wealth, z, is at any time, t, a "state" or predetermined variable at t. Hence, by (1)–(6),

(7) $$a = z + fk = z + (z - \alpha p)k = z(1 + k) - \alpha v(a)k.$$

By equations (6) and (7), a is a function of z and k at equilibrium, and if f, $k > 0$ (the relevant case for our analysis),

(8a) $$\frac{\partial a}{\partial z} > 0,$$

(8b) $$\frac{\partial a}{\partial k} > 0.$$

We immediately see, by (7) and (8b), that a shift way from foreign exchange and into land increases p, that is, appreciates the real exchange rate. Furthermore, since initially z is predetermined, (1) implies that the value of land will rise. Also, by (2) and (3),

(9) $$z = \alpha p + f,$$

and thus, the rise in p implies a fall in f: the private sector will have exchanged foreign for domestic currency leading to accumulation of reserves by the central bank.

In other words, in trying to shift from foreign exchange to land, the public raises the price of land and, consequently, wealth goes up. The latter, in turn, increases the demand for nontradables, leading to an increase in the price level, and thus, to a rise in the demand for domestic currency. The end result is that the central bank accumulates reserves even when originally the public was interested in land, not in domestic money.

To study the dynamics, let us assume that domestic credit grows at the rate ϵM (where $\epsilon \equiv \dot{E}/E$ = rate of devaluation). Thus,

(10) $$\dot{z} = y_T(p) - C_T(p, a).$$

Recalling (6), our assumptions have the plausible implication that p is

---

11. This is not an important constraint unless foreigners *own* all the land.

invariant across steady states.[12] Since, by equation (6), p is an increasing function of a and, by equation (8a), a is an increasing function of z, we can use (10) to obtain a closed stable system. Thus, after the initial appreciation of the real exchange rate, p will start to fall back to its long-run equilibrium.

Let us denote by R_t the stock of reserves at the central bank at t. Let us denote by R^- and M^- the stocks of reserves and money supply, respectively, before the portfolio shift, which is the subject of our analysis (i.e., the increase of k). Hence, under our assumptions we have

$$(11a) \qquad \frac{M_0 - M^-}{E_0} = R_0 - R^-,$$

and

$$(11b) \qquad \dot{R}_t = \frac{\dot{M}_t}{E_t} - \epsilon \frac{M_t}{E_t} = \frac{d}{dt}\left(\frac{M_t}{E_t}\right).$$

Therefore,

$$(12) \qquad R_t = R_0 + \frac{M_t}{E_t} - \frac{M_0}{E_0}.$$

However, by (3),

$$(13) \qquad \frac{M_t}{E_t} = \alpha p_t.$$

But since a change in k was shown to leave steady state p unchanged, it follows that, if the system started at steady state,

$$(14) \qquad \frac{M_t}{E_t} \to \frac{M^-}{E_0}, \text{ as } t \to \infty.$$

Consequently, by (11a), (12), and (14),

$$(15) \qquad R_t \to R^-, \text{ as } t \to \infty.$$

The above arguments have shown, assuming that before the increase of k the system was at a rest point, that the stock of reserves at the central bank will in the long run be invariant with respect to k. Since it can be shown that long-run z decreases with k, it follows, by (9) and steady state invariance of p, that f will fall. Therefore, in the long run the country as a whole will hold less foreign currency than prior to the portfolio change.

To summarize, the model shows that a portfolio shift as suggested by the data explains a temporary appreciation of the real exchange rate and an accumulation of reserves on the part of the central bank (also tempo-

---

12. This is plausible in the present context because these models are intended to explain temporary departures from the long-run levels of the real exchange rate.

rary). One could also show in this model that, even at steady state, reserves would accumulate (decumulate) if the rate of expansion of domestic credit is held below (above) the rate of devaluation (another feature of the Argentine plan).

Notice that in this model a change in the rate of devaluation has no "real" effect. This is essentially the result of our assuming that the demand for money is inelastic with respect to the nominal interest rate. This type of effect, however, will be captured by our next model.

Before closing this section, we would like to sketch a possible extension to the case where k is variable. A simple way would be to make k a function of the rate of return of land in terms of foreign exchange. With rationality, the latter is a function of land rental (a function of p in a two-sector model) and capital gains, $\dot{q}$. In this fashion, the system can now be expressed by a pair of differential equations in z and q, where q_0 is determined by the usual saddle-path condition. The analysis now proceeds along similar lines as those in Calvo and Rodriguez (1977).

9.2.2   The Currency Substitution Model

In this model we assume, together with the "currency substitution" literature (see Kouri 1976; Calvo and Rodriguez 1977), that the menu of assets consists only of domestic and foreign currencies (M and f). We have in mind a situation where the two monies can be used for transaction purposes, but because of, say, legal constraints they are not perfect substitutes.

A possible model strategy is to assume that monies are arguments in utility functions and to proceed from there. This line was extensively explored in Calvo (1980). For the sake of simplicity, and without losing the central qualitative features of the above-mentioned model, I will "tell the story" starting from demand functions.

The production side is assumed to be the same as in section 9.2.1. The demand side is slightly changed in the following manner:

Let us define income, y by

(16) $$y = y_T + y_H p,$$

and "liquidity adjusted" disposable income, y^d, by

(17) $$y^d = H(m, f) + y - \epsilon m + q,$$

where

(18a) $$m \equiv M/E,$$

(18b) $$\epsilon = \dot{E}/E,$$

g is government lump-sum transfers, and H is a function reflecting the "liquidity services" of the two monies. Johnson (1967) appears to be the first one to suggest that liquidity services should be included in the concept of disposable income (see also Fischer 1972). We assume H to be concave and increasing in both arguments and to exhibit decreasing marginal "productivities."[13] The term ϵm accounts for the depreciation of domestic money in terms of foreign currency.

At each moment of time individuals are assumed to maximize y^d subject to the wealth constraint that now becomes

$$(19) \qquad\qquad a = m + f .$$

The next step is to assume that the demand functions depend negatively on p, as in section 9.2.1, and positively on (maximum) y^d (previously we assumed that a was the other argument besides p). Home market equilibrium is now obtained when

$$(20) \qquad\qquad C_H(p, y^d) = y_H(p),$$

which implies that at equilibrium

$$(21) \qquad\qquad p = V(y^d)$$
$$+$$

(compare this with equation [6]).

Now we are ready to study the effect of a once-and-for-all fall in ϵ (a dramatization of the Argentine plan that started January 1979). Obviously, by the "envelope theorem" initial y^d will take an upward jump if $m > 0$ (which we, of course, assume) and g remains unchanged. By equation (16), this leads to an appreciation of the real exchange rate. However, if in order to preserve the invariance of steady state p we assume, as in section 9.2.1, that

$$(22) \qquad\qquad \epsilon m = g ,$$

the impact effect on p becomes ambiguous. Although one could follow the lines of Calvo (1980) to resolve the ambiguity in terms of empirically meaningful concepts, we will content ourselves here to point out a special, but interesting, case where initial g goes up when $d\epsilon < 0$.

Suppose we start from a steady state where inflation (ϵ) is so high that seigniorage from inflation (ϵm) increases when inflation is diminished. This is the type of situation emphasized by Friedman (1971). That is to say,

$$(23) \qquad\qquad \partial(\epsilon m)/\partial\epsilon < 0 .$$

As before, $d\epsilon < 0$ implies $dy^d > 0$, if g is constant. But now since (22) holds, we have by (23) that g rises, implying a further increase in y^d—all of which results, by (21), in a rise of initial p.[14]

13. More generally H should also be made a function of p to reflect the use of monies to transact home goods.

14. This is not intended to be a rigorous proof. However, the reader can easily convince himself of this result by laying out the dynamics of the model.

Another interesting experiment is to study the implications of lowering minimum cash reserves of banks which, as indicated above, was one of the ingredients of Argentina's financial reform.

A simple way to handle the question is to think of m as high-powered money (in terms of foreign exchange). Letting λ denote the "money multiplier," it is natural to rewrite the "liquidity services" function, H, as follows:

$$(24) \qquad H(\lambda m, f).$$

Using the latter in equation (17), we can answer the question we posed.

Clearly, again by the "envelope theorem," a rise in λ leads ceteris paribus to an increase of initial y^d and, hence, p. One can show that the latter holds true if (17) is assumed and if H is homogeneous of degree one (not an unreasonable assumption).

9.2.3   The Credibility Model

In section 9.1 we put a great deal of emphasis on the lack of clarity and credibility that seemed to have prevailed during several subperiods of the stabilization plans. In 1980, for example, there is a sizable spread between the U.S. prime rate plus actual devaluation and the domestic nominal interest rate, suggesting that people were expecting a rate of devaluation larger than had been announced (see table 9.6). So far, however, our models have not incorporated these features.

To keep the discussion within reasonable limits, we will discuss only a special case of the credibility problem where people do not believe that the preannounced rate of devaluation will actually be made effective.

Table 9.6   **Risk Premium: Spread between Domestic and International Interest Rates**

Month	1977	1978	1979	1980	1981
January	—	5.47	1.36	2.57	3.45
February	—	3.69	1.30	2.03	−5.23
March	—	2.67	1.40	1.59	3.75
April	−2.08	2.02	1.48	1.46	—
May	−1.24	3.51	1.61	2.01	—
June	1.71	6.04	1.93	3.51	—
July	0.99	5.54	2.54	4.47	—
August	1.93	4.41	3.14	3.66	—
September	1.54	2.81	3.28	3.15	—
October	2.78	2.30	3.33	3.07	—
November	4.36	1.20	2.38	3.04	—
December	5.08	1.86	2.54	3.57	—

Source: Same as table 9.1. Calculated by subtracting from table 9.5 the ten-day prime rate plus the rate of devaluation.

Furthermore, we will assume that this is the only aspect of the stabilization "package" which is subject to disbelief.

In the first place, disbelief about preannounced ϵ does not necessarily have real effects. One example is the model of section 9.2.1. Another, which is perhaps more interesting because it does not make the assumption that the demand for money is inelastic, is as follows:

Imagine that the demand for home goods takes the following form:

$$(25) \qquad\qquad C_H(\underset{-}{p}, \underset{-}{r}),$$

where r, the (ex ante) "real" rate of interest, satisfies

$$(26) \qquad\qquad r = i - (\dot{P}/P)^e,$$

where i is the nominal interest rate, and $(\dot{P}/P)^e$ is the expected rate of inflation of home goods. Assuming perfect capital mobility, we get

$$(27) \qquad\qquad i = i^* + \epsilon^e,$$

where i^* and ϵ^e are the rest-of-the-world nominal interest rate and the expected rate of devaluation. Thus, denoting the expected growth of p by $(\dot{p}/p)^e$ we get, in equilibrium,

$$(28) \qquad\qquad C_H[p, i^* - (\dot{p}/p)^e] = y_H(p).$$

Making the natural assumption that

$$(29) \qquad\qquad p = p^e,$$

we can, by (28) and (29), obtain a differential equation for expected p; if, as usual, we single out the stationary solution as the one corresponding to "rationality," then we see that the real exchange rate is not affected by changes in the expected rate of devaluation (incidentally, notice that the stationary solution is locally unstable, yielding uniqueness).

Intuitively, what happens in this economy when people expect a higher rate of devaluation, for example, is that the nominal interest rate and the expected rate of inflation will rise in the same amount as ϵ^e does. Hence, the real interest rate remains constant and equilibrium p does not change.

Furthermore, in the context of section 9.2.2, a rise in ϵ^e has ambiguous results for the same reasons that a change in ϵ had ambiguous implications. In fact, one can show that if parameters are such that an increase in ϵ lowers initial p (the case we emphasized in section 9.2.2), then a higher ϵ^e (the relevant case for Argentina) would produce the same type of impact on p as an increase in ϵ—it will go down, a movement opposite to the one we want to be able to explain.

We would get a different implication in a world of price setters for home goods and price takers for tradable goods. Imagine a situation where

(30) $$P_{it} = \alpha E_t^e + (1 - \alpha) P_t^e,$$

where P_i is the price set by firm i in the home goods sector. It is assumed
that P_{it} has to be determined prior to knowing the price of tradables (E_t)
and the average for nontradables (P_t). The index e indicates expectations
at $(t - 1)$, when prices are set. (This model is similar to the one discussed
in Phelps 1979, except that there money supply takes the place of E).
Now, assuming rationality, we get

(31) $$P_t \equiv \int_0^1 P_{it}\, di = P_t^e$$

(where, for simplicity, we assume that each firm is a point in the interval
[0, 1]). Hence, by (30) and (31), we get

(32) $$P_t = E_t^e.$$

Therefore, if, say, $E_t < E_t^e$ (i.e., authorities devalue by less than expected)
then P_t/E_t will be larger than 1, that is, the equilibrium value of P/E if E is
fully anticipated.

Consequently, according to this model, if all of a sudden individuals
expect that a devaluation will occur sometime in the future, but they do
not know exactly when, there will be an appreciation of the real exchange
rate as long as devaluation is not made effective. The model can even
explain a steady increase in observed (P/E) if, in the perception of
individuals, devaluation becomes more likely with the passage of time.

Notice that, if we superpose the assumption that wages are perfectly
flexible, the model implies full employment and excess capacity (or
unwanted inventory accumulation), which is not inconsistent with the
Argentine experience. If, in addition, we append the model with a
demand-for-money function like (3), we also find that the appreciation of
the real exchange rate would be accompanied by an accumulation of
reserves at the central bank.

Independently of whether unfulfilled expectations of the sort examined
above affect the ex post determination of the real exchange rate, there is
also an effect on the ex post real interest rate that appears to have played
an important role in the last stages of the Martínez de Hoz administration. Take, for instance, the first model discussed in this section (equations [25]–[29]). By using equation (28) and recalling that the solution
requires $(\dot{p}/p)^e = 0$, the ex ante expected real interest rate would be i^*.
However, again because ex post p is a constant, $\dot{P}/P = \epsilon$ (the actual rate
of devaluation). Consequently, by equation (27) the ex post real rate of
interest is equal to $i^* + \epsilon^e - \epsilon$.

Therefore, by simply making the expected rate of devaluation larger
than the actual we can increase the actual interest rate over the expected.
Various conditions existed to make this likely to happen during 1980. In
the first place, the closing of major banks in April together with the

Table 9.7   Twenty-Nine-Day Lending Rate

Month	1977	1978	1979	1980	1981
January	—	18.42	7.59	6.70	6.40
February	—	11.14	7.06	6.00	8.00
March	—	9.30	7.03	5.60	10.30
April	4.49	8.34	7.06	5.30	—
May	4.49	8.17	7.14	5.40	—
June	7.43	8.30	7.26	6.40	—
July	7.17	8.02	7.60	7.10	—
August	8.20	7.79	8.10	6.10	—
September	9.17	7.35	8.10	5.50	—
October	12.23	7.38	8.00	5.30	—
November	13.66	7.58	7.00	5.40	—
December	13.58	7.87	6.90	6.30	—

Source: Same as table 9.1.

widespread belief that the peso was overvalued led people to think that the economy was out of control of de Hoz's team, and that any reasonable successor would most likely devalue to restore some kind of "equilibrium" parity. The second, and perhaps most crucial, factor that operated during 1980 was the nomination (by the junta) of a new president (R. Viola) whose term would start on March 29, 1981. It was immediately transparent that Viola disagreed with de Hoz's policies, and to make things worse, he made no clear policy statement before taking over, except for saying that he supported the (loosely defined) basic principles of the 1976 revolution (freer markets, etc.), but it was likely that there would be changes in "instrumentation." This together with the perception that the peso was overvalued led to a belief of an imminent and substantial devaluation (this is dramatically shown in table 9.7 for March 1981).[15] The effect on the real interest rate for the last stretch of the Martínez de Hoz period agrees with the implication of the above theory (see table 9.5).

9.3   Epilogue

The devaluation pressures by the end of the Martínez de Hoz period were practically insurmountable. As indicated above, de Hoz was prompted to make an unexpected 10 percent devaluation in February 1981. The new administration, however, confirmed what almost everybody had predicted by further devaluing the peso by 30 percent a few days after taking the oath of office. The prefixed rate system was continued but it did not stop the outflow of capital. As a consequence, another 30 percent

15. As indicated in note 5, the peso suffered an unannounced 10 percent devaluation in February 1981.

devaluation, this time highly unexpected, was carried out the first week of June 1981. Credibility was lost, capital outflow gathered additional momentum, and a few weeks later the government announced a "dual" exchange rate system: a prefixed rate for most commercial transactions and long-run capital flows; a floating rate for short-run capital and some commercial transactions (like some nontraditional exports and tourism). Taking into account the average of the floating rate for June, the upshot of all this was that the peso was devalued by over 200 percent since January 1981, in striking contrast with the plan of December 1978 that had anticipated a completely fixed rate after March 1981. It is worth noting, however, that over that period the price level (CPI) increased by slightly less than 50 percent and that, for the first time since 1976, the rate of unemployment appears to have overshot the 6 percent mark.

Like physicians, economists should learn from the catastrophes of some economies to try to improve the welfare of many others. In this light, the models discussed in this paper have to be seen as only tentative explorations of a mysterious disease that will require many able researchers to diagnose it adequately.

References

Calvo, G. A. 1980. Financial opening, crawling peg and the real exchange rate. C.E.M.A. (September). Manuscript.

Calvo, G. A., and C. A. Rodriguez. 1977. A model of exchange rate determination under currency substitution and rational expectations. *Journal of Political Economy* 85, no. 8:617–625.

De Pablo, J. C. 1980. Un análisis "ex-durante" de la politítica económica Argentina, 1976–1980. Universidad de Buenos Aires (September). Manuscript.

Dornbusch, R. 1980. Inflation stabilization and capital mobility. Paper presented at the first Latin American meeting of the Econometric Society, Buenos Aires, July.

Fischer, S. 1972. Money, income, wealth, and welfare. *Journal of Economic Theory* 4, no. 2:289–311.

Friedman, M. 1971. Government revenue from inflation. *Journal of Political Economy* 4 (July/August):846–856.

Johnson, H. 1967. *Essays in monetary economics*, chap. 4. Cambridge, Mass.: Harvard University Press.

Kouri, P. J. K. 1976. The exchange rate and the balance of payments: A monetary approach. *Scandinavian Journal of Economics* 78, no. 2:280–304.

Phelps, E. S. 1979. Obstacles to curtailing inflation. In *Essays in post-*

Keynesian inflation, edited by J. H. Gapinski and C. E. Rockwood. Cambridge, Mass.: Ballinger.
Rodriguez, C. A. 1979. El plan Argentino de estabilización del 20 de diciembre. C.E.M.A., Working Paper no. 5, July.
Rodriguez, C. A., and L. A. Sjaastad. 1979. El atraso cambiario en Argentina: mito o realidad? C.E.M.A., Working Paper no. 2, June.
Sargent, T. J., and N. Wallace. 1975. "Rational" expectations, the monetary instrument, and the optimal money supply rule. *Journal of Political Economy* 83 (April):241–254.

Comment   Herminio A. Blanco

The internal consistency of the first and second models presented by the author is beyond dispute. However, since the empirical motivation of the third model is that agents made a significant forecasting error in 1980, the "natural assumption" made in equation (29) (i.e., $p = p^e$) is inappropriate. Instead the formulation of a fully stochastic model is called for. Such a model should specify if the forecasting error was fostered by an unexpected change in the parameters of the underlying stochastic processes, or if it was generated under a stable structure.

My main comment centers around the validity of developing a series of models to "capture" each of the highlights of the Argentine experience during the 1976–1980 period. Is the author listing alternative hypotheses to be tested in a stepwise regression, or is he groping toward a general model?

My general impression is that the answer would be negative to the first question and affirmative to the second. If the author is trying to formulate a general model, he should have developed the implications of each one of the models for the whole period under consideration. Instead of following this initial "testing" procedure, the author only considered the capacity of each model to replicate a particular historical episode.

As a final comment, I would like to stress that one of the most intriguing pieces of evidence presented in the historical background was not incorporated in any of the models. What is the relation between the collapse of the three major banks and the decrease in foreign exchange reserves which occurred in 1980?

Herminio A. Blanco is a professor in the Department of Economics, Rice University.

Comment   Ricardo Ffrench-Davis

The Argentine case offers an interesting example of a new set of economic policies recently being implemented in several developing countries. (LDCs). The set includes the following among its most distinctive features: a reform of the domestic financial market in the direction of liberalizing interest rates and the allocation of credit and of reducing reserve requirements; the freeing of capital flows; a trend toward a fixed unified exchange rate; a generalized relaxation of price controls; the demobilization of labor unions; a public sector increasingly passive on economic matters; and, most often, an authoritarian regime. Actual experiences in LDCs toward an "open economy" have tended to be associated with "closed politics" and repressed social organizations.

This set of economic policies—frequently called orthodox, neoconservative, or free market experiments—is well illustrated by the economic models implemented in the Southern Cone countries, especially Argentina and Chile. They conform better than, for instance, South Korea or Singapore, to a textbook "free market" model. Moreover, Argentina (until mid-1980) and Chile (still by the end of 1981) were exhibited by the supporters of these policies as highly successful and promising cases.

The Southern Cone experiments do not begin from a steady state situation. Actually, they are initiated in a framework characterized by high and variable inflation, large fiscal budget deficits, arbitrary trade restrictions, and a distorted price system. The Southern Cone experiments are intended to "normalize" the domestic economies. But, in contrast with previous stabilization programs, they have also been directed to introduce "structural" changes in the economic organization that was built in previous decades. It is obvious that the title of "market economy" or free market is too vague and general to describe these new experiments.

Guillermo Calvo takes one significant feature of the Argentine case, which was the growing gap between domestic inflation and international rates of inflation (plus variations of the exchange rate) that resulted, between 1977 and 1980, as the rate of devaluation was reduced in the search for a fixed exchange rate. This issue is also quite relevant for Chile, where the formal implementation of a "monetarist approach to the balance of payments" or an open-economy global monetarism has also resulted in a significant appreciation of the real exchange rate.

Calvo sketches some of the relevant features of the implementation of the model imposed in Argentina. Then he presents three models framed

Ricardo Ffrench-Davis is a researcher at Corporación de Investigaciones Económicas para Latino América, Santiago, Chile.

in a general-equilibrium, rational-expectations context. They are intended to explain the real appreciation of the peso against the U.S. dollar, which was close to 100 percent in the period discussed. Model 1 focuses on the impact of a portfolio shift by Argentinians from foreign currency to domestic land; model 2 studies the effects of substitutability between domestic and foreign monetary assets; and model 3 examines the implications of the noncredibility of the official announcements with respect to exchange rate policy.

Here, for the sake of brevity, I will make only two brief comments related to the sketch of the implementation of the Argentine model, and then I will refer briefly to Calvo's discussion of models 1 and 3.

Calvo asserts that the economic policy was not always clearly understood by the public. He rightly says that this "lack of clarity" was partly the result of the dismantling of long-inherited price distortions. But one can go further by following the track of this fact. One can hypothesize that even if the public were able to understand the policy, it might be unable to identify correctly (a) the direction of changes in relative prices and the corresponding reallocative signals, and (b) the range of feasible trends in the effort to stabilize the price level. Many economists place in these two implications a significant explanatory power of the low investment rates or the persistence of domestic inflation with a stagnant or depressed economic activity (see, e.g., Ffrench-Davis 1979; Foxley 1980; and Ramos 1978 on Chile's case). It is a very relevant question whether the reduction of some (not all, of course) "distortions," especially in the conjunctural framework characterizing the Southern Cone countries, has been generating costs overwhelmingly larger than the present value of potential benefits to be reaped sometime in the future.

Second, I want to touch on one point relating to restrictions on capital movements. Calvo calls the maintenance, until July 1980, of the minimum one-year period of permanence for capital inflows an *imperfection*. It can be argued that some sort of intervention in capital movements might be required to improve the performance of the market and to avoid speculative flows. As Dornbusch (1981) puts it, "There is no reason whatsoever to establish linkages to the world capital market for the benefit of speculators," and imbalances "can as well be financed by sterilized central bank intervention or by changes in public sector net foreign assets." In fact, there seem to have been too many experiences in Latin America disturbed by destabilizing capital flows. Free flows, rather than discouraging the mismanagement of policies such as the exchange rate, appear to foster it. That has been the case of the recent experiments of Argentina and Chile: capital inflows larger than the actual current account deficit have pressed for a clearly excessive appreciation of the exchange rate; for a while, the process of appreciation has encouraged further capital inflows.

Now let us refer briefly to model 1. First, it must be recalled that Calvo states clearly that the models have the potential to account for *at least some* of the divergence between the actual and the long-run exchange rates, but *how much* is an open question.

There has clearly been a demand shift from foreign currency to land. (It was subsequently reversed in both countries.) The open questions are how large has this shift been, and how significant is its effect on "wealth," the core variable in model 1; and then how strong is its transmission to the price of nontradables (p). In Argentina's case, we are dealing with differences between the annual changes of CPI and of the exchange rate (plus international inflation) as large as 80 percent (158 percent versus 80 percent, in average, for 1978–1979). And it is not a one-year phenomenon, but it lasted for four years. I think that the strength of "inertia" in inflation and the weakness of the capacity of the exchange rate either to influence inflationary expectations or to influence directly the market of nontradables, are notably more relevant as explanatory variables of the persistently large net domestic inflation.

The boom of the price of land and of other forms of wealth have probably been more significant in contributing to the diversion of investment and mental efforts from "productive" uses to "speculative" uses. These problems of transition introduce complications in the return of p to an "invariant steady state" and most probably modify to a significant degree the long-run equilibrium.

Finally, just two comments in relation to model 3. First, disbelief in preannounced exchange rate schedules, rather than the consequence of the lack of clarity of the government, appears to be the result of the increasing appreciation of the exchange rate and the subsequent effects on the trade balance (Frenkel 1981). Both in Argentina and Chile evidence seems to show that disbelief came after appreciation, not vice versa.

Second, it is true that disbelief about the preannounced path for the exchange rate, in some cases, may not have real effects. Calvo discusses some interesting examples that illustrate this possibility. But that, for sure, has not been the case of Argentina and Chile in their recent experiments. The data suggest that, as a consequence, real interest rates became more unstable, the spread between domestic and foreign interest rates increased, and investment in tradables was discouraged. It is one thing to know that the real exchange rate will be devalued sometime and another to know when it will be done. The actual market exchange rate is a factor that has been affecting the short-run profitability of producers of tradables and actually pushing many to bankruptcy. The actual working of capital markets is not guided by distant horizons, particularly after the sort of financial reforms that have been implemented with these experiments.

References

Dornbusch, Rudiger. 1981. Panel on external financial openness and effects on the national economy. In *Seminar on external financial relations and their impact on the Latin American economies*. Santiago, Chile: CIEPLAN-Ford Foundation.

Ffrench-Davis, Ricardo. 1979. Exchange rate policies in Chile, 1965–1979. In *Exchange rate rules*, edited by J. Williamson. London: Macmillan.

Foxley, Alejandro. 1980. Hacia una economía de libre mercado: 1970–1978. In *Colección Estudios CIEPLAN*, no. 4 (November), pp. 5–37.

Frenkel, Roberto. 1981. Financial liberalization and capital flows: The case of Argentina. In *Seminar on external financial relations and their impact on the Latin American economies*. Santiago, Chile: CIEPLAN-Ford Foundation. Also discussion papers by José Luis Machinea and John Williamson.

Ramos, Joseph. 1978. Inflación persistente, inflación reprimida e hiperinflación. In *Desarrollo Económico*, no. 69 (April–June), pp. 3–34.

10 Interest Differential and Covered Arbitrage

José Saúl Lizondo

10.1 Introduction

This paper deals with interest rate differentials between U.S. dollar denominated assets and Mexican peso denominated assets. In particular, the paper examines to what extent transaction costs can account for deviations from interest rate parity.

In section 10.2, I compare two propositions concerning the relationships between interest rate differentials and other economic variables. One of them is the Fisher hypothesis that relates the differential with the expected rate of change in the spot exchange rate. The other is the interest parity theorem that relates the differential with the forward premium or discount on foreign exchange. The connection between these propositions and the problems in testing the Fisher hypothesis for the Mexican peso are also discussed. In section 10.3, I restate the condition for covered interest arbitrage in the presence of transaction costs. I also discuss the availability of data and the procedure followed to estimate the transaction costs in the foreign exchange market. In section 10.4, I analyze the empirical evidence on covered interest arbitrage between U.S. dollar and Mexican peso denominated assets for the period from July 1979 to December 1980. The results show that only a small percentage of the deviations from parity can be accounted for by the transaction costs as previously measured. Then I examine two possible explanations. One of them is associated with additional costs and obstacles found in carrying out forward transactions. The other one is associated with the exchange gains tax treatment. Some concluding remarks are contained in section 10.5.

José Saúl Lizondo is a professor at Instituto Tecnológico Autónomo de México.

10.2   The Fisher Hypothesis and Covered Interest Arbitrage

The Fisher hypothesis states that nominal interest rate differentials between assets that are identical in all respects except for the currency of denomination can be explained by the expected change in the spot exchange rate between those currencies over the holding period (Fisher 1930). Let S_t be the spot exchange rate at time t, defined as the domestic currency price of foreign currency; let i_t and i_t^* be one-period nominal interest rates at time t on domestic and foreign currency denominated assets, respectively; and let $E_t(X)$ denote the expected value of the variable X, conditional on all the information available at time t. The Fisher hypothesis may then be formally written as:

(1)
$$\frac{(1 + i_t)}{(1 + i_t^*)} = \frac{E_t(S_{t+1})}{S_t} .$$

The interest parity theorem states that short-term capital movements will ensure that the returns on assets that are identical in all respects except for the currency of denomination will be equal when expressed in terms of the same currency after covering the exchange risk in the forward exchange market. This establishes a relationship between nominal interest rate differentials and the forward premium (or discount) on foreign exchange. Let F_t be the one-period forward exchange rate at time t. The condition for interest parity may then be formally written as:

(2)
$$\frac{(1 + i_t)}{(1 + i_t^*)} = \frac{F_t}{S_t} .$$

From equations (1) and (2), it is clear that the Fisher hypothesis and the interest parity theorem are not equivalent unless the forward exchange rate at time t is equal to the expected value at time t of the spot exchange rate that will prevail at time $t + 1$. That is, both propositions are equivalent only if

(3)
$$F_t = E_t(S_{t+1}) .$$

There are theoretical reasons that lead us to believe that equation (3) does not necessarily hold. Several models (Grauer, Litzenberger, and Stehle 1976; Stockman 1978; Frankel 1979; Fama and Farber 1979; Roll and Solnik 1979) imply that, under uncertainty, the forward rate is in general different from the expected value of the future spot rate. That difference may be the result of the existence of a risk premium. This premium depends on people's attitudes toward risk and some characteristics of the probability distributions of the variables included in the model. Moreover, even under risk neutrality, the forward rate may be different from the expected value of the future spot rate. This is because of the presence of a convexity term that arises from Jensen's inequality and the probability distribution of some of the variables included in the model. Jensen's inequality establishes that the expected value of a convex function of a random variable is larger than the value of the function evaluated at the expected value of the random variable. This implies that if the forward rate is equal to the expected value of the future spot rate from the domestic point of view, then they are not equal from the foreign point of view. This implication is known as the Siegel paradox, but it is thought to be of no empirical significance (Siegel 1972; McCulloch 1975).

Even when the implication of several models is that in general the forward rate is different from the expected value of the future spot rate, there are some conditions under which the same models imply that they are equal. Therefore, the validity of equation (3) is an empirical matter. Given that $E_t(S_{t+1})$ is not an observable variable, empirical work on this subject has tested the validity of equation (3) jointly with the hypothesis of market efficiency (Geweke and Feige 1979; Hansen and Hodrick 1980). If equation (3) holds and the market is efficient, the forward exchange rate should be the best forecast of the future spot rate. The tests are concerned both with whether the forward rate is an unbiased forecast of the future spot rate and with whether there is any other information that can be used to generate better predictions of the future spot rate. The information set generally includes past values of the forecast error for the same exchange rate and forecast errors from other currencies. Sometimes the hypothesis that the forward rate is the best forecast of the future spot rate is considered independently of its implications for market efficiency (Bilson 1980), but the results of the tests are nevertheless relevant for that issue.

The results of the tests tend to reject the joint hypothesis of market efficiency and the condition expressed in equation (3). If equation (3) does not hold, the Fisher hypothesis is different from the condition for interest parity. Therefore, there are reasons to test the empirical validity of each of them separately.

To test the Fisher hypothesis is to test whether equation (1) holds. Here, the same problem that was found in testing the validity of equation (3) is present: $E_t(S_{t+1})$ is not an observable variable. This problem is circumvented by testing the Fisher hypothesis jointly with the hypothesis of market efficiency (Cumby and Obstfeld 1980). If equation (1) holds and the market is efficient,

$$[(1 + i_t)/(1 + i_t^*)]S_t$$

should be the best forecast of the future spot rate. In particular, the forecast error should have zero mean and should be uncorrelated at all lags. The results of empirical work on this subject suggest that the Fisher hypothesis does not hold under the assumption of market efficiency.

The procedures used to test equations (1) and (3) are not adequate when studying currencies under fixed exchange rates when there is a positive and small probability of a large change in the exchange rate, either by devaluation or revaluation. The consequences of the existence of a positive and small probability of a drastic event has already been studied (Krasker 1980; Lizondo 1980). Also, when discussing the possible explanations for the rejection of the efficiency hypothesis in their works, Hansen and Hodrick (1980) say:

> Even though economic agents may process information optimally, the correct stochastic specification of government actions may not be consistent with the statistical model underlying our test. For instance, if economic agents correctly perceive that governmental actions will be roughly constant over relatively long periods and yet may change dramatically either at uncertain points in time or by an uncertain magnitude, we conjecture that it is possible that the statistical procedure we employ might yield sample autocorrelations in forecast errors that are large relative to their estimated standard errors even if the simple efficiency hypothesis is true. The cause of this could be a combination of incorrect assumptions we have made in determining the asymptotic covariance matrix for our estimators, a small sample size relative to the movements in government policy variables, and the inappropriateness of an ergodicity assumption in an environment where agents may assign positive a priori probabilities to events that may ultimately never occur.

These warnings are especially important when analyzing the validity of equation (3) under fixed exchange rates. For instance, assume that the level of the spot rate is equal to S_0. Also assume that, at time t, there is a positive and small probability P_t of a devaluation, between t and $t + 1$, that will set the exchange rate at a new level $S_0(1 + \alpha)$ with $\alpha > 0$. Assume that investors are risk neutral, that they know P_t and α, and that the market is efficient. Under those conditions, equation (3) holds and

$$F_t = S_0(1 + \alpha P_t).$$

As long as the devaluation does not take place, the forecast error,

$$e_t = F_{t-1} - S_t = S_0 \alpha P_{t-1},$$

is positive. In other words, the forward rate consistently overestimates the future spot rate and there seems to be a positive bias. Moreover, there is reason to believe that P_t is a variable with positive autocorrelation. The reason is that, in general, the variables that determine P_t, such as the level of international reserves and political stability, are themselves positively autocorrelated. Then, if yesterday's probability of a devaluation was relatively high but it did not take place, today's probability of a devaluation will tend to be relatively high too. In that case, the forecast error will show positive autocorrelation. Therefore, as long as the devaluation does not take place, the results of the usual tests will reject the joint hypothesis of market efficiency and equation (3), even when it is true.

It is also interesting to note that if the devaluation takes place between $t + k - 1$ and $t + k$, the forecast error,

$$e_{t+k} = F_{t+k-1} - S_{t+k} = S_0 \alpha (P_{t+k-1} - 1),$$

will be negative, unless $P_{t+k-1} = 1$, which is very unlikely. In other words, for that period the forward rate will seem to have underestimated the future spot rate. These implications are consistent with the experience of the Mexican peso during the period prior to the devaluation of August 1976.

Even though Mexico has not formally had a fixed parity since September 1976, the exchange rate has been relatively constant since March 1977 and the peso has always been quoted at a discount on the forward market. This suggests that the problems of the bias and the autocorrelation mentioned above may have been always present.

Table 10.1 presents some information about the series of forecast errors $e_t = F_{t-1} - S_t$. The series consists of forty-three nonoverlapping monthly observations for the period from May 1977 to December 1980 using bid rates. The series has a positive mean, and only two of the observations are negative. It also shows positive autocorrelations at the first lags. A first order autoregressive model was estimated for the series.

The results show a significant positive constant and a significant first order autoregressive parameter. The specific model estimated for the series is less important than the general conclusions that the forward rate seems to have consistently overestimated the future spot rate and that the forecast error shows significant positive autocorrelations.

These types of results are generally used to reject the joint hypothesis of market efficiency and the validity of equation (3). As was mentioned above, under fixed exchange rates and positive probability of devaluation

Table 10.1

	Series $e_t = F_{t-1} - S_t$									
Mean	.196									
Standard deviation	.155									
Lags	1	2	3	4	5	6	7	8	9	10
Autocorrelations	.73	.51	.36	.25	.10	.06	.02	$-.04$	$-.05$	$-.02$
Estimated model	$e_t =$	.053	$+$	.733 $e_{t-1} + u_t$						
		(.016)		(.106)						
Number of observations	43									

Note: Figures in parentheses are standard deviations. Monthly nonoverlapping observations for the period May 1977 to December 1980. The S_t and F_t are bid rates. Spot rates are 9 AM New York time quotations, and forward rates are 12 AM New York time quotations. The source of data of exchange rates is the Federal Reserve Bank of New York.

these results should not be interpreted in that way because they are also consistent with market efficiency and equation (3). In other words, these results do not help us test equation (3) for the Mexican peso.

The same reasoning applies to equation (1). Under fixed exchange rates and positive probability of a devaluation, if the market is efficient and equation (1) holds, the domestic interest rate will reflect the expected devaluation. As long as the devaluation does not take place,

$$[(1 + i_t)/(1 + i_t^*)]S_t$$

will overestimate the future spot rate, and the forecast error is likely to show positive autocorrelation. Nevertheless, this reasoning assumes that domestic interest rates are free to adjust, reflecting the expected devaluation. This is not the case in Mexico. Interest rates on peso-denominated time deposits are officially determined, and returns on Mexican treasury bills are regulated through open market operations. In this case, we do not even have a strong presumption about the characteristics of the series of forecast errors

$$e_t = [(1 + i_{t-1})/(1 + i_{t-1}^*)]S_{t-1} - S_t.$$

Table 10.2 presents information on that series. The series consists of forty-three nonoverlapping monthly observations for the period from May 1977 to December 1980. Exchange rates are bid rates, and interest rates are after-tax rates on time deposits. The series has a positive mean, and nine of the observations are negative. It also shows a small positive autocorrelation at the first lag. A first order autoregressive model was estimated for the series.

The results show a significant positive constant and a first order autore-

Table 10.2

$$\text{Series } e_t = \left[\frac{1 + i_{t-1}}{1 + i_{t-1}^*}\right]S_{t-1} - S_t$$

Mean	.027									
Standard deviation	.073									
Lags	1	2	3	4	5	6	7	8	9	10
Autocorrelations	.21	.10	.06	−.03	−.06	.02	.08	−.03	−.02	−.06
Estimated model	$e_t =$	.022	+	.216 e_{t-1} + u_t						
		(.011)		(.154)						
Number of observations	43									

Note: Figures in parentheses are standard deviations. Monthly nonoverlapping observations for the period May 1977 to December 1980. The S_t are bid rates. The i_t and i_t^* are after-tax rates on Mexican peso and dollar time deposits, respectively, for Mexican depositors. The source of exchange rate data is described in table 10.1. Interest rates on dollar deposits are Eurodollar opening rates in London collected from Reuters news service. Interest rates on Mexican peso deposits were taken from "Indicatores Económicos," Banco de México, S.A.

gressive term that is not significant at the 5 percent level. The positive constant indicates that

$$[(1 + i_{t-1})/(1 + i^*_{t-1})]S_{t-1}$$

overestimated the future spot rate for the period considered.

Nevertheless, the extent of the overestimation is considerably smaller than the one found when using the forward rate to predict the future spot rate. Given that interest rates are regulated, these results do not imply that interest rates reflect the expected devaluation better than forward exchange rates do. On the other hand, those who believe that equation (3) holds may interpret the results as evidence that interest rates on Mexican peso deposits were not allowed to adjust by the full amount of the expected depreciation.

Therefore, not only are there technical obstacles in testing the Fisher hypothesis, there is also the issue of interpretation of the results when interest rates are regulated. In view of these problems, I will focus on testing the interest parity condition.

10.3   Covered Interest Arbitrage

The interest parity theory maintains that the returns on assets that are identical in all respects except for the currency of denomination will be equal when expressed in terms of the same currency after covering the exchange risk in the forward exchange market. Otherwise, capital flows would take place from the asset with the lower return to the asset with the higher return, until changes in interest rates or changes in exchange rates insure that equation (2) holds.

The observed deviations from the parity condition have been rationalized in terms of nonmonetary yields (Tsiang 1959), political risk (Aliber 1973; Doodley and Isard 1980), transaction costs (Branson 1969; Prachowny 1970; Frenkel and Levich 1975, 1977), capital controls (Doodley and Isard 1980), differential tax treatment (Levi 1977), and difference between short-run and long-run relationships (Pedersson and Tower 1979). Some of these and other explanations, like default risk and premature repatriation, are analyzed in a survey article by Officer and Willett (1970).

My purpose here is to analyze the deviations from interest parity between dollar-denominated assets and peso-denominated assets. I examine to what extent transaction costs can account for those deviations, and I also consider the effects of other factors, such as regulations on forward market operations and exchange gains tax treatment.

The framework used is based on Frenkel and Levich (1975). It consists of the derivation of a neutral band around the interest parity line. For points within the band, transaction costs exceed arbitrage profits. Therefore, those points do not violate in a meaningful sense the condition of equilibrium expressed in equation (2).

Frenkel and Levich consider four distinct transaction costs for a covered outflow (inflow) of capital: sale of domestic (foreign) securities, purchase of foreign (domestic) currency spot, purchase of foreign (domestic) securities, and sale of foreign (domestic) currency forward. Let the costs in the foreign and domestic security markets and in the spot and forward exchange markets be denoted by c^*, c, c_s, and c_f, respectively, as percentages of the total transaction. The condition for profitable capital outflows is

$$(4) \qquad (1+i) < \frac{F}{S}(1+i^*)\Omega',$$

and the condition for profitable capital inflows is

$$(5) \qquad \Omega'(1+i) > \frac{F}{S}(1+i^*),$$

where $\Omega' = (1-c)(1-c_s)(1-c^*)(1-c_f)$. This assumes that the initial position of the arbitragers is in securities. If the initial position of arbitragers is in cash Ω' should be replaced by $[\Omega'/(1-c)^2]$ in equation (4), and by $[\Omega'/(1-c^*)^2]$ in equation (5).

Due to unavailability of data, I assume that arbitragers begin their position with cash and that $c = c^*$. Under those conditions, I replace Ω' in equations (4) and (5) by $\Omega = (1-c_s)(1-c_f)$.

From equation (4), the lower limit on $p[p = (F-S)/S]$ for which outflows of capital are profitable is:

$$(6) \qquad \underline{p} = \frac{(1+i) - \Omega(1+i^*)}{\Omega(1+i^*)}.$$

From equation (5), the upper limit on p for which inflows of capital are profitable is:

$$(7) \qquad \bar{p} = \frac{\Omega(1+i) - (1+i^*)}{(1+i^*)}.$$

The neutral band is defined by equations (6) and (7). As long as $\bar{p} < p < \underline{p}$, arbitrage flows are not profitable. For $p < \bar{p}$ inflows are profitable, and for $p > \underline{p}$ outflows are profitable.

The empirical implementation of this problem requires the estimation of transaction costs in the spot and forward foreign exchange markets. Frenkel and Levich estimated those costs by studying the behavior of triangular arbitrage. They assume that deviations from triangular arbitrage are due to transaction costs, and their estimates of c_s and c_f are the percentages that bound 95 percent of those deviations.

The estimation of c_s and c_f by this procedure assumes that the various exchange rates reflect a direct exchange of one currency for another. Unfortunately, all the quotations of the Mexican peso with currencies different from the U.S. dollar are obtained through the Mexican peso/U.S. dollar exchange rate. Therefore, this procedure should not be applied in the present case.

In the empirical applications, S and F represent midpoint rates. Therefore, the transaction costs should be at least equal to one-half of the bid-ask spread in the respective market. In addition to that, c_s and c_f should include other costs, such as brokerage fees. This suggests that it is possible to estimate the transaction costs using data on bid-ask spreads.

McCormick (1979) estimated the costs of transactions in the spot foreign exchange market using triangular arbitrage between U.S. dollars, British pounds, and Canadian dollars. The period of estimation was April 26, 1976 to October 22, 1976. When using exchange rate quotations with no time difference among them, his estimate of c_s was .090 percent, considerably smaller than the estimates of Frenkel and Levich that used quotations with some time difference among them.

Table 10.3 presents information on the bid-ask spreads of the British pound/U.S. dollar and the Canadian dollar/U.S. dollar exchange rates for the same period as McCormick's estimation. The average spreads in the spot markets were .060 percent for the British pound/U.S. dollar exchange rate and .022 percent for the Canadian dollar/U.S. dollar

Table 10.3 **Percentage Bid-Ask Spreads (April 26, 1976–October 22, 1976)**

	Maximum	Minimum	Average	Standard Deviation
British Pound/U.S. Dollar				
Spot	.610 (.150)	.011	.060	.055
Forward 3 months	.646 (.212)	.038	.100	.057
Deutsche Mark/U.S. Dollar				
Spot	.103 (.103)	.025	.058	.014
Forward 3 months	.366 (.154)	.025	.111	.029
Canadian Dollar/U.S. Dollar				
Spot	.117 (.078)	.019	.022	.011
Forward 3 months	.158 (.147)	.039	.047	.018
Number of observations: 126				

Note: Figures in parentheses indicate the maximum value of the spread when the largest observation is deleted. The source of the data is the *International Monetary Market Yearbook, 1976–1977*.

exchange rate. In view of McCormick's estimate of c_s and the information of table 10.3, I considered it a reasonable procedure to estimate the transaction costs for the Mexican peso/U.S. dollar spot exchange as one-half the bid-ask spread plus .06 percent.

Another question to discuss is the stability of transaction costs. The triangular arbitrage procedure produces one estimate for the whole period and therefore assumes that costs were stable during the period of estimation. Nevertheless, looking at table 10.3 it is possible to see that bid-ask spreads have large fluctuations. If other components of the costs do not vary inversely with the spread, and I do not see any reason why they would, one should have one estimate of the cost for each of the observations. Therefore, for the Mexican peso I use one-half of the bid-ask spread plus .06 percent for each of the observations. I am aware that this is a compromise because I am still using McCormick's estimate to justify the .06 percent above the half bid-ask spread.

For the estimation of transaction costs in the three months forward market, McCormick assumes $c_f = .96941\ c_s$ for arbitrage between U.S. dollars, British pounds, and Deutsche marks, and $c_f = 1.00913\ c_s$ for arbitrage between U.S. dollars, British pounds, and Canadian dollars. These are relationships found by Frenkel and Levich for the 1973–1975 period using the procedure of triangular arbitrage. On table 10.3, it is possible to see that the spread in the three months forward market is about twice the spread in the spot market. If the other components of the cost are not lower in the forward market, and I do not see any reason why they would be, c_f should be larger than c_s at least in one-half of the differences between the bid-ask spreads of both markets. Therefore, McCormick's procedure seems to me to be inadequate. Therefore, for the estimation of the costs of transactions in the forward market I also use one-half of the bid-ask spread plus .06 percent for each of the observations.

Table 10.4 presents information on spreads in Mexican peso exchange rates for the period for which bid and ask rates are available. It also presents, indirectly, information about the estimates of c_s and c_f. The

Table 10.4 **Percentage Bid-Ask Spreads in Mexican Peso Exchange Rates (July 1979–December 1980)**

	Maximum	Minimum	Average	Standard Deviation
Spot	.35 (.31)	.02	.10	.05
Forward 1 month	2.77 (2.48)	.08	.52	.37
Forward 3 months	4.98 (4.97)	.13	1.18	.70
Number of observations:	354			

Note: Figures in parentheses indicate the maximum value of the spread when the largest observation is deleted. The source of the data is described in table 10.1.

spread in the spot and the forward markets are considerably larger than for other currencies. This may be a consequence of banks assigning a larger risk to take positions in Mexican pesos than in other currencies and widening the spread accordingly. The effects of uncertainty on bid-ask spreads is theoretically considered in Allen (1977). Some empirical evidence on that relationship is provided by Fieleke (1975), Aliber (1975), and McKinnon (1976). Another interesting point to observe in table 10.4 is that the average spread in the forward market is considerably larger, with respect to the spread in the spot market, than for the other currencies. This may be a consequence of the Bank of Mexico intervening actively in the spot market and presumably not intervening in the forward market.

After determining the procedure to use to estimate transaction costs in the foreign exchange market, it is necessary to consider the assets whose returns are to be compared. Ideally, the assets should be identical in all respects except for the currency of denomination. One important factor to take into account is the political risk (Aliber 1973). When comparing the returns on assets denominated in currencies of two countries, the assets should be issued in the same financial center, that is, the same legal jurisdiction, located in a third country. Under those conditions, it is expected that the probability of future capital controls will affect the returns on both assets to the same extent. The empirical evidence shows that assets differing essentially only in their currency of denomination, such as Eurocurrency deposits, conform with the interest parity condition after considering the transaction costs. For the comparison of returns on treasury bills, the transaction costs explain a considerably smaller percentage of the deviations from interest arbitrage (Aliber 1973; Frenkel and Levich 1977, 1979; McCormick 1979).

For the Mexican peso we should use interest rates on deposits in foreign banks placed in foreign countries that are not subject to Mexican official regulations on interest rates. Unfortunately, data are not available on interest rates paid on those types of deposits. Therefore, I use time deposits and Mexican treasury bills as peso-denominated assets. For the dollar it does not matter whether we use Eurodollar deposits or dollar deposits created by the Mexican banking system. The interest rates paid on both types of deposits are the same for the period under consideration.

Finally, it is important to take into account the effect of taxes on the net returns to investors (Levi 1977). I use the after-tax returns on the different assets for Mexican individuals.

10.4 Empirical Results

The period of observation is July 1979 to December 1980, for which there is information on bid and ask exchange rates. During that period, Mexican treasury bills were issued each week. For those days I obtained a series of net returns for a three-month holding period. Data on rates of interest on three-month deposits in pesos and three-month deposits in dollars were collected for the same dates. After deleting some observations for days on which data in some of the variables were not available, there were seventy-five observations left. Based on the prices of the treasury bills one month prior to their expiration, I generated a series of net returns for a one-month holding period. Data on rates of interest on one-month deposits in pesos and one-month deposits in dollars were collected for the same dates. After deleting some days, there were seventy observations left.

Using that data, I computed $\underline{p}$ and $\bar{p}$ from equations (6) and (7) for arbitrage between Mexican peso time deposits and U.S. dollar time deposits, and for arbitrage between Mexican treasury bills and U.S. dollar time deposits. The results are presented in table 10.5.

The first column indicates the percentage of observations that lay within the neutral band, that is, observations for which $\bar{p} \leq p \leq \underline{p}$. It is possible to see that only a small proportion of the observations fall in that category. For all the observations outside the band $p > \underline{p}$. This indicates that for those observations there seems to be an opportunity for profitable capital outflows. The proportions of observations within the band is larger for Mexican treasury bills than for Mexican peso time deposits. This is the result of an official policy of keeping interest rates on time deposits below the rates on treasury bills. This policy also gave rise to a complaint from the commercial banks of "unfair competition" by the government in the attraction of funds. The proportion of observations

Table 10.5   Deviations from Interest Parity Computed from Equations (6) and (7)

	%ONB[a]	Average $\underline{p} - \bar{p}$[c]	Average $\underline{p} - p^{*}$[c]	NOBS[b]
One month:				
Time deposits	10.00	.88	.44	70
Treasury bills	25.71	.88	.44	70
Three months:				
Time deposits	4.00	1.50	.75	75
Treasury bills	18.67	1.51	.76	75

Note: Three-month returns on Mexican treasury bills were taken from "Anuario Financiero y Bursátil" 1979 and 1980, Bolsa Mexicana de Valores, S.A. de C.V. One-month returns were calculated from a sample of prices provided by six brokerage firms. For the sources of the other data used on this table see tables 10.1 and 10.2.

[a]%ONB = Percentage of observations within the neutral band.

[b]NOBS = Number of observations.

[c]
$$\underline{p} = \frac{(1+i) - \Omega(1+i^*)}{\Omega(1+i^*)}; \quad \bar{p} = \frac{(1+i)\Omega - (1+i^*)}{(1+i^*)}; \quad p^* = \frac{i - i^*}{(1+i^*)}.$$

within the band is also larger for one-month assets than for three-month assets. This may arise because in general the discount on the peso increases substantially with the time length of the contract, and this is not completely reflected in the time structure of interest rates on peso-denominated assets. The second column indicates the average size of the band, $\underline{p} - \bar{p}$. The band is wider for three-month assets than for one-month assets, reflecting the larger spread in the three-month forward market than in the one-month forward market. Given that for all the observations outside the band there are incentives for capital outflows, $p > \underline{p}$, I computed the maximum positive deviation of p from "complete" parity consistent with equilibrium. Let $p^* = (i - i^*)/(1 + i^*)$, then "complete" parity means $p = p^*$. Therefore, the maximum positive deviation of p from complete parity consistent with equilibrium is $\underline{p} - p^*$. The third column of table 10.5 provides information on that variable. Those numbers say, for example, that on average the one-month forward discount on the peso needs to increase more than .44 percent above the parity line to present opportunities for profitable capital outflows.

The results of table 10.5 indicate the presence of persistent deviations from interest parity that provide incentives for capital outflows. This leads us to think about the reasons why prices did not adjust to reach equilibrium. Given that domestic interest rates and the spot exchange rate are controlled, and that the Eurodollar rate can be considered exogenous, the only price left to perform the adjustment is the forward exchange rate. One explanation of the results may be the presence of corner solutions in which we observe interest rate quotations for peso-denominated assets that seem to be out of equilibrium, but the quantity of those assets demanded at those prices is zero, that is, nobody is holding peso-denominated time deposits and nobody but the central bank is holding Mexican treasury bills. But this is not the case. Another possibility is to emphasize the difference in time for the different quotations. Spot exchange rates are recorded at 9:00 AM New York time, forward rates are recorded at 12:00 AM New York time, Eurodollar rates are London opening rates, peso time deposit rates are valid for the whole day, and Mexican treasury bill rates are daily averages. Even when there is time difference among the quotations, it seems to me that they do not provide a plausible explanation of the results. In particular, if time differences were the cause of the deviations, we would expect to observe deviations of p above and below the band, but we only observe deviations of p above the band. Therefore, we have to look for other explanations of the results. I examine two possible explanations below; one is associated with additional costs and obstacles found in carrying out forward transactions, and the other is associated with the exchange gains tax treatment.

Mexican investors with an initial position in pesos can make arbitrage operations selling pesos, investing in dollar deposits and selling dollars forward. It seems that Mexican investors were actually doing all those operations through foreign banks. Those banks were in fact creating peso-denominated deposits located in various foreign countries, among them were Panama and the United States. Even when there are not records about the interest rates paid on those deposits, some sources affirm that they were calculated as the Eurodollar deposit rate plus the discount on the peso. Under those circumstances, we expect the parity condition to be very robust, as it happens with Eurocurrency deposits on other currencies. This arbitrage activity may have prompted the Bank of Mexico in April 1980 to ask the foreign banks to abstain from performing those operations. At the same time Mexican brokerage firms were forbidden to intervene directly or indirectly in those type of operations. Only the Mexican commercial banks are allowed to perform those operations. But there is a special regulation for forward transactions. When a commercial bank sells dollars forward, the buyer must deposit in Mexican pesos 25 percent of the value on the contract, without interest, during the life of the contract. Given that commercial banks act as intermediaries, they have to sell dollars in both cases, inflow of arbitrage capital and outflow of arbitrage capital. The foregone interest on the 25 percent deposit is an additional cost that must be borne by the arbitrager. Under those conditions, there are incentives for capital outflows if:

$$(8) \qquad (1 + i) < \frac{F}{S} (1 + i^*) \Omega (1 - .25i).$$

There are incentives for capital inflows if:

$$(9) \qquad \frac{\Omega(1 + i)}{(1 + .25i)} > \frac{F}{S} (1 + i^*).$$

From equations (8) and (9),

$$(10) \qquad \underline{p} = \frac{(1 + i) - \Omega(1 + i^*)(1 - .25i)}{\Omega(1 + i^*)(1 - .25i)},$$

$$(11) \qquad \bar{p} = \frac{\Omega(1 + i) - (1 + i^*)(1 + .25i)}{(1 + i^*)(1 + .25i)}.$$

The additional costs in foregone interest on the 25 percent deposit widen the neutral band. This can be checked by comparing equations (10) and (11) with equations (6) and (7). With a wider band, the percentage of observations within the band should rise.

Table 10.6 presents the results of the computations when using equations (10) and (11) for $\underline{p}$ and $\bar{p}$, respectively. As expected, the costs of arbitrage activity rise substantially. This is reflected in the second and third columns. For example, under the new conditions, on average, the one-month forward discount on the peso needs to increase more than .81

Table 10.6   **Deviations from Interest Parity Computed from Equations (10) and (11)**

	%ONB[a]	Average $\underline{p} - \bar{p}$[c]	Average $\underline{p} - p^{*}$[c]	NOBS[b]
One month:				
Time deposits	52.86	1.61	.81	70
Treasury bills	80.00	1.69	.85	70
Three months:				
Time deposits	38.67	3.82	1.94	75
Treasury bills	58.67	4.08	2.07	75

Note: For the sources of data see table 10.5.

[a] %ONB = Percentage of observations within the neutral band.

[b] NOBS = Number of observations.

[c] $\underline{p} = \dfrac{(1 + i) - \Omega(1 + i^{*})(1 - .25i)}{\Omega(1 + i^{*})(1 - .25i)}$; $\bar{p} = \dfrac{\Omega(1 + i) - (1 + i^{*})(1 + .25i)}{(1 + i^{*})(1 + .25i)}$; $p^{*} = \dfrac{i - i^{*}}{(1 + i^{*})}$.

percent above the parity line to present opportunities for profitable capital outflows through Mexican commercial banks. Also as expected, the percentage of observations inside the neutral band rises considerably. As in the previous case, and for the same reasons, the percentage of observations inside the band is larger for Mexican treasury bills than for peso time deposits, and they are also larger for one-month assets than for three-month assets.

It is unclear if arbitragers actually incur the additional costs of the 25 percent deposit. Sources in Mexican commercial banks affirm that the previous deposit regulation left them out of the market, because individuals prefer to operate through foreign commercial banks located in foreign countries to avoid the regulation. Nevertheless, the results of table 10.6 give us an idea of the costs that arbitragers will be willing to bear before resorting to Mexican commercial banks, that is, the costs they will be willing to bear to circumvent the regulation.

Another factor that may partially explain the results of table 10.5 is the exchange gains tax treatment. If there is a depreciation of the exchange rate, holders of dollar deposits must pay taxes on the increase of the peso value of the deposit. Therefore, holders of dollar deposits must take into account the possible change in the exchange rate. Given that the future value of the spot exchange rate is unknown at the time of creating a deposit, there is uncertainty; hence, it is not formally correct to call the operations we are considering arbitrage. Nevertheless, I will continue using that term. Let t denote the marginal rate of taxation, and let S_1 denote the value of the spot exchange rate at the time when the deposit matures. Assume that investors are risk neutral; they are interested only in the expected returns of their operation. Under those assumptions there are incentives for capital outflows if:

(12)
$$(1 + i) < \frac{F}{S}(1 + i^*)\Omega - E\left(\frac{S_1 - S}{S}\right)t.$$

There are incentives for capital inflows if:

(13)
$$(1 + i)\Omega > \frac{F}{S}(1 + i^*) - \frac{F}{S}E\left(\frac{S_1 - S}{S_1}\right)t.$$

For the construction of a neutral band based on these conditions, we need to know $E[(S_1 - S)/S]$ and $E[(S_l - S)/S_1]$. Assuming that $F = E(S_1)$ and ignoring Jensen's inequality, we can replace those expressions by $(F - S)/S$ and $(F - S)/F$, respectively. Under those assumptions and using equations (12) and (13), we can derive

(14)
$$\underline{p} = \frac{(1 + i) - (1 + i^*)\Omega}{(1 + i^*)\Omega - t},$$

(15)
$$\bar{p} = \frac{(1 + i)\Omega - (1 + i^*)}{(1 + i^*) - t}.$$

There is a substantial difference between the effects of the tax on exchange gains and the effects of the 25 percent deposit. The deposit increases the costs for both capital inflows and capital outflows. Therefore, $\underline{p}$ rises and $\bar{p}$ decreases, widening the band around the parity line. This can be checked by comparing equations (10) and (11) with equations (6) and (7). On the other hand, the tax on exchange gains increases the costs for capital outflows while giving incentives to capital inflows. Therefore, besides affecting the width of the band, the tax displaces the band upward. As the comparison of equations (14) and (15) with equations (6) and (7) indicates, $\underline{p}$ and $\bar{p}$ both increase.

Table 10.7 presents the results when equations (14) and (15) are used to compute $\underline{p}$ and $\bar{p}$. The value assumed for t is .55, which is the highest marginal tax rate for individuals. The percentage of observations within the band is larger than in table 10.5 for each of the categories, and the band size is also larger. In this case, the observations outside the band are distributed above and below it. That is, sometimes there seem to be opportunities for profitable capital outflows and sometimes there seem to be opportunities for profitable capital inflows. The opportunities for capital outflows are present in the first part of the period, in which domestic interest rates were relatively low. The opportunities for capital inflows are present in the second part of the period, in which domestic interest rates have risen considerably. Considering capital outflows, on average, the one-month discount of the peso has to rise more than 1.34 percent above the parity line for them to be profitable.

Once again, it is not clear whether the exchange gains tax is actually paid by holders of dollar deposits. It seems that individuals are able to evade relatively easily the payment of the tax, but that firms are moni-

Table 10.7   Deviations from Interest Parity Computed
from Equations (14) and (15)

	%ONB[a]	Average $\underline{p} - \bar{p}$[c]	Average $\underline{p} - p^{*}$[c]	NOBS[b]
One month:				
Time deposits	85.71	1.93	1.34	70
Treasury bills	74.28	1.93	1.52	70
Three months:				
Time deposits	40.00	3.24	2.98	75
Treasury bills	49.77	3.26	3.52	75

Note: For the sources of data see table 10.5.
[a]%ONB = Percentage of observations within the neutral band.
[b]NOBS = Number of observations.
[c]
$$\underline{p} = \frac{(1 + i) - (1 + i^{*})\Omega}{(1 + i^{*})\Omega - t}; \quad \bar{p} = \frac{(1 + i)\Omega - (1 + i^{*})}{(1 + i^{*}) - t}; \quad p^{*} = \frac{i - i^{*}}{1 + i^{*}}.$$

tored more closely and are less able to evade it. The results of table 10.7 give us an idea of the costs that holders of dollar deposits will be willing to bear to evade paying those taxes.

As a final exercise, I consider the case in which both regulations—the 25 percent deposit and the tax on exchange gains—are present. Under those conditions there are incentives to capital outflows if:

(16) $$(1 + i) < \frac{F}{S}(1 + i^{*})\Omega(1 - .25i) - E\left(\frac{S_1 - S}{S}\right)t.$$

There are incentives to capital inflows if:

(17) $$\frac{\Omega(1 + i)}{(1 + .25i)} > \frac{F}{S}(1 + i^{*}) - \frac{F}{S}E\left(\frac{S_1 - S}{S_1}\right)t.$$

From equations (16) and (17), and under the assumptions made previously,

(18) $$\underline{p} = \frac{(1 + i) - \Omega(1 + i^{*})(1 - .25i)}{\Omega(1 + i^{*})(1 - .25i) - t},$$

(19) $$\bar{p} = \frac{\Omega(1 + i) - (1 + i^{*})(1 + .25i)}{(1 + .25i)(1 + i^{*} - t)}.$$

Comparing equations (18) and (19) with equations (6) and (7), it is clear that $\underline{p}$ is larger than in the first case considered as a consequence of both regulations: the exchange gains tax reduces the denominator, and the 25 percent deposit increases the numerator and reduces the denominator. As previously mentioned, the effects of the two regulations work in opposite directions on $\bar{p}$. The 25 percent deposit reduces it and the exchange gains tax increase it.

Table 10.8 presents the results for the case in which both regulations are present. The band has widened substantially and, as a result, all the observations lie within it. Now, for example, on average it is necessary for the one-month discount on the peso to rise more than 2.16 percent above the parity line for capital outflows to be profitable.

10.5   Concluding Remarks

Domestic interest rates may be linked to foreign interest rates by the Fisher hypothesis through the expected change in the exchange rate, and by the interest parity condition through the forward exchange rate premium or discount. Under a system of fixed exchange rates it is difficult to test the equivalence between the two propositions, and it is also difficult to test the Fisher hypothesis itself. Even more, in the case in which interest rates are officially regulated, interest rate differentials do not reflect exchange rate expectations but official economic policy. Interest parity, on the other hand, may be expected to work even with controlled interest rates if there are no capital controls and if individuals have access to the forward foreign exchange market.

The empirical evidence presented in this paper for the period 1979–1980 suggests that transaction costs in the foreign exchange market account for a small percentage of the deviations from parity. There are several causes that may help to explain this result. Here, I examined two of them: One is the requirement of a previous noninterest-bearing deposit in forward exchange operations, and the other is a tax on exchange gains. The explicit consideration of those additional costs increases the required deviation of the forward discount on the peso from interest

Table 10.8   Deviations from Interest Parity Computed from Equations (18) and (19)

	%ONB[a]	Average $\underline{p} - \bar{p}^c$	Average $\underline{p} - p^{*c}$	NOBS[b]
One month:				
Time deposits	100.00	3.55	2.16	70
Treasury bills	100.00	3.73	2.44	70
Three months:				
Time deposits	100.00	8.31	5.61	75
Treasury bills	100.00	8.90	6.47	75

Note: For the sources of data see table 10.5.
[a] %ONB = Percentage of observations within the neutral band.
[b] NOBS = Number of observations.

[c] $\underline{p} = \dfrac{(1 + i) - \Omega(1 + i^*)(1 - .25i)}{\Omega(1 + i^*)(1 - .25i) - t}$; $\bar{p} = \dfrac{\Omega(1 + i) - (1 + i^*)(1 + .25i)}{(1 + .25i)(1 + i^* - t)}$; $p^* = \dfrac{i - i^*}{(1 + i^*)}$.

parity for capital outflows to be profitable. This helps us to understand the observed deviations. Even when it is not clear if individuals actually incur those additional costs, such costs certainly present obstacles to the free movement of funds.

References

Aliber, Robert Z. 1973. The interest rate parity theory: A reinterpretation. *Journal of Political Economy* 81:1451–1459.

———. 1975. Monetary independence under floating exchange rates. *Journal of Finance* 30:365–376.

Allen, William A. 1977. A note on uncertainty, transaction costs and interest parity. *Journal of Monetary Economics* 3:367–373.

Bilson, John F. O. 1980. The "speculative efficiency hypothesis". NBER Working Paper Series. Working Paper no. 474.

Branson, William H. 1969. The minimum covered interest differential needed for international arbitrage activity. *Journal of Political Economy* 77:1028–1035.

Cumby, Robert E., and Maurice Obstfeld. 1980. Exchange rate expectations and nominal interest differentials: A test of the Fisher hypothesis. NBER Working Paper Series. Working Paper no. 537.

Doodley, Michael P., and Peter Isard. 1980. Capital controls, political risk, and deviations from interest parity. *Journal of Political Economy* 88:370–384.

Fama, Eugene F., and André Farber. 1979. Money, bonds and foreign exchange. *American Economic Review* 69:639–649.

Fieleke, Norman S. 1975. Exchange rate flexibility and the efficiency of the foreign exchange market. *Journal of Financial and Quantitative Analysis* 10:409–428.

Fisher, Irving. 1930. *The theory of interest.* New York: Macmillan.

Frankel, Jeffrey A. 1979. The diversifiability of exchange risk. *Journal of International Economics* 9:379–393.

Frenkel, Jacob A., and Richard M. Levich. 1975. Covered interest arbitrage: Unexploited profits. *Journal of Political Economy* 83:325–338.

———. 1977. Transaction costs and interest arbitrage: Tranquil vs. turbulent periods. *Journal of Political Economy* 85:1209–1226.

———. 1979. Covered interest arbitrage and unexploited profits? Reply. *Journal of Political Economy* 87:418–422.

Geweke, John, and Edgard Feige. 1979. Some joint tests of the efficiency of markets for forward foreign exchange. *Review of Economics and Statistics* 61:334–341.

Grauer, Frederick L., Robert Litzenberger, and Richard E. Stehle. 1976. Sharing rules and equilibrium in an international capital market under uncertainty. *Journal of Financial Economics* 3:233–256.

Hansen, Lars P., and Robert J. Hodrick. 1980. Forward exchange rates as optimal predictors of future spot rates: An econometric analysis. *Journal of Political Economy* 88:829–853.

Krasker, William S. 1980. The peso problem in testing efficiency of forward exchange markets. *Journal of Monetary Economics* 6:269–276.

Levi, Maurice D. 1977. Taxation and "abnormal" international capital flows. *Journal of Political Economy* 85:635–646.

Lizondo, J. Saúl. 1980. Foreign exchange future prices under fixed exchange rates. ITAM (April). Mimeographed.

McCormick, Frank. 1979. Covered interest arbitrage: Unexploited profits? Comment. *Journal of Political Economy* 87:411–417.

McCulloch, J. Huston. 1975. Operational aspects of the Siegel paradox. *Quarterly Journal of Economics* 89:170–172.

McKinnon, Ronald I. 1976. Floating foreign exchange rates 1973–1974: The emperor's new clothes. *Journal of Monetary Economics*, suppl., 3:79–114.

Officer, Lawrence H., and Thomas D. Willett. 1970. The covered arbitrage schedule: A critical survey of recent developments. *Journal of Money, Credit and Banking* 2:247–257.

Pedersson, George, and Edward Tower. 1979. On the long- and short-run relationship between the forward rate and the interest parity. *Journal of Macroeconomics* 1:65–77.

Prachowny, Martin F. 1970. A note on interest parity and the supply of arbitrage funds. *Journal of Political Economy* 78:540–545.

Roll, Richard, and Bruno Solnik. 1979. On some parity conditions encountered frequently in international economics. *Journal of Macroeconomics* 1:267–283.

Siegel, Jeremy J. 1972. Risk, interest rates, and the forward exchange. *Quarterly Journal of Economics* 86:303–309.

Stockman, Alan C. 1978. Risk, information and forward exchange rates. In *The economics of exchange rates*, ed. J. A. Frenkel and H. G. Johnson. Reading, Mass.: Addison-Wesley.

Tsiang, S. C. 1959. The theory of forward exchange and effects of government intervention on the forward exchange market. *IMF Staff Papers* 7:75–106.

Comment   Kenneth Rogoff

Lizondo's paper achieves a significant step toward explaining and quantifying the segmentation of Mexican financial markets from world financial markets. He shows explicitly how to take into account tax laws and forward contract regulations in analyzing covered interest arbitrage between dollar time deposits (in Mexican banks) and peso time deposits or treasury bills.

There is one confusing aspect of Lizondo's otherwise very clear analysis, and most of this comment will be directed toward clarifying it. Lizondo defines deviations from covered interest parity on the basis of net of tax interest rates, but gross of tax capital gains on exchange rate depreciation (see tables 10.2 and 10.5). The taxes on capital gains are introduced only in the latter part of the paper as one major factor which helps explain the author's definition of covered interest deviations.[1] Because these deviations only take into account the taxes on interest income, and because peso-denominated deposits yielded a higher interest rate during the sample period, the deviations are skewed in favor of dollar assets. The deviations would be less skewed if they were based on gross yields, or if they included capital gain taxes on dollar appreciation against the peso. Of these two consistent definitions of covered interest arbitrage, it would probably be better to look first at gross yields. Tax laws and forward contract regulations could then be used to explain deviations from zero, much as Lizondo does.[2] Some aspects of the relationship between gross of tax and net of tax covered interest parity are developed in the analysis below. This analysis also expands on Lizondo's observation that covered interest arbitrage can involve risk because of taxes.

Covered interest parity is defined in equation (1) on a gross of tax basis:

$$(1) \qquad 1 + i_t = F_t(1 + i_t^*)/S_t,$$

where i_t and i_t^* are the interest rates on peso-denominated Mexican bank time deposits and dollar-denominated Mexican bank time deposits. S_t is the spot rate at time t (peso/dollar), and F_t is the forward rate at time t.

Kenneth Rogoff is an economist at the Board of Governors of the Federal Reserve System, Washington, D.C.

The author thanks Dale Henderson for useful suggestions. The views expressed herein are the author's and do not represent the opinions of the Board of Governors of the Federal Reserve System.

1. The size of the bounds in Lizondo's table 10.8 would be smaller if centered on a definition of covered interest deviations which included the tax on capital gains. Incidentally, the one- and three-month bounds in Lizondo's tables differ so much because the interest rate deviations are not annualized.

2. This is really only a suggestion of an alternative way to organize the paper, since it would lead to much the same conclusions as Lizondo's.

The forward rate and the interest rates in equation (1) are of the same maturity.

In equation (2), (covered) interest arbitrage is defined on a net of tax basis for a taxpaying Mexican investor:[3]

$$(2) \quad \begin{aligned} (1 + i) - \tau_i i &= \hat{S}_{t+1}(1 + i^*)/S_t + \phi(F_t - \hat{S}_{t+1}) - \tau_i i^* \hat{S}_{t+1}/S_t \\ &- \tau_s(\hat{S}_{t+1} - S_t)/S_t - \tau_f \phi(F_t - \hat{S}_{t+1}), \end{aligned}$$

where $\hat{S}_{t+1}$ is the expected value of S_{t+1} (which is not necessarily equal to the forward rate when there is a risk premium); τ_i is the marginal tax rate on interest income from peso-denominated deposits and also on the peso value of interest income from dollar-denominated deposits; τ_s is the marginal tax rate on capital gains from exchange rate depreciation; τ_f is the marginal tax rate on capital gains from forward contracts; and ϕ is the quantity of dollars the investor sells forward to cover his exchange rate risk. Because of taxes, he will not necessarily need to cover the principal plus gross interest exactly; we will solve for the appropriate ϕ^* below. The left-hand side of equation (2) represents the principal plus net interest income obtained by placing one peso in a one-period peso-denominated time deposit. The right-hand side of (2) represents the after-tax peso income obtained by converting one peso into dollars and placing it in a one-period dollar-denominated time deposit, while simultaneously selling ϕ dollars forward. The first term on the right-hand side represents the gross expected return from holding the dollar time deposit, and the second term represents the gross expected return on the forward contract. Even though the forward rate may equal the expected value of the future spot rate, it is important to retain this term because we want to analyze risk as well as expected return. The third term on the right-hand side of (2) represents the expected tax on the dollar interest income. This term is uncertain at time t due to the assumption that investors have to pay interest income taxes on the peso value of their dollar interest income. The fourth term represents the expected tax on the expected appreciation of the principal. The final term represents the expected tax on the expected capital gain or loss on the forward contract.

By choosing the size of the forward contract ϕ appropriately, the investor can insure himself of a riskless peso return on his dollar-denominated asset. The appropriate ϕ^* is found by summing the coefficients on the expected spot rate $\hat{S}_{t+1}$ in equation (2), and setting ϕ so that this sum is zero. Performing this calculation yields

$$(3) \quad \phi^* = [(1 - \tau_s) + i^*(1 - \tau_i)]/S_t(1 - \tau_f).$$

---

3. Net of tax interest arbitrage may be relevant even for an analysis of tax-avoiding investors. Lizondo points out that the taxes may provide a measure of tax-avoidance costs.

The expression for net of tax covered interest arbitrage is obtained by using equation (3) to substitute for ϕ^* in equation (2). It is clear from equations (2) and (3) that covered interest arbitrage does not become risky when taxes are introduced as long as the investor adjusts the size of his forward contract to take the taxes into account. The covering forward contract becomes smaller as interest income taxes and exchange rate capital gain taxes rise, and falls as capital gain taxes on forward contracts rise. When all three tax rates are equal, the covering forward contract ϕ^* is $(1 + i^*)/S_t$, which is exactly the size of the covering forward contract in equation (1) for gross of tax interest arbitrage.

The case where the capital gain tax rates and income tax rates are all equal is important because when $\tau_i = \tau_s = \tau_f$, net of tax covered interest arbitrage, equations (2) and (3), implies gross of tax interest arbitrage, equation (1). Thus deviations from gross of tax covered interest arbitrage can only be attributed to taxes to the extent that marginal tax rates on interest income and capital gains differ. Again, this result holds whether or not the forward rate is equal to the expected value of the future spot rate.

In conclusion, I should note that Lizondo's paper contains a useful discussion of a number of methodological issues faced by an empirical researcher who is trying to extract information from exchange market data. The so-called "peso problem" is particularly relevant to the problem at hand. It is worth emphasizing that the "peso problem" refers to the slow convergence to normality of distributions which include the small probability of a major event. Even if the rare event (which in this case is a sudden devaluation of the Mexican peso) occurs in the sample, problems arise. The asymptotic, normal distribution on which most statistical tests are based may still provide only a poor approximation to the sample distribution unless the sample size is very large, perhaps large enough to include many devaluations. The problems posed by Jensen's inequality are also more likely to be significant when there is a small probability of a major intervention.

11   Capital Mobility and the Scope for Sterilization: Mexico in the 1970s

Robert E. Cumby and Maurice Obstfeld

This paper studies the interaction between Mexico's capital account and domestic credit policy during the decade 1970–1980. It seeks in particular to measure the offset to monetary policy caused by interest-sensitive capital flows, and, in doing so, is careful to account for the potential estimation bias introduced by central bank sterilization activities. The empirical record suggests that the instantaneous capital account offset to monetary policy, while substantial, was less than complete in the 1970s. The Banco de México's short-run control of the monetary base allowed it to sterilize international reserve movements, at least over part of the decade.

Empirical studies of offsetting capital flows have concentrated almost exclusively on the industrialized, North Atlantic economies.[1] But the impact of capital mobility on domestic monetary management is of great importance for Mexico, which until August 1982 had allowed relatively unrestricted external asset trading, and for other industrializing economies which have only recently removed impediments to capital account

Robert E. Cumby is a professor at the Graduate School of Business Administration, New York University. While preparing this paper he was with the International Monetary Fund, Washington, D.C. Maurice Obstfeld is a professor in the Department of Economics, Columbia University, and a Research Associate of the National Bureau of Economic Research.

This research was supported in part by the National Science Foundation and was completed while Dr. Obstfeld was a Visiting Scholar in the International Finance Division of the Board of Governors, Federal Reserve System. The authors acknowledge with thanks the helpful suggestions of Pedro Aspe, Rudiger Dornbusch, Jacob Frenkel, Pentti Kouri, and Kenneth Rogoff. All errors and opinions are the authors'. The views expressed here are not necessarily those of the institutions with which they are affiliated.

1. An exception is Miller and Askin (1976), which studies Brazil and Chile and reaches conclusions similar to those reached below for the Mexican case.

transactions. Argentina, for example, experienced substantial capital inflows and real exchange rate appreciation as a result of the disinflation policy it pursued in the late 1970s. Sterilization might mitigate these problems during the transition to lower inflation rates in countries (such as Uruguay) following strategies similar to Argentina's.

Broadly speaking, the econometric approaches taken in the industrialized country studies of the capital account offset may be classified either as "reduced form" (Porter 1972; Kouri and Porter 1974; Girton and Roper 1977) or "structural" (Herring and Marston 1977; Obstfeld 1980a).[2] In this paper, we apply the structural approach to the recent Mexican experience in order to avoid the simultaneous equations bias that may distort reduced-form offset estimates in the presence of a sterilization rule. The structural model estimated is a partial equilibrium model of financial markets, however. As such, it can yield at best a partial picture of the channels through which monetary policy was offset over the longer run.

An additional feature of our econometric technique deserves mention. Along with the standard two-stage least squares estimates of the Mexican structural equations, we present estimates based on the two-step, two-stage least squares procedure proposed by Cumby, Huizinga and Obstfeld (1981). The theoretical advantages of the latter estimator are discussed in context below.

The plan of the paper is as follows: Section 11.1 distinguishes between offsetting capital movements and systematic sterilization as possible causes of an empirical negative correlation between capital inflows and increases in the domestic source component of the monetary base. We briefly review the reduced-form approach to the offset in the light of possible contemporaneous feedback from the balance of payments to the central bank's domestic assets.

Section 11.2 describes our empirical measure of domestic credit expansion and estimates a quarterly Banco de México reaction function relating changes in the domestic source component of the high-powered money stock to the balance of payments and the public sector borrowing requirement. We find that reserve flows were a significant determinant of domestic credit movements in the 1970s and are unable to reject the hypothesis that sterilization of reserve flows was complete, at least over the second half of the decade.

Section 11.3 estimates the parameters of a small, aggregative model of Mexico's money market and capital account. The underlying portfolio balance model of the capital account assumes that peso-denominated, nonmoney assets and covered foreign assets are imperfect substitutes in

---

2. The paper of Argy and Kouri (1974) does not fall easily into either of these categories. See note 8 below for further discussion.

portfolios and allows for the gradual adjustment of portfolio shares to their desired values. The empirical results imply that, depending on how the increase in the money supply was effected, anywhere between 30 and 50 percent of an expansion in domestic credit was offset by capital outflow in the same quarter. The offset would have been higher had asset markets adjusted fully within one quarter.

Section 11.4 briefly discusses the extent to which a systematic relationship between domestic credit movements and the futures premium on foreign exchange might alter the results of section 11.3. The data reveal a pronounced relation between the futures premium and lagged deviations from purchasing power parity. We argue that expectations concerning possible peso devaluation were the major determinant of the premium.[3] The implication is that the external offset to monetary policy was probably exacerbated through channels not captured in our partial-equilibrium, financial-sector model.

Section 11.5 contains some concluding remarks. An appendix describes the construction of the data series employed in this study.

11.1   Sterilization and the Capital Account Offset

When the exchange rate is pegged and international capital movements are sensitive to interest rate differentials between countries, the capital account response to domestic monetary measures diminishes their effect on the monetary base. An expansion of domestic credit, say, exerts downward pressure on domestic borrowing costs, inducing a reduction in net private foreign indebtedness and a central bank reserve loss that offsets some fraction of the intended increase in the base. When domestic and foreign securities are perfectly substitutable and portfolios adjust instantaneously, this offset is complete and immediate: the central bank possesses no control over the domestic money stock.[4]

Both imperfect *substitutability* between interest-bearing assets of different currency denomination and imperfect *mobility* of capital between financial centers may afford a central bank some short-run monetary independence. Neither necessarily enables the central bank to peg the price level or money supply indefinitely (see Obstfeld 1980b). Imperfect

3. The peso was devalued on August 31, 1976. A second devaluation occurred on February 18, 1982; and a third, on August 5, 1982, was accompanied by capital controls and the establishment of a two-tier foreign exchange market.

4. See Keynes (1930, vol. 2, p. 309) and Mundell (1963). A key assumption in deriving this result is that the central bank expands domestic credit through an open-market operation that leaves private wealth unchanged. If domestic credit creation augments private wealth and the public's demand for money is a function of its wealth, the capital account offset will not be complete, even under perfect capital mobility and unlimited asset substitutability. Below, we compute the empirical offset coefficients associated with both types of domestic credit creation.

substitutability can arise if various risks render stochastic the perceived returns on domestic and foreign assets. When this is so, the desired portfolio share of domestic bonds in domestic wealth is an increasing function of the home interest rate; and the central bank can influence this rate (and so, the demand for money) by varying the stock of outside domestic currency debt available to private wealth owners.[5] Costs associated with rapid portfolio adjustment may allow international interest rate arbitrage to occur only over time. Thus, imperfect capital mobility affords the monetary authority a second means of temporarily influencing domestic credit conditions. The model of Mexico estimated below allows for both possible sources of short-run interest rate independence in the presence of international asset trade.

The offset to monetary policy gives rise, empirically, to a negative correlation between the capital account surplus and increases in the domestic component of the base. Figure 11.1 plots the change in Banco de México's reserves against the seasonally adjusted change in domestic credit and is suggestive of such a negative correlation in the Mexican case.[6] But the absolute magnitude of this correlation, by itself, is not evidence of a powerful capital account offset. Central banks frequently take advantage of any short-run monetary control they possess to sterilize reserve flows. Their attempts to divorce the balance of payments from the high-powered money supply introduce an additional source of systematic negative correlation between domestic credit and capital inflows. A sterilization rule increases reserve volatility, but can successfully counteract balance of payment influences on the money supply in the short run when the capital account offset is incomplete. Under sterilization, there is a systematic contemporaneous feedback from the balance of payments to the domestic assets of the central bank. These two variables are jointly, endogenously determined by the preferences of private asset holders and the monetary policy reaction function of the central bank.

Attempts to measure the offset coefficient—the fraction of any domestic credit increase offset by capital outflow over the relevant time horizon—have often failed to account for sterilization, and instead view the domestic source component of the base as a predetermined variable for purposes of estimation. Studies adopting this assumption produce estimates of the offset which reflect the central bank's policy as well as the true capital account response to domestic credit expansion; but they erroneously ascribe the computed correlation exclusively to the latter. This is true in particular of the "reduced-form" approaches to the offset

5. Even when foreign and home bonds are imperfect substitutes, the central bank may be unable to control the monetary base if government debt is not outside debt; see Obstfeld (1982a) and Stockman (1979). We ignore below the problems that can arise when the public internalizes the government and central bank budget constraints.
6. The series are adjusted for reserve requirements as described in section 11.2.

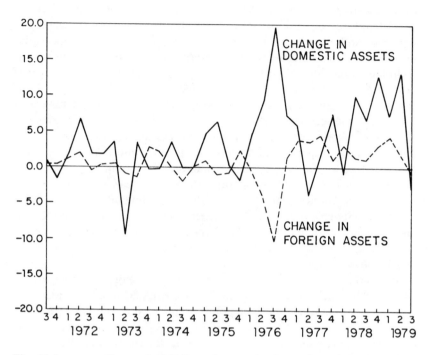

Fig. 11.1   Banco de México: changes in domestic and foreign assets (billions of pesos).

coefficient, which use ordinary least squares to regress the capital account surplus on the contemporaneous increase in domestic credit, the current account surplus, and the exogenous determinants of changes in the external asset position and the domestic interest rate (usually the contemporaneous change in the foreign interest rate and home income).[7] When the monetary authority pursues a sterilization policy, the resulting least

7. The reduced-form capital flow equation, as estimated by Kouri and Porter (1974), is derived in two steps. First, one writes the change in net external lending over a quarter as a function of the changes in the foreign and home interest rates and the changes in income and other determinants of the capital account. Second, one eliminates the change in the domestic interest rate from this equation using the (first-differenced) money-market equilibrium condition, which relates the quarterly change in (base) money demand to the sum of the capital account, the current account, and the increase in central bank domestic assets. It is of course possible that the change in home income is *not* a predetermined variable; and if income is not predetermined, ordinary least squares estimates of the reduced-form capital flow equation are inconsistent even if domestic credit policy is unrelated to the balance of payments. However, the assumption that income is predetermined is traditional in the empirical literature on offset coefficients. A similar problem arises if the current account is falsely taken to be a predetermined regressor. That problem can be avoided by moving the current account variable to the left-hand side of the capital flow equation and estimating an offset equation in which the change in international reserves is the dependent variable. Such an equation captures the current account as well as the capital account offset to domestic credit creation.

squares estimate of the domestic credit variable's coefficient is not a consistent estimate of the offset coefficient, for that variable is correlated with the capital-flow equation's disturbance term. The bias this correlation imparts to the estimated offset is discussed by a number of authors, including Argy and Kouri (1974), Magee (1976), Girton and Roper (1977), Murray (1978) and Obstfeld (1980a, 1982b).

Empirical equations which express changes in foreign reserves as a function of changes in domestic credit, changes in income, and changes in the *home* interest rate (e.g., Cardoso and Dornbusch 1980) are clearly money-demand equations, and thus can give no information regarding the effect of credit expansion on the capital account. (See Frenkel, Gylfason, and Helliwell 1980, among others, for discussion of this point.) Balance of payment equations such as the one estimated by Connolly and Dantas da Silveira (1979), which assume that income is predetermined and that money demand and the money supply multiplier are interest inelastic, assume implicitly that the external offset to domestic credit expansion is complete.[8]

In section 11.2 we estimate a Banco de México monetary policy reaction function. The results provide strong evidence that the Mexican authorities pursued a systematic policy of full sterilization during at least the second half of the 1970s. To avoid the bias this might introduce into reduced-form results, we then estimate a small structural model of Mexico's financial markets. This allows us to calculate estimates of the offset coefficient by tracing the effect on the stock of net external claims of increases in the domestic credit component of the monetary base. The structural model allows for gradual asset-market adjustment, and thus allows us to distinguish empirically between the consequences of imperfect substitutability and imperfect mobility of capital. Accordingly, we report estimates of both the short-run or one-quarter offset coefficient and the long-run offset coefficient. The former gives the fraction of a monetary expansion reversed by capital outflow in the same quarter on the assumption that output, the price level, and the futures premium are predetermined; the latter is a hypothetical construct measuring what the

---

8. If current real income were instead allowed to be endogenous, responding positively to a fall in the home interest rate, the offset could be incomplete even in this interest-inelastic case. It is worth noting that when money demand and money supply are both interest inelastic, the Kouri-Porter capital flow equation is underidentified. Identification is lost also when no variables other than the balance of payments enter the monetary policy reaction function. (The last statement assumes that no prior information is available concerning the degree of correlation between the disturbances of various equations.) If domestic credit responds systematically to variables other than the balance of payments, these variables, if predetermined, may be used as instruments in estimating the reduced-form capital flow equation by two-stage least squares. An instrumental-variable approach, which in principle yields consistent parameter estimates, was suggested by Argy and Kouri (1974). Their estimated offset coefficients were generally similar to those obtained by Kouri and Porter using ordinary least squares.

short-run offset would be if asset holdings could adjust immediately to their long-run desired levels.

11.2 The Banco de México's Reaction Function

In this section we examine the extent to which the Banco de México systematically neutralized the monetary effects of its foreign exchange intervention. To begin, we describe the construction of a domestic credit policy variable which summarizes the effects of a variety of instruments available to the central bank. We next estimate a central bank reaction function relating the level of this policy variable to a number of macroeconomic targets. The central finding is that a policy of systematic sterilization appears to have been followed at least during the second half of the 1970s. Not surprisingly, we find also that credit policy is influenced strongly by the need to finance the public sector's deficit, and that seasonal variation in liquidity preference is accommodated by the monetary authority.

To construct a comprehensive measure of monetary policy suited to the recent Mexican experience, two important adjustments of the published domestic credit series are required. The first involves the treatment of decisions to monetize changes in the peso value of the Banco de México's international reserves. The second incorporates the effects of variations in the reserve requirements imposed on private banks.

The peso value of the Banco de México's foreign reserves may change for two reasons other than actual foreign exchange intervention. The first of these is fluctuations in the market price of gold. Since the second quarter of 1976, the Banco de México has revalued its gold holdings daily to reflect prevailing market prices. As a result, the *dollar* value of gold holdings increased by more than 500 percent between 1975 and 1979, while physical gold holdings declined by 45 percent over the same period.[9] A second source of reserve change in the absence of balance of payments disequilibrium is exchange rate variation. When the peso-dollar rate was altered abruptly in 1976, Banco de México experienced a substantial capital gain, in peso terms, on its holdings of foreign currency denominated assets. Devaluation, like the gold price increases, inflates the book value of reserves.

The decision to monetize such capital gains as a means of government finance is entirely discretionary. The alternative is the creation of a fictitious accounting liability that offsets the increase in the peso value of central bank foreign assets without directly increasing the high-powered money stock. Monetization is thus completely analogous to an increase in

---

9. Calculations are based on year-end data published in the International Monetary Fund's *International Financial Statistics*, lines 1ad and 1and.

the domestic assets of the central bank, even though it presupposes a rise in the peso value of the bank's foreign assets. It should be included in any measure of domestic credit change and excluded when calculating foreign reserve changes.[10]

Minimum reserve requirements for private banks were varied several times during the 1970s, and these changes, too, should enter into a summary measure of domestic credit policy. We incorporate them by assuming that policymakers think in terms of an *adjusted monetary base*, that is, a base adjusted to reflect the effect of average reserve ratio changes on the volume of demand deposits it supports. (We abstract from currency in circulation.) The adjusted base at time t, BA_t, is given by

$$BA_t = \frac{q_0}{q_t} B_t,$$

where q_0 is the base-period (1971:1) average reserve ratio, q_t the current reserve ratio, and B_t the unadjusted base, measured in pesos.[11] BA_t is just the base that would support a money supply equal to B_t/q_t were the average reserve ratio at its base level q_0.

Letting $\Delta FACB_t$ denote the change in central bank foreign assets over period t (excluding valuation changes) and $\Delta DACB_t$ the change in central bank domestic assets over period t (including monetized capital gains on foreign reserves), we may write

$$(1) \qquad BA_t = BA_{t-1} + \frac{q_0}{q_{t-1}} (\Delta FACB_t + \Delta DACB_t + \Delta B_t^*),$$

where $\Delta B_t^* = [(q_{t-1} - q_t)/q_t] B_t$. Because

$$(B_t + \Delta B_t^*)/q_{t-1} = B_t/q_t,$$

ΔB_t^* is the increase in the unadjusted base that would, at reserve ratio q_{t-1}, bring about the same rise in the volume of demand deposits supported by B_t as a reduction of the reserve ratio from q_{t-1} to q_t. The quantity $(q_0/q_{t-1})\Delta B_t^*$ appearing on the right-hand side of (1) thus measures the impact of the reserve ratio change on the adjusted base.

Identity (1) suggests a natural measure of overall domestic credit policy:

$$(2) \qquad \Delta MP_t = \frac{q_0}{q_{t-1}} \Delta DACB_t + \frac{q_0}{q_{t-1}} \Delta B_t^*.$$

We take ΔMP to be the dependent variable in the Banco de México's

---

10. The data appendix provides details on the construction of our central bank domestic asset series. See also Girton and Roper (1977) on the appropriate treatment of capital-gains monetization.
11. Details on the calculation of the average reserve ratio series used in this study appear in the appendix.

monetary reaction function, and turn next to a discussion of the appropriate independent variables.

A central bank reaction function should allow for response to a number of factors in addition to the balance of payments. Monetary policy, as defined by (2), may respond also to real output fluctuations, to changes in Mexico's international competitiveness as measured by the real exchange rate, and to seasonal fluctuations in money demand, for example. Further, in the Mexican case, the public sector's borrowing requirement is a major determinant of domestic credit creation. We therefore specified a reaction function of the form:

$$\Delta MP_t = a_0 + a_1(q_0/q_{t-1})\Delta FACB_t + a_2(q_0/q_{t-1})GOVBOR_t$$

(3)
$$+ a_3 p_{t-1} + a_4 \ln(y_{t-1}/y_{t-2}) + \sum_{i=1}^{3} a_{4+i} Di + u_{1t}.$$

In (3), GOVBOR is the consolidated public sector deficit, $p \equiv \ln(ePUS/PMex)$ the log of the real exchange rate, y the index of real industrial production, and Di a seasonal dummy for the ith quarter. PUS and PMex are the U.S. and Mexican price levels, while e is the peso price of U.S. dollars.[12]

When the central bank pursues a systematic sterilization policy, a_1 is negative. If $a_1 = -1$, the monetary authority seeks to neutralize all reserve flows through offsetting movements in domestic credit: sterilization is complete. A positive value of a_1 indicates that monetary policy is aimed at external balance.

The role of government deficit financing is particularly important in Mexico.[13] The consolidated public-sector borrowing requirement consists almost entirely of the central government's borrowing requirement and the borrowing requirements of "controlled" public enterprises. In general, that part of the public sector deficit not financed through external borrowing must be financed through the domestic banking system. (The Banco de México, since 1955, has induced private banks to hold a large portion of the public sector's debt by allowing certain debt holdings to serve as required reserves.) Because the domestic banking system plays an important role in deficit financing, we expect the coefficient a_2 in (3) to be positive and significant. However, because public external borrowing is important as well, we expect a_2 to be smaller than 1.

If the monetary authority adopts a competitiveness target, the coefficient a_3 of the lagged real exchange rate should be positive. Thus, when domestic prices rise more quickly than exchange rate adjusted foreign

12. All variables are defined in detail in the appendix. Financial aggregates are measured in billions of pesos.
13. We draw on the discussions of government deficit financing in Brothers and Solís (1966) and Ortiz and Solís (1979).

prices, credit policy becomes more restrictive. If monetary policy is used to lean against cyclical activity fluctuations, a_4 is negative.

Finally, as the major seasonal influence on money demand is the fourth-quarter increase, the coefficients of the seasonal dummies should be negative.

The results of estimating the reaction function with quarterly data appear in table 11.1. The endogeneity of the balance of payments makes an instrumental variables estimation technique necessary, and two different ones were employed. The first of these was Fair's (1970) version of two-stage least squares (2SLS), which incorporates a correction for first order serial dependence in the equation's disturbance. The second was the two-step, two-stage least squares (2S2SLS) procedure proposed by Cumby, Huizinga, and Obstfeld (1981). An advantage of 2S2SLS is that the asymptotic distribution theory it uses to calculate parameter estimates' standard errors is valid under assumptions less restrictive than those adopted by Fair.[14] But both estimation methods should yield consistent parameter estimates in the present setting.

Initially, the specification (3) was used; the results are reported as equations (A) and (C) in table 11.1. Both estimates give the competitiveness term the expected positive sign, but they provide no evidence that countercyclical considerations influence domestic credit policy. Equations (B) and (D) present estimates of a reaction function from which the statistically insignificant competitiveness and cyclical variables have been excluded. The remaining coefficients exhibited relatively little sensitivity to this exclusion restriction.

The accommodation of seasonal money demand shifts is apparent in the estimates, with a strong seasonal expansion in the fourth quarter.[15] The public sector borrowing requirement is highly significant in all the regressions. These indicate that roughly 70 to 85 percent of the overall public sector deficit is financed through domestic credit creation.

Most importantly, the balance of payments coefficient $\hat{a}_1$ is negative and has a marginal significance level lower than .05 in all versions of the reaction function. Although $\hat{a}_1$ is usually smaller than -1, it is more than one standard error away from -1 only in equation (D). Thus, one cannot strongly reject the hypothesis $a_1 = -1$. The data suggest that the Banco de México attempted to control the money stock through full neutralization of reserve flows.

---

14. The standard error estimates produced by 2S2SLS allow for a nonzero covariance between the estimates of the structural parameters and the estimate of the autoregressive parameter (denoted by ρ in table 11.1). In addition, 2S2SLS does not require the absence of conditional heteroscedasticity, an important problem in standard error estimation when lagged endogenous variables are used as instruments. Conditional heteroscedasticity is discussed by Dhrymes (1974, pp. 183–184), Engle (1982), and Hansen (1979), and, in a cross-sectional context, by White (1980, 1982).

15. This seasonality is reflected in the money demand equation estimated below.

Table 11.1   **Mexico: Reaction Function (1971:3–1979:4)[a]**

Method	Constant	$(q_0/q_{-1}) \times \Delta FACB$	$(q_0/q_{-1}) \times$ GOVBOR	P_{-1}	$\ln(y_{-1}/y_{-2})$	$D1$	$D2$	$D3$	$\hat{\rho}$	SE	R^2
(A) Fair	20.8	−1.266	0.760	22.7	67.7	−40.0	−18.1	−41.2	−0.82	10.6	0.747
	(10.9)	(0.595)	(0.172)	(22.4)	(73.6)	(20.7)	(5.0)	(21.5)	(0.13)		
(B) Fair	16.8	−1.453	0.834	—	—	−32.9	−17.1	−31.6	−0.73	10.6	0.729
	(7.8)	(0.655)	(0.181)			(14.2)	(4.5)	(14.2)	(0.17)		
(C) 2S2SLS[b]	21.2	−1.153	0.691	21.3	39.7	−40.3	−17.0	−38.2	−0.86	9.4	0.738
	(25.5)	(0.223)	(0.121)	(13.0)	(51.9)	(50.8)	(3.4)	(48.3)	(0.26)		
(D) 2S2SLS	13.0	−1.315	0.737	—	—	−25.4	−14.8	−21.8	−0.69	9.7	0.721
	(3.1)	(0.127)	(0.102)			(4.6)	(2.6)	(3.7)	(0.09)		

[a]Standard errors are in parentheses. Mean of dependent variable is 5.8 billion Mexican pesos. Instruments used were a constant, three seasonal dummies, lagged monetary policy, lagged reserve changes, lagged government deficit, once- and twice-lagged competitiveness and real income changes, foreign income, and the foreign interest rate. When the lagged competitiveness and cyclical terms were dropped in (B) and (D), those variables were also removed from the instrument list. The choice of instruments allows the government deficit to be endogenously determined.

[b]Equation (C) reports two-stage least squares estimates that use a heteroscedasticity-consistent estimate of the parameter estimates' variance-covariance matrix. These results, rather than the more efficient second-step estimates, are reported here because the algorithm for computing the latter failed to converge after 200 iterations. The parameter estimates obtained after 200 iterations were virtually identical to those reported in (C), however. For example, the sterilization coefficient was −1.158 and the government deficit coefficient was 0.692.

To investigate the stability of the reaction function, we split our sample into two subperiods, 1971:3–1975:4 and 1976:1–1979:4. In the first subperiod there appeared to be no significant relationship between domestic credit policy and any of the explanatory variables (other than dummies). The relationship estimated (by Fair's method) over the second subperiod is similar to those reported in table 11.1:

$$\Delta MP = 64.6 - 1.362 \, (q_0/q_{-1})\Delta FACB + .441 \, (q_0/q_{-1})GOVBOR$$
$$(48.7) \quad (0.584) \qquad\qquad\qquad (.174)$$
$$- 122.9 \, D_1 - 29.7 \, D_2 - 114.6 \, D_3,$$
$$(95.6) \qquad (6.8) \qquad (94.8)$$

$$\hat{\rho} = -0.94 \,, \qquad SE = 10.4 \,, \qquad R^2 = 0.904.$$
$$(0.05)$$

These results suggest that sterilization was a more important factor in monetary policy during the second half of the 1970s than during the first half.[16] The finding is consistent with the fact that the range of monetary tools available to the Banco de México broadened considerably after 1975.[17]

We conclude that part of the observed negative correlation between changes in the domestic and foreign source components of the base is likely to be the result of official sterilization policy. An implication is that domestic credit policy responds to the contemporaneous balance of payments and should not be treated as a predetermined factor in estimating the capital account offset coefficient.

11.3   A Structural Model of Asset Markets

In this section we estimate a small, aggregative portfolio-balance model of Mexican financial markets. The model allows the calculation of both the short-run and long-run offset coefficients. It consists of three equations: a demand equation for the net external liabilities of the Mexican private sector, a money demand equation, and a money supply equation. All equations are based on quarterly data and were estimated by 2SLS (with Fair's autoregressive correction when necessary) and by the 2S2SLS procedure. A list of the instruments used is provided in a note to table 11.2.

---

16. Bhalla (1981) computes a positive correlation between the balance of payments and the change in the money stock using annual data for the period 1956–1972. This evidence also suggests that sterilization was of limited importance before the mid-1970s.

17. Business International (1979) reports that Banco de México has used *Certificados de Tesorería de la Federación* since 1978 and petrobonds since 1977 to conduct open-market operations. In addition, the move to market valuation of gold reserves in 1976 allowed greater flexibility in choosing the rate of domestic credit expansion. Prior to these innovations, the monetary authority relied on reserve-requirement changes, special deposits, and operations in government securities within the banking system (see Brothers and Solís 1966). Only the last of these was employed with any frequency.

Both the money and external liability demand equations relate desired asset holdings to the expected return on foreign assets. An important component of this return is the expected depreciation of the peso relative to foreign currency. The presence of a large, discrete devaluation of the peso in 1976:3 poses a problem, for it is unlikely that the devaluation was completely unanticipated, or that anticipations of exchange rate movements were a minor determinant of capital flows in 1976–1977. Indeed, figure 11.1 presents striking evidence that the devaluation of 1976 was preceded by a sizable anticipatory outflow of capital.

To capture the impact of exchange rate expectations, we used the premium on three-month peso futures as an explanatory variable in our empirical equations.[18] This premium does reflect the anticipation of a devaluation for several quarters preceding 1976:3, but was always substantially smaller than the realized parity change. This is not surprising in view of the uncertain date of the peso's devaluation.[19]

Each equation is now discussed in turn. At the end of the section, the implied offset coefficients are calculated.

11.3.1   Net Foreign Liabilities

We assume that the real peso value of the desired stock of net external liabilities, eF^d/PMex, may be written as a function of domestic and foreign interest rates, domestic real income, and domestic real wealth:

$$(4) \qquad \frac{eF^d}{\text{PMex}} = \Phi(r, r^* + f, y, W/\text{PMex}) + u_2.$$

In (4), r is the domestic interest rate, r^* the foreign rate, f the premium on peso futures, and W nominal Mexican wealth.[20] We assume that Mexican participants comprise a sufficiently small share of the world financial market that the foreign interest rate may be taken as exogenous.

---

18. The futures rate is expressed in pesos per dollar; and the futures premium is the percent excess of the futures rate over the spot rate e (on an annualized basis). The futures premium can be interpreted as an indicator of exchange rate expectations or as the cost of forward cover. The two interpretations, of course, need not conflict. We use the futures premium rather than the forward premium used by Lizondo (chapter 10 of this volume) because there is a longer series of observations available for the former variable. Jacob Frenkel has suggested that the futures premium may measure exchange rate expectations with error. The two-step, two-stage least squares estimates (but *not* Fair's method estimates) reported below yield consistent parameter estimates even when all asset returns are measured with random, serially uncorrelated error. See Cumby, Huizinga, and Obstfeld (1981) on the procedure to employ when an equation with errors in variables is corrected for autoregressive dependence of its structural disturbance.

19. Lizondo (1983) shows how the futures premium may underpredict an anticipated future devaluation if agents have rational expectations and are uncertain about the timing (but not the magnitude) of the devaluation.

20. All rate-of-return variables are measured in units of percent per annum. We are assuming here that domestic and covered foreign bonds are imperfect substitutes because of political risk. See Aliber (1973) and Dooley and Isard (1980). After the August 1982 devaluation, the Mexican government did in fact take measures penalizing holders of U.S. dollar denominated assets within its jurisdiction.

In addition, we assume that foreign holdings of peso-denominated assets are negligible, so that we may ignore the effects of foreign income and wealth. To incorporate the possibility of imperfect capital mobility, we suppose that agents need not adjust portfolio shares instantaneously to their full optimum level, but instead succeed in making a fraction λ of the adjustment each period. Thus,

$$(5) \quad eF/\text{PMex} - e_{-1}F_{-1}/\text{PMex}_{-1} = \lambda(eF^d/\text{PMex} - e_{-1}F_{-1}/\text{PMex}_{-1}),$$

where F is the *actual* stock of net foreign liabilities, measured in dollars.

Combining equations (4) and (5) and linearizing, we obtain the equation to be estimated,

$$(6) \quad \frac{e_t F_t}{\text{PMex}_t} = b_0 + b_1 \frac{e_{t-1}F_{t-1}}{\text{PMex}_{t-1}} + b_2 r_t + b_3(r_t^* + f_t) + b_4 y_t + b_5 W_t/\text{PMex}_t + \epsilon_{2t},$$

where $b_1 = 1 - \lambda$, and $\epsilon_{2t} = \lambda u_{2t}$. A rise in the home interest rate induces an inflow of capital or an increase in net external liabilities, so $b_2 > 0$. Similarly, $b_3 < 0$. An increase in domestic real income augments the transactions demand for money and causes a decline in desired holdings of foreign assets, so $b_4 > 0$. Finally, an increase in domestic wealth leads to a reduction in external liabilities, and thus, $b_5 < 0$.

The results of estimating (6) are reported in table 11.2.[21] They provide evidence that capital flows are quite sensitive to the domestic interest rate even in the short run. The two techniques yield very similar parameter estimates, although those obtained by 2S2SLS appear to be more precise. All interest rate coefficients have the expected sign and are significant at the 5 percent level. Equation (B), for example, suggests that a 100 basis point rise in the home interest rate, all else equal, induces a capital inflow of 1.2 billion real pesos in the same quarter, while an equal increase in the covered foreign rate induces a 0.25 billion real peso outflow. Both estimates of the adjustment parameter λ are near 0.35. Again using equation (B), the long-run capital inflow occasioned by a 100 basis point rise in r is 3.9 billion real pesos, while the outflow following an equal increase in $r^* + f$ is 0.83 billion real pesos.

The wealth variable has the anticipated sign and is significant at the 5 percent level in both equations. Equation (B) suggests that approximately 15 percent of an increase in wealth is allocated to foreign assets within one quarter. The long-run portfolio share is 50 percent.

11.3.2   Money Demand

The demand for narrowly defined real money ($M1$) balances is assumed to depend on the domestic and foreign covered interest rates,

---

21. The domestic income variable had a small and very insignificant coefficient. It was therefore omitted from the equation reported in table 11.2.

Table 11.2 **Mexico: Net Foreign Liabilities (1971:3–1979:4)[a]**

Method	Constant	r	$(r^* + f)$	$W/PMex$	$\dfrac{e_{-1}F_{-1}}{PMex_{-1}}$	$\hat{\rho}$	SE	R^2
(A) Fair	4.64	1.46	−0.265	−0.207	0.605	−0.457	3.263	0.935
	(3.14)	(0.29)	(0.103)	(0.064)	(0.073)	(0.158)		
(B) 2S2SLS	3.22	1.161	−0.252	−0.150	0.696	−0.866	3.425	0.916
	(1.08)	(0.146)	(0.066)	(0.032)	(0.025)	(0.131)		

[a]Standard errors are in parentheses. Mean of dependent variable is 6.73 billion 1975 Mexican pesos. As in the regressions reported in tables 11.3 and 11.4, the instruments used here are a constant, three seasonal dummies, the contemporaneous foreign interest rate and real income level, the lagged government deficit, lagged domestic real income, the lagged futures premium, and the lagged dependent variable. This choice of instruments allows the domestic interest rate, the futures premium, domestic real income, and the budget deficit to be endogenous. The use of contemporaneous foreign variables as exogenous instruments is justified if Mexico can be regarded as a small country in world markets for goods and assets. When necessary, the instrument list was augmented to satisfy Fair's minimum criterion (see Fair 1970).

real income, and real wealth. Thus, long-run desired money holdings may be written as

$$\frac{M^d}{\text{PMex}} = \Lambda(r, r^* + f, y, W/\text{PMex}) + u_3.$$

Invoking the partial adjustment mechanism and linearizing as before, we obtain the empirical specification,

$$(7) \qquad \frac{M_t}{\text{PMex}_t} = c_0 + c_1 \frac{M_{t-1}}{\text{PMex}_{t-1}} + c_2 r_t + c_3(r_t^* + f_t) + c_4 y_t$$

$$+ c_5 W_t/\text{PMex}_t + \epsilon_{3t},$$

where $1 - c_1$ is again the adjustment parameter. As usual, we expect c_2, $c_3 < 0$, and c_4, $c_5 > 0$.

The results of estimating (7) appear in table 11.3.[22] As before, the 2SLS and the 2S2SLS estimates are quite similar. Table 11.3 reports two versions of the money demand equation. In (A) and (B) we estimate the money demand equation without imposing coefficient constraints, while in (C) and (D) the two rate-of-return coefficients are constrained to be equal. In neither of the latter two equations is the constraint rejected by the data. When the constraint is imposed, the coefficient on the interest rates is significant at the 5 percent level. In the unconstrained equation only the coefficient on the covered foreign interest rate is significant.

The adjustment of real balances to long-run desired levels is estimated to be approximately 20 percent per quarter. Equation (D), for example, suggests that a 100 basis point increase in either rate of return leads to a 0.3 billion peso decrease in real money demand in the same quarter and a 1.4 billion peso decrease in real money demand in the long run.

As expected, an increase in real income raises real money demand. At the sample means of y and M/PMex, the income elasticity of money demand derived from equation (D) is 0.42 in the short run and 1.94 in the long run. The empirical equation also contains seasonal dummies, which reveal a marked seasonality in money demand. It is this seasonal variation that gives rise to the significant seasonal dummies in the Banco de México's domestic credit policy function.

11.3.3 Money Supply

The model's monetary sector includes a money supply function relating the supply of real $M1$ to the real monetary base. We assume that the supply of money by the private banking system may be written as a function of the monetary base (adjusted for reserve requirements as

---

22. Domestic wealth has been dropped from the equation, as its coefficient was small and insignificant. No evidence of serial correlation was found.

Table 11.3   **Mexico: Money Demand (1971:3–1979:4)[a]**

Method	Constant	r	$r^* + f$	y	$\dfrac{M_{-1}}{\text{PMex}_{-1}}$	$D1$	$D2$	$D3$	SE	R^2
(A) 2SLS	5.877	−0.560	−0.324	0.426	0.828	−28.7	−21.3	−22.1	4.04	0.962
	(6.100)	(1.002)	(0.170)	(0.193)	(0.228)	(5.0)	(2.6)	(2.2)		
(B) 2S2SLS	5.498	−0.723	−0.347	0.446	0.838	−29.5	−21.7	−22.0	3.65	0.961
	(3.279)	(0.952)	(0.121)	(0.050)	(0.134)	(2.8)	(1.6)	(1.8)		
(C) 2SLS	6.201	−0.312	−0.312	0.418	0.801	−28.1	−20.9	−21.9	3.86	0.964
	(5.689)	(0.156)		(0.182)	(0.192)	(4.0)	(2.1)	(1.9)		
(D) 2S2SLS	6.464	−0.306	−0.306	0.440	0.782	−28.5	−21.4	−22.0	3.47	0.965
	(2.383)	(0.086)		(0.056)	(0.050)	(1.9)	(1.5)	(1.7)		

[a]Standard errors in parentheses. Mean of dependent variable is 104.8 billion 1975 Mexican pesos. See the footnote to table 11.2 for the list of instrumental variables.

Table 11.4   Mexico: Money Supply (1971:3–1979:4)[a]

Method	Constant	r	BA/PMex	$\hat{\rho}$	SE	R^2
(A) Fair	10.8	2.249	1.016	0.717	5.620	0.907
	(12.9)	(1.166)	(0.111)	(0.128)		
(B) 2S2SLS	2.7	2.392	1.042	0.829	5.558	0.909
	(11.0)	(0.943)	(0.054)	(0.101)		

[a]Standard errors are in parentheses. Mean of dependent variable is 104.8 billion 1975 pesos. See footnote to table 11.2 for instruments.

described in section 11.2) and of the opportunity cost of holding excess reserves. When linearized, the money supply function takes the form,

$$(8) \qquad \frac{M^s_t}{\text{PMex}_t} = d_0 + d_1 r_t + d_2 \frac{BA_t}{\text{PMex}_t} + u_{4t}.$$

Estimates of the parameters of (8) are reported in table 11.4.[23] The coefficient of the real, adjusted base is quite small, reflecting both high marginal reserve requirements on demand deposits (in place throughout the estimation period) and banks' practice of holding sizable excess reserves.[24] The high interest sensitivity of money supply is also consistent with the existence of significant excess reserves.

11.3.4 The Offset Coefficient

The estimated coefficients of the structural equations may be used to calculate the capital account offset to domestic credit expansion. Two types of monetary expansion are considered. The first is an increase in domestic credit accomplished through an open-market-type asset swap that leaves private financial wealth unchanged. The second is a helicopter-type increase in credit that is accompanied by an equal increase in private financial wealth. Because our empirical money demand function does not include domestic wealth as an argument, we would expect the offset associated with the latter type of operation to be the greater one. Indeed, were b_5 equal to -1, the offset to a helicopter increase in domestic credit would be complete, even with limited asset substitutability.

In both cases the offset coefficient is (minus) the total derivative of net foreign liabilities with respect to an increase in DACB. Table 11.5A contains the short-run offset coefficients for both types of credit expansion, computed from the two sets of parameter estimates using the

23. There was no evidence of a lag in the adjustment of the money supply to its long-run level. The Banco de México discount rate was constant at 5 percent over the sample period, and therefore is omitted from the money supply equation.

24. Business International (1979) attributes this practice to the extremely limited recourse of commercial banks to rediscounting at the central bank. Generally, only certain export bills are discountable.

Table 11.5   **Mexico: Offset Coefficients[a]**

Credit Expansion	Estimation Method	
	Fair	2S2SLS
A. Short Run		
Open-market type	0.37	0.31
Helicopter type	0.51	0.41
B. Long Run		
Open-market type	0.50	0.51
Helicopter type	0.76	0.75

[a]Offset coefficients are calculated at base period reserve requirements. The capital account offset to an open-market-type credit expansion is given by

$$(9) \qquad (q_0/q_t)b_2 d_2/[(d_1 - c_2) + (q_0/q_t)b_2 d_2].$$

The offset coefficient for the helicopter-type expansion is

$$(10) \qquad \frac{(q_0/q_t)b_2 d_2 + b_5(c_2 - d_1)}{(q_0/q_t)b_2 d_2 + (d_1 - c_2)}.$$

constrained money demand equations. The short-run offset coefficients imply that, while substantial, the capital account offset to a monetary expansion was considerably less than complete. At the initial reserve ratio, anywhere from 30 to 50 percent of an increase in domestic credit by the Banco de México was offset by capital outflow within a quarter, with the exact figure depending on the method through which the domestic credit increase was effected. For example, to achieve a 1 billion peso increase in the monetary base through helicopter money creation, a 1.7–2 billion peso expansion of domestic credit was required. As expected, the computed offsets to a helicopter-type expansion exceed those to an open-market-type expansion, in both cases by approximately 10 percentage points. The offset coefficients derived from the Fair's method estimates exceed those derived from the 2S2SLS estimates. This difference is the result of the greater domestic interest rate sensitivity of capital flows implied by the former set of estimates.

It is also of interest to calculate the offset in a hypothetical world in which portfolio adjustment occurs instantaneously. Replacing the parameters in (9) and (10) with their corresponding long-run values, we obtain "long-run" offset coefficients in all cases between 50 and 76 percent (see table 11.5B). The computed "long-run" offsets to open-market-type expansions are in the lower end of this range, and those corresponding to helicopter-type expansions are near 76 percent. It should be stressed that we are using the term "long run" in a limited sense to signify only the complete adjustment of asset stocks to their desired values.

The estimates indicate that the Banco de México could exercise considerable short-run control over the domestic money stock and domestic credit market conditions during the 1970s, but only at the cost of high reserve volatility.

11.4   Expectations and the Futures Premium

The preceding analysis, while recognizing the role of the futures price as an indicator of exchange rate expectations, has negelcted both the possible influence of the home interest rate on the futures premium and the endogeneity of expectations. The offset to monetary policy has been calculated on the assumption that a one-time expansion of domestic credit leaves the futures premium unchanged.

How might monetary expansion affect the futures premium? By lowering the domestic interest rate, monetary expansion would induce capital outflows and, at the initial forward rate, an excess demand for future pesos calling for a rise in their equilibrium price. As an appreciation of the peso on the futures market discourages capital outflow, the offset coefficient would be lower than calculated in the previous section if covered interest arbitrage were incorporated into the model.

Speculative transactions are also an important determinant of the futures price, however, and the activities of speculators would tend to raise the offset coefficient calculated in section 11.3. Monetary expansion raises the likelihood of devaluation by reducing the central bank's international reserves and encouraging domestic expenditure. Speculators would respond by selling the peso forward, thus enhancing the profitability of capital outflows.

Theoretically, the net effect on the futures price of these two types of activity—interest arbitrage and speculation—is indeterminate. But as an empirical matter, we could find no strong evidence that contemporaneous domestic interest rates affected the futures premium during the 1970s. Expectations regarding the future level of the exchange rate did seem to be an important determinant of the futures premium, however. In particular, lagged deviations from purchasing power parity exerted a persistent and strong effect on the futures premium, with lagged real exchange rate appreciation leading to forward depreciation of the peso.

Letting $p \equiv \ln(e\mathrm{PUS}/\mathrm{PMex})$ again denote the natural logarithm of the real exchange rate, we estimated the following relationship between the futures premium on dollars, f, and past changes in the real exchange rate between 1974:2 and 1979:4:

$$f_t = 45.209 - 6.479 \; \Delta p_{t-1} - 14.803 \; \Delta p_{t-2} - 11.669 \; \Delta p_{t-3}$$
$$(12.708) \quad (1.324) \qquad (4.608) \qquad (4.022)$$

$$- \; 6.288 \; \Delta p_{t-4} - 7.175 \; \Delta p_{t-5},$$
$$(3.250) \qquad (2.071)$$

$$\hat{\rho} = 0.930 \ , \qquad SE = 0.927 \ , \qquad R^2 = 0.740$$
$$(0.079)$$

(standard errors are in parentheses). The correlations between the futures premium and lagged values of the purchasing power parity gap are extremely high. They suggest that any decline in the competitiveness of Mexican exports occasioned forward speculation against the peso and a rise in the price of forward dollars.[25]

This strong evidence that expectational factors influenced the forward premium indicates that our offset estimates probably understate the true offset.

11.5   Conclusion

This paper has studied the capital account offset to monetary policy faced by the Banco de México during the decade 1970–1980. Using a small structural model of Mexican financial markets, we found that roughly 30–50 percent of a domestic credit increase leaked away through the capital account within a quarter, with the precise figure depending on the method of domestic credit expansion adopted. This incomplete offset was the result of imperfect mobility of capital as well as imperfect substitutability between peso-denominated assets and assets denominated in foreign currencies. The offset coefficient would have been substantially higher under instantaneous portfolio adjustment.

These findings suggest that the Mexican central bank possessed some degree of short-run control over the monetary base in spite of the fixity of the exchange rate. While short-run monetary control implies an ability to neutralize the liquidity effects of transitory reserve fluctuations, it does not imply an ability to resist the adjustments needed to eliminate sustained disequilibria in the balance of payments. Conclusions as to the scope for long-run monetary control cannot be drawn from our partial-equilibrium, financial-sector model, which neglects the current account effects of international wealth flows and changes in home borrowing costs. The sharp reserve losses preceding the 1976 and 1982 devaluations provide convincing evidence against the hypothesis that the Banco de México enjoyed any long-run independence from monetary developments abroad.

Estimates of a Banco de Mexico reaction function provided strong evidence of official sterilization activities during the 1970s. Although the reaction function exhibited instability when estimated over subperiods of the decade, the Banco de México seems to have pursued a policy of full neutralization of reserve movements, at least since early 1976. The pursuit of sterilization under conditions of substantial capital account

25. The contemporaneous real exchange rate exerted no significant effect on the futures premium. This is probably the result of lags in the reporting of price level figures.

sensitivity helped give rise to periods of considerable reserve volatility during the decade under study.

Appendix

The following data were employed in this study:

B: High-powered money in billions of pesos. The series is the sum of currency and the reserve deposits of deposit banks in the Banco de México, including securities held at the Banco de México in fulfillment of reserve requirements. Source: *Indicadores Económicos*, various issues, for data from 1974:1 to 1979:4. From 1970:4 to 1973:4, currency in circulation is taken from *Indicadores Económicos* and bank reserves from *Informe Anual*.

BA: Adjusted stock of high-powered money, equal to $(q_0/q_t)B_t$.

D_1, D_2, D_3: Seasonal dummies taking the value of 1 in the ith quarter ($i = 1, 2, 3$) and zero in other quarters.

$\Delta DACB$: Change in central bank domestic assets. Calculated as $\Delta B - \Delta FACB$. Included are monetized capital gains on international reserves.

e: End-of-period exchange rate, in pesos per dollar. Source: *International Financial Statistics* (IFS), line ae.

f: End-of-quarter premium on peso futures for delivery three months forward, measured in percent per annum. The premium is set at zero prior to 1974:2. Source: *International Money Market Yearbook*, various issues.

F: Private Mexican net external liabilities, in billions of dollars, calculated as the cumulated STCF + LTCF.

$\Delta FACB$: Change in reserves of the Banco de México, excluding valuation changes. Calculated as $e_t\Delta R_t$.

GOVBOR: Consolidated borrowing requirement of the Mexican public sector (defined as the central government plus "controlled" public enterprises), in billions of pesos. Source: Ministry of Finance.

LTCF: Surplus on long-term private capital account, excluding direct foreign investment, in billions of dollars. Source: *Indicadores Económicos*, various issues.

M: Narrowly defined money $M1$, in billions of pesos. Source: *Indicadores Económicos* and *Informe Anual*, various issues.

PMex: Mexican CPI, 1975 = 1.00. Source: IFS, line 64.

PUS: United States CPI, 1975 = 1.00. Source: IFS, line 64.

q: Weighted average reserve requirement. End-of-quarter stocks of various domestic and foreign liabilities of the Mexican financial system are used to weight the marginal reserve requirement for each type of deposit. When more than one reserve requirement is published for a given type of deposit (depending, e.g., on location of the issuing institution), some effort is made to choose the rate which is likely to apply to the majority of deposits in that category. In addition, the series is adjusted so that $q_t = q_{t-1}$ if no change is made in legislated reserve requirements. Source: *Indicadores Económicos* for 1972:4–1979:4; *Informe Anual* for 1971:1–1972:3.

r: Domestic interest rate, measured in percent per annum. The rate chosen is the gross yield on *financiera* bonds for 1971:1–1973:4 and the gross yield on three-month certificates of deposit from 1974:1–1979:4. Source: *Indicadores Económicos*.

r^*: Three-month London Eurodollar rate, measured in percent per annum. Source: IFS, line 60d.

ΔR: Change in foreign exchange reserves of the Banco de México, in billions of dollars. The reserve series is taken from the balance of payments data in *Indicadores Económicos* and is based on a constant valuation of gold.

STCF: Short-term private capital account surplus, in billions of dollars. The series includes the errors and omissions in the balance of payments until 1977:1, when short-term capital flows and errors and omissions were first published separately. Source: *Indicadores Económicos*.

y: Mexican index of industrial production. Source: IFS, line 66.

YUS: U.S. disposable income (nominal). Source: IFS, line 99a.

W: Mexican financial wealth, calculated as $B_t + (-e_t F_t)$.

References

Aliber, Robert Z. 1973. The interest rate parity theorem: A reinterpretation. *Journal of Political Economy* 81 (November/December):1451–1459.

Argy, Victor, and Pentti J. K. Kouri. 1974. Sterilization policies and the volatility in international reserves. In *National monetary policies and the international financial system*, ed. Robert Z. Aliber. Chicago: University of Chicago Press.

Bhalla, Surjit S. 1981. The transmission of inflation into developing economies. In *World inflation and the developing countries*, by William R. Cline and Associates. Washington, D.C.: Brookings Institution.

Brothers, Dwight S., and Leopoldo Solís. 1966. *Mexican financial development*. Austin: University of Texas Press.

Business International. 1979. *Financing foreign operations* (October).

Cardoso, Eliana A., and Rudiger Dornbusch. 1980. Three notes on Brazilian trade and payments. Working Paper Series no. 451, National Bureau of Economic Research, Cambridge, Massachusetts.

Connolly, Michael, and José Dantas da Silveira. 1979. Exchange-market pressure in postwar Brazil: An application of the Girton-Roper monetary model. *American Economic Review* 69 (June):448–454.

Cumby, Robert E., John Huizinga, and Maurice Obstfeld. 1981. Two-step two-stage least squares estimation in models with rational expectations. Technical Paper Series no. 11, National Bureau of Economic Research, Cambridge, Massachusetts. *Journal of Econometrics*, forthcoming.

Dhrymes, Phoebus J. 1974. *Econometrics: Statistical foundations and applications*. 2d ed. New York: Springer-Verlag.

Dooley, Michael P., and Peter Isard. 1980. Capital controls, political risk, and deviations from interest-rate parity. *Journal of Political Economy* 88 (April):370–384.

Engle, Robert F. 1982. Autoregressive conditional heteroscedasticity with estimates of the variance of United Kingdom inflation. *Econometrica* 50 (July):987–1007.

Fair, Ray C. 1970. The estimation of simultaneous equation models with lagged endogenous variables and first order serially correlated errors. *Econometrica* 38 (May):507–516.

Frenkel, Jacob A., Thorvaldur Gylfason, and John F. Helliwell. 1980. A synthesis of monetary and Keynesian approaches to short-run balance-of-payments theory. *Economic Journal* 90 (September):582–592.

Girton, Lance, and Don Roper. 1977. A monetary model of exchange market pressure applied to the postwar Canadian experience. *American Economic Review* 67 (September):537–548.

Hansen, Lars Peter. 1979. The asymptotic distribution of least squares estimators with endogenous regressors and dependent residuals. Graduate School of Industrial Administration, Carnegie-Mellon University, Pittsburgh, Pa. Mimeo.

Herring, Richard J., and Richard C. Marston. 1977. *National monetary policies and international financial markets*. Amsterdam: North-Holland.

Keynes, John Maynard. 1930. *A treatise on money*, 2 vols. London: Macmillan.

Kouri, Pentti J. K., and Michael G. Porter. 1974. International capital flows and portfolio equilibrium. *Journal of Political Economy* 82 (May/June):443–467.

Lizondo, José Saúl. 1983. Foreign exchange futures prices under fixed exchange rates. *Journal of International Economics* 14: in press.

Magee, Stephen P. 1976. The empirical evidence on the monetary approach to the balance of payments and exchange rates. *American Economic Review Papers and Proceedings* 66 (May):163–170.

Miller, Norman C., and Sherry S. Askin. 1976. Monetary policy and the balance of payments in Brazil and Chile. *Journal of Money, Credit and Banking* 8 (May):227–238.

Mundell, Robert A. 1963. Capital mobility and stabilization policy under fixed and flexible exchange rates. *Canadian Journal of Economics and Political Science* 29 (November):475–485.

Murray, Gordon L. 1978. Monetary policy and capital inflow. *Economic Record* 54 (August):271–280.

Obstfeld, Maurice. 1980*a*. Sterilization and offsetting capital movements: Evidence from West Germany, 1960–1970. Working Paper Series no. 494, National Bureau of Economic Research, Cambridge, Massachusetts.

———. 1980*b*. Imperfect asset substitutability and monetary policy under fixed exchange rates. *Journal of International Economics* 10 (May):177–200.

———. 1982*a*. The capitalization of income streams and the effects of open-market policy under fixed exchange rates. *Journal of Monetary Economics* 9 (January):87–98.

———. 1982*b*. Can we sterilize? Theory and evidence. *American Economic Review Papers and Proceedings* 72 (May):45–50.

Ortiz, Guillermo, and Leopoldo Solís. 1979. Financial structure and exchange rate experience: Mexico 1954–1977. *Journal of Development Economics* 6 (December):515–548.

Porter, Michael G. 1972. Capital flows as an offset to monetary policy: The German experience. *International Monetary Fund Staff Papers* 19 (July):395–424.

Stockman, Alan C. 1979. Monetary control and sterilization under pegged exchange rates. Department of Economics, University of Rochester, Rochester, New York. Mimeo.

White, Halbert. 1980. A heteroskedasticity-consistent covariance matrix estimator and a direct test for heteroskedasticity. *Econometrica* 48 (May):817–838.

———. 1982. Instrumental variables regression with independent observations. *Econometrica* 50 (March):483–499.

Comment   Jacob A. Frenkel

The paper "Capital Mobility and the Scope for Sterilization: Mexico in the 1970s" by Robert Cumby and Maurice Obstfeld represents a significant contribution to the literature on the scope for an independent

Jacob A. Frenkel is the David Rockefeller Professor of International Economics in the Department of Economics, University of Chicago, and a research associate of the National Bureau of Economic Research.

The author wishes to acknowledge financial support from the National Science Foundation grant SES-7814480-A01. The research reported here is part of the NBER Research Program in International Studies. Any opinions expressed are those of the author and not those of NBER.

monetary policy under a pegged exchange rate regime. After pointing out the possible biases in earlier estimates of the offset coefficient (measuring the extent to which the effects of domestic credit policy on the money supply are being offset by losses of international reserves through the balance of payments), the authors develop and estimate a structural model for Mexico and compute the relevant offset coefficient for the decade of the 1970s. My own comments are divided into three parts. The first deals with econometric issues and with the sources of the bias in previous reduced-form estimates; the second deals with the structural model, and the third with the estimated offset coefficient.

Estimating the Offset Coefficient: Econometric Issues

A typical reduced-form equation used to estimate the offset coefficient is presented in equation (1).

$$(1) \qquad \Delta R_t = a_0 + a_1 X_t + a_2 \Delta D_t + u_t,$$

where ΔR_t denotes changes in international reserves during period t, ΔD_t denotes changes in the domestic assets component of the monetary base, X_t denotes a vector of other factors that induce changes in international reserves, and u_t denotes an error term. In equation (1) the parameter a_2 is being referred to as the offset coefficient; it is a measure of the degree to which changes in the domestic asset component of the monetary base (ΔD) are offset by changes in the stock of international reserves (ΔR). A negative value of a_2 indicates that losses of reserves offset the effects of credit expansion, and when $a_2 = -1$, the offset is complete.

As emphasized by Cumby and Obstfeld, to the extent that domstic credit policy is influenced by the state of the balance of payments, ordinary-least-squares (OLS) estimates of a_2 will be biased. The dependence of domestic credit policy on the balance of payments is usually rationalized by noting that the monetary authority may wish to sterilize the consequences of the balance of payments. Such a sterilization function is described in equation (2):

$$(2) \qquad \Delta D_t = b_0 + b_1 Y_t + b_2 \Delta R_t + v_t,$$

where Y_t denotes a vector of other factors determining credit policy, and v_t denotes an error term. In equation (2), b_2 is being referred to as the sterilization coefficient. A negative value of b_2 indicates that the monetary authority attempts to sterilize the monetary consequences of reserve flows, and when $b_2 = -1$, sterilization is complete. As is evident, when the behavior of the monetary authority is characterized by equation (2) with $b_2 < 0$, ΔD_t would be correlated with u_t, and the OLS estimate of the offset coefficient, a_2 in equation (1), would generally be biased downward (algebraically). This is the nature of the bias which has been frequently discussed in the literature (e.g., Magee 1976) and which is also reiterated by Cumby and Obstfeld.

If the monetary authority employs its domestic credit policy to attain a target level of international reserves rather than to sterilize the monetary consequences of the balance of payments, the direction of the bias is likely to be reversed. For example, consider the following reaction function:

(3) $\Delta D_t = c_0 + c_1 Z_t + c_2 (R_t - R_t^*) + \epsilon_t,$

where R_t and R_t^* denote actual and desired stocks of international reserves, Z_t denotes other factors determining credit policy, and ϵ_t denotes an error term. In equation (3) c_2 is likely to be positive, suggesting that when the holdings of reserves exceed the target level, the monetary authorities expend credit and thereby induce a decline in the stock of reserves toward the target level. As is evident, when the behavior of the monetary authorities is characterized by equation (3), with $c_2 > 0$, the OLS estimate of the offset coefficient, a_2 in equation (1), would generally be biased upward (algebraically). A reaction function of the type described by equation (3) was estimated by Ujiie (1978) and Lau (1980). These estimates showed that, for the cases studied, the parameter c_2 was significantly positive. In general, it seems that domestic credit policy is influenced by the considerations which underlie equation (2) as well as by those which underlie equation (3). Consequently, while the OLS estimate of equation (1) may yield biased estimates of a_2, the direction of the bias may not be stated on a priori grounds.

Independent of the detailed specification of the reaction function, the OLS estimate of equation (1) will be biased if the error term u_t is correlated with the error term in the reaction function. It is clear, therefore, that to obtain consistent estimates of the offset coefficient, the simultaneity of the various relationships has to be taken into account. There are, in principle, two ways to obtain consistent estimates. First, one could estimate equations (1) and (2), or (1) and (3), simultaneously as in Ujiie (1978) and Lau (1980); alternatively, one could proceed along the lines of Cumby and Obstfeld and estimate a structural model of the economy and then derive the implied offset coefficient. The choice between the two approaches reflects the usual trade-off between reduced form and structural estimates. On the one hand, estimates based on a structural model permit an interpretation of the results in terms of the structural parameters; on the other hand, however, confidence in these estimates depends on one's confidence in the detailed specifications of the structural model. It might be useful, therefore, to supplement the structural model estimate by an estimate of the reduced form as obtained from a simultaneous estimation of equations (1) and (2), or (1) and (3), or (1)

272 Robert E. Cumby/Maurice Obstfeld

and a combination of (2) and (3). If the two sets of estimates yielded similar results, then the interpretation in terms of the structural parameters would gain credibility. If, however, the two sets of estimates differed greatly from each other, then it seems that some more questions concerning the detailed specifications of the structural model will have to be answered.

The Structural Model

The structural model is composed of three building blocks: a demand equation for the net external liabilities, a money demand equation, and a money supply equation. The model is estimated using quarterly data over the period 1971:3–1979:4. Since, however, the authors provide some evidence indicating instability in the Banco de México's reaction function (evidence which is also documented by Porzecanski 1979), it would be useful to examine whether the structural model remained stable throughout the decade.

Net Foreign Liabilities

In specifying the demand for net foreign liabilities, Cumby and Obstfeld assume that asset holders adjust the *composition* of their portfolios to the desired composition only gradually. Specifically, for a given value of wealth, asset holders are assumed to make up each period a fraction λ of the disequilibrium. This fraction is estimated to be between 30 to 40 percent of the discrepancy between desired and actual composition. As a theoretical matter, it is not easy to envisage the precise nature of the cost which induces this type of adjustment to portfolio composition equilibrium. More importantly, as an empirical matter it is extremely difficult to separate out changes in asset holdings into those associated with the restoration of the desired *composition* and those associated with the attainment of the desired *size* of the portfolio, and theoretically, the former is likely to proceed at a much faster speed than the latter. It is not unlikely, therefore, that the estimated speed reflects both types of adjustment.

Throughout their study the authors provide the results of two estimation procedures. The first procedure is Fair's version of two-stage least squares; the second procedure is a two-step, two-stage least squares (2S2SLS) as proposed by Cumby, Huizinga, and Obstfeld. The two procedures have yielded similar parameter estimates. For the case at hand the similarity among the estimates is especially reassuring since one of the determinants of the demand for foreign liabilities is the futures premium on foreign exchange which is being used as a proxy for expectations. To the extent that this proxy measured expectations with an error, Fair's method would have resulted in inconsistent estimates. The 2S2SLS method yielding similar estimates suggests that in the present case the errors in variables problem is not severe.

One of the interesting results in table 11.2 concerns the different responses of capital flows to changes in the domestic rate of interest and to changes in the covered foreign rate of interest. Other things being equal, a 100 basis point rise in the domestic rate of interest is estimated to induce (using the 2S2SLS procedure) capital inflow of 1.16 billion (real) pesos in the same quarter, while an equivalent rise in the covered foreign rate of interest is estimated to induce an outflow of only 0.25 billion (real) pesos. This difference suggests that for the case of Mexico it would be inappropriate to follow the convention of specifying capital flows as a function of covered interest differential; rather it suggests that one needs to decompose the differential into its components. To gain some idea of the orders of magnitude, one may note by inspection of figure 11.1 that these flows are usually smaller than the typical quarterly changes in Banco de México's foreign assets.

Finally, it is noteworthy that the estimated value of the autocorrelation coefficient, ρ, (using the 2S2SLS procedure) is -0.866. This estimate is much more negative than the customary estimates. It may reflect the difficulties of estimating jointly a speed of adjustment λ and the autocorrelation coefficient ρ.

The Demand for Money

Analogously with the specification of the demand for foreign liabilities, the authors postulate a stock adjustment model of the demand for money. The speed of adjustment is estimated to be about 20 percent per quarter. Since the adjustments of both money and foreign assets are carried out by the same asset holders, it would be useful to provide a formal link between the two speeds. Once such a link is established, it would be useful to estimate the dynamic equations jointly subject to the implied cross-equation constraints. The desirability of this procedure is exemplified by noting that the long-run effects of a rise in the domestic interest rate on capital inflows is about 3.9 billion (real) pesos (based on equation [B] in table 11.2) while the corresponding decline in money holdings is only 1.4 billion (real) pesos (based on equation [D] in table 11.3). It would be useful to account for this long-run difference within the context of the model.

The specification of the demand for money states that money holdings depend on the expected holding cost. The authors stress two relevant costs corresponding to two margins of substitution. They include the domestic nominal rate of interest to capture the substitution between money and domestic bonds, while the inclusion of the covered foreign nominal rate of interest represents the substitution between money and foreign bonds. However, when various parity conditions are satisfied, these two rates of interest are not independent of each other. Specifically, when the requisite conditions for covered interest arbitrage hold, these rates are likely to be highly collinear. It is possible, therefore, that this collinearity might be responsible in part for the imprecise estimate of the domestic interest elasticity of the demand for money.

Finally, it may be noted that the various estimates in table 11.3 suggest that the long-run income elasticity of the demand for money exceeds 2. This value seems to be somewhat high in comparison with corresponding estimates for other countries as well as for Mexico (e.g., Blejer 1975). It is not unlikely that a joint estimation of the speeds of adjustment in the various markets could yield a higher estimated speed in the money market and, correspondingly, a lower value of the long-run income elasticity.

The Money Supply

In estimating the money supply function, the authors have imposed the constraint (which is not rejected by the data) that the supply is not subject to a lagged adjustment process and that the two primary factors governing the supply are the monetary base and the rate of interest. The estimates in table 11.4 reveal a high interest elasticity (exceeding 2.2) and a low elasticity with respect to the base (about unity). The estimated unit elasticity is, however, consistent with other findings (e.g., Blejer 1975).

Of special interest is the estimate of ρ, the autocorrelation coefficient. This is the only case in the study in which estimating the autocorrelation coefficient yielded a positive value of ρ. By the same token, the money supply function is the only building block of the structural model which does not include in the estimation a lagged dependent variable representing a stock adjustment process. I believe that these two facts might be intimately related. The difficulties in estimating a speed of adjustment along with an autocorrelation coefficient are well known, and it is possible that when the lagged dependent variable is included, it picks up "too much" of the serial correlation and thus yielding a negative estimate of ρ (as in table 11.2). On the other hand, when the lagged dependent variable is not included, the resulting positive estimate of ρ captures the "true" nature of the serial correlation (as in table 11.4). These considerations provide an additional reason for attempting a further examination of the estimated speeds of adjustment.

The Offset Coefficient

Having estimated the three building blocks of the structural model, the authors have computed the offset coefficient as (minus) the total derivative of net foreign liabilities with respect to a change in the domestic asset component of the monetary base. Intuitively, an expansion of domestic credit yields a new equilibrium rate of interest that clears the money market. This equilibrium rate of interest, which is found with the aid of the estimated money demand and money supply functions, is then substituted into the net foreign liabilities function from which the offset through capital flows is being determined. It is clear, therefore, that the computation of the offset coefficient, as in equations (9)–(10) of Cumby and Obstfeld's paper, involves all the estimates of the interest rate coefficients. Following this procedure, the "long-run" offset coefficient to open market policy is computed to be about 50 percent. Intuitively, this estimate seems to be somewhat low. The payoff to the authors' structural model estimation is that one can identify the sources of possible biases in the final estimate. Specifically, a given expansion of credit lowers the rate of interest in an inverse proportion to the interest elasticity of the supply of money and in an inverse proportion to the (absolute value of the) interest elasticity of the demand for money. The resultant capital flow, in turn, depends positively on the interest elasticity of the net foreign liabilities function. It follows that an overestimation of the sensitivity of the demand or of the supply of money to changes in the rate of interest, as well as an underestimation of the interest sensitivity of capital flows, will result in an underestimation of the offset coefficient. Since the authors' definition of capital flows includes the item measuring errors and omissions in the balance of payments, it is unlikely that the elasticity of capital flows is being significantly underestimated. My speculation is that to the extent that the offset coefficient is being underestimated, the source of the bias would be found in the overestimation of the interest elasticity of the demand for money. As indicated before, the high value of the estimated long-run elasticity may be attributed, in part, to the extremely low estimate of the speed of adjustment. Furthermore, as recognized by the authors, allowance for the endogeneity of the futures premium on foreign exchange is also likely to yield a higher value of the long-run offset coefficient.

In conclusion, I wish to reiterate my opening remarks. This paper represents a significant contribution to the study of the scope for sterilization. I have found the empirical research extremely well designed and professionally executed. As such, I believe that it could serve as a model for the proper way to study and estimate the offset coefficient.

References

Blejer, Mario I. 1975. Money, prices and the balance of payments. Ph.D. diss., University of Chicago.

Lau, Melanie. 1980. The simultaneous determination of international reserves and domestic credit when the monetary authorities have a demand for international reserves. Ph.D. diss., University of Chicago.

Magee, Stephen, P. 1976. The empirical evidence on the monetary approach to the balance of payments and exchange rates. *American Economic Review* 66 (May):163–170.

Porzecanski, Arturo C. 1979. Patterns of monetary policy in Latin America. *Journal of Money Credit and Banking* 11, no. 4 (November):427–437.

Ujiie, Junichi. 1978. A stock adjustment approach to monetary policy and the balance of payments. In *The economics of exchange rates: Selected studies*, ed. Jacob A. Frenkel and Henry G. Johnson, 179–192. Reading, Mass.: Addison-Wesley.

12   Panel Discussion:
      The Capital Market
      under Conditions of
      High and Variable Inflation

Juan Carlos de Pablo, Miguel Mancera, and
Mario Henrique Simonsen

Remarks   Juan Carlos de Pablo

The following observations on the impact of inflation on the economy in general, and on the capital market in particular, evolve from the Argentine experience, an extremely interesting case on all inflation issues except one, namely, how to stop it.

1. Under high inflation (say, 8 percent per month, per week, etc.) either direct price controls evaporate or the corresponding commodity disappears. This fact does not mean that, as the rate of inflation increases, the evaporation of direct price controls becomes equivalent to the absence of controls. The reason for the difference is that, in general, the evaporation of direct price controls is far from being a resource-free activity. On the contrary, however difficult to estimate econometrically, it seems clear that the evaporation of direct price controls is an activity specially intensive in human resources, a scarce resource indeed (when managers perceive that the private rate of return of designing evasion mechanisms is the most profitable alternative they face, they do not have time for other activities, like introducing technical change, quality improvements, etc.).

In the case of capital markets under high inflation, the mentioned facts imply that the option is not between free interest rates and controlled interest rates that segment the financial market in two sections, but whether in the absence of direct controls the markets develop "efficiently" (i.e., minimizing the spread) or because of the existence of controls on interest rates, the funds are channelled through alternative and inefficient routes, since mainly because of lack of transparency the spread increases significantly.

Juan Carlos de Pablo is a professor at the National University of Buenos Aires.

2. In most cases high inflation implies variable inflation. Logue and Willett (1977) popularized this view, although in my opinion for the wrong reason. The difficulty with the Logue-Willett "demonstration" of the thesis is that in the empirical analysis their proxy for variability is the standard deviation of past inflation, a well-known estimator of *absolute* variability. Question: What is relevant in the estimation of the variability of the rate of inflation, the use of indicators of absolute or of relative variability? No simple answer can be given to this question. On the one hand, it is clear that if you expected 1,000,000 percent rate of inflation, and observed inflation was "just" 999,000 percent, your absolute error is equal to one thousand percentage points, but it does not have any practical difference[1] (which means that relative indicators do matter); but on the other hand, if you expected 0.1 percent rate of inflation and the observed rate was 0.2 percent, your error was 100 percent, but also it does not have any practical difference[2] (which suggests that to a certain extent indicators of absolute error also matter). Some mixed estimator, derived from the percentual gain (or loss) of a loan made at a fixed nominal interest rate on the basis of the expected rate of inflation should be designed. My guess is that when the "correct" estimator is computed, the computation will confirm the popular view that the higher the rate of inflation the higher its variability.

3. What is the consequence of high and variable inflation on the economy, beyond the loss involved in the mentioned misallocation of human resources? High and variable inflation reduces significantly the time horizon of the economy. (In Argentina there is a joke that says, the Argentinian who knows where to spend his next weekend has already solved his long-run problems).

The reduction of the time horizon of the economy affects mainly the level and composition of investment. It is clearly impossible to increase the *volume* of output of a given investment, but under the conditions mentioned the real value of output and profits should be increased (i.e., the payoff period reduced) if the project is expected to be carried out; this means that the inflation-induced increase in uncertainty reduces ceteris paribus the level of investment.

4. Indexed and floating rate loans, bonds, and time deposits are one of the main by-products of the capital market under conditions of high and variable inflation. Under the mentioned circumstances it has proved a useful mechanism, since it combines nonprohibitive administrative costs with the need for almost instantaneous recontracting as a result of the change in economic conditions.

1. If you borrowed money at an ex ante zero real interest rate, you will end up paying a 0.1 percent real rate.
2. If you lent money at an ex ante zero interest rate, you will end up getting a 0.1 percent negative real rate.

5. For the happy few who still live in countries in which inflation is not a problem, the main lesson that emerges from these observations is very simple: DO NOT BE SOFT ON INFLATION. As an Argentinian, I know what I am talking about.

References

Logue, D. E., and T. D. Willett. 1977. A note on the relation between the rate and variability of inflation. *Economica* 43:151–158.

Remarks   Miguel Mancera

During this conference, very interesting points were made on the relationship between taxation and the financing of private business. This relationship is so important that it well deserves further comment.

Obviously, the structure of taxes heavily influences both the development of financial markets and the way in which firms fund their operations. It seems, however, that in a considerable number of countries, tax rules may hinder the financing of business, and consequently, they may also impair economic development. This is the case because such rules were designed for other countries whose economic features are quite different.

The argument can be presented by means of a very simplified model which, in essence, may be applicable to several countries.

The assumptions required for the model to hold are the following: (1) that there are close financial links between the country's economy and international financial markets; (2) that capital can move to and from these markets, whether legally or illegally; and (3) that it is practically impossible to tax or to collect tax on income obtained abroad by individuals.

Under these assumptions, it is clear that, for banking intermediation to be successful, the after-tax yield of bank deposits in the country in question must be competitive with the yield of bank deposits abroad—usually not taxed when the depositor is a foreigner. Thus, other things being equal, any tax on interest from domestic bank deposits brings about an increase in the deposit interest rate, since this is clearly the only way for the after-tax yield to continue being competitive with the rates obtained abroad. Therefore, it can be seen that, even though formally the taxpayer is the depositor, the real taxpayer is most likely the borrower. This holds true except to the extent that the fiscal burden is absorbed by

Miguel Mancera is a governor of the Banco de México.

the financial intermediary when the conditions of the supply and demand for loanable funds do not allow such intermediaries to pass on the tax burden to the borrower. Therefore, under the assumptions made, and with this possible exception, it can be asserted that tax on interest is not an income tax but a tax on the use of credit.

Some comments are also worth making on the way in which taxation may affect the stock market and equity financing.

Let us assume that the tax on corporate profits is 50 percent, that there is no dividend tax, and that the after-tax yield of debt is around 4 percent, as it might well be in a zero inflation economy. In these circumstances, for a firm to be able to raise equity capital, it would be necessary for the after-tax corporate profit to be competitive with the net yield of bank deposits, namely, 4 percent, which implies that an 8 percent before-tax corporate profit is required. In practice, this means that there would be a tax on the use of equity capital equivalent to 100 percent of the net yield for the shareholder.

The fact that, under the assumptions made, an income tax—whether on interest or on profits—becomes a tax on the use of capital may have a serious contractionist effect on investment. This contractionist effect, however, is greatly amplified by inflation, and the higher the inflation, the greater the effect.

Imagine an economy with an inflation rate of 30 percent in which the tax on interest is 15 percent, and where the after-tax yield of bank deposits is 34 percent—4 percent in real terms. In such a case, the loan rate would have to be around 40 percent to cover just the net yield of bank deposits, plus the 15 percent tax—not considering the operational cost and the profit of the financial intermediary. This implies, in turn, that the real loan rate would have to be around 10 percent to cover only the net yield and the tax of bank deposits. Whereas, without inflation, a 4 percent after-tax yield of bank deposits would require a gross interest rate of around 4.7 percent, which would be the real loan rate required to cover the net yield to the depositor, plus the tax. Thereby, as can be seen in this example, inflation implies more than doubling the real loan rate.

The situation with regard to equity, however, becomes much more difficult in inflation, under the already made assumptions that corporate tax would be 50 percent and that the net yield of bank deposits would be 34 percent. Then, profits would have to be 68 percent in nominal terms, at least, to produce a net yield of 34 percent, which would be the minimum required to raise equity capital if the after-tax interest rate corresponding to bank deposits is 34 percent.

One wonders if there might be many investment projects with a return higher than 68 percent in nominal terms, even in an economy with 30 percent inflation. If there are not many, it will become extremely difficult to finance firms with equity capital alone, so that more leverage will be needed. This explains why the structure of balance sheets of businesses has deteriorated so much over the years. Indeed, degrees of leverage that some time ago were unacceptable to bankers, today have to be swallowed by them if firms and banks are to continue to exist. And, even worse, if the rate of return of projects is not above the high real cost of the mixture of debt and equity, investment will tend to contract.

During the first stages of inflation, corporate profits may increase tremendously, enabling firms to raise equity capital in spite of the difficulties imposed by a fiscal system like the one outlined; but high rates of profit are very difficult to maintain for the average firm over long periods of time. They decrease as inflation permeates the markets of inputs or, perhaps, because the government intervenes to control prices.

These reflections make one think that countries which are in a situation somehow resembling this simplified model would be well advised to either suppress or decrease inflation or, else, reform their tax systems. Considerable progress has been made in the latter course of action, especially in connection with depreciation rules that acknowledge revaluation of assets; but this progress—when and where achieved—has lagged tremendously behind the appearance of the problems to be solved and seldom has amounted to a complete solution. Monetary stability, however, would have avoided the distortions mentioned which have implied high social costs and delayed economic development over the years.

Remarks   Mario Henrique Simonsen

Capital market instruments and regulations have been frequently developed under the implicit assumption of long-term price stability. High and variable inflation rates, which are correlated problems of today's world, introduce two types of inefficiencies in such traditional arrangements. The first type is related to the existence of money illusion based regulations, which drag the development of capital markets whenever the inflation rate exceeds a certain limit. Inefficiencies of the second type result from the inability of the traditional capital market structure to deal with widespread price uncertainty.

Usury ceilings provide the most extreme case of money illusion in regulations and might destroy all bond markets, as occurred in Brazil in 1964. Interest rate controls produce the same type of distortions. Conventional accounting, which fails to distinguish between real and nominal profit, spreads misleading information to the markets, underrating the

Mario Henrique Simonsen is a professor at the Fundacao Getulio Vargas, Rio de Janeiro.

stocks of the high debt/equity ratio corporations. High inflation rates transform the capital gains tax into a sales tax. Income taxes subsidize the borrowers at the expense of the lenders. Of course, if tax rates were the same for all economic agents, the above mentioned transfer effect would be offset by an upward adjustment of nominal interest rates. Yet, a number of distortions might arise as a result of different economic agents being taxed at different rates, a natural outcome of a progressive income tax. Moreover, usury ceilings and interest rate controls might prevent the adjustment mechanism from working.

Even in the absence of money illusion in the regulations, price uncertainties challenge the efficiency of the traditional capital market instruments. Since most economic agents are risk averse the most immediate effect of price uncertainty is to destroy the market for long-term bonds with fixed nominal interest rates. Because of the exacerbated risk premium, any nominal interest rate which might attract the lender becomes too high for the borrower and vice versa. Housing industries, which are heavily dependent on long-term mortgages are the first to be hurt by the uncertainty trap.

According to economic theory, there is one single way to restore the efficiency of the competitive markets under uncertainty, namely, to make every contract contingent on the state of nature. Of course problems of moral hazard and costs of listing and checking all the possible states of nature prevent the world from behaving according to the Arrow-Debreu model of general equilibrium under uncertainty. This, incidentally, explains why price and real interest rate uncertainties, which appear in practice as an inevitable by-product of chronic inflation, always create some troubles to capital markets. Yet, if one is bound to live with inflation, indexed bonds might emerge as a good proxy to the Arrow-Debreu contingent claims. In fact, fully indexed contracts would solve the Arrow-Debreu equations with uncertainty if shocks were purely nominal. Of course, full indexation ceases to be optimal when real shocks are brought onto the stage.

To sum up, high and variable inflation rates have never been the ideal setup for the development of capital markets since they introduce price and interest rate uncertainties which cannot be properly offset by enforceable contracts. Yet, if one has to live with inflation, the foregoing analysis suggests some steps to take to minimize the market frictions. The first step is to abolish all money illusioned regulations, which may include usury ceilings and interest rate controls. The second step is to make inflationary accounting mandatory, to convey to the stock market the correct information on the economic performance of the corporations.

Regarding the market for indexed bonds, one should let it choose its own course. When shocks are basically nominal, such bonds provide the best answer to price uncertainties, especially in the long run. Therefore, one should not hinder the development of the market for indexed bonds by artificial regulations or by inappropriate fiscal treatment. But there is no point in forcing the market, that is, making bond indexation mandatory, since they are a poor instrument when inflation rates are substantially affected by supply shocks. Regulations should favor the coexistence of both indexed and nominal bonds. Moreover, some additional flexibility would be gained if contracting parties could freely chose their preferred price indices.

A more advanced step is to index both the income tax and the capital gain tax. Income tax indexation involves much deeper changes than the simple automatic adjustment of the personal income tax brackets according to observed inflation rates. It also involves the tax distinction between nominal and real interest rates, as well as the taxation of the corporate profits on the basis of the inflationary accounting results. Of course indexation here requires a complete tax reform to avoid revenue losses. It is not a faultless step, since it eliminates the fiscal drag on inflation provided by the conventional income tax structure. Yet, one must recognize that chronic inflation sooner or later forces a trade-off between economic efficiency and price drags. Fixed exchange rates also produce a very important drag on inflation rates, but are obviously inconsistent with chronic price increases.

Contributors

Andrew Abel
Department of Economics
Harvard University
Cambridge, MA 02138

Carlos F. Díaz Alejandro
Department of Economics
Yale University
New Haven, CT 06520

Pedro Aspe Armella
I. T. A. M.
México 20, DF, México

Olivier Jean Blanchard
Department of Economics
Harvard University
Cambridge, MA 02138

Herminio A. Blanco
Department of Economics
Rice University
Houston, TX 77005

Michael Bruno
Department of Economics
Hebrew University
Jerusalem, Israel

Guillermo A. Calvo
Department of Economics
University of Chicago
Chicago, IL 60637

Domingo F. Cavallo
Instituto de Estudios Económicos
Fundación Mediterranea
Cordoba, Argentina

Robert E. Cumby
International Monetary Fund
World Bank
Washington, DC 20431

Rudiger Dornbusch
Department of Economics
Massachusetts Institute
  of Technology
Cambridge, MA 02139

Stanley Fischer
Department of Economics
Massachusetts Institute
  of Technology
Cambridge, MA 02139

Ricardo Ffrench-Davis
CIEPLAN
Santiago 9, Chile

285

Jacob A. Frenkel
Department of Economics
University of Chicago
Chicago, IL 60637

Peter M. Garber
Department of Economics
University of Rochester
Rochester, NY 14627

Nissan Liviatan
Department of Economics
Hebrew University
Jerusalem, Israel

José Saúl Lizondo
I. T. A. M.
Rio Hondo Num. 1
Mexico 20, DF, Mexico

Miguel Mancera
Banco de México
México 1, DF, México

Charles E. McLure, Jr.
Senior Fellow
Hoover Institution
Stanford University
Stanford, CA 94305

Michael Mussa
Graduate School of Business
University of Chicago
Chicago, IL 60637

Maurice Obstfeld
Department of Economics
Columbia University
International Affairs Building
New York, NY 10027

Guillermo Ortiz
Banco de México
México 1, DF, México

Juan Carlos de Pablo
Paez 2608
1406 Buenos Aires, Argentina

A. Humberto Petrei
Instituto de Estudios Económicos
Fundación Mediterranea
Cordoba, Argentina

Kenneth Rogoff
Board of Governors
Federal Reserve System
Washington, DC 20551

Thomas J. Sargent
Department of Economics
University of Minnesota
Minneapolis, MN 55455

Mario Henrique Simonsen
Fundacao Getulio Vargas
Praia de Botafogo 190
Rio de Janeiro 20000, Brazil

Author Index

Subject Index

Absorption approach, 32
Adjusted monetary base, 252
Appreciation, and borrowing, 132–33
Argentina: debt service, 26–27; financial policy, 160–75; fiscal policy, 18–22; inflation, 157–58; monetary policy, 17, 21, 201–2; real output, 8–9, 159–60; sources of finance, 160–75; stabilization policy, 153–61, 200–204
Arrow-Borch condition, 127, 129
Arrow-Debreu model, 95–96, 124–25
Asset market model, 256–64
Automatic adjustment, and exchange rate policy, 145

Balance of payments, 137; and capital inflow, 6–7; and inflation, 157
Balance sheet, of banking system, 138; of firms, 165–75
Bank failures, 18
Banking decontrol, 201, 204
Basic balance, 135
Bid-ask spread, 236
Bimetallism, in Mexico, 73
Black market, in foreign exchange, 47
Bond market equilibrium, 112–13
Border transaction, 82
Borrowing, and development, 131–33
Box-Jenkins technique, 90
"Brain drain," 43–44, 50. See also Factor mobility
Brazil: current account deficit, 187; debt service, 27–29; fiscal policy, 23; real output, 8–9

Bretton Woods system, 48
Budget constraint, government, 60, 62, 99; household, 60

Capital account, 137
Capital controls, 46, 103. See also Capital mobility; Exchange controls
Capital flight, 37
Capital import tax, 145
Capital inflow, and devaluation, 141; effect of, 12; and interest rates, 258; in Latin America, 6–7
Capital markets, under inflation, 277; regulated, 281–83
Capital mobility, degree of, 137; and economic integration, 53–55; and flexible exchange rates, 143–46; limited, 138–42. See also Capital controls; Exchange controls
"Cash in advance" constraint, 97
Central bank reaction function, 251–56
Cobb-Douglas utility function, 61
Coffee price maintenance, 23
Colombia: exchange rate controls, 17; monetary policy, 17; real output, 8–9
Commodity market, 134; and exchange expectations, 144–45
Commodity trade, and factor mobility, 52–53
Compensation, and welfare change, 43
Consumption function, 189–91
Consumption loans, as inside debt, 99
Consumption loans model. See Overlapping generations model

290